D1144644

The Lake Counties
from 1830 to the mid-twentieth century

The Lake

J. D. MARSHALL and JOHN K. WALTON

Counties

*from 1830
to the mid-twentieth century*

A STUDY IN REGIONAL CHANGE

Manchester University Press

© J. D. MARSHALL and J. K. WALTON 1981

Published by Manchester University Press, Oxford Road, Manchester M13 9PL

British Library cataloguing in publication data   Marshall, John Duncan
The Lake Counties from 1830 to the mid-twentieth century.
1 Cumbria, Eng. – Social conditions
I. Title II. Walton, John K
309.1′427′8081   HN398.C/

ISBN −7190−0824−7

*The authors and publishers gratefully acknowledge
the financial support
of* Cumbria County Council
and the Curwen Archives Trust

Phototypeset by Northern Phototypesetting Co., Bolton

*Printed in Great Britain
by* Butler & Tanner, Frome and London

CONTENTS ෨

ILLUSTRATIONS ᔰ

PREFACE

This volume is a study of the changing fortunes of Cumberland, Westmorland, and Lancashire (or Lonsdale) North of the Sands during the Victorian and Edwardian periods, with a final excursion deeper into the present century. The area thus covered is today the administrative county of Cumbria, and, as a matter of convenience, this title, and the adjective 'Cumbrian', are together used throughout the text to denote the whole of this region.

Such a usage may be thought to be anachronistic, and a native of Victorian Westmorland would certainly not have employed it when talking about the natives of his own county. The historian of a region or regions, however, must always bear geographical considerations in mind when first embarking upon a study of this kind, even if other data ultimately lead him to reject them. When, in 1961, the late Canon C. M. L. Bouch and Professor G. P. Jones published an earlier volume, *A Short Economic and Social History of the Lake Counties, 1500–1830,* to which the present work is a successor of a somewhat different kind, they had no doubt that the region studied by them, the one covered in the following pages, had 'a geographical unity'. Likewise, a distinguished geographer, Professor A. E. Smailes, has remarked that the Lake District 'is incontestably a unit by reason of distinctive physical characteristics, reflected in its human development and destiny'.[1] In other words, the shape of the Cumbrian massif, west of the North Pennine barrier, has been of more historical consequence than a mere administrative boundary or two, and it remains true that the life of its hill farmers has long had some relationship to the towns of the region's lowland fringes. It is interesting to note, too, that the broader 'Cumbrian' region, including Furness, was the one annexed by the scholars of the Cumberland and Westmorland Antiquarian and Archaeological Society following its foundation in 1866, and it is clear that an area so readily recognised by a great learned society, however pragmatically, as having some kind of inherent unity can be treated, also pragmatically, as a fit and suitable subject for examination. The founders of the 'C & W' evidently sensed a cultural coherence in their chosen territory, although other considerations suggest very persuasively indeed that industrial West Cumberland was developing some of the characteristics of a separate 'region' in these same mid-Victorian years, and much the same can be said of the Furness area. These observations are of the greatest importance, for it is no purpose of the authors of this book to appear to give some kind of theoretical justification for the local government reorganisation of 1974. A cultural and social region may not make a good administrative one.

Not surprisingly; for, whatever criteria one uses, a 'region', in the rapidly developing world of modern history, can scarcely be seen as a fixed and static entity. It is, to say the least, a mass of overlapping and sometimes conflicting or interlocking economic and social relationships, influenced or shaped by occupation or workplace, by religious persuasion or organisation, by agrarian activities and customs, by population movements, by political bodies, by voluntary organisations of innumerable kinds, and by commercial activities almost as numerous. Relationships in each of these broad spheres tended to produce what were often self-conscious social groups within the region itself, and, just as individual groups inside Cumbria might develop an apparently distinctive historical character, like, let us say, Methodists in the Eden Valley or in transplanted Cornish mining settlements, so the entire pattern of group activities assumed, at different periods, a complex chemistry which gave the region its unique nature. These social groups were not, of course, sealed off from the economic and social influences of the nation itself, nor always from the international scene and its more indirect forces. It is certain, moreover, that to study any group in isolation, without reference to its regional, national or international context, results in inadequate history, and this is, of course, a prime argument for regional and inter-regional historical study. The effeteness and disorientation of much local history seems also to be a consequence of the lack of organised information bearing on the relevant region as seen at several levels, and, equally regrettably, of the absence of a clearly structured body of information relative to regions and localities viewed comparatively.

The present volume has been much concerned with surveying and organising what appears to be fundamental in the history of the Lake Counties between 1830 and 1914. This work of organisation has been pursued in the light of major economic and social questions, but it can, of its nature, attempt to answer only the most obvious and basic ones: what were the major factors which shaped the region's economy, in what ways did its economic and social life change most signally, and, above all, what were the distinctive characteristics of the Lake Counties in some of the specialised spheres which have been mentioned? It is this last question which many readers will find to be of the greatest interest, and the ability of regional study to answer it should at once provide a test of the effectiveness of the study itself, and a justification for the challenging remarks at the end of the preceding paragraph.

The Lake Counties, then, represented a region of unusually small farms and, by contrast, of a few unusually great landowners; of an agrarian economy which withstood the late Victorian depression in agriculture almost more effectively than that of any other part of Britain; of rapid industrial development which took place in spite of the steady drain of educated or intelligent people from Cumbria itself to other parts, and in spite of lack of capital and initiatives within the region; of markedly low marriage rates, and bastardy rates which were almost the scandal of the nation; of exceptionally high literacy which had deep roots in the past but which may well have had some connection with the pronounced tendency of Cumbrians to migrate; of a tradition of deep local and regional patriotism which, if anything, tended to increase when natives diffused themselves about England and the world; of a unique and developing tourist function – in an area of memorable beauty – which drew comfortably placed visitors into its dales as the natives left; of capacious hotels, and stark overcrowding in some rural areas and towns; of an increasingly effective conservationist movement, driven along primarily by outsiders, which eventually contributed to the broader stream of opinion which produced the National Parks; of a theatre of protest which saw fighting against railways and reservoirs, and which now finds itself facing the incursions of British Nuclear Fuels. It will be seen that several of these dual considerations carry within them an element of paradox, sometimes of a decidedly grim nature. Other instances are less painful to consider. The powerful transforming agency of the Victorian railway system not only proved to be fundamental to industrial development but, in making modern forms of recreation and sport more easily accessible, also gave a new lease of life, or incidental stimulus, to certain traditional sports. Hence Cumberland and Westmorland-style wrestling gained new popularity as the railways took contestants into Lancashire towns, and attracted much larger crowds through the same agency. Special trains were laid on by local companies to take spectators to Workington to view the traditional, and violent, Easter town football games there.

Railways certainly did not destroy awarenesses of regionality, even when they carried away their thousands of out-migrants, and brought in contingents of workers from other counties or countries. They transported newspapers, with their vast accumulations of local and district news, to many a country station and dales railhead, and they nurtured the group self-consciousness that has been mentioned, even in the act of bringing the nation's doings to the rural doorstep. Other forms of regional identification were perhaps much more singular, and could gain strength and colour from the activities of the Earls of Lonsdale, employers and estate-owners on a massive scale, and, like the 'Yellow' Earl, Hugh Lowther, creators of legends and leaders of local regiments. The authors regret that they have been unable to say much about the military history of the Lake Counties, for volunteer companies and war service knitted people together. The Cumbrian, however, was not a mere follower of notables, and was reputed, perhaps rightly, to have a strong streak of independence – understandably in a world of small property-owners, although, as is shown later, modest property did not necessarily make for radicalism. Industrial workers were capable of rebellion, even against the Lowthers, and instances of this have been traced in some detail, if not always fully explained. As the following study shows, other forms of political conflict have more visible roots, and West Cumberland industrialists gave new life to county politics after the formation of the County Councils in 1889, just as labour movements had similar effects in the towns in the new century.

Inevitably, a study of this kind must raise as many questions as it answers. If it gives a sense of direction to at least some forms of regional and local historical research, then it will have achieved its purpose. The authors' approach throughout has been conditioned by the need to explain social change in relation to economic factors, not in any deterministic manner but rather in the course of a cautious journey through a jungle of variables. Accordingly, some economic forces have received much stress; others very little. Some aspects of social history, too, have been left in the safe hands of other authorities. Dr R. N. Thompson has so thoroughly studied the Cumbrian poor law and its operation[2] that no detailed reference has been made to pauperism, which hardly seemed to call for development as a separate theme. Similarly, Dr L. A. Williams' work, *Road Transport in Cumbria in the Nineteenth Century* (1975), has had its very real uses, but does not deal directly with most of the major questions raised in this volume. It is a pleasure to acknowledge the generosity and meticulous help of Dr Oliver Wood in several matters relating to the statistics and development of West Cumberland industry, just as Professor R. H. Campbell afforded information giving a clearer view of the origins of the Scottish ironmasters who 'invaded' West Cumberland after 1870. Dr D. J. Rowe freely gave of his wisdom in the matter of interpreting census occupational data, and Mr C. F. O'Neill and Mr Paul McGloin have made available the results of their researches on Whitehaven and Keswick respectively; and Mrs June C. F. Barnes's studies of the weavers of northern Cumberland showed that all was not sweetness and light there in the age of the Chartists. Mr Roger Tufft and Mr Bruce Hanson have provided great help in matters of local government. Mr David Joy and Mr A. W. H. Pearsall provided helpful guidance on some crucial points of railway history, and Mr Rowland Atkinson provided material which could well have resulted in an adequate study of regional banking – a luxury which has had to be largely eschewed. There are other considerable debts: to Mr O. M. Westall for reading parts of the manuscript, and for making available the results of his work on moneyed settlers by Windermere, to the late Professor G. P. Jones, whose kindly encouragement led to the production of this book, to Mr T. G. Goodwin, whose work on Furness literacy was highly apposite to what is said in Chapter 6, to Mrs Margaret Capstick, whose knowledge of the recent economic development of Cumbria is in a class of its own; and to Mrs Marion McClintock and Mrs Helen Shaw, whose labours helped forward the production of a substantial typescript through a succession of stages. The County Record Offices at Carlisle and Kendal played their usual indispensable and unfailingly helpful parts.

The authors' gratitude to their wives calls for more than a perfunctory or formalised acknowledgement; it has a reality which could not receive adequate expression in print. Although the authors have worked closely together as colleagues, in order to give the book such organic unity as it possesses, J. D. Marshall takes full responsibility for Chapters 1 to 7 inclusive and for the Epilogue, and J. K. Walton is totally and completely the author of Chapters 8 and 9. Both are wholly responsible for the use of information placed at their disposal.

The Lake Counties, 1830–51: the changing face of the region

The Cumbrian scene of the years following 1830 was already becoming a stereotype in the minds of many people who lived outside the region. For two generations, guidebook and (later) directory compilers had, through their united efforts, formed a powerful public impression of a district 'so highly valued for its picturesque scenery'.[1] This last was treated as an asset even more valuable than its lead, copper, silver, slate or iron ore, even though Parson and White's lavish 1829 directory of the region was well enough aware of economic and social realities other than the delights of tourism.[2]

Wordsworth's magnificently written *Guide to the Lakes* was about to reach its fifth and best-known edition in 1835, and in it the Poet Laureate laid stress, like his less distinguished forbears, on scenery rather than on people. However, he did make reference to a Lakeland 'society' that was other than literary, and showed concern over 'an alteration in the circumstances of the native peasantry',[3] a concern which had of course dated from the wartime years, when the guide was conceived.[4] Meanwhile, the casual visitor or reader could have been forgiven for supposing that Lakeland, and Cumbrian, society consisted wholly of the inhabitants of limewashed farmhouses at the foot of the bracken-covered steeps. In fact, the people of the Lake Counties were represented by a great variety of social groups, themselves created by an ever more extensive economic alteration. Canon Bouch and Professor Jones, in their earlier volume on this general subject, rounded off their narrative by stressing the decreasing homogeneity as well as the greater variety of the early nineteenth century region: 'the societies of the hill, the plain and the coast, the communities of the shepherd, the corn growers, the millhands, miners and sailors, not, of course, completely isolated from each other but nevertheless with different interests and to a large extent a differing outlook'.[5]

Notwithstanding this, the region had become, over three centuries of development, more stable in the conduct of its social and political affairs, just as its population had become more mobile, more aware of other societies and communities, and, above all, more willing or able to accept ideas conveyed by the printed word. Indeed, it is a paradox that a society which was in flux in so many important respects was also becoming more unified in a variety of complex ways, as well as more heterogeneous. Turnpikes and improved postal services conveyed information and fashionable consumer goods as never before,[6] and the railway system was soon to make beauty spots in innermost Lakeland accessible to industrial workers on the region's coastal fringe. Industries themselves, whether growing or declining, led to the movement of people within the region as well as the migration of Cumbrians beyond its boundaries, and these same people often studied a more widely circulating newspaper press for news of trade near home as readily as they did for details of events abroad. It should be added that the local newspapers themselves, increasing in number in these years, certainly grew to contain more district and regional news, and this is a contention that can be verified mathematically. As families became more widely distributed than they had been one or two centuries before, so their ability to communicate in writing, or to exchange news of different parts of the region, was undoubtedly augmented. Those who left the region to work elsewhere did not, in the short term, become less consciously Cumbrian, but were probably even more aware of their origins. Finally, the rates of social and economic change in the region, although quickening variably, were not yet so rapid or all-embracing as to undermine many traditional views, attitudes, customs or forms of speech. Those who were not forced to tear up their roots were becoming more conscious of them, and those who did experience or suffer the tearing process were of course only too well aware of what was taking place. Cumbria was not only becoming a more completely integrated part of a nation, but also a more self-conscious one.

It is true, indeed, that the world of the individual Cumbrian, in so far as the latter clearly saw 'Cumbria' (rather than, say, 'canny auld Cummerlan') as a horizon, was very largely a rural world, with all the restrictions of view that situation implies, and in the case of the last-mentioned county, scarcely more than one-fifth of the 1831 population was to be found in the main towns of Carlisle, Whitehaven, Penrith and Keswick, while rather under a third of the inhabitants of Westmorland, in the same year, lived in Kendal, Appleby, Kirkby Lonsdale and Kirkby Stephen.[7] As population movement intensified, however, most of these towns came to develop complex and manifold inter-relationships with their neighbouring countrysides, and some, like Kendal,[8] had been forming such relationships for a considerable period. Such towns certainly did not represent microcosms with a sense of abiding separation from the rural reality beyond their streets. People were far less likely to be separated by any town–country distinction of view than by differences of occupation, origin, or physical situation as defined by mountain barriers and the vicinity of roads. Further, a great part of the population of Cumbria occupied the relatively fertile areas of the Eden Valley or the Solway plainland and coastal lowlands, and were, of course, primarily aware of these sub-regions or localities as their essentially home territory, the 'country' of the seventeenth-century gentleman or yeoman, defined by journeys to market, visits to family and friends, or even the far-ranging movements of the fox-hunts to which all rural groups passionately adhered. Social custom, market areas, roads, sports, town distribution, river crossings, occupations, village densities and other geographical or social considerations no doubt 'determined' these home areas, just as it is quite certain that administrative boundaries hardly ever did so except where the law and fiscal requirements pinched the victim.

As Bouch and Jones implied, there were considerable differences between agricultural and industrial communities within these areas. But there were common cultural elements also – a man did not change overnight because he moved from a farm servant's attic to a coalmine – and, likewise, there was an element of cultural homogeneity throughout large parts of the whole. There need be no mystery about this; the major industry of Cumbria, agriculture, not only had deep-seated traditions and practices, but had long stimulated the movement or migration of individuals as a necessary part of its way of life. The Cumbrian farmworker was not tied to his parish, like so many further south are said to have been, and the magistrates and village rulers had long seen to it that he was hired – as a living-in 'servant' – for six months at a time, in order that farm servants, given to free-ranging movement, could not obtain poor-law settlements.[9] Some of this movement was regularised, if not wholly confined to Cumbrians, and, as though to demonstrate the frequent irrelevance of purely administrative boundaries, there was a powerful and traditional link between Furness and West Cumberland forged by travelling reapers, who came to work in the early harvests of Low Furness from their small farms at the bases of the western fells.[10] Some of the reapers were, indeed, Irish, noted for their voracious appetite for heavy labour, and doubtless blamed for 'the drunkenness, quarrelling and fighting, which (had) defied all law, civil and ecclesiastical' in the hiring town of Dalton-in-Furness.[11] Local and regional consciousness, however, could be strengthened, if in a chauvinistic and illiberal direction, by the presence of these useful aliens, who were to play such a powerful political and social role in parts of West Cumberland, and who were already working in the mines of Whitehaven in fair numbers.[12] Meanwhile, the Cumbrian farmer was given to following, both mentally and physically, the movements of cattle. 'Most of the North Cumberland farmers', wrote William Dickinson, 'from their adjacency to the great driving-roads, have a smattering of trade in either cattle, sheep or horses',[13] and the great cattle traffic from Scotland, which continued to affect the regional and national economy, was enjoying its Indian summer.[14]

A countryside's culture must necessarily have its basis in trades and crafts, and the farmers of the region spoke, on the whole, a common language coalescing around the sheep, with its references to the fold-bitted, ritted or sneck-bitted lugmarks of the *Shepherd's Guide* (1819), or the drystone walling of thousands of acres of rough fell, with its heartings, its footings and its throughs. Dialect and accents, although displaying many subtle differences, were not barriers to understanding within the region, and stood as recognisably rugged as the mountains to anybody outside it; the use of *lile* (little) by a man from Furness, and *laal* in the more gritty speech of West Cumberland, would not be noted easily in London. But the outward or physical manifestations of regional culture would have struck a traveller readily enough, so that a visitor to Dalton-in-Furness would have seen, in squat vernacular buildings, the heavy stone window-posts and lintels of West Cumberland, and a man entering the region somewhere beyond Lancaster, the round drystone chimney stacks of South Westmorland. The pele towers of Beetham and Arnside would have pointed to a troubled world of past centuries, sharing common terrors with border areas scores of miles northward.

There would have been plenty of evidence of more recent changes written into the landscape. The traveller pressing onward into the region would have noted closes and dales of ploughland or stubble alongside nearly every lane, just as research would have shown him ancient town and common arable fields tucked into corners of Bannisdale and Longsleddale. The signs of cultivation were recent, often no older than the Napoleonic Wars, when the acreages under the plough must have been vast indeed. A generation later, the tithe and corn rent schedules could still show proportions of arable land that seem unbelievable by present-day standards; although 62 per cent (1839–47) of a group of Solway Plain parishes, and the 46 per cent of another group in the West Cumberland plain may not be entirely incredible, the 18 per cent of some upland or dales parishes is certainly more impressive.[15] Some of the ploughing was for the purpose of improving moorland pasture, as James Losh noted when he rode by the bleak Stainmore hillsides in the early 1820s,[16] and much of this land, over-limed and greedily taken in, had lapsed back to rough grazing. But where the sharper greens of the improved pasture met the russets and browns and streakier greens of the rougher land, the ruler-straight walls soared everywhere. By the 1830s, fewer wallers were at work, rood by rood, and the enclosure fever was seemingly a memory; the Cumbrian farmer was passing through a period of relative quiescence and stability. There had been a steady but limited incidence of Cumbrian enclosure from 1760 to the onset of the French Wars, a great burst in the early years of the new century to 1816, and a recession after that year. Some enclosure was certainly proceeding in the few years after 1830, but it hardly represented the state of excitement of the Cumberland of 1793 to 1816, when some 200 000 acres were enclosed,[17] or of the massive operation in the parish of Cartmel (1796–1809), when the entire scenery was transformed from limestone fell to mossland grazing, and wheatfields appeared in formerly undrained land by Morecambe Bay.[18]

In 1830, the farmer of the region stood on the eve of another phase of agricultural transformation, this time more steady and less dramatic. The state of his mind and pocket was knowledgeably described by William Blamire, nephew of the great J. C. Curwen and M.P. for East Cumberland, before the Select Committee on Agriculture of 1833;[19] Blamire himself was to achieve fame through his work for tithe commutation, which in turn produced the maps and schedules we have mentioned. The evidence put forward by Blamire, in so far as it is possible to summarise it fairly at all, is broadly as follows: the prosperity of the wartime period had not altered the frugal habits of the Cumbrian farmers, who suffered from high rents, over-demanding labourers — 'now they have tea and coffee often for breakfast; formerly they never had anything but porridge'[20] — and undue competition for land or better farms. However, their houses were comfortable, dry and warm, and 'pretty well furnished', and the archaeological evidence supports his claim, for many of the solid double-pile, double-fronted farmhouses of West Cumberland and the Eden valley belong to this age.[21] What is more, the census schedules of 1841 and 1851 show these farmhouses to have been sheltering not only large families — for young men still stayed under the family roof to help their fathers — but strikingly large teams of labourers. For this was a period and region of plough-culture and horse-culture as well as sheep-culture, and in the heavier clays of the lower territories one needed an extra man for every 60 or 70 acres.[22] Since the local farmworker in this labour-intensive economy demanded, and got, money wages which were relatively high when viewed nationally,[23] the farmers and their Cumbrian spokesmen told the Poor Law Commission of 1832, almost unanimously, that their capital was 'diminishing'.[24] Blamire's doubtless well-informed commentary paints a picture of frugality on the part of the larger farmers — 'the family are up about five in the morning . . . and they generally have their breakfast soon after six, which consists of oatmeal-porridge with milk, barley, bread and cheese'.[25] Men farming up to rentals of £600 a year still lived and worked in humble fashion.[26] But frugality on the part of the better-placed did not mean pauperism on the part of the labourers, in what was then a corn-exporting region[27] which needed nearly every able-bodied man it could find. The corn went to Lancashire and Northumberland,[28] and in this sense Cumbria was part of a great food-supplying area for the industrial north, even though, as was later admitted,[29] its soils and character were not really shaped for the supply of cereals beyond its own needs. Yet circumstances change, and the Cumbrian farming society of the time of Victoria's accession merely struggled with its own prejudices and limitations.

It quite evidently believed in keeping men employed, so much so that the threshing machine made little headway in the Lake Counties;[30] in the hard periods of the winter, the indoor labourers swung the cumbersome flail on the threshing floors. The farms themselves were smaller than even Blamire suggested in his commentary, the mean size being considerably less than 100 acres, and yet the number of farm labourers per employer was appreciably more than two in

1831.[31] It is easy to assume that the smaller farmers or yeomen were 'backward' by the standards of their time, but remaining family evidence relating to such persons does not suggest that the patronising remarks of agricultural reporters were necessarily justified; one group of yeomen, whose farmhouses remain in part to be seen in the modern Barrow suburb of Salthouse, were in fact using a threshing machine in 1830, utilising an improved iron plough in the following few years, and experimenting with shorthorn cattle, clover and chaff-cutters in the period we now describe,[32] while the surviving diary of John Grainger of Southerfield, a yeoman's son from the Solway plain, indicates a keenly intelligent and informed interest in the agricultural world (1828).[33] These, of course, were men working in the arable and exporting districts, and the sheep farmers of the dales necessarily lived in more isolated and restricting worlds. The general evidence for technical advancement in farming shows a certain slowness in reacting to the need for basic improvement, and threshing machines were being introduced in fair numbers only in the 1840s and 1850s,[34] while tile drainage was spreading steadily in the same decades.[35] The social gain, of course, lay in the low pauperism of the region in the 1830s,[36] and notwithstanding any labour-intensifying effects of work on the threshing floor and with cereals, turnip and potato cultivation, the demand for able-bodied labour necessarily increased as extractive industries developed and as railways were built in the 1840s.[37] The population of rural Cumbria continued to increase during this period, albeit at a strikingly diminishing rate. The rate of increase in local rural districts of Cumberland and Westmorland (excluding 'towns' of more than 2000 inhabitants), was less than 0.4 per cent per annum, or only about one-third of the rate for the rural districts of England taken *in toto*.[38] Yet, simultaneously, the earlier returns of the Registrar-General show high rates of natural increase in Cumbrian country districts,[39] and it is clear that the net loss by migration was considerable.

Hence, the region appears in two further striking, if not distinctive, guises or roles. It was a supplier of labour for the industrial areas, towns and manufacturing industries; and it was at the same time a relatively high-wage area in agricultural terms, although the statistics of money wages for the time, region and nation, often quoted, can be misleading – the farm servants who made up more than half of the wage-earning agricultural labour force were paid substantially in kind, and these allowances for keep and accommodation could be variable, and were often Spartan. But a frugal way of life, accepted by both farmer and labourer, was dedicated to the supplying of food to more distant markets, as we have seen, and a competitive economy was offering some opportunities to the hard-working farmer's son or farm servant. Finally, the yeomen about whom Wordsworth had written, with their peasant republic in the inner valleys,[40] were still falling out of the race and slowly diminishing in numbers; although directory entries are imperfect statistical sources,[41] the land tax lists of owner-occupiers support the argument up to 1831,[42] and William Blamire, the knowledgeable contemporary, was in any case definite on this point. '(Their) number has considerably diminished', he remarked in 1833, 'and the situation of those who are still in existence is considerably worse than it was'.[43] As Professor Jones suggested, the yeomanry of 1829 made up about one-third of all listed occupiers as given by Parson and White,[44] but their apparent survival does not manifest any particular geographical or economic logic.[45] Those persons designated as 'yeomen', who were conceivably manorial customaryholders or copyholders of the old style, or simply long-established small freeholders, were apparently disappearing rapidly in the Windermere area, but were numerous in the eastern lead-mining territories, and they continued to appear in the remoter dales until well into the twentieth century.[46] But a great mystery surrounds their supposed disappearance. The 1873 *Return of Owners of Land* shows that tiny Westmorland had no fewer than 4376 owners of land, many of them with small acreages, and many with fair-sized farms. Plainly these were not the decimated yeomen; and equally plainly, such persons were not being absorbed in great numbers by large landowners. Small freeholders and owner-occupiers were there in strength, just as hundreds of them remain in the present century.

It would be improper to conclude this part of the survey without referring to the great landowners of the region. As is shown in Chapter 3 (see especially Table 3.1), the proportion of small farms in Cumberland and Westmorland in the middle of the century was considerable when viewed against a national norm or background. Yet the region also contained a number of great landed estates, like those of the Lowthers, Grahams, Howards, Leconfields (or Wyndhams) and Tuftons, with well over 10 000 acres in either Cumberland or Westmorland, or, as in the case of the Lowthers, four to five times that number of acres in both counties together. As Professor F. M. L. Thompson has suggested in his *Landed Society in the Nineteenth Century* (1963), it was in the middle ground, that of the landed gentry, that the region was weakest when compared with other English counties. Hence, although the great landowners might indeed have influenced more general agricultural practice beneficially, through experimentation with improved breeds of cattle or sheep, or, as in Sir James Graham's case, through the diffusion of drainage techniques from the 1820s, it is reasonably clear that their role in the region's agrarian life was limited by the existence of large numbers of small farmers with little capital. As is argued in Chapter 5, their influence was primarily political and social. The Second Earl of Lonsdale, and Sir James Graham of Netherby (through their roles in Peel's government) were of course major figures in the national scene. The Lowthers in particular represented Cumberland and Westmorland impartially in parliament, in the latter case apparently irremoveably. In travelling about the southern and western parts of the region, it would hardly have been possible to ignore the existence of the Lowther mansions at Whitehaven and at Lowther Castle in north Westmorland.

Their pervasive influence which reached into innumerable corners in both counties, and had a powerful industrial connection, was constantly reflected in the newspaper press, and was, too, another factor making for a more general regional consciousness. Cumbria had been, in effect, their political kingdom in the eighteenth century, and informed members of the political nation had taken this state of affairs for granted.

Industry was manifesting itself in scores of Cumbrian settlements, not always, it is fair to say, 'on the fringes of the region'. Some of its activities were hidden away in country factories, invariably water-powered, and it was not of the kind that thrust great chimneys into a greying sky from greyer towns. Towns did, however, play a larger part in its development than could easily be appreciated, and many of its domestic and other industries had some kind of urban stimulus or base, just as the majority of its towns lay on its plainland or coastal periphery. It is clear that there was some centrifugal movement of migrant labour towards this fringe territory, and soon after 1830 an Assistant Commissioner on the Poor Laws, who had been noting some evidently very visible transformations in the region,[47] made the following remarks:

> the extensive coal-mines and the large manufacturing establishments have continued to afford a great demand for labour. The enclosure of common and waste land, and (the) bringing (of) it into cultivation, has been very great; at the same time canals and new roads have been constructed, particularly a very fine road across the fells from Aldstone (*sic*) to Hexham, and a superb railroad is in progress between Carlisle and Newcastle. It will be evident, therefore, that there must be a demand for labourers, and scarcely any who can be called able-bodied are on the poor-rates.

Some of these points have already been made, and are of course supported by other evidence from the time and region. Assistant Commissioner Pringle indulged himself in apparent hyperbole on the subject of 'extensive coal-mines' because he had no doubt seen the impressive Howgill and Whingill pit complexes at Whitehaven, the property of the Lowthers, or the Curwen mines at Workington. In both places miners worked beneath the sea. Nevertheless, coalmining supported only a few hundred miners, even in these major coastal centres, and in no sense could the coalfield area of West Cumberland, stretching from St Bees to the countryside near Aspatria, be regarded as a separate industrial world, cut off from the rest of Cumberland by occupation and self-awareness. In much of the field, miners went to work by lonely field paths and *lonnins* to small pits hidden behind hedges, and their spoil heaps remain to be traced by the industrial archaeologists of today. The Census of 1831 is reticent on the numbers of people engaged in the collieries of this area, and its most significant entries relate to an increase in population in Camerton because of 'the Coal Mines in the Parish', or in Plumbland, 'ascribed to additional Collieries and Limeworks'. Both were rural places of the kind indicated. But, as is implied, changes were slowly taking effect, and the division of Allerdale Above Derwent, in which many of the mines were found, did indeed contain more than the regional average number of non-agricultural labourers. Yet, even in this division or ward such workers were outnumbered by agricultural labourers, and its saturation level of non-agricultural workers was roughly matched by that of Leath Ward, in the east of the region, where the Alston and other lead miners were to be found. In both divisions mentioned, roughly one in every ten males of all ages was an industrial worker, but in other wards of both Cumberland and Westmorland, the proportion was likely to be nearer one in thirty.[48]

The 'superb railroad' mentioned by Pringle was, too, very much in evidence, and, like the improved turnpike and other roads, it was doubtless training footloose migrants as well as giving the employment which caused navvies to move into the Carlisle locality.[49] But this was still very much an age of the horse, and the county's rulers evidently regarded any threat to equine dominance, as represented by the Newcastle and Carlisle Railway, with distaste. The bill for that line prohibited locomotives (1829), and even stationary engines 'within view of the Castle of Naworth or Corby Castle' and other mansion houses.[50] It is true that the outlook of the Howards of Corby was about to be drastically modified by the soaring railway viaduct at Wetheral (1833), made out of the red sandstone of the Eden gorge, and the local magnates soon grew used to the plumes of steam which replaced the horse-drawn waggons. Their attitude, however, was scarcely one which was likely to question the industrial limitations of the region itself, and only the Lowthers and the Curwens, with a very few others, were steeped in the ideas of industrial enterprise – and the mining of coal and ore in their sub-region, West Cumberland, merely produced raw material to feed fires in Ireland or furnaces in South Wales, just as its fields helped to fill the bellies of Lancashire. Cumbria would not utilise its own resources to develop its industries in any decisive manner until the 1870s. Even the tiny Ulverston Canal (1796) and the Lancaster Canal from Kendal (1819), with the Port Carlisle canal link with the old border city (1823) tended to guide raw materials seawards or outwards. The Port Carlisle Canal, however, had its uses as a means of transportation for local cotton imports, required in nearby mills.

The textile industries, indeed, were widely diffused within the region, in towns and countryside, and their most advanced development was doubly epitomised by the massive cotton mill of Peter Dixon in Shaddongate, Carlisle, open in October 1836, and by the mill's 305-foot chimney, still a remarkable feature of the Carlisle skyline.[51] The mill's spinning activities depended on the labour of perhaps 3500 weavers scattered through the north of the region, and many others, weaving in linen as well as cotton, disposed of their yarn to other manufacturers. In Carlisle itself, up to a quarter of the population still depended upon the employment offered by its seven mills and 122 000 spindles.[52] But by 1844, the weavers of the yarn had suffered more than a generation of steady

1 'The textile industries were widely diffused within the region'. A glass plate print showing workers' cottages (long disappeared) and the mill at Backbarrow.

impoverishment, and some were yet to struggle on starvation wages at the time of the Cotton Famine. Handloom weavers long remained numerous in several of the smaller towns of northern Cumberland, and their difficulties posed problems for the early Victorian Poor Law authorities or magistrates in Longtown, Wigton, Cockermouth and Brampton.[53] Even Allonby, which lived largely by fishing, agriculture and sea-bathing, had one in twelve of its household heads engaged in weaving in 1841.[54] Further south, the Penrith of *c.* 1847 still had 'about 100 weavers, who are employed . . . by the Carlisle manufacturers'[55] while handloom weaving, employed by other spinners or agents, remained important in Kendal and its environs,[56] and it is significant that the main centres of social and political unrest in Cumbria developed where these poor but often organised and politically conscious groups bulked largest. Carlisle, especially, maintained a well-earned reputation for radical militancy into the Chartist period, while Wigton and Cockermouth saw angry stirrings of the adherents of physical force.[57] By contrast, the miners in the Lowther industrial fiefdom of Whitehaven, and elsewhere on the west coast, were almost completely quiescent after some bitter strikes in Whitehaven in 1831 and 1843, when troops had to be called in to quell

10

would-be trade unionists.[58] Kendal, with a more mixed economy, and perhaps a more mobile population than was common in most of the regional towns, met and turned a Chartist challenge of very limited sharpness,[59] and conflict was keener elsewhere in the 1830s and 1840s, in localities where the economic decline of the weavers stood out clearly. In Kendal this was certainly not the case in 1831, and there 'between 500 and 600 Males (were) variously employed there in making Cotton-checks, Kerseys, Linsey, Blanketting, Fancy-Waistcoating, Carpets, Girths, Hosiery and Sacking'.[60] Of these, the blankets, to be used by railway travellers as well as horses, and the carpets were to play their part in keeping the local economy buoyant.[61]

Elsewhere, there was a striking diffusion of small industries across the countryside, and even the most rugged fellsides had their mining and quarrying. Travelling from Kendal, one would have found 'Canvas and Linens at Holme, Kirkby-Lonsdale and Orton; Bobbin is *(sic)* made at Stanley (Staveley), Strickland-Roger, Hugill and a few other places; Gunpowder at Sedgwick and Langdales'.[62] The rather fastidious 1831 Census did not mention quarrying, or basketmaking, but Parson and White's *Directory* for 1829 more than makes up for its omissions by giving a convincing picture of these industries, and several others, in the Furness area.[63] As we shall see, it is equally informative about the remainder of the region, and there is at least enough information about the industrial, and to some extent the occupational, structure of the countryside to show why it was able to sustain a measure of population growth, however modest the latter might be. There was an increasing specialisation of trades and industries within the fabric of rural life, and among the side-effects of the trade cycles of the age was an enhanced movement of people, some of it enforced, and, probably, a greater social and political awareness. Hence, it is unsurprising to find that handloom weavers were flung into the passionate debates of the age, but more noteworthy to find that hoopmakers in North Lonsdale were capable of organising a strike in the turbulent year of 1848.[64] The mere fact of movement necessarily widened social horizons, even though the latter were often on a regional scale only, and the census enumeration schedules for 1851 show lead-miners from Alston working in the copper mines of Coniston, while those for 1861 demonstrate that persons from both of these places were employed at the lead-mining settlement of Glenridding (Greenside) by Ullswater. None of these centres maintained very large populations, and the major and more developed mining centres, like the industries of the seaboard, exported their raw materials to other regions, just as the slate of the Lakeland mountains went to the industrial towns. However, the economic development of the rural parts of Cumbria, and of its smaller towns, did not depend wholly upon external demand, markets and industries, and developing agriculture within the region exerted a steady influence through its ancillary crafts and industries.

This was especially the case where the iron-using or metal-using trades were

11

concerned, and a search through the Parson and White *Directory* for 1829 produces six scythe and sickle-makers in Cumberland and Westmorland, six spade-makers in the same counties, eight plough or machine-makers and no fewer than 435 blacksmiths. The building trades gave employment to 56 nail-making establishments, and maritime activity supported ten anchor and cable makers. Generally speaking, these industries were diffused; hence, there were spade-making establishments, using modest supplies of water power, at Dalston, Cleator and in Furness. It was enough that they were near to an agricultural district, or to mines of some kind. Other local industries clustered near their sources of supply, and this was especially true of the bobbin-making industry, with its small mills occupying sites near the coppice woodlands of southern Lakeland, and, in one case, concentrating together in the Westmorland market village of Staveley. The latter accordingly grew in status, and had acquired its own cattle fair by 1831.[65]

There is no mystery about Staveley's development at this time; abundant water-power was available at the meeting point of three small rivers, and it was on a main turnpike route down which light products like bobbins could easily be sent, in this case to the industrial towns of Lancashire and Yorkshire. The growth of other Cumbrian country towns, which was very much a fact of this age, presents more complex problems of interpretation. The larger market centres grew, between 1801 and 1841, considerably faster than the smaller ones, and it is clear that the concentration of minor industries aided this process in, for example, Wigton, Cockermouth and, to a lesser extent, Brampton. But, whether the region's 35 or so identifiable market centres were supported by an industrial infrastructure or not – and at least 17 of them were[66] – their social and service functions were of vital importance to what was still largely a rurally related or rurally thinking population – and one, moreover, which frequently and characteristically lived in small, scattered settlements. The numbers of shops and services which appear in small centres like Egremont, or even the tiny port of Harrington, in 1829 or 1841, are striking, and it is apparent that for many local people they represented sharply defined horizons of economic, social and recreational activity; that is to say, most people satisfied most of their needs at these particular points. So, equally, the medium-sized towns with concentrations of more than a thousand people at a given urban centre were at the high noon of their importance, and sometimes considerably smaller places like Burton-in-Kendal or Milnthorpe show a signal range of functions. Hence, Burton had a striking variety of shops and workshops (and we can take ten shops or over as constituting a shopping centre), attorneys, doctors, agricultural repair and services facilities in the form of wheelwrights and blacksmiths, petty sessions, a grammar school, several public houses and coach, carrier and canal services.[67] If we add to this array of desiderata the possession of a banking service, and the existence of other religious edifices than a parish church, we have a list of requirements that can be applied usefully to a list of Cumbrian towns and market centres at this period; and out of the 35 that have been noted, at least 26 of them could satisfy seven of these services or needs. Yet we may take warning from the case of Burton-in-Kendal, which even in 1829 was reduced to 'small importance' as a market centre, and which had its corn market and inspector moved to Kendal on the opening of the Lancaster Canal.[68] The railway system of a generation later

2 Main towns and social or industrial centres in Cumbria, c. 1830.

13

was to have profound but subtle and variable effects on local markets and cattle fairs.

How far did residents of different parts of Cumbria look beyond the local horizons which these market towns, and their array of services, represented? Surprisingly, there is evidence that localism of this kind did not preclude the growth of wider awareness, if only because physical movement, or the lack of it, is not to be equated with a limitation of information and interests. It is true that during the period of which we write there is evidence of greater internal migration, if not more regular travel, within the region, and primary sources like parish registers suggest a greater flux of people within localities. This impression is reinforced by sources like the farm attendance book kept by the small landowner Roger Taylor of Finsthwaite in Furness (1822–41), which shows a steady turnover of casual labour during the whole of that period.[69] Yet the 1851 Census schedules demonstrate that the overwhelming majority of country people in sample areas of Westmorland were either born in their own parishes, or had originated a few miles away,[70] and the truth seems to be that much of the movement of people related to certain occupations or activities – those of farm servants, reapers, drovers, tailors, carriers, carters, navvies, mariners or pedlars – and that this type of movement was largely a surface phenomenon, if a growing one. Even by 1861, the total number of Cumberland and Westmorland-born people living in Furness did not exceed 12 per cent of the total population there.[71]

How, then, can we conceive of the growth of regional consciousness, even at the period under discussion? There are several considerations here, one of them unexpectedly obvious, and several more subtle. The obvious consideration is that of the visible environment, the distinctive nature and shape of the Cumbrian landscape. Most Cumbrians are keenly aware of the shape of the central mountains, visible from all points of the compass, so that a man in the Eden valley sees, on the western skyline, the unmistakeable form of Saddleback and the central dome of hills rising above distant fields. No man or woman who travelled only a few long journeys within the region could doubt its general topography, just as the same person could have little doubt about the eastern boundary of the Cumbrian world, with Mickle Fell, Dufton Fell and Cross Fell rearing like a wall to mark its limits. A man in Furness is constantly aware of Black Combe as his looming companion; a farmer on the higher hillsides of south Westmorland has the Old Man of Coniston rearing before him. More than this; people who travelled close to the hard ground were aware of its shape far more keenly than are the imprisoned travellers of today, and knowledge of countryside and landmarks was hard won and long remembered.

A genuine enough attachment to a broad tract of hill and dale was understandable, and local, even regional patriotism began to find a voice in the later eighteenth century, through the words of poets like Robert Anderson:[72]

Yer buik-larn'd wise gentry, that seen monie counties,
May preach and palaver, and brag as they will
O' mountains, lakes, valleys, woods, watters and meadows,
But canny auld Cummerlan' caps them aw still.

The nineteenth century saw a multiplication of Cumbrian dialect versifiers,[73] and it is not the quality of their writings that need concern us here, but rather the evident fact that they had a literate and widespread public, who celebrated their Cumbrian patriotism by reading, in the printed word, the speech of their forefathers. About the literacy there can be no doubt at all, and it was accompanied by an unusually high provision of schools (see Chapter 6 below), suggesting a clear relationship of one occurrence to the other. Table 1.1 is taken from the Registrar-General's recordings of marriage signatures or marks for 1839–45.[74]

Table 1.1 Marriage signatures (mean figures 1839–45)

	Percentage of men		Percentage of women	
	Signing with marks	Signing their names	Signing with marks	Signing their names
Metropolis	12	88	24	76
Cumberland	16	84	36	64
Northumberland	19	81	37	63
E. Riding Yorks.	20	80	39	61
Westmorland	20	80	35	65
England	33	67	49	51
Herts.	51	49	56	44
Beds.	51	49	64	36
Monmouth	51	49	65	35

It will be seen that high apparent literacy (and ability to sign is clearly not the same thing) was a border phenomenon, and the region had much in common with Scotland in the educational sphere. But no southern Scottish county, for all the kirk-inspired scholarship of its *Statistical Account* entries, had the same reasons for self-awareness as the Lake Counties, which had long been the subject of a steady stream of topographical studies and guides. Many of these, it must be recognised, were read outside rather than within the region, but there can be little doubt that they were also read within an educated stratum in Cumbrian society. The antiquarian work of Nicolson and Burn or Hutchinson[75] had given way to more popular studies like John Housman's *Topographical Description of Cumberland, Westmorland, Lancashire and Part of the West Riding* (1800), which had run through six or more editions by 1830. Guides to the Lake District, which did not pay much attention to county boundaries, were now appearing in profusion, and those by William Green[76] and Hodgson[77] purported to examine local society and its traditions, whilst the classic fifth edition of Wordworth's *Guide* (1835) enriched the sightseeing and sensitivities of generations. Nor is it merely naive to assume that such books remained unread inside small-town societies; the majority of the market towns of the region had one or more booksellers in 1829,[78] and the better-known topographical studies were advertised in the regional press.

The public which read books also read newspapers, and this age saw a steady growth of the newspaper press, modest at first, and inhibited by the so-called 'taxes on knowledge',[79] but fairly influential throughout large tracts of the region. A news-sheet could be read by more than one person, and political conflict necessarily stimulated interest. The influential Whig *Carlisle Journal* (1798) was later challenged by the Tory *Carlisle Patriot* (1815), just as the radical *Kendal Chronicle* (1811) was afterwards brought into combat with the Tory *Westmorland Gazette* (1819). The *Cumberland Pacquet* (1774), however, had fired the first Lowtherite Tory shots long before, and it will be noted that much of the political and electoral controversy transcended county boundaries in spirit, and surrounded the great magnates of both Cumberland and Westmorland, the Lowthers, Earls of Lonsdale. Even though the 'stamp-duty' readership of all these newspapers barely exceeded 5000 *in toto* at this period, they percolated, through reading rooms and other means of sharing, to a much wider public. Some of the readers were poor men and weavers, and in between elections, when the newspapers inevitably reflected a multitude of less partisan preoccupations, there was an increasing tendency to display regional cultural self-awareness through the publication of dialect poems, or to portray local traditions or ceremonies which were peculiar to an area. It may be no accident that Robert Anderson's collected poems were prepared for the press by Robert Perring, editor of the *Carlisle Patriot*.

There can be little doubt, too, that the regional newspapers reached a group which has not hitherto been mentioned – the substantial communities of Cumbrians, migrants from the region, residing in the great cities, especially in London. It is noteworthy that Anderson's poem on 'Canny Auld Cummerlan' was originally recited to the Cumberland Anniversary Society in the metropolis, and throughout the nineteenth century there was a flourishing Westmorland Society in London also, which was evidently connected with displays of Cumbrian-style wrestling there.[80] This distinctive sport appeared in the industrial towns of Lancashire also, to appeal to a partly migrant audience. Meanwhile, it is often observed that patriotism, local or other, will develop roughly in proportion to one's distance from home territory, and men from the Lake Counties, measuring themselves, sometimes very successfully, against strangers and southerners, did not lose in self-consciousness as time passed by.

It may be that some of this regional awareness appealed to a bucolic past which was already becoming a memory in parts of the region itself. Certainly, Cumbria's societies and localities were themselves changing, slowly in the rural setting, and more rapidly in the industrial one. The changing industrial scene is examined in the following chapter.

The economy of the region: its changing shape and structure, 1830–1914

As we have seen, industry was already well established in parts of western Cumbria by 1830. Yet the visitor, even had he confined his activities to surveys of the mines of the Whitehaven district or of Workington, or to listening to the clack of looms in Wigton, would hardly have been conscious of encountering the forms of industrialisation which had, by that date, spread across southern Lancashire. He would have been justifiably astonished had he visited West Cumberland and Furness towards the end of his own lifetime – say, after a lapse of forty years – and been precipitated into an area of winding railway lines, greasy spoil heaps and gaunt headstocks; flaring furnaces and beating blast engines; and, above all, redbrick or stone terraces and busy streets. By that time, of course, tourists were entering the Lake District in fair numbers, and were made aware of this new and alien world beyond the mountain barrier only by their occasional encounters with excursion trains. As the latter creaked into Keswick, Coniston and Lakeside stations, visitors heard the speech, harsh or outlandish, of workers from Scotland, Ireland, the North-East or Cornwall. These men (who were, at that time, often without womenfolk) represented the new industrial world that had mushroomed out of sight of the polite, comfortably mobile and moneyed, a coastal microcosm and sub-region with its own peculiar mixture of manners, customs, religious affiliations and ways of life. They represented not only a different world, but new wealth and a great accession of population to parts of the Lake Counties.

Despite such development, and sometimes because of it, much of Cumbria was understandably barren and empty. As late as 1891, Westmorland was the most sparsely populated county in England, with a mean population of 81 persons to a square mile, measured against a national mean of 497, and the upland or mountainous areas of Cumberland were likewise thinly peopled. Only remote Welsh counties like Radnorshire and Montgomery had fewer people per square mile or acre.[1] It will, however, be easily understood that population densities can vary greatly within the compass of a mile or two, and averages are for that very reason misleading. A pleasantly fertile dale like the Lyvennet valley in Westmorland might have three or four hundred people in a square mile, especially in the areas of villages like Crosby Ravensworth or Maulds Meaburn.[2] These rural localities were capable of maintaining a high rate of natural increase (excess of births over deaths), and thereby producing a steady outflow of young people without themselves experiencing great absolute loss during the course of the nineteenth century.

Thinly populated regions are also likely to be poor ones. But it must always be understood that poverty, like population density, is relative and variable, and that potential or exploited wealth may lie in unexpected places. Cumbria's most barren mountains contained, *inter alia*, silver, lead, copper, tungsten, and iron, and produced the finest of building slates,[3] just as they were able to attract to their wilder ridges not only sheep, foxes and ravens, but also dedicated visitors and, later, impassioned climbers. The upland fringes of the mountains bred hardy dalesmen and daleswomen who, as has been indicated, were fertile in their production of families, and helped to swell an out-movement of people which was one of Cumbria's greatest contributions to the national economy. Hence, a comparatively slow absolute growth of total population could be accompanied by rapid industrialisation in given localities, especially when persons from within the Lake Counties migrated to local urban districts during the course of their journeyings; and it is worth noticing that Cumberland, during its period of unprecedentedly rapid town and industrial development in 1851–81, evidently partially halted its outward drift, and at least did not fail contemptibly in its overall increase of people (Table 2.1).

Table 2.1 Relative population growth; northern and national rates compared

	1801	1851	1881	1911
Cumberland	100	166	214	227
Westmorland	100	143	157	155
Lancashire	100	301	513	706
Durham	100	262	581	917
England and Wales	100	201	292	406

The Cumbrian out-migrants followed a familiar pattern in settling, for the most part, in nearby counties and in industrial towns within those counties. Hence, the heaviest Cumberland out-migration was to Northumberland and Durham, especially on the part of males, and the most marked movement of Westmorland-born migrants, who were more noticeably female, was one into industrial Lancashire and Yorkshire, between the middle of the century and the census of 1891.[4] In addition, a substantial number of Cumbrians settled in London, and many of them did not lose their original patriotism in the process (see the Epilogue, pp. 221–2). The cardinal point here is not that nostalgia

19

growth of towns had consequences for the countryside in providing markets for food or labour, or in creating flows of tourists, and, *per contra*, that great landlords had much involvement in transport or industry or both. It is, indeed, with landlords and railways that the more detailed story of the region's Victorian economic development must commence. Moreover, one fact must be seen as fundamental: agriculture, in all its forms, remained Cumbria's major industry throughout the entire period covered by this volume, in that it employed the largest single section of the occupied population as revealed in census years. The reader will perceive that this revelation may not in itself mean very much in an economy which embraced a multiplicity of industries and occupations, and the significance of the observation is made palpable only if one compares the two main Cumbrian counties with the rest of the counties of England and Wales. The 'agricultural class' of both Cumberland and Westmorland, taken as a proportion of each 1000 persons occupied in 1891, for example, was markedly larger than the average for England and Wales (61 such persons per 1000), Cumberland having 93, and Westmorland 143. The latter was the ninth most 'agricultural' county in all the English counties. Meanwhile, Cumberland, notwithstanding the changes outlined, had a below-average proportion of persons engaged in industry (303 per 1000), as against the England and Welsh average of 333.[12]

This last proportion relative to Cumberland merely demonstrates how misleading county averages can be (or, indeed, how fallible are all averages for large areas), in that it masks the impressively rapid urban and industrial change which took place in the western districts of Cumbria in 1861–81. Otherwise, however, the drift of the 1891 census calculation[13] is a sound one; if we analyse in detail the agriculturally-related occupations[14] given in the census breakdowns classifying all persons 'occupied' or employed, then agriculture, despite a decline in its relative status over time as an employer, remained the most important single field of activity in the region throughout the Victorian period and beyond. It engaged 26.5 per cent of all occupied males and females in both Cumberland and Westmorland taken together in 1851, and nearly 14 per cent in the two counties in 1911. (See Appendix 3 p. 243–7.) Although several primary occupations associated with agriculture either increased little or suffered a relative decline, like quarrying or working in wood and timber, the fundamental factor at work in this fall-away was the selective out-migration of farm labourers, a matter discussed at greater length in Chapter 4 (pp. 68–79). Domestic service, too, was a vast and widespread giver of employment. The Cumberland of 1851, for example, had just over 38 per cent of its occupied workers engaged in domestic service and agriculture together, with 14 per cent in the former, and just over 40 per cent engaged in the other main forms of industry, cloth or textile manufacture (then the largest employer in the county with 15.5 per cent), clothes and shoes production and sale, working in metals (then only 3.26 per cent), food and drink industries, building and coalmining. In Westmorland, these industries, or non-agricultural, non-domestic service activities, understandably occupied a smaller sector, just over 31 per cent (1851) whilst domestic service and agriculture together occupied nearly 48 per cent of the working population there. Domestic service employed increasing numbers in both counties for the following forty or so years, and may, indeed, have played its part in drawing girls and women from the countryside, but, following national trends[15], it declined thereafter relatively and absolutely, holding up its numbers more firmly in Westmorland than in its neighbouring county, as a possible consequence of the growth of residential settlement and tourism together. By contrast, it had much less relative significance in Cumberland throughout, and in this respect it seems to have shared a common characteristic with the heavily industrial County of Durham; it had fallen to less than 10 per cent of all occupied persons there by 1891, and was little above that figure in Cumberland by 1911. It need only be added that the quite independent figures in the published Census of 1891[16] support these trends and positions, and show the industrial counties to have had relatively fewer people in the 'Domestic Class', Cumberland being below the national norm of 86 per 1000 with a figure of 80, and Westmorland being well above it with 100.

To return to the industrial front: Cumberland's transformation in the early and mid-Victorian decades was not wholly in the direction of a major swing to the largely localised production of iron, steel, and coal. It was accompanied by a serious decline in the textile industries, which was shared with the County of Westmorland, but which was experienced principally in the cotton industry of Carlisle and its sub-region. This affected both factory workers and domestic handloom weavers, and the decline was also responsible for the non-development of towns like Wigton, which after 1841, swung away from the production of coarse checks, linens and ginghams. By 1851 it was remarked that 'The stoppage of a calico manufactory' had contributed to its decline of population.[17] The extent of the more general collapse may be gauged from the fact that the proportion of Cumberland persons engaged in cloth manufacture fell from 15.5 per cent of all those occupied in 1851 to 5.7 in 1871. The Cotton Famine helped to bring about the bankruptcy of the great cotton firm of Peter Dixon in Carlisle,[18] which had employed many hundreds of handloom weavers in the north of the region, and there can be no doubt that the events of the 1860s stimulated a fateful downward slide in that district which was only checked by a limited recovery and stabilisation between 1891 and 1911.[19] Westmorland's and Kendal's woollen and cotton industries failed to develop after similar setbacks, and the Westmorland town was saved from a worse fate in the 1860s, and later, by the development of a famous shoe manufactory by the firm of Somervell.[20] Cumbria as a whole had, in the early and middle years of the century, developed a pattern of water-powered rural woollen, cotton, linen, and other industries[21], and although the absolute sizes of the labour forces involved were certainly not large in any one area, and embraced country colonies and mills like those still to be seen at Warwick Bridge[22], Cleator, and Dalston, their vicissitudes had short-term but serious consequences for country people. A cotton worker, with soft hands and specialised skills, could not simply transform himself into a railway or ironworks labourer or a coalminer overnight.

Several Cumbrian rural or market centres, like Wigton, Penrith, Cockermouth and Keswick, had placed some reliance on domestic or small-scale textile industries, and, almost without exception (Keswick benefited from the expansion of railway-borne and other tourism), it was towns of this type which showed slow or halting population growth after the middle of the century, despite their relationship with relatively prosperous agricultural districts. As we have seen, Carlisle textiles alone made some kind of convincing part-recovery. Other firms in the area of the city, like Ferguson's at Holme Head and at least three others in the locality, continued to work on a diminishing scale, and even in 1871, 20 per cent of the occupied population of Carlisle was engaged in the various textile branches of cotton, linen, woollens and general finishing. Between 1881 and 1901 there was a considerable contraction of cotton spinning in the city and its immediate district, partially offset by some development in wool and worsted, linen, rug, carpet and felt manufacture.[23] Indeed, the city area remained fairly strong in what had originally been widely distributed regional industries, with some additions – the fabric printing firm of Stead, McAlpine and Co. at Cummersdale, Messrs Robert Todd, woollen spinners at the former Dixon Mill in Shaddongate from 1888, and the establishment of Morton Sundour Fabrics (1900) by Alexander Morton, a former Ayrshire handloom weaver.[24] In 1911, Carlisle, with a total of 2121 workers in textile bleaching, dyeing, printing and finishing, had two-thirds of all the textile workers in Cumberland. Far more than this, however, it had become in the previous 50 years, a service centre of an even more influential kind than before, a role enhanced by the elaborate system of rail communications for which it was a focus during that period.

Economico-social impact cannot be measured invariably and accurately by occupational figures alone. The latter, in their more localised implications, go far to explain the relative rates of population growth for Cumbrian towns (see Table 2.2), but they are only broadly indicative of major changes in the regional economy, and they pose as many questions as they answer. They do not tell us precisely why entrepreneurial decisions were taken at a given time, and they point only in the broadest manner to the influence of national movements in industry, trade or fashion, just as they fail to tell us why individual workpeople not only entered the towns, but also left them, often between census years. One consequence or side-effect of the national or northern textile industry, one which had considerable local impact in rural Cumbria, was the development and rise, if not the subsequent decline, of the southern Lakeland bobbin-making industry. This was, until about 1870, of a far more direct utility to the cotton and woollen interests of Lancashire, Yorkshire and elsewhere than the mere outliers of fabric

Table 2.2 Urban growth in Cumbria, 1841–1911: populations (and percentage changes)

Main iron, coal or shipbuilding towns or areas, with ports

	1841	Change (%)	1851	Change (%)	1861	Change (%)	1871	Change (%)	1881	Change (%)	1891	Change (%)	1901	Change (%)	1911
Cleator(a)	763	*(133·1)*	1779	*(124·5)*	3995	*(76·7)*	7061	*(48·4)*	10420	*(−9·2)*	9464	*(−14·3)*	8120	*(2·2)*	8301
Egremont(b)	1750	*(17·1)*	2049	*(69·8)*	3481	*(30·1)*	4529	*(31·9)*	5976	*(2·2)*	6105	*(−5·6)*	5761	*(9·4)*	6305
Whitehaven(c)	17420	*(18·5)*	20636	*(2·1)*	21073	*(0·6)*	21208	*(5·8)*	22435	*(−3·8)*	21811	*(−1·0)*	21593	*(−0·6)*	21484
Total	19933	*(11·8)*	22464	*(27·1)*	28549	*(14·9)*	32798	*(18·4)*	38831	*(−3·7)*	37380	*(−5·1)*	35474	*(1·7)*	36090
Workington(d)	6045	*(3·9)*	6280	*(3·0)*	6467	*(30·1)*	8413	*(70·7)*	14361	*(65·1)*	23749	*(10·1)*	26139	*(−4·1)*	25065
Barrow(e)	—		—		3135	*(503·2)*	18911	*(149·9)*	47259	*(9·4)*	51712	*(11·4)*	57586	*(10·7)*	63770

Regional service centres of long duration

	1841	Change (%)	1851	Change (%)	1861	Change (%)	1871	Change (%)	1881	Change (%)	1891	Change (%)	1901	Change (%)	1911
Carlisle(f)	24488	*(19·7)*	29320	*(11·6)*	32723	*(5·5)*	34628	*(14·1)*	39509	*(6·4)*	42195	*(14·0)*	49088	*(0·9)*	49551
Kendal(g)	11447	*(0·6)*	11516	*(0·6)*	11588	*(12·0)*	12983	*(0·8)*	13088	*(3·5)*	13553	*(4·8)*	14183	*(−1·0)*	14033
Cockermouth(h)	4940	*(16·9)*	5775	*(−6·7)*	5388	*(−5·0)*	5115	*(4·6)*	5353	*(2·0)*	5464	*(−2·0)*	5355	*(−2·8)*	5203
Total	40875	*(14·0)*	46611	*(6·6)*	49699	*(6·3)*	52826	*(9·7)*	57950	*(5·6)*	61212	*(12·1)*	68628	*(0·2)*	68787

Main tourist centres and areas

	1841	Change (%)	1851	Change (%)	1861	Change (%)	1871	Change (%)	1881	Change (%)	1891	Change (%)	1901	Change (%)	1911
Bowness & Windermere (i)	1479	*(41·0)*	2085	*(43·3)*	2987	*(16·4)*	3478	*(19·3)*	4148	*(11·2)*	4613	*(9·7)*	5061	*(1·7)*	5147
Ambleside (j)	1281	*(24·3)*	1592	*(0·7)*	1603	*(24·0)*	1988	*(0)*	1989	*(18·7)*	2360	*(7·3)*	2536	*(0·7)*	2553
Keswick (k)	2442	*(7·2)*	2618	*(−0·3)*	2610	*(6·4)*	2777	*(15·3)*	3201	*(17·5)*	3760	*(19·7)*	4500	*(−2·1)*	4403
Total	5202	*(21·0)*	6295	*(14·4)*	7200	*(14·5)*	8243	*(13·3)*	9338	*(14·9)*	10733	*(12·7)*	12097	*(0)*	12103
England and Wales		*(12·6)*		*(11·9)*		*(13·2)*		*(14·4)*		*(11·6)*		*(12·2)*		*(10·9)*	

Notes:

(a) Cleator and Cleator Moor kept a stable acreage, modified only slightly by the Divided Parishes Acts of 1876 and 1879.

(b) The same applied to the parish of Egremont, with extensions 1881–1901, when it had become a borough.

(c) Whitehaven is represented (1841–91) by the township of Whitehaven, the chapelry of Hensingham, and the township of Preston Quarter, including the Ginns. The two latter expanded in acreage, c. 1861; when Whitehaven became a municipal borough in 1894, its total area was only 229 acres less than the combined areas of the original three divisions, and embraced much of their territory.

(d) Workington township showed a slight increase in acreage after 1891.

(e) Barrow was merely an ecclesiastical district in 1861, but became a municipal borough in 1867. Its population was concentrated in the same areas within the latter.

(f) Carlisle is represented by the parishes of St Cuthbert and St Mary, which together embrace much of the area of the modern town south of the River Eden.

(g) Kendal township, given here, experienced a slight increase in acreage as between 1871 (2116) and 1881 (2242).

(h) Cockermouth chapelry, given here, kept the same acreage (2425) during the period here shown.

(i) Windermere comprises the townships of Applethwaite and Undermillbeck.

(j) Ambleside township was divided between Grasmere and Windermere parishes. The two parts are combined for this table.

(k) Keswick is represented by the township of that name.

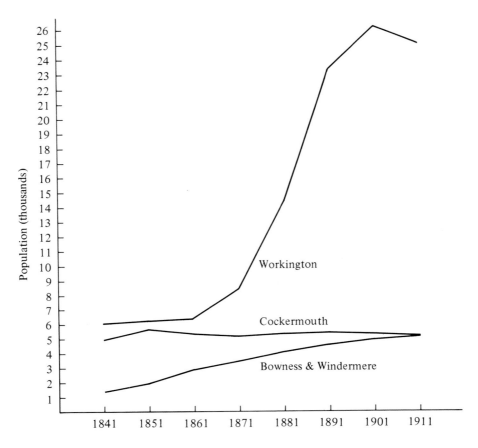

Population (thousands)

Workington

Cockermouth

Bowness & Windermere

1841 1851 1861 1871 1881 1891 1901 1911

3 Population of three Cumbrian towns, 1841–1911.

weaving or thread manufacturing which were dispersed about Cumbria itself, even though it employed a labour force which was, in terms of magnitude, so unimpressive that it accounted for possibly less than 2 per cent of the regional total, scattered in between 60 and 70 small mills and workshops from Sedbergh to Santon Bridge, or Skelwith to Spark Bridge. The trade of 'bobbin turner' is not even clearly distinguished in the 1851 and 1871 census lists of occupations, although local enumerators' schedules use the term regularly enough, as in Staveley near Kendal,[25] and yet the nature, scope and working conditions of the industry were alike clearly evident to a visiting investigator for the Children's Employment Commission in 1864.[26] One reason for the underestimate in the census occupational lists was demonstrated during his visit; the bobbin mills made much use of boy labour, partly because Cumbria was an area of labour scarcity and high wages, and such young labourers were liable to be entered as 'scholar' in the enumerators' sheets.[27] Although some excellent business records, like those of the Horrax Mill in Ambleside, demonstrate that the bobbins, and other wooden products, went to textile mills all over the north of England,[28] turned in their untold millions from the ash, birch, alder and willow coppices of High Furness and elsewhere, it has required much local and industrial archaeological research to establish the scope and distribution of the industry. As has been implied, the latter began its rapid decline *c.* 1870, when cotton and woollen firms more commonly made their own bobbins, and as local timber became scarcer, at a time when Scandinavian competitors were learning to shape theirs into bobbins, also by water power.[29] Yet the industry had played its part in providing employment in relatively remote areas, thus helping to maintain the fabric of dales life in putting a brake on unduly heavy out-migration; and it had provided a market not only for local millwrights, but also for the still surviving firm of R. H. Fell, woodworking machine-makers of Troutbeck Bridge, and yet another form of customer for Messrs Williamson of Canal Head, Kendal, which manufactured the Thomson vortex turbine on licence. This firm became Messrs Gilbert Gilkes (1881), another major employer in Kendal, supplying turbines to a variety of regional water-powered industries.[30]

The impact of these minor rural industries, like that of bobbin-making, cannot be easily estimated. The bobbin industry was only one of a varied group of small water-powered industries scattered throughout the Cumbrian countryside during much of the nineteenth century – gunpowder, snuff, sawmilling, blacking manufacture, paper-making, spade-making, the manufacture of coconut matting, printing, engineering and silk, flax and woollen manufacture, with, later in the century, the generation of electrical power.[31] Few of these are adequately accounted for in the occupational tables of the census volumes, and gunpowder-making in southern Lakeland, which was regionally and nationally important, suffers the fate of the bobbin workers by missing classification in the mid-Victorian census lists. The numbers employed in this occupation, as in bobbin-making, were not so large as to distort the percentages for the broad categories of labour so far discussed, but the point remains that rural industry and economy alike were in reality much more complex than casual sampling of enumerators' sheets would suggest, especially in parts of Westmorland and Furness. The original sheets do, however, reveal the deficiencies of the published lists.

The gunpowder industry, in five main centres of south Lakeland (Sedgwick, Lowwood, Elterwater, Gatebeck and Black Beck in Furness) was a major producer of black blasting powder for quarrying, and was at the height of its effectiveness between 1860 and 1918,[32] a singularly fortunate circumstance in view of the decline of bobbin manufacture in the same broad area. The transfer of labour from one to the other was sometimes practicable for those who were not deterred by an industry with a record of spectacular explosions,[33] and, for the rest, the availability of cheap water power seemed frequently to attract small local entrepreneurs to equally small, capital-intensive industries which had no long-term ability to maintain rural populations, but which at least provided some temporary support for village and parish economies. Nor should we forget that some of these industries, like paper-making in the Kendal district, have remained rooted until the present time, even though the regional gunpowder manufacture disappeared between the wars.[34] In the agricultural districts of the Solway Plain there were, throughout the Victorian age, tileworks, limekilns and manure or minor chemical plants; and limeburning and moorland collieries were found extensively near Brampton and in remote localities of Stainmore, further tile-making was carried on in the upper Eden Valley (the relevant sites, again, have had to be explored by industrial archaeologists in the substantial absence of business or other records), and the mining of gypsum, like the paper-making at Beetham and Burneside, and the snuff manufacture at Helsington, is still pursued at Kirkby Thore. It should also be remembered that even had all of these industries been fully and comprehensively recorded for posterity, it is unlikely that they would have ever, at any point, accounted collectively for more than 5 per cent of the occupied regional population. Their significance, as should have been made sufficiently clear, has been social rather than economic. A countryside with powerful propensities to depopulation needs its brakes, checks and alternative or new employments more keenly than an area subjected to lesser pressures.

Water-power was also much used in the various categories of mining which were well established in the Lake District and the Pennine slopes of Cumbria. Here, again, the economic record was a mixed one, with a remarkable story of continued success and development in the case of the major silver–lead mine at Greenside near Ullswater,[35] with its steady production of silver for the use of the Bank of England, and with more variable but still effective productive activity at mines operated by the London Lead Company at Dufton (the Silver Band mine) and Nent Head. Generally, however, the story of lead mining in north-eastern Cumbria, especially, in the Alston district, was one of socially disastrous decline in c. 1831–2,[36] and the fluctuating fortunes of the mines of Alston Moor are thereafter sadly reflected in the population figures of the high and wind-blown market town of Alston itself, which indicate very clearly the collapse of the local mining industry in the 1870s and 1880s. As can be seen from the occupational tables (Appendix 3(i)), lead-mining in the County of Cumberland occupied a fairly small and diminishing category of the total of all employments throughout the period now discussed, but impersonal statistics should not be allowed to obscure what was little less than a social tragedy affecting an entire community. In the case of the almost equally famous copper mines at Coniston, their virtual closure in the 1880s[37] was in some measure offset by the rise of the tourist industry in that district, which was beginning to produce noticeable though not easily measurable benefits, as lodging houses began to appear in a village which had hitherto been in effect a railhead colony devoted to the extraction of copper and the export of slate.

Generally speaking, the effects of tourism in rural locations were not as clearly manifested as this, and they emerge most clearly in the comparatively sharply marked if somewhat fluctuating growth of tourist centres like Bowness, Windermere, Ambleside and Keswick, which partly indicates the settlement of lodging house keepers, whose main concern was, of course, the satisfaction of demand limited to three or four months of the year. The subject of tourism is explored in greater detail by Dr Walton in Chapter 8, but it should be noted here that the comparative rates of urban growth indicated in Table 2.2 suggest that total urban development in one parish of West Cumberland, Cleator, in, say, 1861–81 (when railways were established and were catering for Lakeland tourist traffic), could far outstrip that of the specialised tourist townships. Important qualifications are nevertheless called for. The tourist industry continued to develop when other, more volatile industries in the coastal towns were subject to dangerous instabilities, and did so to such an extent that the Furness Railway, for example, came to regard it as a valuable if secondary source of income;[38] and, although it has not been possible to estimate the multiplier-effects of the spending of visitors to the Lake District, its benefits cannot have been other than appreciable to the tradesmen and sometimes the farmers in the most popular areas. The rise of tourism accompanied the decline – as we have seen – of a number of regional rural industries, and if the palliative effects of the former were not generally felt by the sufferers from the latter, comparatively few economically troubled regions of England were enabled to enjoy the advantageous effects of such unparalleled scenery.

As can be seen from the bare urban record in Table 2.2, the most spectacular developments were to be seen in west-coast towns like Barrow and Workington. The transformations in these centres, and in numerous smaller places like Aspatria and Millom, were not of course limited to one narrow coastal strip; they had implications for a great part of Cumbria, and represented the identification of the heavy-industry area of West Cumberland not only with what we may call the Northern and Irish Sea Economy, but with international trade and industry also. For a few brief years, the western industrial periphery became a major Bessemer iron and steel centre of Europe and the world. Thereafter, as we have seen, the same districts became intensely vulnerable to economic fluctuation, and they failed to engender the varied factors which might easily have led to a more complex but also a more resilient industrial structure. Growth in the iron, steel and associated industries, was so marked in West Cumberland that 'workers in metals' (Appendix 3(i)) increased from some 3.3 per cent of all occupied persons in the county in 1851 to 12.56 in 1891, and 13.53 in 1911, a higher proportion of the labour force than in County Durham during a similar period,[39] but engineering, which could easily have grown alongside the production of its raw materials, metals (and which showed promising signs of doing so effectively in Barrow at one stage), appeared only modestly in an otherwise important iron and steel area like West Cumberland. Hence, from the 1860s, firms developed in the Workington harbour area making bridges and boilers, or were engaged in wagon-building, forging, brass casting and finishing. Likewise, Barrow's Hindpool Estate began to provide space for foundries, firms of millwrights, and jobbing engineers' workshops.[40] These, however, were highly localised areas of diversification, and Cumbria as a whole had a proportion of persons engaged in factory or workshop production – if we include textiles and other occupations – which was well below the average for workshop and factory employment throughout England and Wales. Indeed, if we take the north of England generally, it was only in Lancashire and the West Riding that coal and iron went comfortably side by side with a diversity of other industries, a conclusion which can be very clearly drawn by 1895.[41] Cumbria had well under 7 per cent of occupied people engaged in such work, and it is this simple consideration which throws light on the imbalance as well as the vulnerability of its economy. Its major ports, which also became iron centres, did in fact possess a shipbuilding tradition even before their stages of rapid development, but only in Barrow did a major ship-construction industry survive across the new century, thanks to its late-Victorian role as a builder of naval vessels,[42] and the story elsewhere was one of decline or failure, with only 362 males in Cumberland engaged in this industry in 1891, and 174 in 1911, a small fraction of 1 per cent of those employed in the county.

Of all the Cumbrian towns, only Carlisle can be said to have had a genuinely varied and consistently developing economy, one which was enabled to withstand the winds of national and international economic change, and this is reflected in its modest but persistent growth rates (Table 2.2). Even the strains placed upon its textile industries did not, after the conflicts and privations of the 1830s, 1840s and 1860s, permanently damage its prospects, and the border city, which became a centre of railway communication for the extreme north of England, developed in strikingly differing directions; as a home of food processing and biscuit manufacture (Messrs Carr), of light engineering from the manufacture of agricultural implements and bicycles to the building of cranes (by Messrs Cowan, Sheldon), and the iron and brass founding which existed creatively alongside this work. Carlisle was a centre of banking and commerce not only for Cumberland, but for the border country well into south-west Scotland and towards the Cheviots, and it was a market for farm labour as well as a retailing centre with an exceptionally wide range of goods and services for its region. Not a large place in physical extent – it grew primarily into the flat marshy land by the River Caldew, known as Denton Holme, beneath the old city walls where the railway lines also converged – it concentrated a mass of activity into a few streets and a multiplicity of yards. Much of this activity was concerned with processing and retailing the food which came from a wide countryside, or clothing the latter's population; and in consequence, other, smaller market centres like Wigton and Brampton suffered, and even Penrith merely held its own. However, a more refined economic analysis than has been possible here would almost certainly show that whilst railway development helped Carlisle by providing modest direct employment on the part of railway companies, and also by widening its market area, it produced few by-industries directly connected with this form of transport, and was thus in the main indirectly contributory to its growth as a town. There was, by 1901, one firm of railway signal makers there, and Carlisle did not even acquire a private railway wagon works, as did Barrow for a few years.[43]

In any case, as was demonstrated in several instances of town development on the Cumberland coast, the transport of goods or raw materials did not in itself lead to urban growth unless a railway company took deliberate land-control and planning decisions, as happened in the cases of Barrow and Silloth, and, as a minor example, of Seascale.[44] For the rest, the railway history of the region requires separate consideration, if only for the reason that the analysis of labouring populations, a major topic in this chapter, of its nature deals with only one factor of production, that of labour. The introduction of railways, and the complex of investment decisions that it engendered, which in turn brought about the involvement of landed wealth as well as that provided by a wider investing public, was a necessary and basic preliminary to the Victorian development of West Cumberland. It is dealt with here as the first significant phase in the large-scale application of capital. Railway-building is of course easily measurable, both physically and in terms of actual cost. The more gradual growth of the West Cumberland coalmining industry had considerable local economico-social effects, and was a more reliable sector of the regional economy than the secondary industries mentioned; but its effects were long term, and were not always directly connected with the more spectacular changes which are here described. By the first decade of the new century it had become the greatest single employing institution in Cumberland after agriculture, with some 10 122 workers in 1911, having had only one-third of that number in 1851, and, of course, it remained a sub-regional staple well into the twentieth century. The story of its failure belongs to a study of the last four or five decades; it is also best studied in its curious relationship to the local Victorian iron industry in a short survey of this kind, and the Cumberland coalfield was in any case a minor producer in national terms, and certainly did not reproduce the scale of related capital developments in railways, iron and steel. It is certain that, lacking a railway system, the regional iron and steel industry could never have developed, for a few years, into an institution of world importance.

The story of Cumbrian rail transport is best surveyed in a semi-narrative form,

31

if only because railways, and the economic developments they help to stimulate, follow their own peculiar logic. Although the history of regional lines has received much attention and called forth lively writing,[45] railway historians find recreation in particularities. Generalisations are more dangerous, and a few will be essayed here. Firstly, then, Cumbria was late to develop an effective network of lines, and its true 'industrial revolution', based essentially on the needs and markets of what became the Age of Steel, occurred late in the day when compared with that which had taken place in Lancashire two or three generations before; and this 'revolution' also rested in railway promotion, not only locally but internationally.

The regional coalfields had long understood the advantages of rail transport as such, and Whitehaven coal had been transported by wagonway to the harbour of that town in the seventeenth and eighteenth centuries, whilst the Tindale Fell wagonway had carried the coals of the Earl of Carlisle, in the late eighteenth century, from the Midgeholme district to Brampton for the Carlisle market.[46] The coal trade of the region, and of North England as a whole, habitually looked towards the sea, however, and the opening of the Newcastle and Carlisle Railway, a line mentioned in the last chapter, which did not in fact take place until June 1838,[47] was in fact the partial culmination of a long-term policy drive, firstly by canal and then by rail, to bring Newcastle as well as local coal to the Irish Sea. This campaign was ultimately effective not only because the corporations of Newcastle and Carlisle backed it,[48] but because the terrain of the Solway Plain encouraged bold ideas, and the Senhouses of Maryport, major landowners further west, avidly seized hold of a chance both to develop their own port (an idea which had been long discussed[49]) with the help of such neighbouring landowners as the Dykes family and the Lawsons of Brayton. They also took a leading part in a much more momentous campaign which affected the whole of the north-west at that time, namely, one for the promotion of a through line to Scotland via the Lake Counties, and, in particular, along the Cumbrian coast.

This campaign had its origin in the mid 1830s, when national railway construction was already, in the form of the Grand Junction Railway, reaching towards the north-west[50] as far as Warrington (1835), and when, within three years, the Preston to Lancaster line was surveyed as part of a direct route through Lancashire. This approach towards Cumbria stimulated a wave of discussion throughout the towns of this region, and the newspaper press is in any case explicit in the matter.[51] There were two main camps, one of which wished for the continuance of the line over Shap and towards Carlisle and Scotland, and a second, formed as early as 1836, with Sir H. le Fleming Senhouse as the moving spirit, which argued for a 'Caledonian, West Cumberland and Furness Railway', along the Cumbrian coastline. Ambitious plans for crossing Morecambe Bay by embankment were put forward by George Stephenson (1837) and John Hague

RAIL ROAD.

PUBLIC MEETING.

Golden Lion Inn, Whitehaven, 7th Dec., 1835.

At an Adjourned Public Meeting, held this Day, to take into further Consideration the Expediency of forming a RAIL WAY from the PORT of WHITEHAVEN to the CITY of CARLISLE,

R. JEFFERSON, Esq., in the Chair,

Upon the Motion of Mr. WILSON, of the Retreat, Seconded by Mr. MILLER,

RESOLVED—That it is, in the Opinion of this Meeting, necessary for the Commercial, Manufacturing, and Agricultural Interests of Cumberland, that a Rail Road be formed between Whitehaven, Maryport, and Carlisle.

Upon the Motion of Mr. PETER FISHER, Seconded by Mr. CURWEN,

RESOLVED—That this Meeting recommend the Committee to apply to Sir John Rennie, in conjunction with Mr. Stephenson, for Advice and Assistance to carry such Measure into effect, and to make a Survey, Estimate, and Report.

Upon the Motion of Mr. BUCKHAM, Seconded by Mr. SPITTALL,

RESOLVED—That a Subscription be entered into, and the Sums subscribed be deposited in the Whitehaven Joint Stock Bank and in Messrs. Hartley & Co.'s Bank, to defray the Expense of Surveys, and all other Incidental Expenses : the money so paid to be Part of the Purchase of the Shares or other Interest in the Undertaking held by the Subscribers.

Upon the Motion of Mr. BUCKHAM, Seconded by Mr. ANTHONY BELL,

RESOLVED—That the following Gentlemen be appointed a Committee to carry the said Rail Way into effect, viz. :—Lord Viscount Lowther ; Henry Curwen, Edward Stanley, M.P., Samuel Irton, M.P., Matthias Attwood, M.P., Robert Jefferson, Milham Hartley, James Robertson Walker, Thomas Hartley, John Harrison, and Joseph Harris, Esquires ; and Messrs. George Buckham, Alexander Spittall, Richard Barker, jun., James Bell, William Miller, John Dawson, Peter Fisher, John Jackson, John Spencer, Anthony Bell, Robert Curwen, William Randleson, Robert Jackson, James Nicholson, Dickinson Birkett, Thomas Milward, John Bell, George Harrison, John Benn, John Wilson Fletcher, and John Peile, with power to add to their numbers in Whitehaven or elsewhere, and Five to constitute a Quorum.

Upon the Motion of Mr. JAMES BELL, Seconded by Mr. ANTHONY BELL,

RESOLVED—That Mr. Hodgson be appointed Solicitor, and Mr. Heywood Secretary, to whom all Communications be addressed.

Upon the Motion of Mr. FISHER, Seconded by Mr. ANTHONY BELL,

RESOLVED—That these Resolutions be Published in the Newspapers printed at Whitehaven, Carlisle, Newcastle, and Liverpool, and that the same be also Printed for Circulation.

Upon the Motion of Mr. BARKER, Seconded by Mr. BUCKHAM,

RESOLVED—That Application be made to the Earl of Lonsdale, Henry Curwen, Esq., and other Land-owners, for Permission to go upon their Estates to make the necessary Surveys, and also to solicit their Support to the Undertaking.

ROBERT JEFFERSON, Chairman.

Upon the Motion of Mr. MILLER, Seconded by Mr. W. JACKSON,

RESOLVED—That the Thanks of the Meeting be given the to Chairman for able and impartial conduct in the Chair.

4 A poster marking the local agitation in Whitehaven for the formation of a coastal railway line to Scotland (1835). Such agitation did not depend wholly on major landowners.

(1838), amidst much controversy and some acclaim.[52]

The agitations of the period achieved little, even though they are well worth study as an example of the operation, or non-effectiveness, of public opinion in unripe circumstances. The obstacles to the rapid realisation of a coastal route may be simply set out. There were formidable physical barriers in Morecambe Bay and the Duddon, and these remain unconquered at the present day. Next, the Senhouses, and north and west Cumbrian business interests, were in no position to influence events in the Furness peninsula, and a railway from its shores round the coastline to Carnforth was not completed until 1853–7. Just as relevantly, the affairs of the Earls of Lonsdale were passing through a period of transition, in 1840–44, although the Lowther family still found time to involve itself in the vital plan for a through railway route over Shap, this despite the fact that the influential Baron Lowther, successor to the Earldom in 1844, was only awakening to the responsibilities and possibilities of his inheritance. He had shown only the mildest of interest in Whitehaven's fortunes in 1839[53] as his personal diary suggests. Finally, the inland Cumbrian towns on the whole favoured the Shap route.

5 Whitehaven in its late Victorian heyday, 'the finest harbour between Liverpool and Glasgow'.

What *was* clear to all the great landlords of the seaboard, however, was the need to get minerals to the local ports with as much expedition as possible; the rest could wait. As the Maryport and Carlisle line was constructed, section by section, to be opened in February 1845,[54] the pressures of the Great Railway Mania were simply telling the main actors to 'get something done'. The new Earl of Lonsdale, the second in his line of succession, caused the Whitehaven Junction Railway to be carried a few miles down the coast from Maryport, and made his position very clear at its opening in 1847 by declaring that Whitehaven 'possessed the finest harbour between Liverpool and Glasgow', and that it 'might be made still more so by developing the Irish trade in coal and merchandise'.[55] In Furness, meanwhile, the Earl of Burlington and the Duke of Buccleuch, each with his entourage, had been planting the tiny acorn of the Furness Railway (1843–6), soon to become a formidable tree, and the Earl of Burlington's private diary[56], again manifests the very limited objectives in the minds of the main movers. The latter were not blind to the likelihood of a completed coastal line, but the concern of the Earl, before long to be the dominant capitalist in his district, was primarily that of transporting his slate, and growing quantities of the superb iron ore of the west coast, to a suitable anchorage by the village of Barrow.

Although, as we have seen, the business communities of towns like Kendal, Penrith or Appleby could agitate for a main inland line,[57] much more powerful interests, including a phalanx of northward-reaching railway investors on the Lancashire and southerly side of the region, were pressing for its completion. This took place in 1844–6, with the brilliant Joseph Locke as engineer and the formidable Thomas Brassey as contractor, following one of those taut and violent battles against nature, geological and human, which characterised the most outstanding Victorian railway construction campaigns. There was the added spice of competition with an east-coast route scheme to reach Scotland first via Berwick, and Locke, driving long sweeping inclines up the Grayrigg and Shap summits, and full of faith in the locomotive engineers of the future, broke through to Carlisle by December 1846,[58] beating the east-coast rivals by nearly two years. He had not constructed a single tunnel on the way, but, with his ultimate total of nearly 10 000 labourers and masons, he had made 155 bridges *en route* from Lancaster to the border city, and had not, as far as we know, permitted even the most sustained and serious navvy rioting to shake his nerve. The general and forbidding costliness of the project, £21 400 a mile, was surpassed in Cumbrian terms only by the single-track Ulverston and Lancaster Railway (1857), which cost £22 000 a mile, over a much shorter route, in opening a southern exit for the railways of the regional seaboard.[59] This, of course, emphasises the original unrealism of the earlier project for a coastal through line, but the complex story of regional railway development carries a more profound moral. In this, as in other significant instances, outside capital had to play a major role if railway or industrial schemes were to be effectively furthered, although there is little doubt, too, that in the Cumbrian setting landlords, great and small, played their respective parts. The Earls of Lonsdale were most certainly interested in the Lancaster and Carlisle line, to the extent that they could always nominate one of its directors, and the railway of course passed through their vast Westmorland territories.[60] Most of the landowners along the route of the line were persuaded

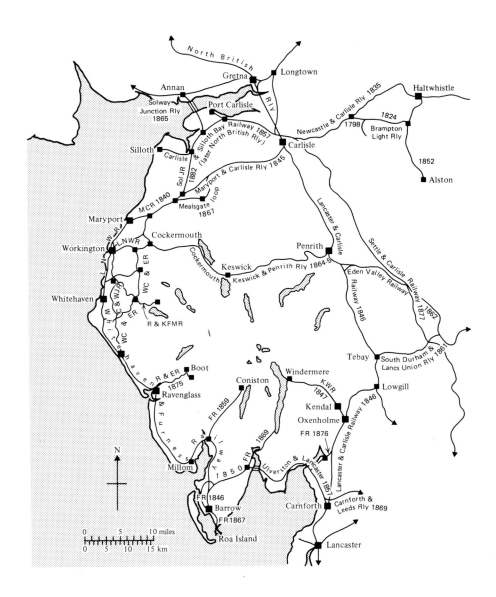

6 Cumbrian railways. Key: C & WJR, Cleator and Workington Junction; KWR, Kendal and Windermere; LNWR, London and North-Western; R & ER, Ravenglass and Eskdale; R & KFMR, Rowrah and Kelton Fell Mineral; WC & ER, Whitehaven, Cleator and Egremont. The Cockermouth and Workington Railway and the Whitehaven Junction Railway were taken over by the LNWR in 1866.

36

to take the value of their land in shares, but they did not react quickly, and no doubt rallied behind Col. E. W. Hasell, chairman of the company from 1844 to 1872.[61] As regards Cumbrian railway history generally, landed gentlemen, some of them with a military background, not infrequently took directorates. In this vital instance, however, the greater part of the capital came from the Grand Junction Railway (£250 000), the London and Birmingham (£100 000) and the North Union and the Lancaster and Preston lines (which gave £65 000 each), the whole share capital of the line amounting to £900 000 in the first instance.[62]

On no previous occasion had such vast sums of money ever been poured into any Cumbrian enterprise (the Newcastle and Carlisle line, which cost £800 000, had been financed mainly, as we have noted, from Newcastle, and only a short section of it lay in Cumberland). But the emphasis of the investment sources presaged something of far greater moment; the control of the main route through inland Cumbria was to lie, within a very few years, in the hands of a single great railway company, the London and North Western, which in 1859 took control of the Lancaster and Carlisle line on a 900-year lease.[63] For the rest, this remarkable transport enterprise – rivalled in historical terms only by the M6 motorway, which accompanies it on much of its journey – probably brought little *direct* economic benefit to the region, save in one important particular. From its junction at Oxenholme (then known as Kendal Junction) a group of Kendal and Westmorland businessmen and gentry – the Gandys, J. J. Wilson, and G. B. Crewdson of the Quaker banking family among their leaders – promoted a short but highly significant line to the hamlet of Birthwaite near Windermere, the Kendal and Windermere Railway (1847).[64] The consequences of this enterprise are made explicit by Dr Walton in Chapter 8, and it will be immediately apparent that travellers from Euston could find themselves by the side of that most magnificent lake within 7 or 8 hours. Table 2.2 reveals some interesting effects upon Bowness and Windermere.

The significance of the Kendal and Windermere line lay also in another direction. It was one of a group of town-promoted or civically controlled enterprises within Cumbria, or associated with the region. Clearly, the Newcastle and Carlisle Railway came within this category, but the Carlisle and Silloth Bay Railway (1855) (see also Chapter 8, pp. 197–8) was a corporation-controlled venture of a remarkable kind, and it should on no account be assumed that the region's townsmen or native capitalists were unable to act on their own initiative. But, in the matter of railway promotion and investment, the region was one of contrasting groups and centres of power, expressed in the formation and running of quasi-feudal railways, industrialists' railways, and civic-inspired lines of the type indicated. The interests and attitudes of all three types of interest or control were thrown into high relief, as opportunity, scale and scope of action ordained in the febrile atmosphere of the Great Railway Mania.

The three forms of railway inspiration or control were not of course mutually exclusive, but it was the quasi-feudal type of control or interst that completed the West Cumbrian Railway system, thereby virtually making a ring of railway lines round the central Lakeland massif. Lord Lonsdale, as we have seen, promoted the Whitehaven Junction Railway (with George Stephenson, who had supervised the Maryport and Carlisle project, as engineer), and then went on, somewhat amateurishly,[65] to nurse his cheap and ill-tracked line down the south-west Cumberland coast, the Whitehaven and Furness Junction Railway, opened in 1850.[66] Here the Earl and his Whitehaven business associates made contact at Broughton-in-Furness with another of the quasi-feudal lines, the Furness. The latter enterprise, after a halting start, grew steadily more profitable in the 1850s by working as a straightforward mineral line,[67] but also demonstrated that without a deliberate policy of town-creation, railways and transport systems did not create substantial towns by their mere operation – for Barrow, *pro tem*, remained a village. For the rest, the word 'feudal' implies that major aristocratic landlords wielded *force majeure* in the promotion and working of a given line, often by or through a chairmanship, by dint of extensive land-ownership in the vicinity of the line, by the capital they injected, and through the general prestige and influence they bestowed or deployed. In the case of the Furness Railway, the Cavendish motto, *Cavendo Tutus*, and part of their heraldic bearings, were also the company's, and the Earl of Burlington's presence was at least visible to employees. The matter of public influence and power-wielding is further explored, however, in Chapter 5. Far more important, at this stage of the economic development of the seaboard, was the escalating demand for the rich haematite iron ore of Furness and the Cleator Moor district, and the Second Earl of Lonsdale took a major part in the formation of the Whitehaven, Cleator and Egremont Railway (1854–5),[68] and this began to compete with the Furness in the promise of its dividends, which rapidly rose to 6 per cent, as the ore was taken to Whitehaven for shipment.

It should be added that as far as can be ascertained, and excluding the Ulverston and Lancaster line, coastal lines, which occupied fairly level territory, were relatively cheaply constructed, and that, using the broadest of estimates, the Furness, the Whitehaven and Furness Junction, and the Whitehaven Junction were built at between £10 000 and £14 000 a mile, the Maryport and Carlisle being exceptional in costing nearer £16 000. Each was soon to do more than earn its keep.

The chief value of the haematite, at this time, lay in its unusually high iron content, usually more than 60 per cent. This meant that when it was employed in smelting, less fuel was used in iron furnaces, and so it was carried long distances by sea, to South Wales or Scotland or to ports within reach of Staffordshire or Shropshire furnaces. At this time, the railway iron of England was of the malleable puddled variety, and no way of making cheap steel in quantity had been devised. Hence, of the ore shipped at Barrow in a boom year, 1856, when the entire produce of the Furness haematite mines was some 445 000 tons, about 200 000 tons went to South Wales, and a large part of the remainder to the puddling furnaces of Staffordshire.[69] These inter-regional connections are of the utmost importance, for they betoken the existence of what has already been called a Northern and Irish Sea Economic Community, a network of trading and producing relationships which underlay much of the economic development of West Cumberland itself. Capital, and capitalists, will often travel down lines of supply. Just as, near the beginning of our period, Anthony Hill of Merthyr, with extensive puddling furnaces in South Wales, had iron mines in the Cleator district,[70] so H. W. Schneider, incomparably the most astute capitalist in Furness, and the Brogden family (who took it upon themselves to complete the outer ring of Cumbrian railways by pushing through from Ulverston to Carnforth in 1857) had considerable industrial connections on the South Wales coast.[71] Nor was this the only potentially fateful trade route, for by 1857 small but significant quantities of haematite ore were being sent by sea to Scotland, and this connection, chiefly with iron works and ironmasters in Ayrshire and Kilmarnock, was to prove increasingly important for Cumberland's future.[72]

The regional export of iron ore remained of considerable and growing moment for at least a decade longer, and it reached a new intensity with the invention of the Bessemer process in 1856, especially after Sir Henry Bessemer had ascertained that the haematite ores of Cumberland and Furness were almost ideal for his method of large-scale steelmaking by converter; in his own words, when he had been very busy 'endeavouring to discover all the non-phosphoric iron ores in this country . . . the chief were found to be the haematites of Lancashire and Cumberland'.[73] The manufacture of Bessemer steel, however, became largely concentrated in Sheffield in the 1860s, and although Furness and Cumberland began to make coke-smelted pig-iron on their own ground, at Cleator Moor (1841), Seaton and Harrington (1857), and Barrow (1859), there was no suitably direct route for supplying these furnaces with the essential hard-structured coke from Durham ovens. Furness, it must always be remembered, had no workable coal whatsoever, but in Whitehaven, on Lord Lonsdale's former land on the north shore, the remains of batteries of coke ovens dating from the 1840s can still be seen, the proof of an experiment which did not reduce the danger of heavy dependence on Durham supplies, even though there was coal beneath this very spot.

The local capitalists of the age did not see their tasks and opportunities in this light. Firstly, the region was in a position to supply non-phosphoric ore or 'Bessemer iron' to any suitable market in England, Wales, Scotland or Europe. Secondly, at this very period, what became one of the richest iron ore mines in the world, at Hodbarrow in south-west Cumberland, began its rapid development from early prospectings in 1856; and this continued to mine a large proportion of the ore raised in the county, producing more than a quarter in 1872, and roughly a third by 1883 out of nearly 1.5 million tons. Thirdly, the opening of the South Durham and Lancashire Union Railway (1861), winding through its cuttings high above Stainmore, made Durham coke available through a somewhat circuitous passage from Tebay down to Carnforth and thence to Furness; and this vital event was followed by the opening of the Cockermouth, Keswick and Penrith Railway (January 1865, somewhat earlier for goods), which meant that low-phosphorus coke fuel could travel from east to west, into the central coastline district of Cumberland.[74] This line, too, was to carry some significance for the tourist industry, and was yet another feeder reaching into the lake country. But the economic potential of the railway network for heavy industry was at this time immense. Cumberland's coalmines were also beneficiaries of improved rail communication, and it should not be forgotten that they had provided the necessary justifications for the original stretches of railway line; but the coal of the Whitehaven and associated localities still looked to Ireland, and to seaborne traffic generally, for its markets.

Huge quantities of iron ore continued to leave the Hodbarrow and other mines by sea.[75] Indeed, the small port of Borwick Rails on the Duddon Estuary, serving Hodbarrow, was enabled to clear as many as 1457 vessels in one year (1867), and the Hodbarrow Mining Company maintained stockpiles at Ellesmere Port and Saltney on the Dee, which supplied customers in North Wales and the Midlands by rail and canal. Meanwhile, the vast South Wales connection remained, with the haematite ore, for hundreds of puddling furnaces, going to Cardiff, Newport, Swansea and Briton Ferry, and these markets persisted through into the 1870s[76] during which decade nearly half of the Hodbarrow produce of roughly 200 000 tons came to be used in Cumberland itself. All this can be learned from the extensive business records of the great mining company,[77] and the transition from exportation to the smelting of the haematite ore in the locality betokened much more than a simple and sensible change in investment strategy. It was at least partially the work of outside investors, working in conjunction with the greater landlords of the coast, and has to be seen as part of an inter-regional movement of capital, technological expertise and skilled labour.

Barrow provides the first, and in some ways the most striking example of this multiple stimulation. The ironworks (1859) put into action there by H. W. Schneider, international mines speculator, and Robert Hannay, the Kirkcudbright landed gentleman-merchant, was by 1863–4 provided with a Bessemer steel plant[78] and turned into a mighty company with financial support from the new Duke of Devonshire (the former Earl of Burlington), his Furness Railway and mining entourage, and representatives of the Midland Railway.[79] The technological skills were provided by one of the country's few genuinely sophisticated ironworks managers, J. T. Smith of Dudley and Stanton, and experienced ironworkers were brought from Staffordshire. Two factors weighed heavily in the minds of all those who were financially involved: the availability of the direct rail route for Durham coke into Furness, and the glint of opportunity afforded by a future market for steel railway rails, which would last three to four times as long as the puddled iron ones, then still almost universal. The ironworks, near to limestone, water, superb ore and to the Irish Sea, was already a resounding success, and the Furness Railway, with its elaborate infrastructure of business and town-developing activities, was far more than a mere carrier of coke in an area devoid of coal.

H. W. Schneider, Smith's original employer, who had made an ore deposit discovery of remarkable magnitude in the Furness field, at Park in 1850, had had business connections with Cornish tin mining,[80] and within a few years Cornish tin miners were working in the Furness haematite mines, at Hodbarrow and in settlements in West Cumberland, like Moor Row. Certain basic skills, and even a way of life, were transferable. Meanwhile, Cumberland ore had gone to the great ironworks at Dowlais in the 1860s,[81] and the chief chemist there (1867), G. J. Snelus, later a Fellow of the Royal Society, found himself attracted to West Cumberland by 1872, and became a powerful motivator and innovator in iron and steelmaking development on the coast.[82] Such men, as D. L. Burn has shown, had been rare in the previous generation or two,[83] and there was much to do in Workington and district, where open-topped, stone-built blast furnaces wasted their gases during the 1860s.[84] More than this; as though to indicate that the Furness capitalists were not semi-omnipotent (and Smith had carried them technologically ahead of Cumberland in the 1860s), the gifted and hardworking Barratt family had entered the region from Cornwall, via the Duke of Devonshire's lead mines at Grassington, to manage the Coniston copper mines, and then to help to make Hodbarrow the startling success that it became.[85] The Northern and Irish Sea Community had more subtle and varied strands and connections than is suggested here, and just as the Brocklebanks and Ismay went from Cumberland to Liverpool to become major figures in shipping history there, so Nathaniel and W. S. Caine, major iron merchants, came from that city to further guide the fortunes of Hodbarrow.[86]

The ironfields themselves, if we count Furness and Cumberland together, now had a monopoly of the finest ore in Britain, and could look forward to the production of 'Bessemer pig' *ad libitum*. They remained the major producer of this form of iron, which was not only used for steelmaking. During the late 1860s, iron shipbuilding was coming into its own, and it may be significant that the West Cumberland Haematite Iron Company at Workington, established in 1860, received finance from Teesside ship-builders, as well as from a Quaker group which included one of the Peases of Middlesbrough, famous for their coke, and an Albright of Birmingham. This firm expanded its activities into puddling iron and rolling plates in the mid-1860s, but by 1871 it was making steel rails. It

41

was this company that gained the services of G. J. Snelus.[87] Before that time, however, the Barrow Haematite Steel Company was making rails in quantity, was recording even more massive profits, and was receiving rail orders that could 'scarcely be filled as fast as they are received' (1869).[88] These orders came increasingly from the New World, but, inevitably, a sector of the market was in the home country, for the Midland Railway had not invested in 'Barrows' for nothing, and the Furness Railway itself relaid its own tracks with steel by degrees. Cumbria's real contribution to the development of an international economy was not negligible, however. From 1869 onward, iron ore rumbling in the railway wagons which ran from thirty-odd heavily producing west coast haematite mines was likely to be tipped into one of 17 furnaces in blast in Cumberland, and 16 in Furness,[89] and of their output, perhaps a quarter was made into steel, some to become rails for export. By 1873, Cumberland alone had 39 blast furnaces, and by 1875, the two associated districts had more than twice as many furnaces in blast.[90]

Nevertheless, the region did not become a major steel producer without difficulty. Its principal problem was a lack of willing local investors, who could act with sufficient determination and force to take full advantage of the region's temporary monopoly as a Bessemer iron producer, and thereby use local influence to organise other forms of productive experiment without delay. There were, for example, few local capitalist groups which had the resources, the confidence or the connections of the Barrow Haematite Steel – Furness Railway interest, which was not only furthering major industries and planting a substantial town, but which, above all, controlled its own transport system and its ore and limestone supplies.[91] The Seventh Duke of Devonshire, the leader-figure of this group, was unlike his neighbouring fellow-aristocrats and great landowners in Cumberland in that he was willing to invest heavily in both the steel and the shipbuilding industries, and he was not content merely to accumulate massive mineral royalties. The Cumberland royalty owners drew from the *Iron and Coal Trades Review* (1885) the comment that 'in no other county had such enormous sums been returned to the owners of minerals as in Cumberland',[92] but in no known case did they use this wealth, once the railway system had been established, to invest in the newer forms of local industry. It is highly likely that the Second Earl of Lonsdale, an ageing man, had totally lost interest in his railway and other enterprises by the mid-1860s. Whatever the case, it is clear that the *Review* was not wholly exaggerating the Lowther type of income, and the family royalties of the Earl and his successor, as between June 1869 and June 1878, amounted to rather over £208 000 in the ten years inclusive,[93] and those for coal royalty rents, derived from Lonsdale leases to colliery operators, to nearly £126 000 in the same period.[94] The family's colliery profits at Whitehaven, which could vary considerably from year to year, came to approximately £250 000[95] in the same decade – and even after they had leased out the same collieries in 1888, the family income from that source, spent with *panache* by Hugh Lowther, the 'Yellow' Earl, could be even greater.[96] There is no reason to believe that Lord Leconfield, who had rich ore mines on his estate in the Cleator district, drew much less money towards his seat at Petworth in Sussex – and it certainly did not return in bold and invigorating investments of the kind suggested.

These men of influence, then, did not always act when action was needed; and, indeed, the Earl of Lonsdale failed to fend off an invasion of the central coastal district by the LNWR in 1866, as this great company secured control of the Whitehaven Junction and the Cockermouth and Workington railways.[97] As we have seen, the LNWR already controlled the Lancaster and Carlisle line, and it thereby had a direct interest in the coke traffic from Durham, via Tebay, that had to pass over part of this route and into the other sections of railway that were now within its empire. As local observers noted, directors sitting in Euston were hardly likely to exhibit the degree of local enterprise shown in Furness, even though it was not in their interest to inhibit traffic in coke and pig-iron. It is only fair to add, too, that within a few years the West Cumberland landlords (Lonsdale, Leconfield and H. F. Curwen), seeing an enormous development of the iron trade before their eyes, did take part in a fight back against 'outside' railway encroachment. They challenged both the Furness Railway, which had penetrated far into West Cumberland by taking over Lord Lonsdale's Whitehaven and Furness Junction line in 1866,[98] and, even more, the LNWR, by promoting in 1874 a rival line to carry ore out of the Cleator field towards Workington, known as the Cleator and Workington Railway.[99] The 'encroaching' lines, together with the ore-carrying Whitehaven, Cleator and Egremont Railway, had all increased their freight charges in the early 1870s, and landlords, ironmasters and some traders were able to unite in pushing forward the new line, which opened in late 1879.[100] The supporting elements within the WC and E company were led by Henry Jefferson, of a noted Whitehaven merchant family, and examination shows that they, too, were composed of varied groups of tradesmen, shipowners and merchants from along the coastal conurbation, who understandably supported a railway that was paying a $13\frac{1}{2}$ per cent dividend by 1872![101] Since Lord Lonsdale had at least encouraged the promotion of the WC and E, and had been an early director of it, it is clear that local railway politics had reached such a degree of complexity that exceptionally careful analysis of the contending groups and their motives will in future be called for.

The salient fact for our present purposes is that the West Cumberland industrial district had become a complex mass of competing interests in rail transport, coal, iron and iron-ore mining, often narrowly preoccupied or wasteful in their actions, and the Bessemer boom of the late 1860s and early 1870s found the sub-region ripe for exploitation by yet another intrusive or contending group. The gate had long been slightly ajar in this particular case by virtue of the operation, for the major part of a century, of the Jacktrees Mine at Cleator Moor by the famous Carron Company of Scotland, and the value of the local ore was of course well known in that country. In 1863, two former employees of the then largest Scottish ironworks, William Bairds of Gartsherrie east of Glasgow, had restarted the original Harrington furnace of 1857, and formed a firm styled Bain, Blair and Paterson.[102] James Bain, the senior partner and sometime Lord Provost of Glasgow, was also to become the lessee of the Whitehaven mines from the Lowthers, and was, with his sons, to leave a major impression on the economic and social history of the Whitehaven district. The Bain incursion was quickly followed by a very different but equally significant event, the promotion of the Solway Junction Railway (1864–9),[103] which entailed throwing a viaduct over the estuary as part of an imaginative scheme to convey ore to Lanarkshire ironworks.[104] Nor was this a pipe-dream, for the Whitehaven, Cleator and Egremont line was soon carrying Scotland-directed ore traffic,[105] and the garrulous Samuel Griffiths, the iron trade publicist, writing of the year 1872 disparaged the 'Scotch Ironstone . . . as being unfavourable to the production of pig iron of the sort most desirable for manipulation in the Bessemer pots, owing to the presence of phosphorus in Scotch mineral'.[106] It is hardly surprising that ironmasters from north of the border rapidly followed their lines of supply as the haematite pig trade beckoned, although, as we shall see, the Bains and their partners were hardly representative of their fellow-countrymen who arrived in West Cumberland.

The Scots were mainly from Ayrshire, Kilmarnock in particular, and their enterprises were on the whole fairly short-lived and modestly capitalised. Nevertheless, it would be wrong to underestimate their impact; by *c.* 1880 some 25 iron furnaces on the Cumberland coast were Scots-owned or controlled, as against 26 which were built with the aid of local or northern-English capitalists.[107] Hardly any of the Scottish investors appear to have thought seriously of large-scale steel or even puddled iron production, and only one firm, the Lonsdale Iron and Steel Co. (1870–1903), promoted by Barclay and Craig of Kilmarnock, left its options open, but did not exploit them by making steel. Another Barclay-financed works, the Lowther Ironworks at Whitehaven (which remained Scots-controlled between 1872 and 1905, and which, as its name implies, was set up on Lord Lonsdale's land), made only pig-iron, as did other works at Distington (financed mostly from Kilmarnock), Maryport (an enterprise by the Gilmours of the same district), and the Derwent Haematite Iron Co. at Workington (1874), which yet again had the support of Kilmarnock capital. None of these works was as ambitious as the time and place seemed to demand, and an unsuccessful Scottish-formed ironworks at Parton (1872) was the most strongly financed of the group, with a capital of £120 000.[108] Such a figure can be compared with £600 000 capital of the English-controlled West Cumberland Iron and Steel Co., reconstituted in 1872 as a major steelmaker, or even the £350 000 capital of the highly durable Moss Bay Haematite Iron

Company fixed as it began to make steel in 1881. This last enterprise was largely locally inspired, and guided by the experienced Workington ironmasters Kirk and Valentine.[109] Such an example, unhappily, goes to show how far one of the most important iron districts in England was dependent upon outside initiative and stimulus. Nor was the dependence confined to the Bessemer iron trade; the Scots invasion was accompanied by a remarkable banking 'raid' into West Cumberland in 1874. This incursion was largely the work of the Clydesdale Bank, which, with the Union Bank of Scotland, broke into a Cumbrian system hitherto largely dominated by a few families and partnerships, chiefly associated with the names of Head, Heysham, Mounsey and (in the case of the Kendal Bank), Wakefield.[110] Unfortunately, when hard times brought the Kilmarnock-inspired Maryport Haematite Iron Co. into difficulties in a few years before 1882, its largest creditor was the native Cumberland Union Banking Co., who were owed £124 826. The Union Bank of Scotland escaped with a mere £36 239 in moneys advanced.[111] It cannot thereby be argued that the Scots bankers shielded their colleagues south of the border against risk, and it is much more likely that the latter were forced to undertake dangerous gambles during the boom period of 1869–74.

Cumberland iron-making sites were not only attractive at this propitious time because haematite or Bessemer pig-iron was readily saleable; local furnaces used only three-quarters of the average fuel input of a British furnace, by virtue of the extreme richness of the ore itself.[112] Both Scottish and English investors were aware of this, and no firm seems at first to have resisted the idea of bringing coke from Durham into West Cumberland. Nevertheless, improvements in furnace design and heat conservation ensured that whereas the average Cumberland furnace used some 2.4 tons of coal or coke per ton of iron produced in 1872, the fuel input had fallen to less than 2 tons in 1877.[113] But it was the major steelmakers, with their converter shops, who led the way in discussions on economies, and the Barrow and West Cumberland enterprises began to see the point of taking molten metal from the blast furnace directly to the converter; indeed, J. T. Smith and Snelus addressed the Iron and Steel Institute on this subject, but it was Barrow, with Schneider as its mouthpiece, which most readily fell into self-recrimination in the matter of 'sharpen(ing) the Barrow wits' at the wastage of heat,[114] especially when the idea of falling iron prices, and the awareness of the lack of coal in Furness, began to bite deeply into the local consciousness.

The rest of the story, a sadder one, is well known; and it will be in place to stress, at this point, that the great boom of the early 1870s did not affect the iron-producing localities of the Lake Counties only. It brought more than a stirring of economic activity to Carlisle, as a building boom in houses for railway workers took effect there, and as local foundries flourished,[115] and if we take the dividends of the Maryport and Carlisle Railway as part-indicators of the economic state of its operating territory,[116] then prosperity reigned by the shores of the Solway when some ironmasters were already in desperation. Generally, however, a large part of the population of Cumbria – perhaps well over half of it, if we bear in mind the population distribution of the region as sketched at the beginning of this chapter – was now directly affected by the vicissitudes of the heavy and extractive industries of the coastal areas, and even in country districts the townward and other movements of labour were responsible for high wages as the farmers had to make do with fewer and fewer men. This subject is explored further in Chapter 4 (pp. 79–80). For the rest, one major West Cumbrian steelworks now had more significance for the regional, national and even international economy than the whole of the industries of inner Cumbria or Lakeland. Even so, a serious regional study cannot simply dismiss the latter, and what was a temporary crisis for the coastal towns was a tragedy for the lead-miners of eastern Cumberland or the copper-miners of Coniston. From 1873, coal and iron prices, as quoted in the Cleveland pig-iron market, slid downwards until 1878, rose again in 1878–80, then meandered downwards to 1887. There was again a part-recovery in 1888–9, and a flattening in *c.* 1890, with depression following for several years.[117] Copper prices, as quoted in the London market, fell downwards more or less steadily from 1872 to 1886,[118] by which time Coniston's mining was virtually ended, and lead prices demonstrated a similar but less painful trend.[119] Although there was much failure and re-starting of regional lead-mines, the working population engaged therein tailed off in the closing decades of the century, and only the famous Greenside mine carried itself through the period triumphantly,[120] the first electrified and fully modernised mine of its type in England.

As deduced from the census occupations of the region, its economic balance tipped increasingly westwards, and the vicissitudes of the iron and coal industries made the region itself more vulnerable. Yet, even in 1889, after two recent periods of depression, Cumberland and North Lancashire together still produced one-fifth of England's total pig-iron output,[121] and, even more memorably, its steelworks at Barrow and Workington had created a powerful reputation in the world rail market, by that time greatly aided by the firm of Charles Cammell. This firm had uprooted itself from Dronfield, south of Sheffield, because a combination of high railway rates, distance from ports, and distance from iron supplies had threatened its business position. In 1883 it performed the remarkable feat of transporting its steel-making gear piece by piece to the former Derwent Works at Workington, originally (1873) Scottish-inspired. There, it had a port near at hand, and it was near iron furnaces producing Bessemer pig; moreover, it almost immediately set about the purchase of iron mines in the nearest part of the Cumberland ironfield, north and east of Cleator Moor,[122] like Eskett Park and Frizington Parks. Just as the Barrow Haematite Steel Co. had in 1872 supplied rails to the Grand Trunk Railway of Canada,[123] so Cammells reached out even farther into the world, gaining orders not only from that country, but South America, Japan, Australia and India, and contriving to sell to home railways at the same time.[124] But such passages of triumph were not consistently maintained, even though Cammells steered resourcefully through the grim patch of the early 1890s, managing to add blast furnaces to their works and to improve the productivity of existing ones in their plant. A firm with a capital of over a million pounds ($£1\frac{1}{4}$ million in 1897) was able to purchase the efficient Solway Ironworks for a mere £12 000 (1895).[125] Cumberland pig-iron output, which had passed the million-ton mark in 1882, was maintained, in most years,

7 View of the Derwent Iron and Steel Works, Workington, apparently after the change of name of the owners to Cammell, Laird and Co. in 1903.

at well over the 800 000-ton level during the following two decades, just as Cammells made useful net profits in their combined works during the same period.[126] Yet the coastal iron industry as a whole suffered from some appreciable shocks, which were transmitted earthquake-like through the local railway system. In 1885, Cammells were congratulating themselves on the wisdom of their move from Dronfield;[127] William Fletcher, chairman of the Cleator and Workington line, spoke very differently a few months later:[128] 'Out of a total of 40 blast furnaces in one immediate district, there are no less than 20 out of blast — a single furnace gives rise to at least 125 000 tons of traffic to us, in the shape of coke,

47

pig-iron and limestone; so you can easily conceive the result on the railways.'

Nevertheless, the numbers of local useable furnaces declined only slightly, from 51 to 44 for Cumberland proper between 1880 and 1900, and a majority remained in blast, producing more iron per furnace than before.[129] The impact of the 'basic' or Gilchrist–Thomas process was undoubtedly felt, as was that of increasing world competition, and after having been recorded apprehensively by the Furness Railway directors in 1879,[130] the Gilchrist-Thomas process was made, ten years later, the subject of an emotive appraisal by Barlow-Massicks of the Millom and Askam Haematite Iron Co.; 'the Middlesbrough people have succeeded very fairly in making basic steel out of the worst ore in the world, and it has pretty nearly ruined the works of this country(side)'.[131] (It is only fair to add that Massicks was attempting to frighten intending strikers,[132] and the output of Hodbarrow haematite, from the great mine near the Millom ironworks, increased more or less steadily between 1886 and 1895.)[133]

In the remainder of the ore field, iron ore production tended to fall, especially in Furness (see Table 2.3), and this, too, had repercussions for railway receipts. The Whitehaven, Cleator and Egremont Railway did disastrously in the late seventies, and the Cleator and Workington was driven to the wretched expedient of declaring a $1\frac{1}{2}$ per cent dividend in 1885. The Furness Railway's average dividend of $9\frac{1}{2}$ per cent in 1870–73 had fallen to $2\frac{1}{2}$ per cent in 1888, although it recovered to $7\frac{1}{4}$ in 1881, but fell steadily in 1882–6.[134] The Duke of Devonshire, who was heavily committed to the Furness system, spoke as grimly about its prospects in 1879[135] as Fletcher afterwards did about the Cleator and Workington line in 1885. It is striking, however, that the Cockermouth, Keswick and Penrith line, which brought the vital coke to the West Cumberland furnaces, and which regularly paid less than 4 per cent in dividends during the early 1870s, recovered a measure of prosperity during the last two decades of the century, so much so that it refused to sell out to the London and North-Western Railway (which otherwise, as we have seen, controlled its route).[136] The most interesting paradox of all is provided by the case of the persistently independent Maryport and Carlisle Railway, which held up its dividends remarkably to 6, 7 and 8 per cent during the depression years, and which was just as committed to its local countryside as was the Furness line; it had (1889) 1075 shareholders, many of them from the Solway Plain, with an average holding of £723 each. In that year the company divided at $7\frac{1}{2}$ per cent.[137] It was not tied to iron furnaces or to the ore field, although it did carry coke from the east, and it helped to maintain the Irish coal supply through Maryport. Above all, it was a carrier of varied freight and of passengers in fair numbers, and was not, like the Furness Railway, deeply and even embarrassingly involved in the promotion of great and uneconomic docks, as at Barrow.[138] Its ventures at Maryport were, in the matter of dock improvement, more successful.

The other coastal lines were all more committed to iron, steel and ore, and lines

Table 2.3

(a) Iron ore production (quinquennial average)

	Cumberland			Furness		
	Output (millions of tons)	Persons employed	Output per head (tons)	Output (millions of tons)	Persons employed	Output per head (tons)
1855–9	0·310			0·455		
1860–4	0·606			0·589		
1865–9	0·920			0·702		
1870–4	1·209	3771	321	0·899	3222	279
1875–9	1·287			0·954		
1880–4	1·533	5478	279	1·294		
1885–9	1·427			1·149		
1890–4	1·353			0·908		
1895–9	1·236	4674	264	0·764	2694	258
1900–4	1·093	4625	236	0·475	1975	240
1905–9	1·245	4652	268	0·359	1692	212
1910–14	1·294	5142	252	0·390	1791	218

(b) Cumberland and Westmorland coal production (quinquennial average)

	Output (millions of tons)	Persons employed	Output per head (tons)
1855–9	0·925(b)	3579(a)	258
1860–4	1·293(b)		
1865–9	1·468		
1870–4	1·266		
1875–9	1·388	5938	234
1880–4	1·738	6146	283
1885–9	1·762	6612	266
1890–4	1·743	7678	227
1895–9	1·994	7745	357
1900–4	2·128	8879	240
1905–9	2·216	9336	237
1910–14	2·258	10617	213

(a) Year 1854 only
(b) Cumberland figures only
See note (152) to Chapter 2.

(c) Some examples of the interrelationships of Cumberland iron production, and uses of coal and haematite ore

	Cumberland ore produced (tons)	Coal produced (tons)	Coal exported (tons)	Cumberland iron output (tons)	Blast furnaces built	No. in blast
1856	267 256	913 981	643 140	25 530	8	3
1869	1 047 819	1 410 808	679 548	129 107	18	9
1880	1 491 383	1 680 841	517 893	790 343	51	40
1882	1 725 478	1 747 317	461 148	1 001 181	55	45

and mines were, from the 1870s, in competition with seaborne non-phosphoric ore imported from Spain through local harbours and docks, although, of course, much of this was circulated on short-distance hauls by rail. It was here, in the sphere of port facilities that the greatest weaknesses of the western sub-region's transport structure began to manifest themselves, and a further pattern of seeming paradoxes appeared. Whitehaven, historically Cumberland's leading port, remained largely tidal, and although it continued to export coal in quantity it could not handle large steamers, the most effective carriers of ore from Spain and North Africa. Moreover, its prospects were damaged in 1872 by a strike and by a shift in the direction of ore travelling to furnaces, and it is ironic that a leading ore mining proprietor, S. J. Lindow, welcomed the importation of Spanish ore as a solution to problems of ore supply and cost.[139] In the event, the Duke of Devonshire saw the far superior advantages of Barrow docks for accommodating large or varied shipping,[140] and Spanish ore was coming into this port in 1873–4,[141] and did so thereafter, into all the main Cumbrian ports, in increasing quantities. The real significance of its use, however, lay not only in the competition if offered to increasingly costly local haematite mining, especially in Furness, but in its employment by South Wales and Cleveland steelmakers,[142] who could build Bessemer plants and take advantage of its non-phosphoric quality. The Workington steelmakers were of course sensitive to their rivals in these other districts, and were, in the absence of adequate docking facilities in Workington itself, largely dependent upon Maryport's superior wet dock, the Senhouse (1884), which could take vessels of 6000 tons. The Lonsdale Dock, Workington (1865) could accommodate ships of only a third of this tonnage. Meanwhile, the major Workington steelmakers, Cammells and the Moss Bay Iron and Steel Company, were in turn obliged to use the small port of Harrington to send away steel rails by coaster for trans-shipment to larger vessels at Liverpool.[143]

Just as these resourceful enterprises survived to become the bastions of an even more concentrated West Cumberland iron and steel industry, so the great Hodbarrow mine, worried by the competition of imported ore, nevertheless surmounted it. This it achieved by selling its 'blast ore' for mixing with the imported variety,[144] and there was still a wide market for both, if only because 'acid' or Bessemer-type steel was still the most commonly encountered form in the pre-1914 United Kingdom. Although its Welsh market had diminished, it could still sell in Scotland and the Midlands.[145] This great company maintained its productive level at around half a million tons per annum until three or four years before the Great War, and reached its record output, nearly 546 000 tons, in 1907. By that time, Hodbarrow alone had far outstripped the total production of the Furness iron ore field, which was hindered by the exhaustion of ore deposits, water and pumping problems and, outside the mines controlled by the main iron and steel companies, lack of capital (see Table 2.3). Cumberland ore production, partially underpinned by that of Hodbarrow, remained fairly stable by contrast. Hodbarrow's story has well deserved its separate and definitive study,[146] and is one of allied resourcefulness and good fortune, boldness, technical skill, and not a little concern with community building and the institutions of a flourishing small town, Millom. Cedric Vaughan, the company manager, was virtually the town's manager as well, until trade unionism and public opinion alike overtook him.[147] The mine he controlled was one of the most remarkable of its kind in the world. It is worth noticing that it continued to operate its own small port of Borwick Rails in the Duddon estuary, and so it was independent of the region's competing but unsatisfactory docks and harbours.

The survival of one of the larger iron and steel firms, the Moss Bay company, was not achieved without pains and alarms, and in 1890 the latter became bankrupt, to be resuscitated by what had then become a strongly locally-identified group of ironmasters, including J. S. Randles, William McCowan, David Mallalieu, C. J. Valentine, William Burnyeat and R. E. Highton. In 1909, this company became amalgamated with yet another deeply rooted local firm, the Workington Iron Company, and also with the former Bain enterprise at Harrington, and, most important of all, with the Workington undertaking of what had become Messrs Cammell, Laird and Co. The whole group then became known as the Workington Iron and Steel Company, and controlled coke ovens, collieries and iron mines in a system of integration more complete than any that previously been witnessed in the region. It remained under the control of the directors listed, or of their sons, and after the First World War it came to control the Cleator and Workington Railway,[148] by which time the giant combine had been taken under the wing of the United Steel Companies Ltd. Only the Barrow Haematite Steel Company wielded a remotely comparable influence in its own district. Meanwhile, the mortality on the part of the less well directed or less adequately capitalised ironworks, nearly all Scots-inspired, had been heavy; the Parton works and the West Cumberland plant at Workington (both closed in the grim year of 1891); the Maryport ironworks, shut down in 1893; the Lowther Haematite Iron and Steel Co. at Workington, which went into liquidation in 1903, but which was temporarily resuscitated in 1911; and the Lonsdale Iron and Steel Co. at Bransty, Whitehaven, which was wound up in 1904.[149] By 1913, only 17 furnaces were in blast in West Cumberland (and a further 10 in Furness and Carnforth), as against 45 in the former district in 1882, but it is important to note that the later furnaces were of much larger capacity. In the earlier year, production had been of the order of 22 000 tons per annum per furnace, but in 1913, the average output was over 40 000 tons. Accordingly, there was nothing like the catastrophic drop in production that might otherwise be deduced, and it is an arresting thought that even in 1900, West Cumberland alone was responsible for roughly one-tenth of UK iron production.[150]

The coal industry of the region, by contrast, produced little more than 1 per cent per annum of the coal output of England and Wales during much of the period under review. It is yet another paradox that it was, and remained for several decades, the major single employer in industrial Cumberland with an increasing workforce and overall production from the mid-century to 1914, and a further climb, albeit with a heavily flagging output per year per man, in the first of the inter-war decades.[151] The statistics for Victorian years, however, are to be regarded with some suspicion as regards their literal accuracy relative to the coal and ore-mining industries,[152] and, as given in Table 2.3, they indicate trends only. The coal industry has been notoriously labour-intensive, and, whereas many millions of pounds of capital investment went into Cumbrian railways, iron and steel, the region's collieries were often small and were often likewise controlled by small companies of limited capital. So much attention has been directed to the historically important Whitehaven collieries, which employed over 2000 men during much of the period now examined, that it could easily be forgotten that the average Cumbrian coal mine outside that district employed in that same period, considerably fewer than 200 men.[153] In 1885, there were some 40 collieries in the small Cumberland fields,[154] including that isolated outlier near Brampton and another at Alston, and 43 in 1900.[155] Although the West Cumberland Iron and Steel Co. was probably the first to acquire a colliery for use in iron production, at Clifton (1873), the fashion for the purchase of such mines by the iron companies did not spread rapidly, and only five pits were owned in the names of such companies in 1885.[156]

There was an understandable reason for this slowness to integrate the working of collieries and ironworks. Cumberland coal was not considered to be suitable for coking, as we have seen, and not until the new century, when more scientifically designed by-product coke ovens (originally imported from Germany) were installed widely, did the local colliery output find itself increasingly used in the coastal iron furnaces. The first collieries to build their own ranges of modern ovens were at St Helens, near Workington, (1894), and at Risehow, near Flimby (1908), whereupon the Workington and Barrow steel interests acted rapidly and acquired these and other collieries and their ovens, developing into major coalmining employers by 1930.[157] By 1912, roughly a third of Cumberland coal was transformed into coke for local use,[158] and it should be remembered that the iron-masters of the coastal district had already suffered a severe shock when a major strike in Durham interrupted their main source of supply in 1892,[159] thus no doubt stimulating the St Helens experiment. Yet it is probably fortunate that the coalmining and iron-making interests of the coast were not too closely inter-related during certain periods in the late Victorian year, for there was a ready market for the local coal elsewhere – it is a striking fact that Cumberland coal was nearly the lowest-priced in England, costing 5s. 6d. per ton at the mine in 1882 and 7s. 7½d. in 1891.[160] Only Durham and Northumberland coal was generally cheaper; in 1891 the England and Wales average was 8*s*. 3*d*. per ton at the mine. It is interesting to find the local collieries supplying not only Ireland, their long-established and historic customer country, but also London, to the quantity of over 200 000 tons by rail and sea in 1882, whilst the London and North-Western Railway distributed larger quantities about England for domestic use. Each of the Cumbrian ports except Barrow continued to find coal a vital staple[161] in its handling trade and the Irish export remained significant well into the new century.[162]

The economic structure of regional coalmining, and industry, was to have profound social consequences. Small mines meant small colliery settlements, often in the countryside, and a man leaving agricultural work did not always find his surroundings totally transformed. This subject of migration into urban or quasi-urban surroundings is discussed in Chapter 4. Even the heavily capitalised iron and steel companies contributed only piecemeal to the growth of towns, so that the Barrow Haematite Steel Company dominated and helped to stimulate the suburb of Hindpool, and the Workington companies between them produced isolated areas of building development at the 'Marsh', Oldside, Northside and Barepot (the site of a Welsh-inspired tinplate works, formerly a famous foundry). Only Cammells had sufficient impact to weld the whole into a self-conscious and self-respecting industrial town.[163] Elsewhere, a group of collieries might produce a thriving small town, as in the case of Aspatria, or other works might engender genuinely 'company' towns or villages like Millom, Harrington or Askam-in-Furness. Frizington and Cleator Moor acquired, as ore-mining settlements, a civic self-awareness which can be too easily under-rated. Such developments and achievements implied the existence of settled men of influence and power, rather than the incidental interest of distant investors, and, just as importantly, they called for a stable labour force which acquired or transmuted local social traditions and which could help to form new ones. Some of the region's most important investors and industrialists – Schneider and Ramsden in Barrow, Valentine and Randles in Workington – stayed to throw down roots, and many lesser men imitated them. They became part of a process which is considered at greater length in Chapter 5.

The major implied argument within this chapter will be apparent enough. Sounding through the complexities of economic change within the Victorian region was a keynote or theme of contradictions and almost continual paradoxes. When its textile industries, factory and domestic, were under pressure or threat as the first major phase of the northern industrial revolution wound to its close, a remarkable and localised by-product of that revolution, the bobbin industry, was burgeoning in southern Lakeland dales. Like a dozen other rural industries, which also died or struggled to survive in their turn, it represented a skilful use of water power which has lessons for the twentieth century. Several branches of hill-country mining, like copper and lead, with centuries of prospecting and practice behind them, virtually perished during the century, and yet the gunpowder industry, which supplied mines and quarries with black blasting powder, continued to flourish. The railways, which should have increased the chances of survival of many of these rural industries, did so only intermittently, and the very construction of their lines seems to have increased population movement away from rural or dales hamlets. As those railways conquered distance and moved loads with speed, the lines nearest to the coastal mines, ore deposits and ports prospered incommensurately; and as the Age of Steel transformed relatively small coastal districts into centres of heavy industry, an already unsufficiently varied or balanced regional economy was given a heavy westwards list. One of the most important steel-producing areas in England, and, for a short time, in the world, lay on the edge of a thinly populated massif which yet provided thousands of out-migrants for a developing national economy. Yet that massif, recognised as the most beautiful area in England, was increasingly drawing in tourists, carried by the railways that were taking Cumbrian work-seekers to other counties.

Throughout all these transformations, the region, as we have seen, remained predominantly and visibly agrarian by comparison with most other regions or counties of England. The basic changes in its agriculture are discussed in the next chapter.

Cumbrian farming, 1851–1914

As we have seen, agriculture remained the most important single industry in Cumbria during the whole of the period covered by this book. Necessarily, it diminished in importance as urban industry and commerce burgeoned, and it experienced major changes in character and structure between the early Victorian Age and the Edwardian; some of these changes were understandably common to northern and upland farming in England and Wales. In terms of persons employed in field and farm it had reached the height of its regional significance at the time of the 1851 census. Well over 20 per cent of the occupied regional population earned its living in agriculture in that year, whereas the national proportion so engaged was under 9 per cent. Thereafter, the numbers of persons classified as 'farmers, graziers' remained at roughly the same level, between 7000 and 8000, in Cumberland and Westmorland combined until 1911, but the remainder of the agricultural non-family labour force declined drastically (Appendix 4). This decline, which is clearly an important topic, is discussed more fully in the next chapter. This short chapter attempts to outline the general history, character and structure of regional farming within the period.

Its economico-social structure was somewhat unusual, in that the sizes of landed estates, and of farms themselves, were unevenly distributed down the social scale. At the upper end were several great landed estates, like those of the Earls of Lonsdale, the Howards, the Hothfields, the Lords Muncaster and the Grahams; and much lower down was a large number of small farms and freeholds, with a smaller-than-average intermediate class of minor gentry or substantial freeholders. The large or comfortable farmer of the Cumbrian plainlands and lower valleys could, especially if he was under the tutelage of an improving landlord or steward, lead the way in progressive farming, and there is no doubt that the greater or aristocratic landlords, like the 2nd Earl of Lonsdale and the 7th Duke of Devonshire, were at heart more deeply committed to the management of their estates than they were to the administration of railways or industries. However, as is implied here and elsewhere in this book, such great regional figures were far more than mere heads of estates, and they are considered in their roles of powerful public personalities in Chapter 5. Their agricultural influence is not only difficult to examine in isolation from their other functions; its extent is decidedly unclear, if only because many Cumbrian farmers or freeholders lacked capital to drain their land, rebuild farms or purchase breeding stock, and so their power of emulation was restricted. Yet their intelligence was not always lacking, and, like the Salthouse yeomen described in Chapter 1 (p. 6) they were capable of pursuing types of improvement which were within their reach. It may be significant that the Salthouse occupiers were living within a short distance of the Duke of Devonshire's leading tenants in their own district just outside Barrow, the Pattersons of Holbeck. It would be wrong, however, to generalise too firmly from this. Cumbria was a region of small capitals and small farmers, many of them working or tending farms of fewer than 100 acres, even when the advantages of moorland common (not usually taken into account in these calculations) are given due allowance. Nor do mere average acreages tell us much, for land varied greatly in quality, from the patches of rich but heavy wheat-growing land in Low Furness or the lower Eden Valley to the thin soil coverings of the fellside lands recovered by recent enclosure, and, even when fairly regularly limed, fit only for sheep and a few cattle.

At the beginning of our period, it would have been true to say that the Cumbrian lowland farmer was generally a mixed farmer, employing the members of his own family, farm servants, and – in areas like the Solway Plain – day labourers to get the more demanding tasks performed. This heavy use of labour was noted in Chapter 1 (see p. 5), and even small farms of 40 or 50 acres in a relatively remote dale like Ravenstonedale, might, according to the census enumerators' schedules of 1851 or 1861, employ a farm servant – a worker hired for a six-monthly term who lived in on the farm itself. In a case like that, much depended on how many grown sons or daughters the farmer was likely to have at his command; but farm servants were so widely employed throughout the Lake Counties that their sheer numbers set Cumbria apart from most of the counties or distinctive regions of England. At the end of our period it had become abundantly clear that much of the work on a Cumbrian farm was done by the farmer and his family, with only occasional help from a member of a much-diminished farm servant labour force.

By that time, perhaps fortunately, the nature of the productive work of many a Cumbrian farm had altered radically, and had moved away from any pretension to regular or extensive arable farming towards a concentration on dairying and beef or wool. Such altered preoccupations necessarily called for less physical toil engendered by jobs like sowing, ploughing, turnip-lifting, harvesting, carting, manuring and the like. The major part of the transformation from mixed farming (with a fairly heavy stress on arable) to largely pastoral and livestock management, occupied only about a generation (1851–1881), with a slower rate of conversion to pasture taking place thereafter. It will be noticed that the transformation, or part of it, corresponds with the well-known depression period in English agriculture (which commenced seriously in 1879) and therefore we may consider in the course of this chapter how the Cumbrian farmer, used to a market for a variety of products, especially in the industrial towns, fared during these gloomy and sometimes apparently disastrous times for English agriculture. It was noted in Chapter 1 that he had a reputation for frugality; but were his skills, or agricultural education, equal to any sharp challenges placed before them? It is not claimed that this brief survey can hope to produce a mathematically perfect answer; but it can throw out a few suggestive considerations.

Even in the 1850s, the stress given to beef production, as distinct from cereal-growing, was becoming evident on those parts of Cumberland where adaptation was easily stimulated. It is important to emphasise that the region as a whole was inevitably affected by its position near to the industrial areas of Lancashire, Yorkshire and the north-east, and the railway system was to have locally varying but decisive effects on an agriculture which was shot through with traditionalism. One of the most interesting of contemporary commentators, William Dickinson of Arlecdon, of an old yeoman family, who saw the agrarian world of his time from the standpoint of the middling farmer (1853), witnessed the beginning of the change: 'many arable farms now feed annually their twenty or thirty or more head of cattle, which are mostly sent off as they become ready, by steamship or rail, to the great markets of Liverpool, Newcastle & C.'. Cumberland, he remarked, was 'a cattle-breeding county to a large extent . . . Feeding cattle for the shambles'.[1] As we shall see, this was by no means a fortuitous process, nor did the farmers concerned neglect their arable fields; the middling and larger farmers of the Cumbrian plainlands were using corn (which they would have exported not many years previously), and turnips, as well as hay fodder, for fattening cattle in the stalls. Dickinson went on: 'It is always the object of the Cumberland grazier and winter-feeder to make his cattle pay for the food they consume', and the farmer's own swede, turnips, hay, straw and oatmeal were used for fattening, whilst even wheat was used for that purpose when, as in 1851–2, prices of that commodity were low.[2] Indeed, it is to relative price movements that we must now turn, for they go far to explain what was preoccupying the Cumbrian farmer and his national counterpart.

Dr E. L. Jones has characterised the period running from 1853 to 1873 as one of agrarian prosperity.[3] From the Crimean War, wheat showed little or no tendency to rise in price, as against prices of livestock products, which rose with little pause. There is little doubt that these national economic trends affected the Lake Counties profoundly, sometimes in such a way as to give a positive advantage to the small upland farmer; wool prices, for example, gained very considerably from 1850 to 1875 despite some marked fluctuations.[4] An examination of market prices in the regional press can be revealing. Hence, beef retailed in Ulverston market climbed from a median figure of $4\frac{1}{2}d.$ a pound in 1849 to $6\frac{3}{4}d.$ in 1859, again to $7\frac{1}{2}d.$ in 1865, and $8d.$ in 1866 — increases broadly in line with national figures,[5] which demonstrated almost a doubling of general beef prices between 1851 and 1875. Meanwhile, market prices for butter more than doubled in the Ulverston market between 1850 and 1875, and veal and mutton showed increases of a similar order.[6] Cereal prices, by contrast, remained fairly stable, and in consequence fell far behind those of the products described. It is an interesting commentary on the age, for example, that the cost of flour in the Kendal market, in this same span of years, rarely increased significantly at all.[7]

Here, then, was a challenge to the Cumbrian farmers to follow the famous dictum re-popularised in the writings of Lord Ernle, 'down corn, up horn'. All that can be said here is that they were, on the whole, fairly slow to react. Only occasionally is it possible to measure the extent of the reaction, and such a measurement is available in the estate accounts of the Seventh Duke of Devonshire at Holker Hall in Cartmel,[8] where — on the Cavendish estate in the immediate vicinity — beef cattle increased more or less steadily both in number and value during the 1850s and 1860s. Unfortunately, there is no indication that the tenant farmers and small landowners in the nearby Westmorland countryside reacted with similar firmness of policy. Nor was this inertia simply the outcome of ignorance or foolishness. But the former existed, and a Westmorland gentleman farmer, W. E. Maude, put in a plea to the Kendal Farmers' Club in 1862: 'must we make, on the generally thin soils of this county, immense efforts to grow grain to compete in quality and quantity with the grain grown in the United States, Canada, the countries round the Black Sea and the Baltic, to say nothing of the sunny lands of Europe, and our own southern and Midland counties? . . . grass lands and grazing are for the future to be described as the proper course for Westmorland farming'.[9] Both Maude and the Duke of Devonshire were, amongst the larger farmers or landowners of the region, in a position to exert considerable influence over their fellows and tenants. But the existence of a multitude of small landowners and tenant farmers is indicated in the county lists in the 1873 Return of Landowners,[10] and these, who worked in many hundreds throughout the Lake Counties, were probably out of reach of direct pressures to improve or reform their farming methods.

This point was very clearly brought out in the late 1860s by the Westmorland land agent and surveyor Crayston Webster: 'All kinds of rural reform are slow to accomplishment, so hard is it to move out of the accustomed track, and numerous are the excuses why land, under the above circumstances, is not turned to grass.'[11] In fact, the 'excuses' were often very good ones, and Webster himself listed them: 'an outlay for seeds, manure, subsequent top-dressings, and years of patient waiting, with little return, which very few farmers can afford'. He added, with his struggling small farmer in mind: 'neither, even if they had the capital, could they be fairly expected to lock it up in the absence of a proper lease or security.'[12] There was another cost-accounting factor which Webster failed to mention directly; as a 'Cumberland Landowner' put it in 1873, returns to the arable farmer came in through the year – 'in short, he can, as it were, live from hand to mouth on comparatively less capital'.[13] Stock farming, for the larger farmer, could easily, profitably and conveniently be carried on in close relationship to arable cultivation, but the small man lacked the capital to make the best use of his grassland. In 1873, by contrast, Thomas Farrall's report on Cumberland to the Royal Agricultural Society[14] was at pains to condemn the small farmers who 'plough(ed) out far too much land ... under-fertilised and under-capitalised'. There was still a desperate need for a regular income.

The agricultural commentators of this age, as of the Georgian one, looked to the great landlords for leadership, but their criticisms of the less strongly placed show how insecure farming for the many could often be, and how many stresses these small farmers must have experienced in an age of transition. Nevertheless, the Cumbrian farmer, whether large or small, seems to have effected the great transformation to a largely pastoral system, and we must bear in mind that he was assisted by industrial development, by improvements in transport, and by accidents of geography or topography. The farmer of the plainland fringes was often fairly near to urban markets, or found himself comparatively close to a railway station or siding, and any efforts at improvement were likely to be rewarded as markets widened. Nearness to the urban world was no unmixed blessing, for, as we shall see (Chapter 4), discontented labourers might rapidly be tempted to migrate, and William Dickinson commented on the slovenly smallholders often to be found near towns, where 'the utmost efforts of man and horse are requisite to gain even a scanty livelihood'.[15] But there was – in Cumbria as elsewhere – a farming ladder of upward mobility and competition, whereby the 'spirit of advancement' caused some of the more industrious farm servants to acquire small but workable farms. Unfortunately, the number of rungs in the ladder was limited, the rungs themselves were tolerably wide only at the base, and the number of available farms remained restricted and finite, allowing landlords to pick their tenants with some care from a number of applicants. The number of large farmers and owner-occupiers was, by contrast with the numbers prevailing in many parts of England, small, and it is worth remembering that the poorly capitalised small farmer was also a determined or even desperate one, 'anxiously and painfully mak(ing) farming the main business of (his) industry'.[16] Not only this; as agricultural labour became more expensive, and more difficult to come by, the sheer toil of farm work became greater, and so the thousands of Cumbrian rural labourers found their opportunities for self-advancement restricted as the supply of small farms remained limited, and found farming itself becoming less attractive. However, it is also important to bear in mind that since most Cumbrian farms were small, they could often manage without hired labour, especially when the conversion to grassland was in full progress. Between 1851 and 1881, the numbers of male and female labourers of both the 'indoor' and the 'outdoor' kinds, in Cumberland and Westmorland, decreased by well over 5000 in the census totals.

Dickinson (1853) described the farmers of 150 to 400 acres as a relatively stable and homogeneous group – 'a large number of these are the descendants of farmers from generation to generation, some of whom are tilling the same farms, along with additions, which their grandfathers, and even great-grandfathers, held in tenancy under the same race of owners. Others are yeomen, cultivating the patrimonial estates in whole or in part.'[17] He agreed that a few in this group had 'risen from servitude', but the rungs of the ladder were clearly much narrower at this social or agrarian level. Table 3.1 will acquire more social meaning with this consideration in mind and it should also be remembered that the distributions of Westmorland farm sizes, at the Census of 1851, show an exceptionally marked skew towards the small farm, with roughly 70 per cent of all separate holdings under the 100 acres. A sample taken by Canon J. S. Simpson (1869) from the rate books of 62 parishes and townships of Westmorland, and accounting for perhaps two-thirds of the operative substantial farms in the county, found 56 per cent under the 100-acre level, but this count ignored smallholdings of 50 acres and under.[18] A set of figures for Westmorland, given by F. Garnett in his monumental study of the agriculture of that county, and also ignoring the under-50-acre group, shows distributions for three selected years up to 1885,[19] and, in so far as it is roughly accurate, suggests little throwing together of farms (see Table 3.1 (b)). Compared with the census totals for farmers, however, it indicates that some under-50-acre holdings may have been consolidated into medium-sized farms, if not amalgamated into big estates like Underley and Netherby, which were alleged to be the engrossers of small properties.[20] But it is clear that figures for actual holdings, and figures for persons who described themselves as male or female farmers or graziers, do not coincide, and the figures for Cumberland (1851) in Table 3.1 give holdings only, and show much more exactly the shape of the farming ladder down to the 5-acre level, comparing it in percentage terms with the national distribution.

The large surplus of persons professionally denominated 'farmer' strengthens the case for keen competition in the lower levels of the ladder, unusually wide enough though the rungs may have been, and it is likely that horse-leaders, farm servants and labourers with smallholdings swelled the multitude. The Victorian self-help philosophy made much of the abstemious farm servant who saved hard, married a woman servant rather late in life, and slowly built up a moderately prosperous small farm of his own – and Wilson Fox, in his 1895 report on Cumberland and Westmorland agriculture, stressed that many tenants on small farms were men of this type.[26] The labourer could be encouraged to become a

Table 3.1

(a) Distribution of Cumberland farms by acreage, 1851[21]

	5–49	50–99	100–299	300–499	500–999	1000-plus	Total
No.	1466	1513	1569	208	75	58	4889
Distribution (%)	29·9	30·9	32·1	4·25	1·5	1·1	
England (%) (comparative)	8·6	13·0	44·6	17·6	11·5	4·5	

Acres

Total persons described as 'farmer, grazier' (both sexes) in Cumberland in 1851: 5556.

(b) *Westmorland: size distributions of farms at selected dates*[22]

	50–99	100–299	300–499	500–999	1000-plus	Totals
1851	711	555	76	35	9	1386
1875	821	575	66	26	2	1490
1885	790	641	64	31	3	1523

Total persons described as 'farmer, grazier' (both sexes) in Westmorland: 1851, 2719; 1881, 2589. Classifications as given by Garnett, slightly adjusted.

farmer by the availability of sheep flocks for hire at 4 to 4½ per cent, and it is worth noticing that in 1880–86 the numbers of under-50-acre Cumberland holdings increased in number,[24] and were thereby placed within reach of scatterings of such men.

As will have been made fairly clear, the ladder of opportunity and social mobility could develop a steep slope beyond a certain level. The cardinal point must remain that a world of small farmers, which turned increasingly to livestock, had less and less obvious need for labour hired at money wages which were, on paper at least, amongst the highest in the kingdom. A Cumberland labourer might get one-third as much again in such wages as his southern counterpart.[25] Moreover, we must not overstress the completeness of any agrarian transformation, nor the completeness of any changes in attitude which accompanied it. Conservatism remained in this world of small occupiers, despite the continued existence of agricultural societies and their shows, and of pockets of notable experiment or improvement.

The Board of Trade crop returns (see Appendix 5), for 1867 and 1900 respectively, make possible a straightforward comparison of the apparent style of farming between one generation and another; between those dates, the Westmorland farmer reduced the amount of his arable land by roughly one-fifth, and he cut down heavily on cereal growing, keeping only substantial oats acreages, for here was food for man and beast. But, as Crayston Webster might have predicted, he did not greatly increase the amount of his permanent pasture, perhaps fearing the expense of so doing. Cumberland, by contrast, maintained much of its arable land, losing only 13 per cent between the two dates, but increased its permanent pasture by nearly 50 per cent – largely, it would appear, by reclamation of former commons and by seeding and liming. It increased its sheep and its cattle markedly, but grew more oats, and nearly as many turnips as before, with the clear purpose of producing feed for its animals. At bottom, its agriculture had not changed much in half a century. Yet its record in the depression years, and that of Westmorland, was almost unmatched in the whole of England. The remaining comments in this chapter cannot pretend to offer the full explanation that the historian always seeks, but they will put forward some simple hypotheses which may help further research.

Cumbrian farming and the depression

The depression in farming may be taken as running from the late 1870s to an unspecified date well beyond the First World War. Its commencement is associated with a collapse of cereal prices at the beginning of this period, made more serious in its impact by increased grain imports from North America and Argentina.[26] More generally still, the depression was part of a deflation of prices which affected the whole of the British economy, although it is important to recognise that this had its advantages for the small farmer who had to purchase feed for his stock — moreover, as we have seen, many Cumbrian farmers were growing theirs. The essential thing to remember is that, regionally, corn was grown for use and not for sale, and here is a sharp contrast with the south-eastern counties of England, which depended heavily upon cereal production for sale. Next, the Cumbrian lowland farmer was usually not far from some kind of railway connection with not-too-distant industrial towns and districts, which provided ready if fluctuating markets for milk, butter, cheese and meat. Even when these products fell in price, as they often did, the Cumberland and Westmorland farmer's outgoings were low, and he could somehow get by. Hence, in 1881–3, agricultural bankruptcies in the south-eastern counties were five to six times more frequent than in the two Cumbrian ones where, *pro rata*, such misfortunes occurred probably less often than anywhere else in England.[27] But the rural inhabitants of the Lake Counties were not really aware of their relative good fortune, and the newspaper press of the period is full of references to 'dull' hiring fairs, indifferent stock prices and the effects of poor weather. In 1886, at the Cartmel Show, Lord Edward Cavendish 'regretted that the farmers had had to contend so long against falling prices and bad seasons'.[28] Yet this type of landlord awareness of the struggles of the numerous small occupiers brought its positive results, and accordingly the great landlords, Cavendishes, Muncasters, Lowthers and Grahams, were willing to reduce their rents, so that between 1882 and 1894, their estate rentals were reduced by between 15 and 25 per cent. Cattle and sheep prices (1874–94) went down by between 12 and 27 per cent.[29] However, smaller landlords were less likely to make such handsome reductions, and we must remember that a group of the greatest estates, those of the Grahams, Lowthers, Lawsons and Howards could (1894) count only 372 farms between them in the two counties,[30] not more than 5 per cent of all known farms there —

although, of course, the largest and most progressive farms were to be found on these estates.

Generally speaking, however, this is scarcely a picture of dynamic or highly adaptable agriculture, and to paint such would be to falsify the world of the sheep-farming dalesman or his cattle-rearing plainland counterpart. Indeed, Wilson Fox noted that the hill sheep farmer of the region rode the depression well[31] – and this was the man with the fewest outgoings, who was often farthest from railway stations and, therefore, from the greater industrial and urban markets, and who was often also an unenterprising dairy farmer. Nevertheless, the relative security, if not prosperity, of such farmers has to be explained, and part of the answer is undoubtedly to be found in a railway system which was sufficiently extensive to enable the hill farmer to send milk to the towns – and milk and wool were the commodities that suffered least from the general deflation of prices.[32] Likewise, he was able to resist the influx of refrigerated meat and dairy products of colonial origin, and, in particular, there was a demand for small lambs and lightweight mutton which was unaffected by foreign competition.[33] However, it is certainly unwise to see the survival of the many hundreds of Cumbrian hill farmers as a simple response to the relatively inelastic demands of increasingly urbanised markets, and the somewhat glowing picture of the triumphant emergence of the small Lancashire farmer from the depression, as painted by the late T. W. Fletcher,[34] certainly cannot be applied *in toto* to Cumbria. It is true that Crayston Webster had written enthusiastically (1867) that 'so long as the tall chimneys of Lancashire and Yorkshire smoke, so long will the Westmorland farmer have a never-failing demand for all his produce – beef, mutton, butter, cheese and wool.'[35] However, Webster also praised Westmorland butter without reserve, stating that it was keenly sought in the manufacturing towns.[36] But in the mid 1880s butter prices collapsed, and, moreover, Garnett – the historian of Westmorland agriculture – felt bound to admit that the product was 'irregular' in quality.[37] In 1886, a controversy in the *Westmorland Gazette* drew attention to small and overcrowded dairies, unhygienic churning and pressing, and rank tastes imparted by sour and weedy meadow plants.[38]

Yet the hill farmer had advantages which even dairy farming of this description could not wholly nullify. He could use family labour; his rents were often modest; and his outgoings on feed for stock were low and falling. The farms themselves were of a basic and sometimes primitive design, commonly consisting, accrording to Webster, of 'a house, barn and cow-house, all joined together, with a bank-barn arrangement in the steeper situations, and the mowsteads or hay-storage above the byre or shippon. Webster went on to remark meaningly that 'farmers cannot afford to pay interest in much building, nor, indeed, is it expected of them',[39] so we may assume that there was little capital expenditure on rebuilding or extension, even at a prosperous period. As Dr Perry

8 Hill farms were of a basic design. A West Cumberland hill farm with a detached shippon and the double-pile farmhouse common in the area.

has written of hill farmers in general during the depression, 'the small farmers who survived did so by accepting very low standards of living and farming practice . . . (e.g.) in such small-farmer counties as Cumberland'.[40]

The Cumbrian farmer of a more ambitious description, usually the man farming on the Solway plainland, enjoyed another advantage which often permitted him to escape from anything approaching voluntary poverty. The long local trade connection with Ireland, firstly through Whitehaven and later through Maryport, brought a return traffic in cattle which partially compensated for the historic and (by the 1880s) long-diminished traffic from the Scottish glens, and the centuries-old business of fattening animals continued unabated. As the *Cumberland Pacquet* put it on 7 March 1889, 'the Irish cattle traffic is a most important one to Cumberland farmers, furnishing as it does a regular and unfailing supply of store beasts all the year round; and animals, too, that have been vastly improved in breed in the past few years.' The great landowners, of

64

course, had done much of the planning in improving breeds. The use and establishment of shorthorn herds had become widely diffused by Edwardian times, and they were no longer the experimental playthings of mid-Victorian industrialists like the Brogdens of Lightburn, Ulverston, or the retired merchant George Moore of Whitehall near Wigton. By 1914, store shorthorns from the Wigton district were being sold to buyers in Durham, Yorkshire and the Midland counties. Meanwhile, by that date, Board of Trade restrictions had in any case put an end to the movement of Scottish cattle into England, and although the trade in Irish beasts continued, Cumbrian-bred animals were dominant in local marts.[41] There was also far more experimentation in the crossing of sheep, and in the breeds accepted and encouraged by local farmers; the familiar Herdwick was of course commonly encountered in southern Lakeland (deliberately bred and fostered for the best results by small landowners like the Brownes of Troutbeck), but Cheviot, Scotch and Blackface sheep had long spread through western Cumbria,[42] just as the Rough Fell sheep was firmly established in Westmorland.

Yet, even on the better-run lowland estates, the basic rules of self-denial and grinding work seemed to prevail. John Coleman, before the Richmond Commission in 1882, described the case of George Leece, a former farm servant renting land at Aynsome near Cartmel. George Leece had not really felt the depression, despite the payment of a very high rental, 'mainly because his outlay was small and his labour was all done without actual cash payments, and by those whose interest it was to make the most of their time'. Leece was essentially a stock farmer, who sold nine or ten fat beasts annually.[43] A neighbour of his, John Backhouse, who was also near the Furness Railway, complained about 'the inequality of railway rates', whereby American meat was conveyed from Barrow to London at 30s. a ton less than English meat to and from the same places.[44] This, it should be added, was a result of the activities of Barrow industrialists, who attempted to turn Barrow into a major transatlantic cattle port; the outcome was abortive.[45] Most Cumbrian farmers can hardly have seen a local railway route in this light, but, just as certainly, they must have worked unremittingly against the uncertainties of a hazardous future.

For the rest, the paradoxes at the roots of Cumbrian rural life remained. It is true that tourism, not always welcomed by local countrymen and landowners, began to create additional sources of income for increasing numbers of farming families, especially those whose farms were situated in the more popular scenic areas. Yet their labourers and female farm servants were leaving the countryside in great numbers after the 1850s and 1860s, thereby throwing more work on to the farmer's wife and family, and there was certainly no great increase of farm lodging accommodation until near the turn of the century – this despite the frequent references to farmhouse lodgings in literary sources throughout the nineteenth century.

Meanwhile, the sad paradox of the Cumbrian labourer leaving his native countryside, and meeting tourists on their way in, calls for further discussion. Some of the economic and social forces surrounding his migration are considered in the next chapter. Tourism is discussed, as a separate topic and force, in Chapter 8.

The search for better things: migration from the Cumbrian countryside, 1841–1914

Some attention has so far been given to the nature of the changes that were shaping the lives of Cumbrian people after 1831, and to the development of the region's industries and its agriculture. Its main industries were sustained not only by capital and enterprise from elsewhere, but by supplies of skilled or experienced labour from other counties. Meanwhile, the main contribution of the Lake Counties to a national economy lay in the region's own steady supply of people to other parts of England, mainly to centres of industry and commerce. This contribution was, in turn, made possible in part by fundamental changes in the agricultural structure and economy of the rural areas as characterised and outlined in the last chapter. Cumbria, despite constant allegations that land and farms were being 'amalgamated', kept its high proportion of small farmers and modest landed properties side by side with the great aristocratic landed estates, and it was principally the farming population which produced, in the middle decades, both a relatively high birth rate and an accumulation of sons and daughters surplus to the requirements of the countryside. Indeed, the former group remains a fertile one even at the present day, as is shown by data recently collected for North Westmorland.[1]

Accordingly, a remarkably sustained outflow of Cumbrian people between the early Victorian years and the Edwardian period was made possible by two factors: low crude mortality (including child mortality) rates in the rural areas, and crude birth rates which were steadily maintained and even increased (as industrial towns grew) during the middle and later Victorian periods. It should be added that these annual rates were in general between 10 and 15 per cent lower than those obtaining for England and Wales in the period between the beginning of civil registration and the end of the century,[2] but the gap or differential between them produced an impressive natural increase which enabled the country districts to maintain their own populations, whilst contributing to the stream of outgoing migrants during decade after decade. If the birth rates of rural Westmorland were lower than those common in the more industrially developed areas of England, it must also be borne in mind that the region, and these same country districts, had unusually high proportions of unmarried people *pro rata* of population, a matter which is discussed below (pp. 80–82). Marriage in the farming communities was not, it is plain, contracted early or easily, and it is all the more remarkable that the children of the latter, farmers' progeny and those of labourers, continued to be born in such large numbers. Nor is the adjective 'large' used lightly; well over 100 000 Cumbrian-born people were distributed about other counties of England and Wales by 1891,[3] scarcely less than a third of the total population of Cumbria at that time. This mass of distant settlers had attained its then magnitude over half a century or more, and it is important to bear in mind that an uncertain proportion had gained some experience of industry or commerce in Cumbrian towns or industrial districts – a matter which will only be resolved when large numbers of census enumerators' schedules, and the often indicative places of birth of children that they contain, are satisfactorily analysed throughout England.

Although migration from country to town was a major fact in the economic and social history of nineteenth-century Britain, the rural areas of the Lake Counties were not merely typical in the part that they played nationally in this movement. Rural Westmorland can safely be taken as representative of the countryside of the remainder of the Lake Counties (including Furness or Lancashire North of the Sands), and it was noted in 1881 that it was amongst the English counties 'that retain the smallest proportion of their natives . . . in which the stationary proportion of the enumerated natives was less than 65 per cent'. It should, meanwhile, be borne in mind that the pronouncing deity of the Census Office, who made this judgement, was referring to the proportionate relationship between the Westmorland-born persons within that county, and all those scattered throughout England,[4] and at that census only 60.6 per cent of such persons were resident in Westmorland itself. The counties of Buckingham, Huntingdon, Oxford, Hereford and Berkshire were, using the same criteria, more prone to lose people by out-migration,[5] but it will be seen that Westmorland stood very high in the list. Other demographic data make clear that the rural districts of Cumberland and Furness must also have done so, given that pastoral farming, to which they were increasingly committed after 1870, made a large outflow of labour inevitable. Nevertheless, economic and social movements are never quite as simple as they may seem in the light of a cursory examination, and it is necessary to examine such contemporary regional evidence as may be available.

Every region has its peculiarities, and Cumbria's own agricultural institutions and farming practices, far from 'tying the labourer to the soil', tended of their very nature to make him footloose. The institution of farm service permitted him to offer his services at hiring fairs, held twice-yearly at Whitsuntide and

Martinmas, and to change his master on those occasions. Not all labourers did this, but many changed their employers frequently, even when staying in the same locality. The farm servant 'lived in', often in a garret in the farm buildings, and received roughly half his payment in kind in the form of bed and board, and occasionally in the shape of certain perquisites which defy analysis. Broadly speaking, the remoter farms and districts used the system of farm service, if only because day labourers were not available in the small and sparsely settled hamlets of the inner dales, whilst day labourers were for obvious reasons more common in the more thickly populated, arable-oriented areas like the Solway Plain, with their labour-intensive field culture. However, too sharp a line should not be drawn, especially at the beginning of our period, between the hill farmer and his plainland counterpart, for, as was noted in Chapter 1 (p. 4), some arable cultivation was pursued in the hillier country in the 1830s and 1840s; hence, villages in the Pennine foothills, like Milburn, had both farm labourers and farm servants in 1851, with an accent on the former (for it is clear from the census schedules[6] that labourers in Milburn had their own family cottages, not always available in the bleaker places), whilst Troutbeck in Westmorland[7] had a preponderance of farm servants in that year, usually on the larger farms. Since Troutbeck was not especially isolated, it is evident that tradition influenced employment practices also. Farm servants (see Appendix 4) were nearly 11 per cent more numerous than day labourers in the county of Westmorland (1851), but were marginally less numerous in Cumberland, an unsurprising if interesting commentary on the greater area of arable plainland in the latter county. In this census year, meanwhile, there were at least three labourers (of either kind) to every farmer enumerated in Cumberland, but only two in Westmorland, a reflection of the more limited needs of the hill farmer. The two types of farmworker did not, meanwhile, pursue their respective forms of labour independently of each other, for a farm servant was generally, within the constraints of his society, obliged to remain unmarried, and he might graduate to day-labouring and married status if cottages were available. The age distributions demonstrated in Appendix 6 show this change of status within the life-cycle reasonably plainly. As was noted in the last chapter, some farm servants became small farmers by dint of hard saving as well as hard work and delayed marriage; however, by any working statistical estimate the efforts of these men did little to stem the outward flow of agricultural labour from the regional countryside. In any case, some experiments with successive census schedules[8] for Westmorland and upland parishes suggest that a considerable contribution to the outflow of migrants was made by the young or adolescent members of families on the smaller farms of those localities, whose parents were unable to support them, and whose own employment opportunities were becoming limited in the middle years of the century. The size of rural population losses cannot, in other words, be accounted for simply in terms of the reduction in the numbers of established farm servants or day labourers – a caveat which is highly necessary, since much in the following discussion necessarily bears on the influences working upon the labourer himself. The attitudes of farmers are, of course, considered.

The small farmers of the region not only supplied out-migrants from their own families; they were themselves an unstable or footloose element, in the sense that they sometimes occupied marginal and badly-run holdings near the industrial towns and districts,[9] but also in the sense that the younger small farmers from the more remote localities, who had limited field work to occupy their attention, were in the habit of undertaking harvesting expeditions (in c. 1850) 'from the bases of the western mountains to the early harvests of Furness, where their extraordinary exertions have in some seasons been recompensed with from 5s. to 7s. a day, and victuals in abundance'.[10] Finally, there was sometimes an interconnection between smallholding in the Pennine districts and an industrial activity like lead-mining,[11] the instability of the latter necessarily affecting the fortunes of the smallholders themselves. The decline of rural industries in given areas has already been touched upon (Chapter 2, pp. 53–4), and was a clear stimulus to out-migration.

Much of the out-migration from the hill country of Cumberland and Westmorland was at first local in scope and range; that is to say, it consisted first of all of an 'acclimatisation-move' to an industrial district or main town within the same general region, or fairly near at hand; the direction of the move would of course be influenced by the experience or skills of the migrants. For example, a farm labourer could adapt himself easily enough to railway labour or to work in the iron ore mines, and the results of this type of transference were noted by Crayston Webster, the Westmorland agricultural report-writer, in February 1867: 'Emigration, and the attraction of large public works, railways &c., and the iron-works of Furness, have tended to increase the cost of all kinds of labour, and good servants, male and female alike, are becoming a scarce article.'[12] It should be added that the 1871 Census, examined in conjunction with the birth and death statistics in the Registrar-General's Reports, tends to bear out Webster's assumptions, and the intercensal period 1861–71 saw an estimated net loss by out-migration of nearly 3000 people from the rural districts of adjoining Furness, many of them, as the census schedules show, heading for the Barrow district and nearby ore-field.[13] However, it should not be assumed that such moves, which were often advantageous to family income, were always undertaken lightly. Lead-miners, who were, of all men, the most likely to accustom themselves to other kinds of mining, at first moved only when they were forced to do so by unemployment, 'although by removing only 20 miles down into the coal country a young man might nearly double his income';[14] and we should also bear in mind that most of the scores of Cumbrian parish officials who supplied information to the Poor Law Commissioners of 1832 did not regard their local labourers as especially migration-prone.[15] In other words, the habit of migration took time to grow, and developed under a variety of pressures, economic and psychological. Commissioner Mitchell, commenting to the 1842 Commission on Child Employment (Mines), referred to the lead-mining dalesmen's 'attachment to their native land and their own people', and the same fact was drawn to the attention of the Poor Law Commission of 1834.[16] Only in the mid 1860s was a 'wind of change' distinctly noticeable in the lead-mining areas, and Thomas Sopwith, leading mines agent and engineer in the north Pennines, drew attention in his diary (1866) to two factors of vital importance:[17] 'The young and active depart . . . this wish may gather strength as railway works afford demand for labour when they are in construction, and when finished will give facilities for movement and for interchange of opinions respecting wages such as have not hitherto been known in these secluded dales.'

Sopwith was here surely right in commenting on the disturbing influence of railway construction; yet it must seem strange that in a region of high literacy, which was in the 1860s, reading more newspapers than ever before,[18] men should be ignorant of wage-levels, and that 'interchange of opinions' was necessary. As is shown below, there is evidence that farm labourers in western Cumbria read the newspaper press, and it may be that information was slow to penetrate the inner dales. An exercise in reconstruction also suggests that migrating workers needed more than details of workplaces and wages; they wished to know about transport and accommodation, and to have news and guidance from kin and friends.[19] For the rest, it seems reasonably clear that the north-eastern and Cumberland coalfields absorbed many of the lead-miners between 1860 and the end of the century, although emigration to Australia, Canada and even 'Spanish America' had been no means unknown[20] even c. 1830. There is, also a further implied paradox in the items of evidence that have so far been given, in that the 'scarcity of labour' caused by this migration-drain led to very high wages in the countryside. The money wages of rural Cumbria were, indeed amongst the highest in England between 1861 and 1907[21] but, as has been indicated, the limitations of farm service, and the payment in kind that was implicit, make any statistics misleading. What is certain is that the upward pressure on money wages did little to stem the flow of outward-travelling migrants; the poorer and smaller farmers of the region simply tried to carry on their business by using members of their families to perform essential labouring tasks. More is said on this subject below. Meanwhile, it is clearly wrong to see migration in purely economic terms.

If miners, under the pressure of necessity, could use their occupational skill or experience to ease their adaptation to new and similar work in a new environment, then what of those in other occupations? The textile industries of northern Cumbria were declining from the 1840s onward, and a man or woman trained on the loom or in the factory would certainly not seek rougher work needing hard hands. In this respect, such work was to be found farther afield in

71

the growing Lancashire textile towns, and Professor Anderson's work on Preston in-migrants is illuminating, showing that, by 1851, a scattering of workers had already migrated from the Carlisle district to that town, and that others had travelled there from Kendal and Ulverston, both places containing textile factories.[22] Both Kendal and Carlisle were then on or near the direct railway route into Lancashire, and the implication here is that the movement was a direct one out of the region. Moreover, it was certainly maintained in more general terms, and the main Lancashire cotton towns all contained between 500 and 1500 Cumbrians by 1891, with a marked preponderance of women,[23] suggesting that girls had been travelling away from possible domestic or farm service in their own region to find more congenial work. Not all of the 1851 out-migrants to Preston, however, were from known textile centres, and a significant scattering came from West Cumberland[24] – an item of evidence which reinforces the argument for stage-by-stage migration, since there was then no direct rail connection into mainland Lancashire (see p. 35).

By far the largest centre of attraction for Cumbrians, in the momentous stretch of time between 1851 and 1891, was the port and city of Liverpool, with 5801 Cumberland and Westmorland-born people in its bounds in the latter year.[25] However, it is important to recognise that there had long been a connection between Cumbria, with its local grammar schools supported by yeomen ambitious for their sons, and the main centres of commerce. The constant movement of coastal vessels between the Cumbrian ports and Liverpool of course aided this transference of people to the great port,[26] and William Dickinson wrote eloquently (1852) about the part played by the Cumberland yeomanry in supplying educated migrants to other parts:

> It is from the savings of this class that their younger sons have been educated, and spread over the kingdom as clergymen and in other professions . . . The successful and wealthy inhabitants of London, Liverpool, Manchester and other commercial and manufacturing towns, are not sparingly intermixed with the offshoots from the vales of Cumberland; and the British colonies, in all parts of the world, have numbers of the progeny of the Cumberland 'statesmen' among them . . . from almost every parish of this county has the spirit of adventure sent them forth; the army and navy have had their share too, and these are some of the causes of the comparatively small increase of population in the rural parishes.[27]

This interesting and significant rhetoric draws attention, however, to the selectivity of certain kinds of out-migration. Professor Lawton's study of the population of mid-nineteenth-century Liverpool, also based on samples from the census schedules of 1851, shows a scattering of domestic servants as having been born in Cumberland and Furness, a handful of merchants, brokers, bankers or accountants, but only two dock labourers or stevedores, one from the Kendal area and one from Carlisle.[28] Generally, Liverpool was a place which was likely to attract in-migrants following a wide range of occupations,[29] but plainly it was more sensible for Cumbrians to travel to Workington or Whitehaven to perform dock work, and if unskilled persons travelled as far as Merseyside, this was, paradoxically, because they were in competition in West Cumberland with the very Irishmen who were so numerous in Liverpool. The subject of in-migration into Cumbria must necessarily be dealt with separately below, but it cannot be considered in isolation because its very nature affected the choices made by natives when they followed their own movements. Many of the movements made by Cumbrians were of very short distance, and it is with these that we must be primarily concerned in a study like the present one. The long-distance transferences are of interest in showing generalised movements of labour, the attractions of given areas, like coal-mining and textile districts, and the types of aspiration that they imply.

What other influences and motivations lay behind the migratory propensities of local people? Some light, of a rather variegated and scattered kind, is thrown on the general movements from and to given places by the mid-Victorian census enumerators' printed comments; and intrinsically much more interesting, if partisan or biased, data are afforded in letters from labourers to the newspaper press. Many of the enumerators' comments either confirm what is already known, or add small areas of insight into local economies. Railway-building on, for example, the North British Railway (which began to connect Carlisle with Hawick after 1859[30]) not only collected a large and temporary population of labourers, but saw them depart from the Longtown district in the 1860s,[31] and the construction of the Settle and Carlisle line was clearly about to have a similar effect at Culgaith, Lazonby, Langwathby and Hesket in the Forest in 1871.[32] As Thomas Sopwith had implied, railway-building was the greatest single source of disturbance to, and a cause of the movement of, labour in many a remote country district and there are, of course, hundreds of instances of its operation. It contributed very greatly to local 'surges' of one or two years in collection and departure, and longer flows affecting a whole stretch of new line. Although Irish navvies often made up the greater part of the labour force used, dalesmen also joined the railway gangs,[33] which offered advantageous rates of payment for carting as well as shovelling. It is hardly surprising that the construction of Cumbrian railways, between 1840 and 1877 (when the Settle and Carlisle line was completed), was a concomitant of much movement of local labourers. However, this movement had still deeper connections with maladjustment or deprivation that was already felt, and was not an autonomous factor. Much more fundamental influences, that produced the implied dissatisfactions or job shortages, are touched upon by the census enumerators. These were the conversion of arable land to pasture, which was especially effective after the 1870s, but which was certainly operative in 'patches' before that decade; secondly, the demolition or shortage of cottages; and, thirdly, the destruction of local or rural industries.

73

The theme of loss of population through conversion of land from arable to pasture was taken up by enumerators (1871) in localities as various as Watermillock, Askerton, Irthington, Bootle and Whitbeck,[34] and such instances suggest that the arable cultivation line in the foothills was being moved downward to the valley bottoms or plainland. Meanwhile the upward pressures on wages near the towns and industrial districts, and the ever-present fear of pauper maintenance charges even in a relatively well-placed Cumbria,[35] were two obviously disparate influences which appear in different guises and places: at Melmerby with Kirkland and Blencarn (1841–51) a loss of population was attributed to 'fewer labourers being employed by the farmers',[36] but at Kirkandrews-upon-Esk near Carlisle, the decrease in 1831–51 was put down to the incorporation of farms 'and the removal of cottages',[37] whilst at Skelton in 1841, it was noted that the houses had become 'dilapidated'.[38] Later, Oulton near Wigton had apparently suffered a 'demolition of cottages'[39] (1871), although the land there belonged to a variety of proprietors, and the region had few closed villages of the classic kind. That a cottage shortage had become endemic in rural Cumbria was an argument put forward by J. H. Tremenheere in 1868[40] and again by Arthur Wilson Fox in 1895.[41] Great landlords like the Earls of Lonsdale and Lord Hothfield had attempted to act beneficially in the matter, but, nevertheless, the large number of small farmers and landowners meant that there was little general investment in labourers' housing.[42] This lack of building, in turn, was clearly one of the several factors bearing on the propensity or ability of young country people to marry. Yet it must seem strange that the cottage shortage persisted even after many hundreds of labourers had left the Cumbrian hills and valleys.

The failure of rural industries has already been touched upon in general terms (Chapter 2, pp. 53–4). In the Wigton and Woodside Quarter (1871) 'the depressed state of handloom weaving' was stated to have led to loss of people,[43] and this tallies with more general trends in northern Cumberland. That the effect of the failure of lead mining in Alston was noted[44] need hardly surprise us, but the closure of country coal mines, as at Hayton and Mealo, and High and Low Bolton near Cockermouth,[45] demonstrates an element of the fortuitous, and the effect of trade fluctuations on Furness bobbin mills[46] – sometimes serious for local communities – supports an earlier argument that their economic importance has been inadequately measured or recorded (see pp. 25–6). Each of these types of force, or incident, would present a group of people with a crisis, and oblige them to act. Nearby opportunities, or economic development, as well as the predilections or training of the individual, might then 'determine' the movements of migrants. In many cases, however, their motivations were hardly very complex; they were, to quote the title of this chapter, in search of better things, and when the labourers of Sebergham were reported to be 'in search of more remunerative employment' (1871)[47] this was probably nothing less than the truth.

The 'remunerative employment', however, must preferably be certainly known, visible or reported to be reliable, in which case its attractive force will be at a maximum. It is for this reason that the late T. H. Bainbridge was almost certainly correct in suggesting that there was considerable movement of local people, and local labour, into the northern part of the West Cumberland coalfield in 1871–81. Bainbridge also pointed out that the total migration from Cumberland as a whole in that period was markedly less than the migration into the western districts, which was large enough to account both for movement from other counties, and for a considerable influx from 'the rural central and eastern parts of Cumberland'.[48] Those industrial communities, like Cleator Moor, which attracted substantial non-Cumbrian groups, are in any case well known,[49] and it was colliery settlements like Aspatria, Brayton, Flimby, Brigham and Moresby which seem to have brought in local labour, and several of these were gaining in population by virtue of their coalmines in 1861–71.[50] The immigrant ironmasters, like those from Scotland, tended to bring their own skilled labour with them, and the case of Cammells was described in Chapter 2.[51] Indeed, the point of much localised Cumbrian population movement lies in the ease with which it was possible for a country worker to adapt himself to certain mining tasks, whether underground or on the surface; but this is not to suggest that he would readily work in a locality which was heavily settled by immigrant Irish or Cornishmen, or that he would not prefer to leave the harsher ironworks labour, like pig-lifting, to Irishmen. In any case, as we shall see, the in-migration of such groups was at times intense and heavy, and the native Cumbrian might, by further stages, leave his region.

Having accepted, with these reservations, that localised population movement was a marked feature of Cumbrian life in the mid-Victorian decades, we shall note that it was in general characterised by short-period surges, like those engendered by railway construction, and that such surges cannot normally be identified by that somewhat clumsy instrument, the decennial census. The detailed observations of the newspaper press in West Cumberland, and incidental data from the Annual Reports of the Registrar-General, together indicate that there was such a surge into the coastal districts in the early 1870s, rather than in that decade as a whole, and that this movement coincided with a rapid rise in industrial money wages and considerable discontent on the part of rural labourers who followed local economic developments in the press. Nor was the situation as simple as is suggested here, for the farm labourers' discontent was partially fomented by a more general movement, the formation of the National Union of Agricultural Labourers under the leadership of Joseph Arch, but also by growing tensions between local farmers and their labourers antedating the formation of the National Union (which took place in March 1872). Farmers and landowners resented the growing independence of the labourer, assisted by out-migration and the local labour shortages which have been described. 'The men are becoming our masters', claimed the land steward of one of the principal proprietors in Westmorland (1868), 'and if the present deficiency of labour should increase we shall speedily change positions in this county'.[52] However, discontent was certainly not confined to one side, and the West Cumberland Farmers' Club reacted to a worsening labour shortage of the early 1870s by challenging the timing, if not the existence, of the traditional Whitsuntide hiring fairs as inconvenient for haymaking.[53] This sign of unrest coincided almost exactly with the beginning of Joseph Arch's effective campaign in Warwickshire in early February;[54] nor is this a *non sequitur*, for, as Mr Dunbabin has shown, the farm labourers' agitation was not confined (as is so often assumed) to the Midlands in its early stages, but spread rapidly northwards,[55] and the critical atmosphere between masters and men was general in England. The point here must be that there was no one formula for the creation of tension, region by region, and Cumberland grievances assumed their own form even when local agitations coincided with those taking place elsewhere. In the West Cumberland case, one of the stimuli came from the example of striking industrial workers, just as Northumbrian farm labourers almost simultaneously wished to follow the example of striking miners.[56] Cumbria, the North-East and southern Scotland did, moreover, share one common characteristic in that their rural agitations tended to be concerned with working hours and conditions rather than wages as such.[57]

The *Whitehaven News* and other newspapers were filled with reports of trade union agitation along the coast in the early spring, and the *News* rapidly drew attention to the activities of the Warwickshire labourers, evidently seeing Arch and his union as *à propos*. The local farmworkers already had one manifest grievance (which was distinguished from those of other districts); farmers had tried to impose upon farm servants a system of character references, which was held to cut into the trusting relationship between the farmer and his labourer,[58] and which, to the student of agrarian history, makes something of a nonsense of William Dickinson's sentimentalised view of that relationship. (In *Cumbriana* (1877) he claimed that 'o' fare't alike . . . In eatin' and drinkin' or wark', a statement which was probably true enough for the smaller hill farms.) Significantly, however, the issue of working hours rapidly became dominant, and a farm servant from Egremont wrote a published letter in the March to say that many of the industrial tradesmen had 'been out on strike for shorter hours . . . I don't see that there is anything to hinder us from doing the same'.[59] A farmworker from St Bees argued that 'from seven to five is quite long enough in the fields',[60] whilst another, 'a constant reader of your paper', argued for 'a couple of hours shorter time, say from six to six, instead of from five to seven, and sometimes eight'.[61] It was a characteristic of farm service that the 'indoor' labourer was at the disposal of the farmer during his waking hours, or nearly so.

Farmers, for their part, argued that they were feeling the effects of the rising cost of food, and a farm servant's wages amounted, as one of the former claimed, 'to only half of what he costs his master'.[62] This, published in the newspaper press, raised the tension, and a labourer replied:[63] 'I think a shilling a day will pay for all; for barley bread, when it gets a fortnight old, is more like pig-meat than for Christians . . . We would starve to death if we were not made of good stuff.'

Other servants' arguments were less crudely expressed than this, and were the work of men of some self-education. One put a case for leisure as a good in itself, but also as conducive to health:[64]

> There are very few servants but who would much prefer a day of rest sometimes, with the forfeiture of their wages, to being forced to stand out at some dirty work on a thorough wet day, to the ruin of both their clothes and health . . . There are places where a servant could not desire any better treatment than he receives, but these places are generally (with) the poorest and the smallest of our farmers. The places where we receive the worst treatment are the largest and most wealthy, and yet in this class there are some exceptions to the rule.

The region produced no more than a demonstration or a public meeting or two, like that held at the Wheatsheaf Inn, Gosforth, on 14 May 1872, which urged that farmers should treat their servants kindly, that six to six were reasonable working hours, and that wages should move with the state of the labour market. Labourers, thought the meeting, should be allowed away from work for special or family reasons.[65] The very moderation of this meeting is far more eloquent than the more sophisticated and perhaps inspired letters that appeared in the press, and one can conclude either that the claims of ill-treatment were not generally true, or that – in terms of the issues which were here quite calmly discussed – a great deal was expected of the farm servant, and that discontent was certainly, for the time being, as large a factor in his life as the lure of the higher wages in the mines and ironworks. One influence, of course, fed on the other.

How many labourers migrated towards the new world of coastal industry? There is no doubt that some were so tempted, to become victims of the later, post-1874 recession, and an East Cumberland correspondent of the *Agricultural Gazette* remarked in 1879 that the then overcrowded hiring fairs were in that state because 'many agricultural labourers who were tempted away to the coal and iron districts when work was plentiful there . . . have now returned to seek employment in agriculture but have found their places filled up by others'.[66] In other words, the amount of actual movement within registration districts, and within the region, was probably markedly greater than any calculations for net intercensal out-migration would indicate, although it is interesting that the Penrith registration district, situated between the coalmines of the east and west coastal areas, showed the highest net loss in 1871–80 (see Table 4.1).

77

Table 4.1 Effects of migration in Cumberland and Westmorland

Registration District	Natural gain	Intercensal loss/gain	Net gain or loss by migration (numbers)	Net gain or loss by migration (%)
Cumberland				
Alston				
1861–70	741	−724	−1465	−22·8
1871–80	528	−258	−786	−9·3
Penrith				
1861–70	2254	+1410	−1244	−5·6
1871–80	2693	−487	−3180	−13·4
Wigton				
1861–70	2347	−607	−2954	−12·6
1871–80	2475	+775	−1700	−7·5
Carlisle*				
1861–70	4060	+1838	−2222	−5·0
1871–80	4863	+6095	−1232	+2·7
Cockermouth*				
1861–70	6491	+5265	−1226	−2·9
1871–80	8416	+10232	+1816	+3·9
Whitehaven*				
1861–70	6009	+7602	+1593	+3·9
1871–80	9000	+11740	+2740	+5·7
Bootle				
1861–70	985	+2645	+1660	+28·2
1871–80	2068	+3700	+1642	+19·1
Westmorland				
East Ward				
1861–70	1542	+1527	−15	−1·0
1871–80	1791	−2423	−4214	−24·9
West Ward				
1861–70	986	+174	−812	−10·0
1871–80	1144	−21	−1165	−14·1
Kendal Ward				
1861–70	5177	+2478	−2799	−7·5
1871–80	5965	+1633	−4332	−10·4

Notes:
Asterisks indicate urban registration districts.
There were high migration rates from Kendal Town

Source: Annual Reports of the Registrar-General, Census Reports.

There can be little doubt that as extensive cereal production became uneconomic (see Chapter 3, pp. 57–8), farmers were finding less employment for labourers, although it may be that the former sometimes did this as a deliberate reprisal, and in 1872, some arable farmers in Hexham were signifying their intention of putting down their land to grass in order to cut down labour.[67] Something of a menacingly combative spirit emerged on the side of Penrith landowners and employers (1872) who urged the tightening up of contractual arrangements in the employment of footloose labourers,[68] and one such employer appealed to members of the bench: 'he hoped, when cases came before them of a servant leaving in the busy season of the year, because they could make a little more somewhere else, they would know how to do their duty'.[69] The farmer, indeed, had his problems, and, as a Furness correspondent of *The Agricultural Gazette* (1879) observed, 'the prosperity of the iron trade and agriculture are closely allied here, as good wages mean good prices for farm produce'.[70] But the farmer without a family of grown sons and daughters on the farm could not always organise the productive work that would enable him to take advantage of growing demand, and, as we have seen, young members of farm families, especially in the hill areas, were likely to decamp as a matter of course. Nor were their reasons for departure always simply concerned with monetary gain *per se*; small landowners bred in their children a sense of social status and aspiration which can be traced in regional literary references and family records,[71] and Francis Grainger, the Solway-side political leader, yeoman and local historian, asserted to the Royal Commission on Agriculture in 1895 that the tendency of yeomen's children to seek genteel or quasi-genteel occupations had been growing for some forty years:

> Now (they) prefer to go out as clerks, shopmen, governesses or nurses ... A man possessing say £5000 in real property feels bound to give his family a good middle class education. Naturally the family, especially the females, object to menial and manual work. In consequence the yeomen lets his farm to a working tenant, whose family are accustomed to take their part in farm work, and the yeoman's family drift into town situations.[72]

What of the small farmers, who were less well off than the type of man described by Grainger? As was argued in the last chapter, they managed to adapt themselves to the conditions of the later Victorian depression years through a dogged willingness to accept low incomes, and through the use of family labour. When such farmers were obliged to employ a labourer, they would expect value for money, and so the working conditions of the labourer were not likely to improve with great rapidity – the more so because the older farmers remembered the early Victorian years, when labourers and others had 'three meals a day ... and did not think of five meals, and they ate porridge and did not think of tea or coffee'. This witness,[73] Mr Tom Newby of Muncaster Head, who recalled the Crimean War period, also held the view that 'It would not be more difficult to make both ends meet now if everyone did not live better' – a revealing remark which points to some of the economico-social contradictions of the age, for a small farmer or labourer who held his earnings or income at the same level also benefited from a rise in purchasing power. But such gains were not always deeply felt by those who lived to reap their benefits, the more so when a farming family deliberately kept its outgoings low, often by exploiting its younger but able-bodied members. An especially vivid assertion came from a Kirkbride farmer, who claimed in 1895 that he worked a 16-hour day:[74]

We all work far harder than labourers, and I am sure that I do not feed or dress as well as a labourer. The small farmers have meat twice a week and some three times. Labourers have it two or three times a day . . . All round here the farmers' sons and daughters work for nothing. I do not know one case where a farmer pays his sons and daughters wages. They give their sons a shilling or two sometimes to buy tobacco. A girl is far better off in service than staying at home.

Nor was this man alone in his views. An Irton farmer, also giving evidence to the Royal Commission, claimed 'that the only class of men who are doing well are those whose families work', and two Keswick farmers agreed that 'The sons and daughters are working for nothing.'[75]

The idea of migration, then, could at varying times be attractive to farmers and their families as well as to labourers, and in 1886 a landowner in the Penrith district was encouraging local farmers to move to Warwickshire,[76] although the census birthplace data cannot be said to suggest that many of them did so. However, although the population of 'farmers and graziers' in the region remained at roughly the same level between 1851 and 1911, it is highly likely that this apparently stable group, as given census by census, in fact concealed some turnover of marginal farmers,[77] especially in periods of relative hardship. But it was in the farm labouring group that the stark loss of people was most evident during the same period, and, allowing for both 'indoor' and 'outdoor' labourers, and for the vagaries of census classification, the numbers of the former fell from over 21 000 in 1851 to some 8 500 in 1911. It is little wonder that a burden was thrust upon the sons and daughters of farmers, and that the families concerned felt some strains in their closer relationships. One type of long-experienced 'strain' has been observed, in comparatively recent years, as being operative within some farm families in a Cumbrian village,[78] and this has to do with the problems for individuals which were created by farm succession or the inheritance of land or tenancies; an eldest son might have to wait for years to take over a farm from his father, and so be obliged to delay marriage. As we have already noted, marriage rates for the main Lake Counties were strikingly low, and this cardinal point calls for illustration.

The proportions of unmarried persons in both Cumberland and Westmorland were exceptionally high, in national terms, in 1851, 1881, and 1891, to take only sample years. In the earliest year, the numbers of bachelors in both Cumberland and Westmorland (given as a proportion of all males of more than 20 years of age), exceeded 35 per 100, whereas the national average was 31. Similarly, and unsurprisingly, the same two counties had numbers of spinsters well in excess of what was common in England, with 32 per 100 in Cumberland and 33 in Westmorland, as against a national average of 28.[79] The Census of 1881, using a different base calculation, demonstrates that the two counties had the highest proportions in England of unmarried persons per 100 000 of each sex.[80] The Census of 1891 is more illuminating in that it gives particulars of

Table 4.2 Illegitimacy, spinsters and excess males in Cumberland and Westmorland

Registration District	Illegitimate births per 1000 live births	1871 Unmarried women 15–35 as % of all females	1871 Excess of unmarried males over unmarried females (15–35)
Cumberland			
Alston			
1855–60	124		
1861–70	142		
1871–80	118	32·1	114
Penrith			
1855–60	114		
1861–70	132		
1871–80	108	31·9	429
Wigton			
1855–60	118		
1861–70	138		
1871–80	108	34·1	23
Carlisle*			
1855–60	98		
1861–70	98		
1871–80	84	33·3	596
Cockermouth*			
1855–60	114		
1861–70	103		
1871–80	82	29·1	552
Whitehaven*			
1855–60	90		
1861–70	83		
1871–80	58	28·3	1318
Bootle (semi-industrial)			
1855–60	106		
1861–70	108		
1871–80	50	29·2	273
Westmorland			
East Ward			
1855–60	113		
1861–70	108		
1871–80	90	29·3	848
West Ward			
1855–60	113		
1861–70	124		
1871–80	98	30·7	125
Kendal Ward			
1855–60	80		
1861–70	92		
1871–80	67	33·4	39

Notes:
Asterisks indicate urban registration districts.
There was a low bastardy rate in Kendal Town.
In country districts of Northumberland, where illegitimacy was less common, there was an excess of unmarried females aged 15–35 (1871) in Berwick, Alnwick, Glendale and Rothbury registration districts. Farm service was a much less common arrangement there.

81

married, unmarried and widowed persons by registration districts, and there it is made clear that unmarried persons in their early twenties were encountered in unusually high proportions (in both regional and national terms) in country districts like Alston, Penrith, Brampton, Longtown and the West Ward of Westmorland. Hill-farmers or other farmers with working families were likely to be encountered in all of these areas. Meanwhile, the distributions of the numbers of the married inhabitants by age-groups leaves little doubt that ages at marriage in these localities tended to be high.[81] A scrutiny of Table 4.2 will also show that registration districts of this type, a decade or two earlier, displayed remarkably high bastardy rates; it should be added that Longtown and Brampton, not there given, had exceptionally high rates of illegitimacy.[82] During the middle decades of the century, Cumberland and Westmorland together produced bastardy rates some 80 per cent above those obtaining for England as a whole, but it was these remoter county districts which contributed the most arresting statistics during the course of what is plainly a most complex story, which cannot be dealt with adequately in these pages. The subject was not debated readily in the Lake Counties themselves, and when moralising attacks were made, they were (when they were specifically aimed at all) directed at a dual objective: the institution of farm service, and the farm servant himself.[83] The farmer's sons and daughters were rarely or never mentioned, but it is most unlikely that they were totally unconnected with the activities which led to the creation of these statistics. In other words, both the farmer's progeny and the diminishing band of labourers were oppressed by institutional arrangements which delayed marriage and kept them in the countryside with little money and little prospect of a separate residence. Even an elder son, as has been noted,[84] might seem to produce an extra-marital pregnancy in his desperate need for married status.

Yet this is a field of research fraught with difficulties. Farm servants were being steadily reduced in numbers in Cumbria from 1851, but regional bastardy rates did not seriously begin to fall until some twenty years later, when the swing from arable cultivation (and hence to the self-sufficient family farm) was becoming effective. Courtship customs and traditions must enter into the story,[85] and nearness to south-western Scotland, where rural illegitimacy was even higher, suggests a complex of roughly comparable influences, in which a high incidence of farm service stands out as a major common element.[86] Victorian moralists on the Cumbrian side of the border blamed the 'immodest' arrangements in farmhouses which threw men and women servants together, whilst Scottish critics stressed the generally permissive attitude to pre-marital conception.[87] Cumbria, meanwhile, presents a striking case, seen from any point of view, whereby high literacy and high illegitimacy rates appear as sharp if unconnected regional peculiarities, and it can be argued that both were related, however indirectly, to mass migration from the countryside, the first because they provided a basis for personal ambition and the gaining of information, and the second because they represented a symptom of strain and frustration within individual lives and within families. Literate men, certainly, must in many cases have had wider social horizons, and have exhibited a desire to travel farther, but this is a matter calling for serious exploration in time to come.[88]

Did the towns ease those frustrations which might have been caused by delayed marriage? Cumbrian industrial districts contained more young married persons during the middle and later Victorian years now under review, as is abundantly clear from the available statistics, especially those relating to the Whitehaven and Cockermouth registration districts,[89] which included towns like Cleator Moor and Workington. But not only must this topic await detailed research into a significant sample of known marriage histories; it must also take into account the large element of Catholicism in places like Cleator Moor, and the high incidence of young unmarried males in rapidly growing centres like Barrow-in-Furness.[90] For the rest, it is clear that marriage rates were comparatively far higher in the non-local industrial districts to which many Cumbrians migrated,[91] and that a medical officer for the Whitehaven rural sanitary district (which was also largely industrial) saw the great local migration surge of 1871–4 as the creator of several evils, among which imprudent marriage occupied a prominent place:[92] 'the prosperity, in 1871–4, from the coal and iron industries, was the cause of an excess of early marriages and of an increased mortality of infants'. The same commentator referred to 'deplorable overcrowding – houses being hastily run up without proper sanitary arrangements',[93] and, since temporary overcrowding of a painful kind was also encountered in the Barrow district,[94] it is clear that the migrant in search of both marriage and a suitable residence might in the short term be disappointed. Perhaps fortunately, surges of local country–town migration were replaced by periods of stagnation or out-migration from the region, and, as we shall see, the new industrial towns eventually produced more accommodation, judged in terms of low ratios of individuals per room, than the older towns and country districts. Meanwhile, there were many underlying influences making for dissatisfaction in districts confined to heavy or extractive industries; for example, a family in a textile area, which might have several male and female members working, and which might therefore endure overcrowding where family earnings were high, might in Cumbrian conditions find its counterpart only in a town like Carlisle or Kendal. In the rest of industrial Cumbria, wives and daughters clearly had difficulty in finding paid work, and, indeed, Barrow's leading town organiser, Sir James Ramsden, evidently sought to provide such employment by the promotion of a Jute Works from c. 1870.[95] While Carlisle had nearly half of its womenfolk over 20 years old in gainful occupations in 1871 (those in textiles actually exceeding women in domestic service by a few dozens), Whitehaven had only one-third so employed, a large proportion of the latter being milliners or domestic servants.[96] The industries of the coastal districts were overwhelmingly male-oriented; there was, for example, no tradition of woman labour in iron-ore mining as there had been in the coal industry. The womenfolk had, in the majority of cases, to stay at home in unsatisfactory conditions, at a time when clean water supplies and adequate sanitation were only beginning to be provided. Otherwise, the problem of finding mothers, kin or friends to look after children probably did not arise in a significant number of instances.[97]

We now come to the question of the impact of the often crucial act of removal to an industrial environment — at work and in the home — on the persons who migrated within the region itself. This is an important topic, if only for the reason that understanding of the motivations behind further migration, often out of the region altogether, may thereby be vouchsafed. It is neither invariably relevant nor especially helpful to use a blanket phrase like 'the urban experience', if only for the reason that much of West Cumberland industry was still situated in a semi-rural *milieu* during the period discussed, and in 1871, only Carlisle was of any real magnitude or extent as a town. Workington, as was noted in Chapter 2 (see p. 53) consisted of a series of iron works settlements loosely related to the old town and port, whereas Maryport and Whitehaven were made up of small areas of tightly packed grid-iron housing, with scattered suburbs and colonies in their environs. Barrow in the 1870s had a high population density in an area of less than a square mile, but was not an undifferentiated mass of people. Certainly, the effect of removal into one of these areas of high density, combined with that of introduction into an industrial occupation carried on in dark, strange, fiery or simply alien places, full of groups of persons using strange speech and outlandish terms, must at first have been sharp and salutary, and have brought with it a form of culture shock. Plainly, too, the shock was likely to be far less in the case of an experienced metalliferous miner from the dales, and was diminished still more if neighbours and their families accompanied him. The dominant factor in the creation of a sense of strangeness and insecurity, on the other hand, would lie in the unfamiliarity and the unpredictability of behaviour of new workmates and neighbours who were from very different backgrounds, and this sense of insecurity could well have obtained when former country acquaintances and relatives were only a few miles away. Victorian working hours and conditions, after all, tended to tie a man to his workplace and locality for most of his working life in any particular place and occupation.

It will be appropriate, at this point, to introduce discussion of a highly relevant topic, that of migration *into* the region, which was mainly industrially stimulated, and which reached its peak in the 1870s and 1880s (see Table 4.3). It was occupationally related, for the most part, and was quite strikingly concentrated in small localities, mostly industrial settlements. Cleator Moor provides the most memorable example, and was, in the light of a sample from the census enumerators' book,[98] occupied by an Irish contingent so large that they accounted for nearly 60 per cent of the population there by 1861. Whilst there

Table 4.3   Cumberland in-migrants from other counties

	1851	1861	1871	1881	1891	1901	1911
Population of Cumberland	195 492	205 276	220 253	250 647	266 549	266 933	265 746
Birthplaces of in-migrants (as % of total population)							
Ireland	5·05	5·13	5·39	5·62	3·64	2·38	1·66
Scotland	3·81	4·40	4·70	4·87	4·44	4·02	3·74
Lancs. (incl Furness)	1·99	2·38	2·56	2·78	3·07	3·03	1·63
Westmorland	2·00	1·91	1·23	1·77	1·85	1·85	1·79
Northumberland	1·24	1·28	1·29	1·36	1·25	1·25	0·88
Yorkshire	0·62	0·70	0·78	1·01	1·31	1·32	0·72
Durham	0·46	0·54	0·68	0·90	0·93	0·99	0·84
Cornwall	0·04	0·06	0·52	0·78	0·59	0·43	0·28
Wales & Monmouth	0·12	0·20	0·42	0·49	0·45	0·36	0·31
Derbys., Notts., Cheshire, Staffs., Warwicks. (combined)	0·34	0·36	0·68	0·85	1·31	1·21	0·70
All other English and Welsh counties	1·40	2·09	1·38	2·89	3·15	3·30	5·06
Total percentage of Cumberland population	17·07	18·75	20·63	23·62	21·99	20·16	19·01

were few other cases of such intensive concentration, this one was significant in a number of ways; it was built around a major occupation, ore mining, and it had repercussions of a political as well as a religious nature. Yet the Irish, like Scottish-born people, were not new to Cumberland. They had provided a substantial part of the mining labour force in Whitehaven long before 1830, and had entered the region in some numbers in the early nineteenth century to assist in harvesting, increasingly staying in the area permanently to work in mines and docks.[99] There were 4175 of them in the Whitehaven registration district by 1851,[100] but of these, only a few scores were in Cleator Moor,[101] which, indeed, had no more than 161 houses. Both Cockermouth and Carlisle districts had attracted appreciable numbers of Irish-born, 1897 in the former, and the evidence in both cases points strongly to the effect of railway construction. The next largest immigrant group in Cumberland consisted of Scottish-born persons, with 3241 in Carlisle alone, or nearly 44 per cent of all such persons in the county, and the concentration in the border city can hardly be seen as surprising. In this census year, 1851, some 17 per cent of the population of Cumberland consisted of persons born in other counties, the main counties of origin, in order of the size of settler groups, being Ireland, Scotland, Westmorland, Lancashire (including, of course, Furness) and Northumberland.[102] In this period, Furness was the only other economically developing area in the region, and it had attracted comparatively few in-migrants even by 1861, mostly from neighbouring areas.[103]

The implied reasons for the in-migration are, in the most striking cases, not difficult to trace. As we have seen, the mining of coal and iron led to Irish settlement, and the rapid development of the Hodbarrow haematite iron mine in south-west Cumberland eventually attracted 'experienced and well-tried miners . . . from Cornwall, Scotland, Ireland and other mining (*sic*) localities'.[104] Moor Row, near Cleator Moor, acquired a significant concentration of Cornishmen,[105] whilst the development of Cumberland iron-smelting in the 1870s attracted Scottish labour as well as Scottish capital (see pp. 44, 85). Barrow became the most polyglot of all the Cumbrian towns, first of all attracting ironworkers from Staffordshire,[106] the largest single in-migrant group there in 1861 and 1871, followed in order of magnitude by settler contingents from Westmorland, Ireland, Cumberland, Yorkshire, Worcestershire and Scotland.[107] Just over 40 per cent of the settlers (1871) were from counties other than Lancashire, and many of the Lancastrians had travelled in from the nearby countryside. This pattern of inward movement was not typical of Cumberland, although the nearby Furness iron-ore field, in attracting Cornishmen – some of whom settled in a small but solid colony at Roose, near Barrow[108] – displayed one of the characteristics of Cumberland iron mining.

The changing pattern of migrant settlement in Cumberland is fascinatingly displayed in successive census enumerations between 1851 and 1911, and is set out in percentage terms in Table 4.3. It should be noted, first of all, that Cumberland had, *pro rata* of relative populations, more Irish within its boundaries than any county except Lancashire, and that the Irish group remained a very strong one until the Census of 1891, from which point it declined in size steadily. Meanwhile, the proportion of locally-born people in Cumberland increased in relative terms, and we must assume that more native Cumbrians had become established in local industry at the side of the groups of in-migrants. The Scottish contingent was widely diffused about the county, and was, perhaps significantly, little affected, until 1901–11, by the contraction of the coastal iron industry; and it still remained the leading settler group even when several Scots-inspired iron firms closed down in that intercensal period (see Chapter 2, p. 51). The coal industry of the east and west coasts seems to have engendered some exchanges of people between Cumbria and the north-eastern counties, but the most striking movement of all (to take place within a relatively short period) was that from Yorkshire and Derbyshire in 1881–91, involving a total of some 1863 persons. This was brought about by the virtual uprooting of the town of Dronfield, on the border of these counties, by the removal of the firm of Cammells from Dronfield to Workington.[109]

In this instance, Cammells employees had their minds virtually made up for them, and an entire industrial community moved *en bloc*, adding yet another element to the already existing diversity of West Cumberland life. More generally, however, migrants from a distance, sharing the same outlook, occupations, experiences and (perhaps) religious life, seem to have chosen to live as well as to work together – although it is never clear how far decisions were imposed upon such migrants by inflexible circumstances, like the availability of given housing, or whether they made such decisions in the light of news passed on to them by friends, and by free choice subsequently. What *is* clear is that long-range migrants formed or settled in colonies, or tended to do so, and that there was steady short-range movement, much of it from the Cumberland dales, but comprehending a steady trickle from Westmorland. This in itself suggests the geographical limit of regional migration towards the coast. The area of immediate attraction, which must have affected metalliferous miners and experienced quarrymen more than others, had a radius of perhaps 30 miles. There is no sign that the attractive forces altered during 50 or so years, and one must also remember that there was a powerful countervailing force, which drew Westmerians southwards or towards Furness. As we have seen, the great majority of the Westmorland-born out-migrants travelled considerable distances. But these adventurous folk were not by any means alone, and it is a remarkable feature of Cumberland in-migration that as the main 'long-range' groups became reduced in size between 1891 and 1911, so the numbers of in-migrants from 27 English counties and 13 Welsh ones began, *in toto*, steadily to swell. This inward movement of people from diffused areas represented something new in kind, and was, as a reasonable hypothesis indicates, the result of the professionalisation of increasing numbers of occupations, the growth of services requiring skilled knowledge, and the general development of specialised labour markets, assisted, beyond question, by such agencies as trade union reports and the still growing habit of railway travel. The retirement of moneyed people into areas of natural beauty must, even at this stage, have played some part, as did tourism and the transport industries.

It is certain that the erosion of the main long-range in-migrant groups did not take place without much social disruption, and without a mass of painful decisions involving whole families. The insufficiently varied economy of West Cumberland was, as we have seen, inherently unstable; meanwhile, its ethnically grouped and sometimed incompatible occupational, social and religious elements, which produced for some settlers an uncongenial or unfriendly environment, caused social as well as economic instability to be added to its disadvantages. Only in this way can we begin to explain the attractiveness of emigration to the New World or to the British colonies. Such emigration is taken for granted as a feature of Victorian life and history, but it was clearly born of an unhappy mixture of hope and disappointment, and, locally, and in some instances, of an ultimate and determined rejection of the industrial world which was springing up on these coasts. An especially striking and well documented case may help to make the point clear. In 1872–3, a group based on Barrow and Furness, and consisting mainly of artisans, decided to establish a colony in Minnesota, at the height of boom conditions there.[110] Recent research[111] has shown that these would-be Furness emigrants were in fact atypical, and were strongly motivated

87

by temperance ideals as well as by the idea of rugged self-reliance in the prairies. Yet their courageous expedition, which took place aided by the North Pacific Railroad and led to the building of a permanent colony, without doubt represented a rejection of an environment which was, in the emigrants' eyes, unstable, brawling and drunken.[112] Certainly such an atmosphere reigned in Whitehaven at the height of the population surge of 1871–4, and gave occasion for condemnatory police reports,[113] dwelling mainly on a spectacular increase in drunkenness. Meanwhile, emigration was not always stimulated by depression or unemployment alone, although, at this stage, it was more often discussed in the newspapers during depression periods. Hence, it was reported in early 1879 that 'there is not so much distress in Barrow as is reported from other towns',[114] yet, only a few months later, emigration from Furness was continuing 'on a considerable scale'.[115] It has to be borne in mind that emigration was organised and institutionalised during this age, and was also frequently advocated by trade unionists; the far-reaching decision to go overseas, meanwhile, was often taken as the result of cumulative experience, and was by no means simply a reaction to the downswing of the trade cycle. Iron-miners, in particular, were ready candidates for the emigrant vessels,[116] and their decisions were not merely reactions to the urban environment *per se*, although, as output from some mines tended to flag towards the turn of the century, there developed a strong tendency on the part of the haematite-miners to go to South Africa, where their special training could be applied in the gold mines.[117] Numbers of such Cumberland miners were setting off for this colony in 1889, when production at the local haematite mines was by no means flagging.[118] It should be added that tempting prospectuses, provided by United States and other agencies, as well as by emigrant organisations in this country, sometimes acted as effective bait. The likelihood remains that a receptive man was almost invariably a discontented man, or even a desperate one.

Depressions, and their effects, are certainly not to be discounted. In 1879, there was rapid provision of soup kitchens in both Whitehaven and Workington,[119] public services in Whitehaven in 1885 estimated that there were 'about 2500 mouths to feed at the present time',[120] this out of a population of some 19 000. Nor was depression felt only in the heavy-industrial coastal towns, and the same year brought 'unusual distress in our midst' in the town of Kendal, with 'dirty and ragged boys' importuning passers-by.[121] Several observations are here germane. Firstly, the industrial towns brought unemployment of the able-bodied of a kind rarely or never before encountered in nineteenth-century Cumbria.[122] Secondly, this unemployment was rapidly eased by the facility with which industrial workers migrated, and the removal of the burden in other directions, or its reduction, was clearly assisted by the rootlessness of many of the settlers; single men in lodgings, tramping artisans, and young couples not incommoded by children.

So far, the picture has been one of movement, impermanence. But, as we have

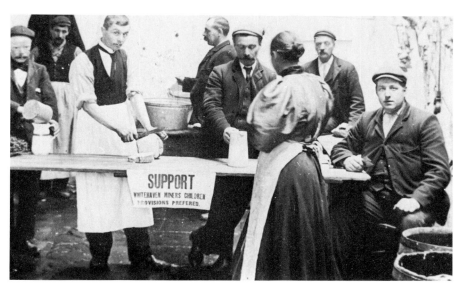

9 Distress in Whitehaven. A soup kitchen during a nineteenth-century strike.

10 The footwear store of W. Sanderson in Main St, Aspatria *c.* 1900. The immigrant but locally rural family name is significant.

seen, many Cumbrians stayed within their native counties as the latter became more industrialised and diversified in economic activity, and it is here necessary to make a distinction between those locally born persons who were in a position to take advantage of opportunities in industry and commerce in a nearby town, and those whose fate it was to travel far in order to seek a living by wage-labour. The wealth of West Cumberland, as displayed in terms of Schedule D tax returns (see p. 20 above), was not restricted to a few fortuitously successful capitalists by the 1870s or 1880s, but was diffused throughout several strata of society, all possessing considerably more potential for permanent residence than the artisan or labouring groups. Moreover, it is abundantly clear, from an analysis of common regional surnames in relation to occupations (or, where it has been convenient or possible, from samples of data in census schedules), that native Cumbrians took full advantage of opportunities on their doorsteps. If we look through the lists of bakers, grocers and confectioners, or warehouse clerks or solicitors' clerks, or joiners, masons and builders, or blacksmiths and braziers, or policemen or mining engineers, or local shipowners, profoundly characteristic Cumbrian surnames, many of them from the border countryside, stare out of the pages. In Maryport, Dixons, Messengers and Nicholsons were well established in trade;[123] in Cockermouth, Bells, Bowmans and Huddarts;[124] in Workington, Armstrongs, Coulthards and Littles;[125] and in Whitehaven, Braggs, Burnyeats, more Coulthards, Fishers, Kitchins and Mossops.[126] Every one of these names goes far back into Cumbrian history, and nearly every one can be found in abundance in the present-day regional telephone directory. A remarkable directory of Barrow-in-Furness for 1875, which gives the address, name and occupation of every householder irrespective of occupation,[127] affords an overview of the occupations and distribution of the people there which makes recourse to the census books virtually unnecessary for the purposes of this survey. There it is made clear that the holders of clearly marked Furness surnames, like Ormandy, Postlethwaite, Casson and Tyson, were seemingly struggling for existence in a sea of Scottish, Manx, Irish and south-Lancashire names, and that the in-migrants from the neighbouring countryside reflected roughly in their jobs the occupational structure of the town as shown in the 1871 census, with one very vital qualification; more of the native Cumbrians were shopkeepers, skilled workers (e.g. in the building trades) or holders of clerical posts. From this we must conclude, however tentatively, that many native Cumbrians or Furnessians did in fact reach journey's end more or less satisfactorily without going to London or to Liverpool. In so doing they often translated the terms of their lives in remarkable fashion, even if they did not emulate the career of William Gradwell, Barrow's leading builder, whose family origins were in the Furness village of Lowick.[128] A little yeoman or landed capital could help signally in setting up a business in a time of opportunity, and we must not forget that kin-inspired aid from the countryside must have saved many a small capitalist when times were hard.

It is, then, almost platitudinous in our present terms, and within the Cumbrian setting, to conceive part of our migratory story in terms of some movement from country to local town.[129] A logical question then follows: did the move, in a significant number of cases, mean a genuine improvement in living conditions? Even though the question itself must provoke so many qualifications as to seem meaningless, a number of major environmental and other changes which have a profound bearing on the subject at issue remain to be briefly discussed. These include, clearly, the matter of sanitary conditions in town and country, and the risks to health encountered in one situation as compared with another. But risks to health are not conditioned or determined merely by the built environment, occupations and their effects must ideally be taken into account; and this is a subject on which local evidence is often regrettably lacking. We must also touch upon the consequences of rapid urban growth, and, associated with them, inter-group tension between employers and employees, or between in-migrant settlers and natives. These tensions in turn affected the quality of life of the 'masses', and, somewhat less directly, those of the middling strata in the urban social structure, whose prosperity and well-being were influenced in some measure by the visible evidence of social ills and strains around them. Generally there was no very easy retreat into a comfortably removed suburbia in the case of most Cumbrian urban districts, although the richer families had their rural residences, and Carlisle's Stanwix was exceptional in this respect, as was Whitehaven's Hensingham. Finally, the matter of a more varied religious and recreational life, which was most emphatically a feature of the urbanising districts, is discussed in later chapters.[130]

The tradesman or middle-class town settler did not necessarily move directly from the countryside; the market towns provided training grounds in commerce for such men, and further research could well show their staging-post function to have been a considerable one. Existing businesses would, in any case, seek to expand into developing localities. In these instances, the migrating individual, whether tradesman or clerk, would have found little difference in sanitary conditions during the middle years of the century as between the old market centres and the newly industrialising ones. This absence of contrast was revealed during a typically abrasive campaign conducted by (Sir) Robert Rawlinson of the General Board of Health and by his lieutenant G. T. Clark, mainly in the spring and autumn of 1849. Although Whitehaven was Rawlinson's first object of attack in the January of that year, and although this sanitarian said of the inhabitants of the poorer properties there that 'the pen of novelist never yet depicted such depths of utter wretchedness',[131] his colleague Clark was not long in directing a series of thunderously schoolmasterly admonitions at the complacency of Kendal's leaders: 'long-continued neglect of attention to public health or convenience . . . ill-paved, close and crowded alleys, its utter deficiency

91

of all proper drainage ... filth, drunkenness, pauperism, sickness, and an excessive rate of mortality'.[132] As Kendal reeled before this verbal whipping, Rawlinson turned his eye upon Carlisle (7 November, 1849, the date of his public enquiry there), and Penrith (14 November).[133] In Carlisle, Rawlinson chose to act diplomatically and even persuasively: 'with proper sewers and drains, systematic regulating and cleansing, the wise, benevolent and philanthropic citizens will see the physical condition of the working man improved'.[134] In Penrith, he found an estimated crude death rate of 26 in the thousand, some sympathy, some skulduggery, and a wholesomely widespread fear of the cholera which had struck at Maryport, Workington and Carlisle in the same year. For all that he had had to say (almost certainly correctly) about filthy, overcrowded Whitehaven, Penrith's estimated death rate was only two or three units – or human beings – in the thousand lower, even though it displayed a modicum of civic enterprise and had gasworks for public lamps in 1830, and a water supply of sorts in 1847. In fact, all those main Cumbrian towns with a measure of antiquity as market centres – Carlisle, Kendal, Ulverston and Keswick – suffered from intense overcrowding in their yards and alleyways, and this unhappy development was largely a product of the inflexibility of pre-existing building forms and the multiplication of trades and crafts within such areas. Further revelations by Rawlinson were printed in the early 1850s, when he returned to the offensive (January, 1852) at Keswick, refusing to make any concession to sentimentality on the subject of Lakeland rustic charm: 'The whole place is encompassed by foul middens, open cesspools and stagnant ditches, or by still fouler drains.'[135] Ulverston, which he visited in the following year, he found just as open to criticism, and redolent with 'nuisances injurious to health which are removable ... there are neither proper sewers nor drains ... cesspools are crowded amongst cottages ... fevers prevail in the houses of the poor'.[136] These were, of course, the exclamations of a powerful propagandist for sanitary reform.[137]

A Westmorland or Furness man migrating via Ulverston to Barrow in, let us say, the 1860s, would have found little enough to choose between the two towns: both lacked sanitation, water supplies of a clean and regular kind, and a variety of civic amenities which were to be taken for granted by the end of the century. Nevertheless, the death rate in Dalton-in-Furness parish, which admittedly contained large open spaces as well as a rapidly burgeoning Barrow, was less than 21 per thousand living in 1864.[138] On the other hand, the iron-mining settlements within its boundaries, including those within the town of Dalton, were badly sewered and insanitary.[139] Yet such a state of affairs was common in town and country wherever people lived, and Victorian attitudes to cleanliness, or the absence of it, cannot be explained in terms of the proclivities of industrialists as such. But the newer industrial towns, by attracting people in large numbers, also exposed them to dirt and disease on a much larger scale, and in so doing laid bare some problems of social pathology which were rehearsed and explored in the newspaper press in some detail. The present survey cannot, of its nature, probe deeply into the complex interplay of developing sensitivities to legislative pressure increasingly shown by town rulers, the moral and publicised involvements of groups of industrialists in local government, and their concern, interested or disinterested, with the welfare of immediately relevant labour forces. Such influences, working in varying combinations, brought emulation with them, and shaped and motivated civic awareness and sanitary improvement in towns like Barrow and Workington, and in lesser places like Cleator Moor, Dalton and Millom; but their exhaustive exploration belongs to a field of comparative urban history which remains to be worked in the future. Such examples as are given here, however, may be useful pointers. Meanwhile, if the countryside of Cumbria enjoyed low death rates, which it did, then the latter were hardly the rewards of virtue. The indefatigable Rawlinson did little in the way of providing an advertisement for Lakeland residential amenities when, in the course of his examination of Keswick, he made a near-vicious side-thrust at the charming nearby village of Braithwaite, which contained, he asserted, 'in proportion to its population more dirt, disease and death than any decent town. It is one of the most romantic and filthy villages in England.'[140] In 1875, the *West Cumberland Times* bluntly described what was clearly a common rural state of affairs: 'At hundreds of farmhouses the families have no other supply of water than that which is supplied from wells sunk beneath the adjacent manure heaps, the cesspools and cattle folds and piggeries.'[141] The newspapers of an urbanised area were ready enough to patronise country cousins, but farmers in rural vestries could resist the idea of paying rates for clean water supplies, like the Papcastle farmer, Mr Benn, who (1875) 'had got his daily water supply from the millrace for the last sixty years, and he defied anybody to say that he was the worse for it'.[142]

It is a striking fact that between 1871 and 1890, Cumbrian death rates fell steeply in both town and country. In the leading industrial towns and major settlements there was significant sanitary improvement, which goes far to explain the declining mortality figures in their immediate districts. In the case of the countryside, explanation is more difficult. We can give a little weight to the consideration that the rising tourist industry was provoking a response from local boards of health in Keswick, Ambleside, Bowness, and Windermere,[143] but this does not account for a 13 per cent drop in mean death rates, as between each of the two decades, for the East Ward of Westmorland, or for a drop, over similar periods, of nearly 10 per cent in the Longtown registration district. The Registrar-General, in pointing to largely rural Westmorland as one of the healthiest counties in England (1895), identified as least one major and significant factor in its remarkable record, namely very low infantile mortality (1881–90). Indeed, its incidence of scarlet fever, whooping cough and measles was so slight that it was held up as a case for admiration.[144] The permanent and, presumably, always powerful factor of low density of population was undoubtedly operative in the background during the whole of our period: diseases of a kind dangerous to young children were not transmitted easily where they occurred. But a generalised background factor does not satisfactorily explain the marked fall in mortality and its degree, and one can only conclude that improved nourishment, at a period of rising real wages, rather than effective sanitation (of which there is no real evidence), and the fact that married women were withdrawn from field labour in an appreciable number of instances,[145] provided a further combination of circumstances which worked beneficially. Any improved nourishment, meanwhile, also benefited adults. For the rest, it has to be remembered that this transformation took place before the County Councils had begun their work of tutelage (1889), and long before villages and hamlets had piped supplies of clean water, which in many cases did not reach them until after 1932.

Migrants moving to the towns frequently put their children at risk until the century was nearing its end, although by the close of the decade 1881–90 the contrast in types of mortality between Wigton and Whitehaven registration districts, or between those for Longtown and Carlisle, or between Brampton and Cockermouth, were in no sense as stark as they had been two or three decades earlier. Nevertheless, children were still more likely to die from the effects of scarlet fever, whooping cough, diarrhoea and dysentery in the towns and urban districts, and the relative mortality of children under five was markedly higher there.[146] The difference in general mortality rates between urban and rural districts is largely explained by this greater relative loss of children, which was not, in national terms, to be considered as unduly serious during the decade under discussion. We must continually bear in mind that urban settlements in West Cumberland often lay in open situations exposed to the sea breezes, and the working man's home and children may accordingly have benefited. The fact remains that the mean death rate of Whitehaven registration district (1881–90) was 19.7, that of Cockermouth 18.5, and that of Carlisle 19.7, but the similar rates for Longtown, Penrith, Brampton and Wigton were 15.3, 14.6, 15.2, and 14.9 respectively, and for the West Ward of Westmorland the death rate, which was not then inflated by a geriatric invasion, was a striking 12.5.[147] Not all of the relatively high 'industrial' rates can be attributed wholly to the exposure of children to disease, and Whitehaven suffered from a higher than average incidence of respiratory diseases which led to death.[148] Yet, even here, in a coal-mining area, the figures are unsensational, and the occupation of ironstone mining was seen by the Registrar-General's statisticians as producing 'rates of death . . . lower than those of occupied males of all age-groups between 20 and 65 years'.[149]

In sanitary matters, the urban areas and districts made great strides in the course of twenty or so years. It need not be a cause for wonderment that because disease was known to cross social barriers, action was probably prompter than it might otherwise have been; as the Mayor of Carlisle somewhat artlessly remarked (1875), 'when . . . even members of this Council had found (a) disease manifesting itself in their own families . . . they must endeavour to find out causes'.[150] The fact remains that a great change in attitude, as well as sanitary organisation, took place in this period, even though it was still possible for the Whitehaven Sanitary Authority as late as 1885, to be 'furnished with medical reports that were productive of . . . amusement at its meetings',[151] and the *Whitehaven News*, in a stinging commentary, represented growing opinion in criticising over-sensitivity to the rights of property.[152] Elsewhere, there was a struggle against inertia. In 1872, rapidly growing Workington was tolerating a water supply that was 'most filthy',[153] whilst in Cockermouth 'sanitary action was in abeyance until the appointment of a medical officer in 1873'.[154] This last event, when it did take place, was to be a significant one for the region, for Dr John M. Fox, the officer appointed, was one of the most formidable sanitary campaigners to leave an imprint on Cumbrian history. Fox saw straight away that the unfiltered water drawn from the River Cocker was a danger to the public, and local sewers made in 1867–8 were already blocked.[155] Fox's campaign developed into a battle for a supply of clean Lakeland water for the entire coastal sub-region, and he was aided in this work by the parsimony of the local government bodies concerned, which permitted the Keswick and Cockermouth local boards to share his services with the Cockermouth Rural Sanitary Authority. His sphere of influence was accordingly widened.[156] His main idea, eventually realised, was that of a supply of water from Crummock Water via Whinlatter. In the course of time Workington, which drew its 'filthy' water from the Derwent, identified itself with the campaign, and by 1879 its local board had joined the Cockermouth authorities (urban and rural) in securing a supply from Crummock, with a reservoir at Stainburn.[157] It is a matter of no little interest that these developing activities in the Cumbrian coastal area could well have given some retrospective moral justification to Manchester in its descent upon Thirlmere.

The 1880s, which brought new self-confidence to Workington as the firm of Cammells became established there, saw a rapid development of local government activity and resultant sanitation, culminating in the town's acquisition of borough status in 1887. Two years later, the medical officer of health for the town was able to claim that – with a death rate down to under 15 in the thousand – 'at no time in its history (had) a lower or more uniform death rate prevailed'.[158] Barrow, which had experienced in the early 1870s even more sustained and drastic inrushes of people than Workington, nevertheless managed to institute a major system of town sewerage in that decade. The effects of this were being clearly indicated during the 1880s; by 1885, the death rate was hovering between 15 and 18, and by 1888 it was just over 14 in the 1000, a remarkable achievement in a town which was rapidly becoming distinguished for the spaciousness of its layout,[159] and, whatever critics might say, for the roominess and utility of many of its houses. As migrants settled in these newly developing towns, and houses continued to be built, the occupying and youthful families multiplied; birth rates, as in Barrow, were high, and natural increase prevented any major losses of total populations. Meanwhile, the death rates in such recently 'mushroomed' redbrick towns were already so low as to compete with those of rural Westmorland.

Nor were smaller towns or industrial settlements inactive. Local boards of health were performing modestly impressive work in such places by the end of the 1880s, when the Arlecdon and Frizington board was enabled to enforce the use of water-closets,[160] and when Millom, another new town, was similarly bringing about hygienic advance.[161] Cleator Moor[162] had long shown the growing civic sense to which allusion has been made (see p. 53), and nearby Egremont, which had reduced its nuisances to those of 'a trifling and remediable nature' (1889) had actually recorded a death rate of scarcely over 12 by the spring of that year,[163] an achievement of which its local board had every right to be proud. Carlisle, Kendal, and Whitehaven, notwithstanding some advances in civic organisation, found the thickly crowded areas of their towns more difficult to deal with, and the latter had, in the same year, to report a death rate of nearly 25 for the packed streets and alleys of the old township of Whitehaven, and 23 for the whole sanitary district surrounding it.[164] These were hardly figures which inspired confidence, and as late as 1902, Whitehaven had to face what amounted to a denunciation from an official of the Local Government Board, Dr Bulstrode — the worst parts of the town had changed little since Rawlinson's critical comments of half a century before.[165]

The exposure to risk of the late Victorian settler in Cumbrian towns, then, clearly depended, partly at least, upon where he chose or was obliged to live. But death rates are not the only means of estimating the pressures or pains which in-migrants may at some stage have experienced, although these data do tell us much about states of sanitation, and, therefore, something about the most unpleasant aspects of the immediate environment. But overcrowding, too, brought its dangers as well as its discomforts, although the available census statistics on this subject are far from satisfactory in that they specify a type of house only by the number of its rooms and the occupants therein[166] without providing crucial additional information on cubic capacities, or types of house arrangement or their local densities. Fortunately, perhaps, an intimate knowledge of a region and its local housing will help to explain the apparent peculiarities in the statistics presented by the compilers of the 1891 Census report, which produced, *inter alia* the startling information that Cumberland was one of the most 'overcrowded' counties in England, with just over 13 per cent of its people living more than two to a room.[167] Westmorland, by contrast, had a good record, with under 5 per cent of its population in that position, as against an English and Welsh average of 11.23.[168]

Why was this? The more specific data for urban sanitary districts and municipal boroughs strongly indicate that overcrowding – reckoned by this very useful yardstick of tenements with more than two persons per room within them – was markedly a feature of the more inbuilt major towns and market centres. These, places like Whitehaven and Carlisle (the two worst cases in the region, with well over 30 per cent of all tenements overcrowded), but also Cockermouth, Maryport and Brampton, were largely responsible for the very high Cumberland county figure. Next in order of seriousness came the new industrial towns, Workington, Barrow, and Cleator Moor, which lacked the yard-and-alley overcrowding of those centres mentioned, but which had their own specific peculiarities and problems affecting considerable masses of people. Cleator Moor, with its large stock of two-up-and-two-down terrace cottages, some of which still remain to be seen, had long been inclined to pack large families into little space,[169] and Barrow's notable percentage of two-roomed tenements (12.9) reflected the existence of its Scots-type flats for shipyard workers.[170] Indeed, Barrow's housing stock of this period was inadequate to meet the needs of its labour force, which was obliged to seek accommodation in Dalton or even Ulverston,[171] just as, in the inward population surge of the early 1870s, Workington looked towards Cockermouth under the stress of pressure on accommodation.[172] During its rapid expansion of the 1880s, Workington managed to create a stock of housing which more than kept place, during the intercensal period involved, with a striking population increase of over 65 per cent,[173] and the relative short-term inflexibility of housing accommodation was only one problem afflicting the area as a whole. Where a locality had a solid basis of regular industrial activity and employment, as at Millom, where the Hodbarrow iron ore output climbed steadily from the early 1870s to the mid 1890s, then its housing problems (which, in the case of this new town, were acute at first)[174] tended to disappear. By 1891, Millom urban sanitary district had the proudest accommodation record in Cumberland, with less than 5 per cent of overcrowding, and a remarkable stock of tenements with more than four rooms – even though the houses themselves were not always monuments to style and elegance.[175] (See Appendix 8.)

Just as there was variation, and variability, between towns, so there were some remarkable contrasts in the countryside. As we have seen, rural Westmorland had little overcrowding, and, of the agricultural areas, only Hereford, Somerset and several of the home counties had a better record. A scrutiny of the classifications of houses in terms of numbers of rooms shows that the Westmorland countryside, measured against the data for other agrarian counties, had a relative shortage of two- and three-roomed tenements, and the common argument that there was a shortage of residences for young couples or families can therefore be sustained.[176] Population drain had evidently prevented any overcrowding developing by 1891. Nevertheless, much depended, in more general rural Cumbrian terms, on traditions of occupancy and building as well as economic advance or decline, and the Brampton and Longtown rural sanitary districts showed a startling contrast with those for Westmorland, each of them possessing a surfeit of two- and three-roomed residences or tenements, and manifesting overcrowding percentages of 22.6 and 28 per cent respectively. These were former handloom weaving areas which had experienced not only a decline in their domestic industries, but had also suffered economic 'overrunning' by virtue of the centralisation of industry

11 The face of labour; the workers in an engineering shop of a Workington ironworks c. 1900. How many of these men had migrated from the countryside?

and commerce in Carlisle. In addition, the Scots-type single-storey cottage was and sometimes is encountered in these border areas, and may have had the effect of making the overcrowding figures appear even worse than they were. Finally, as is hardly surprising, the tourist towns or centres of the Lake District had little in the way of accommodation problems by 1891, although Keswick, earlier condemned by Sir Robert Rawlinson, had a considerable number of three-roomed tenements, and its closed yards and alleys still remained at this time.[177]

The migrating countryman might, then, unless he had very special skills or training, find that he had moved into an uncomfortable and sometimes an unhealthy environment, especially if he went into one of the local towns as a labourer and a lodger; and the most that can be added by way of qualification is that some country towns and districts would give him a very useful and an equally overcrowded induction. Industrial work and town life together must at first have been the occasion of a considerable degree of culture shock; the strange terms and accents of the coal mine or the haematite working, the danger and heat of the ironworks and the sheer brute labour of pig-lifting, and the arguments, tensions and uncertainties. The social statistics that have been given in these pages can give no idea of the true atmosphere in any time or place; to convey the latter would need the imaginative skill of the poet or novelist as well as the training of the historian. Millom, for example, may have had its steadily improving amenities, but its locality saw a battle between Irish, English and Welsh labourers in 1866,[178] a strike at Hodbarrow mine (1880) and a prolonged ironworks strike in the early months of 1889,[179] and much trade union agitation and civic conflict during 1893,[180] the feeling of local workers being partially directed at the paternalism of the Hodbarrow mineowners. Such incidents, far from being mere ruptures in long periods of tranquility, speak of deeper tensions, and the 1889 strike had its roots in a long-term dissatisfaction which had affected the ironworks of the entire Cumbrian coast, a loathing of the two-shift system of working then operative. This, however, is discussed further in the next chapter (see pp. 133–4). The migrant into the Whitehaven district would, especially if he was a Catholic or a strong Anglican, have been brought into an area of religious tension and bigotry, of the kind described by George Jacob Holyoake when recounting the story of a visit to that town in 1851; he was told 'they will come armed with stones'.[181] Nor was the famous secularist exaggerating, and Orange groups in Whitehaven readily enough supported the anti-Catholic demagogue William Murphy in 1871, when he was violently attacked by Irish miners in the coastal town; Murphy died in the following year.[182] The local Orangemen saw fit, as late as 1884, to march provocatively through Cleator Moor and to stir up a mass riot which involved the use of firearms,[183] the Irish population resisting forcibly. A search through the regional press would reveal similar incidents of a less serious kind, and the point to bear in mind regarding them is that they relate to specific localities; the region as a whole was distinctly law-abiding, and, for this very reason, the intra-regional migrant to the coastal districts would have felt a sharp contrast, even a shock. Westmorland was one of the most lightly policed areas of England, and magistrates themselves could see the rural areas of the region as being notably peaceful.[184]

Since the people of the region continued to show every sign of being highly literate (a subject which receives fuller discussion in Chapter 6), and since they were clearly able to read a widely circulated newspaper press, it is a matter of some importance that they continued to leave the hills and dales for the attractions and opportunities of town life. When we learn that a Whitehaven coal miner could earn 6s. per shift in the 1870s,[185] and, if he was in full employment, earn twice as much as a country labourer for distinctly shorter hours (no more than eight daily from 1877 into the new century)[186] then it is easy to see why the less salubrious town districts found their recruits. Other movements, or their rationale, are less susceptible of explanation; many urban-related occupations were ill-regulated and exhausting, and the *Whitehaven News* of 22 January 1872 commented on 'the overworked classes', amongst which it counted shopworkers, railway servants and omnibus drivers, the first group being exposed to unlimited hours, and the remaining two to the weather. Although shop assistants were becoming organised in their own defence in the early years of the new century, their lot was not enviable; and many were, of course, local migrants by origin. Again, builders' labourers in Barrow earned 27s. to 29s. 3d. weekly in 1907,[187] whereas farm day labourers in the nearby Lake Counties received just over 19s. in the same year,[188] and some economic attractions to the urban world are easily explained. But shipyard and engineering labourers in the Furness town were paid no more than a farmworker of the region[189] in the same year, and we are again back to the truism that the occasions for migration were manifold and sometimes complex.

One background factor stands out increasingly; the palpable variety and apparent range of opportunities offered by life along the industrial fringe of the region, with its multitude of voluntary associations, its constantly more variegated evening life, its religious fellowship, its amusements and recreations, and, in a word, its deepening social richness. If a workman managed to hold his earnings – in some phases, never certain or regular *in toto* – at much the same level over the years, his effective purchasing power grew in the later Victorian decades, just as opportunities for acquiring a wider range of goods were appearing; and his life could at last extend towards wider horizons in the most literal sense. He could forget that he had once been a refugee from Lakeland dales, and visit that same unique countryside as a man of leisure in an excursion train, or, as many did after the 1880s, purchase one of the bicycles advertised in the local newspapers for £2. 10s. Sir Wilfrid Lawson, whose own home was on the edge of the industrial district, and who was elected to parliament by liberal-minded workers in Cockermouth and Workington, said publicly in 1889 that 'there never was a period when the working people had such good times and were able to provide the means of life and comfort at as cheap a rate as now'.[190] Notwithstanding strikes, tensions and slumps, it is clear that many agreed with him.

Property, authority and the pressures from below

This chapter, as its title implies, is concerned with the influential or leading personalities who helped to shape the Cumbria of the mid-nineteenth to the early twentieth century. We have surveyed, very briefly, the fortunes of those who laboured, and we now examine those who made decisions and wielded authority. At the end of this period it became fashionable to publish volumes of biographies of county and social 'leaders', like Ernest Gaskell's *Westmorland and Cumberland Leaders*, published in the early years of this century, or the joint work of W. Burnett Tracy and W. T. Pike, *Lancashire at the Opening of the Twentieth Century* (Brighton, 1903). The subjects of these works were, significantly, men who came into prominence through a variety of channels; through landed society, the armed forces, commerce and industry, local government, medicine and the law, the church, national politics, and even trade unions.

An examination of the careers of scores of eminent Cumbrians shows that few of them gained positions of local influence or authority through one such institution alone. Since we are also obliged, in the space of a brief study, to generalise, compare and classify in the broadest of senses, it follows that these men (women were completely ignored) must be seen in relation to a variety of institutions, if only to demonstrate some of the ways in which power was exerted and influence wielded. It need hardly be said that much power, as the twentieth century approached, was utilised invisibly, through increasingly complex industrial and administrative bodies. In the mid-nineteenth century, powerful individuals were almost invariably far more visible; and their activities were in any case made known through an ever more widely circulating newspaper press. Yet the ways in which they exercised that power were manifold, depending upon the machinery they used, the social purpose and impact of decisions, and the administrative levels at which these major personalities worked. A brief historical survey of this kind must be concerned primarily with fundamental decision-making, by groups and individuals, and the social consequences of those decisions. Nevertheless, it would be foolish to deny that there are other aspects of power and 'leadership' which are interesting in themselves, and which call for some kind of classification. A cursory look at some examples may be suggestive.

The seemingly autonomous power and influence of the great landowner — often much augmented by industrial involvement and indirectly supported by administrative responsibility through government, local and national — might in fact draw strength from a number of blended factors; the respect accorded to his position, the efficiency with which he administered his areas of interest and chose his underlings, and his own business and organisational creativity. Much the same applied to the employer and organiser in industry and commerce, with one important difference; the latter often took decisions which might not have been in themselves spectacular, but which had direct and visible effects upon the working-class public and (sometimes) on their long-term fortunes and environment. But, as the world of a growing middle class became administratively and technologically more complex, so its leading members gave increasing quantities of time to local governmental affairs, which might indeed be controversial from time to time, but which did not involve them in conflict with a wider mass of people, but raised their status within localities. Sections of the town middle-class groups became detached from the world of the more powerful landowners, or consciously fought great-landowner influence, as in mid-Victorian Whitehaven. Despite this, there was an enormous desire within the ranks of the richer middle class groups to emulate great-landowner living styles, and for this reason, the great estate-owners continued to stand high in esteem even when the economic base of their wealth and position appeared to be cracking. Meanwhile, beneath the traditional Victorian structures of middle- and upper-class power and influence, other independent forces were appearing. The emergence of a labour movement in remote Cumbria, never itself totally divorced from accepted political values, but still deriving its strength from genuinely deep grass-roots, properly provides a concluding topic for this chapter.

In the pre-1914 world, landed property was still an ultimate determinant of influence and standing, and riches and business success were merely a means of achieving the property, the influence or both together. Worldly success was still apt to be measured in terms of a country house, an estate, a mention in Burke or Walford, the leisure for the demonstrative pursuit of country sports, and the acquisition of armorial bearings. It follows that the greatest landlords, and especially those of aristocratic lineage, represented or were made to represent the fullest embodiment of authority and standing in county or regional circles, and their touch, or patronage, brought an automatic bestowal of social grace. *His Grace* the Duke of Devonshire was aptly addressed, even though the Earls of Lonsdale carried considerably more direct influence over affairs in Cumbria as a whole — largely because they had much more land within the region. Both represented values and standards to which the rest of county landed society aspired, or to which they simply related themselves without further thought.

Nevertheless, our period was one of profound transformations at work beneath these very obvious social assumptions. Industrial and urban growth brought with them both social responsibility and administrative power, expressed through parliamentary representation (which ceased to become the prerogative of certain landed families), political parties, local boards, boards of guardians, and, later, the county councils and district councils. Whilst there can be no possible doubt that the gentry continued to rule in country areas, sections of the gentry themselves went through subtle and not so subtle changes; and, in the industrial districts, control certainly did not stay exclusively with the industrialists. The new urban world, moreover, brought a mass of voluntary associations, from religious bodies to trade unions and sporting organisations, all of which threw up their own particular kinds of leadership. By 1914, the leading trade unionists of (for example) West Cumberland were men to be reckoned with, and some of them sat side by side with the old-fashioned county leaders in committees of the County Council.

It is too easy to talk vaguely of power and influence or 'leadership' without specifying the exact channels through which they took effect. Let us, then, attempt to establish our points of reference by commencing with a brief study of the two most powerful figures of the mid-Victorian North-West, William, Second Earl of Lonsdale (1787–1872), and William, Seventh Duke of Devonshire (1808–91). The Earl owned some 67 457 acres in Cumberland and Westmorland at the time of his death, and had considerable economic and other power in Whitehaven, while the Duke of Devonshire owned much land (certainly over 6000 acres) in Furness and Cartmel, and was deeply involved in the development of Barrow-in-Furness and its industries.[1] Yet, as the personal diaries of both men demonstrate, many of their duties or leanings drew them out of the region both physically and spiritually. In consequence, they were very often in the position of titular or remote leaders, controlling church livings, giving formal or ceremonial support to religious bodies, and influencing committee decisions or local government bodies through underlings. It remains true that the Earl paid regular shooting-season visits to Lowther Castle,[2] while, of his six Cavendish family seats, the Duke loved Holker Hall the most. His strongly developed sense of duty ordained that he should (as Earl of Burlington) become Chairman of the Ulverston Guardians from 1836,[3] and his attachment to the Furness district played no little part in the complex of events that led to its industrial transformation.

Both aristocrats were essentially estate-owners[4] with an intelligent interest in railways and industry, willing enough to perform such official county or other duties as came their way, and willing, too, to take good advice from the lesser magnates and skilful stewards who surrounded them. Yet only for certain periods did they experience any deep involvement in industrial or railway decisions, and they, of course, depended upon the technical expertise of others. In estate administration, however, a landowner could make decisions directly, taking full responsibility for action on rent adjustments, drainage policy and the securing of tenancies. Moreover, he had little enough control, beyond a certain point, over urban multitudes (as the Earl's successor but one, Hugh Lowther, soon found), and only in the countryside was his 'leadership' assured, reinforced by audit days and tenants' dinners, sports ceremonials, volunteers' and military activities, and so on. However, it remains true that the Lonsdale and the Devonshire estates came to depend very considerably upon industrial or railway income or both before about 1875, even though this income could be very unreliable over a longer time-span.[5] Nor should it be denied that the quasi-feudal or ceremonial aspect of a great landowner's influence, as well as the economic, could be extended into the industrial setting, and there was a very real sense in which many of the miners of Whitehaven (before about 1880), and the staff of the Furness Railway, felt some identification with an aristocratic chairman or owner. The Cavendish motto, *Cavendo Tutus*, was displayed by the FR, the Duke had a private coach on the line and was treated very much like royalty, and the company's 'servants' were encouraged to behave accordingly. Nor should we forget, as our theme develops, that several of the substantial gentry of Cumbria

12 Company togetherness; the staff of Ulverston Station on the Furness Railway, before the First World War. The patriarchal Mr Woolgar, the stationmaster, is in the front centre.

who were also railway-promoters or directors had private railways halts or stations. They were good imitators.

The Second Earl of Lonsdale, however, as an older man who was earlier in the field, managed to insert himself into railway folklore through a public association with George Stephenson in the surveying of the West Cumberland coastal route.[6] Certainly the *Whitehaven News* (not a pro-Lonsdale newspaper) remarked of him at his death in 1872 that 'he was the mainspring and mainstay of the coast lines of railway'.[7] The Earl's major investment in the Whitehaven and Furness Junction Railway (1845), which brought him into contact with the later Duke of Devonshire, was not very profitable, and, as the *News* revealed later, the Earl was 'not ... very frequently at Whitehaven'.[8] Yet, as his rather laconic diary indicates, his influence may well have been necessary to secure the passage of railway bills through parliament, and the same source demonstrates his keen vigilance where railway activities near his own territory were concerned,[9] while the Duke was successful in maintaining good relations with important railway companies like the Midland,[10] which had an interest in Furness traffic and connections. However, the Earl distilled within himself some of the traditional quasi-feudalism of the Lowthers in business matters, and it is unsurprising to find him using patronage not only at the local level, but also when in national office – he was, as Baron Lowther, Postmaster-General in Peel's second administration of 1841, and seems to have used his position to secure posts for Cumberland men in the Post Office.[11] The Duke, a Liberal Whig of much personal rectitude, represented a different standpoint altogether, and it is interesting to note, too, that he was related by marriage to another Whig house, that of Howard; the Howards, Earls of Carlisle, appear as the third most important noble family in Cumbria in this age. They provided some of the Whig counterbalance to the Tory Lowthers, and, throughout our period, influenced East Cumberland politics much as the Lowthers were a major force in the west.

Politics and industry could, given the right chemical mix, produce a source of great power, and the Howards lacked local industrial involvements outside the small coalfield near the Northumberland border. Acreages alone, or industries alone, did not guarantee decisive influence, whereas those qualifications combined with local, visible activity generally did. By contrast, the Wyndhams, Lords Leconfield, owned rich iron-ore bearing territory in West Cumberland, and gained much in royalties therefrom, just as they provided parliamentary representation there, of a sort, in the second half of the century. Yet, apart from isolated political encounters, and the constant facts of royalties and wayleaves and manorial ceremonies, the family made little impact in the region, and despite their ownership of Cockermouth Castle, spent much of their time far away at their main seat of Petworth in Sussex.[12] Much the same could have been said of the Duke of Buccleuch in Furness, who sought only limited political representation there. When the time came, there were no Wyndhams on the

Cumberland County Council (a useful indicator), and the Second Lord Leconfield's agent, writing in 1896 after unsuccessful and difficult negotiations with the Cleator Moor UDC and a local railway company, remarked ruefully upon 'Lord Leconfield's small influence with the local boards'.[13] On the other hand, the Duke of Buccleuch was powerfully represented in Barrow and Furness local government by his agent Edward Wadham, who administered further ore-bearing property of great value. Occasionally a great and noble landowner would identify himself wholly with his county, like the Hon. H. C. Howard of Greystoke, the first chairman of the Cumberland County Council, a nephew of the Duke of Norfolk, and a man with many-branching family connections. Conversely, Sir James Graham of Netherby (d. 1861), Sir Robert Peel's former lieutenant, was a notable agricultural improver, with some 25 000 acres, but was largely identified with national politics, serving as MP for East Cumberland in 1832–7 and as Palmerstonian MP for Carlisle in 1852–61.[14] The impact of such a man could be surprisingly localised in the regional context, although it is essential to bear in mind that as opportunities for local political activity increased, so great landowners could place themselves more resoundingly before a regional public.

This certainly happened in the case of the owners of a great Westmorland estate, Underley, who came there as comparative *arrivistes* after Alderman William Thompson, a local man who made good in the City of London and elsewhere, had purchased the estate in 1840. For the next half-century his descendants, the Earl of Bective and the latter's son Lord Kenlis, played a large part in Westmorland county life and ceremonial, until the estate of more than 25 000 acres passed to Lord Henry Bentinck by marriage in 1892.[15] It was as though they had been called upon to fill some tribal vacuum. Yet much of the real work of Westmorland county leadership, through the magistracy as well as through local railway administration and politics, came from men like Colonel E. W. Hasell of Dalemain, whose estates comprised less than 5000 acres, but whose family's connection with the area went back to the seventeenth century. There was certainly no significant correlation between acreage and esteem, assuming that the latter can be measured accurately, but ancient landownership, if not riches, was a factor of much weight if associated with the performance of duties in the public eye.

So far, we have mentioned great landowners who for the most part carried local, regional and national standing. However, it is a point of some importance that a group of lesser landowners, beneath the former in social status, wielded localised but very real influence within given districts of the two counties. It was this group that showed the greatest contrasts within its own ranks; it included relative *arrivistes* like the Marshalls of Patterdale and Monk Coniston, the Croppers of Burneside and the Wakefields of Sedgwick in Westmorland, each of whose estates were derived from trade and industry, the Curwens of

13 Dalemain near Ullswater, the seat of the Hasell family.

Workington, who were already well established but who wielded manorial and industrial influence in one, and relatively old families like the Wilsons of Dallam Tower in Westmorland or the Briscoes of Crofton in North Cumberland (see Appendix 7). All of these owned estates of from 3000 to 10 000 acres (with the exception of the Croppers, who were philanthropic paper-makers, and whose influence was derived from sources other than land). Generally speaking, the pattern of large estates within the region is striking for its 'county-exclusiveness', and only three great landowners out of 21 had extensive territories in both Cumberland and Westmorland, allowing for scattered fragments beyond the county borders. This, of course, had implications for their other involvements, like membership of the Commission of the Peace in the two counties; hence, the then Lord Lonsdale was Lord Lieutenant and therefore chief magistrate for both counties in 1847–51, and Colonel E. W. Hasell, besides being chairman of Quarter Sessions for Westmorland, was also a Cumberland JP, while Sir George Musgrave was a JP for both counties.[16] Each of these, not surprisingly, was a great landowner with estates in each county. The rest of the membership of the respective Cumberland and Westmorland benches consisted of persons with purely local property and involvements. Yet there had long been joint administrative co-ordination of Cumberland and Westmorland in matters military (through the Lieutenancy), and the police for the two counties were placed under one chief constable after 1856.[17] The county boundaries were certainly no barrier to family contacts, and a study of special occasions, like coming-of-age parties or Freemasons' gatherings, shows that these lines could very easily be transcended. But we also have to remember that, railway trips to Carlisle, Kendal or even Seascale apart, the radius of social intercourse was very largely determined by the horse, and the railway system was to provide a solvent only by degrees. Hence, as far as the nobility and gentry were concerned, the idea of county leadership and county commitment was a very real one, although it was based far less on family and personal ties than on administration and politics.

Politics, landowners and parvenus

We must now ask ourselves to what extent the greater landowners, and their lesser colleagues, saw themselves as political leaders at county level, and to what degree they were apparently accepted by those persons who had the vote. About the Lowther dominance in the county of Westmorland, outside Kendal, there can be little doubt, and members of this family occupied at least one of the two county parliamentary seats more or less continuously from the eighteenth century to 1880, the other being shared, after 1841, with a representative of the Underley estate, mainly the Earl of Bective.[18] Colonel H. C. Lowther represented Westmorland between 1812 and 1867, as a virtual absentee who shared a keen and abiding family interest in the Cottesmore hunt,[19] although it is fair to add that he served as an officer of the Cumberland militia. This man's eldest son, Colonel Henry Lowther, was MP for West Cumberland between 1847 and 1868, and this too was a constituency in which the family had a continuous interest, but which they shared with others, including minor gentry like the Irtons of Irton, or the Stanleys of Ponsonby, and, after 1857, members of the Wyndham family, representing the Leconfield interest. (Sir Wilfrid Lawson's subsequent and characteristic jibe was that 'Lord Lonsdale used to put one in at one election, and one at the other, and a friend of mine said that the one went out to grass while the other was working' (laughter and cheers).[20] However, the solidity of the voting in these Tory constituencies calls for serious examination (Sir Wilfrid could never be serious for long), and rough calculations from the polling figures, actual and potential, show that the Conservative vote for West Cumberland was one of the highest in the region, approaching 50 per cent.[21] This fact should be borne in mind when later figures for the region's constituencies are examined. Similar figures for Westmorland are unavailable because it was apparently considered improper to challenge the Lowthers, and there was no contested election there between 1832 and 1880!

The Lowthers, then, as the greatest landowners in the two counties, held an unchallenged position until late Victorian times, one which they shared with Lord Bective and his father-in-law in Westmorland. Something of the same

14 Cumbrian political leaders. *Top left*, the seventh Duke of Devonshire (1808–91); *bottom left*, H. W. Schneider, the Furness ironmaster and magnate, in his prime; *top right*, Patrick Walls (1847–1932), pioneer leader of Cumbrian labour and General Secretary of the National Federation of Blastfurnacemen; *bottom right*, Sir Wilfrid Lawson (1829–1906), the avuncular chairman of the Maryport and Carlisle Railway and leading Cumberland radical teetotaller.

pattern appears in Whitehaven, where there was no contested election between 1832 and 1868, although here the Lowther representatives, like Matthias Attwood, a Birmingham insurance director, were imported. The seat passed (1865) to Lord Lonsdale's nephew, the Hon. G. F. Cavendish-Bentinck, and stayed in the latter's hands until his death in 1891. But nowhere else in the Lake Counties did the same degree of domination, or inertia, manifest itself. Whiggism and even occasional radicalism marked the rest of the region in the nineteenth century. East Cumberland, the province of the Howard family interest, remained Whig on the whole, a tendency attributed by Dr Pelling to the existence of numbers of hill freeholders,[22] but tottered towards the Lowther interest in 1886 and after (when the Penrith division was formed). The remaining towns were firmly Whig–radical. Kendal had taken the lead in combating the Lowther influence in 1818, and, when enfranchised in 1832, it elected a series of carpet-bagging Whigs, and then a home-grown industrialist Liberal in John Whitwell (1868–80). The Redistribution of Seats Act (1885) submerged the town in rural Conservatism once more as Westmorland, North and South, assured Conservative success. Carlisle tended to favour home-grown radical candidates, from the Whig–radical Joseph Ferguson, the local manufacturer (1852–7), through Sir James Graham (1852–61) to Sir Wilfrid Lawson (1859–65), and it did not acquire an outside carpet-bagger until the appearance of Edmund Potter, Glossop manufacturer, in 1861. From 1885 it continued to elect Liberals, Gladstonian or otherwise. Cockermouth, absorbed into a county division after 1885, tended to favour Liberals throughout, and its inclusion with Workington and Maryport from that date brought in a strong Irish and Home Rule influence which carried Sir Wilfrid Lawson to victory there (1886).[23]

These well-known and straightforward items from electoral history serve to underline the point made in our opening paragraph; that a region of great landowners was certainly not dominated by them, especially after semi-urban constituencies were created from 1885, but that there was, nevertheless, a strong element of rural Conservatism, contradicting the notion of the independent small landowner's supposed leaning towards Liberalism. Nor were Whiggish or radical great landowners automatically followed, as Sir Wilfrid Lawson found in Cockermouth division in 1885. The steadily Conservative tendency of many rural and some urban voters is brought out in Table 5.1.

Although the band of land-occupying and middle-class Conservatism, running from the mid-west coastal area to the rural east and south of Cumbria, is easily visible here, it is also clear that industrial Barrow could, at certain periods, bow the electoral knee to magnates just as easily as could Whitehaven, and that regional radicalism found a more regular home in a zone covering northern Cumbria. Barrow had its C. W. Cayzer, a wealthy shipowner, before it ceased to feel reliant upon the givers of shipbuilding orders and turned to Labour in 1906, and there is, perhaps, something of a parallel in Whitehaven's election of its colliery owner, Sir James Bain, in 1891.[25] The latter did not hold his seat for long, but the town remained Conservative until 1906; up to that time, whatever the direction in which Whitehaven chose to turn, its local *bourgeoisie* and professional men ruled where the Lowthers had ruled before. The working-class voter certainly does not appear as a marked force, in town or country, before 1906. He could, however, exert influence in other ways.

Table 5.1 Cumbrian constituencies, 1885–1910; Conservative and Unionist vote as a percentage of the total poll. (After Pelling[24])

Constituency	1885	1886	1892	1895	1900	1906	Jan. 1910	Dec. 1910	Six election average
Barrow	46·9	63·1	53·4	56·9	(53·6)	39·7	44·8	47·1	49·2
Whitehaven	54·3	52·3	45·4	55·3	63·9	44·2	–	46·3	51·5
Carlisle	(44·4)	46·8	48·7	47·4	(50·3)	(40·1)	46·6	49·5	46·2
Cumb., Eskdale	40·0	44·0	44·3	49·0	54·7	48·6	49·8	52·1	47·7
Cumb., Cockermouth	50·1	43·1	45·4	48·5	51·3	47·2	45·2	47·3	48·1
Cumb., Egremont	53·6	51·2	46·7	50·9	53·7	44·5	50·7	51·6	50·0
Cumb., Penrith	46·8	54·8	50·9	54·2	(56·5)	(46·0)	(49·8)	–	50·7
Westmorland N. or Appleby	50·1	51·8	56·8	58·7	44·3	50·0	53·8	54·9	52·3
Westmorland S. or Kendal	52·6	–	56·2	57·5	(54·2)	47·7	54·2	52·7	53·7
North Lonsdale	51·4	55·5	44·9	59·4	(51·1)	51·1	51·1	50·5	50·6

Figures in brackets are computed (from the average swing) for uncontested or otherwise inapplicable elections. A dash means that an extra candidate (e.g. Labour) intervened.

Radicalism and the independent landowner

Before turning to the new industrial middle class which was gaining in weight and influence throughout the region from the mid-Victorian years, it will be well to look briefly at the rural out-voters who, in Dr Pelling's view, gave a markedly Conservative bias to the voting even in so semi-industrialised a division as Egremont, and who apparently produced such a strong right-wing bias in North Westmorland. Pelling tentatively relates such trends to the 'ownership' voting partially made up of 'statesmen',[26] and is puzzled by the anti-Liberalism of what was undoubtedly a largely pastoral economy – one in which nonconformity, as in the Eden valley, was at least more noticeable than in any other rural part of the region. However, there are indications that the 'old' yeomanry, enjoying special fixity of manorial tenure, were in decline throughout the nineteenth century, and numerous sets of crude statistics have been adduced in support of this argument, e.g. by Francis Grainger before the Royal Commission on Agriculture in 1895. He bemoaned the loss of these established rural or village leaders – 'there is not the same interest taken in parish affairs', he complained. He himself belonged to a yeoman family which had inhabited Abbey Holme since the seventeenth century,

111

and was a Liberal, a magistrate, a leader of the poll in a local board election, and a pioneer county councillor.[27] The effect of leadership of this kind is very difficult to gauge, nor is there any evidence that old-established owner-occupying or farming families were necessarily Liberal in inclination. However, there is some evidence that a deeply-rooted independence or sense of status played its part in forming opinion, and in the extreme northern or radical zone of Cumbria, men or families who appear as small landowners in the *Return of Owners of Land* (1873) appear as district or parish councillors some twenty years later, like Waugh and Gardhouse of Dalston, Graham of Beanlands (Irthington), the Hodgsons of Burgh by Sands, the Simpsons of Riggfoot, Hethersgill, and other scattered examples. Directory entries for 1901 suggest that this zone had the largest proportion of individuals designated 'yeomen' in Cumbria (17.7 per cent of 'Farmers' in 26 sample parishes or townships),[28] and it is interesting that a certain radicalism in voting patterns does indeed appear in this border countryside. Likewise, such territories often contained few parishes with dominant landowners, and in 1847 and 1901, nearly every township or parish for 10 miles round Carlisle had a variety of landowners, while a substantial number of scattered or isolated townships had no resident gentleman or person of consequence, even where intensive middle-class house-building was taking place within the area.

Yet, it is also clear that mere analyses of ownership-patterns, viewed at close quarters or more broadly, produce little reliable guidance to electoral behaviour. Westmorland, with its Tory bias and its traditional affection for the Lowthers, had a great mass of small landowners in 1873, counted in the 2662 persons who owned land above 1 acre, and the 1714 who owned pieces of land of less than 1 acre.[29] Some of these persons called themselves 'yeomen', and many did not; those who have been positively identified as persons who also styled themselves as yeomen in directories, might own land or farms of between 50 and 150 acres, but it is also clear that many of them were not of old lineage like Francis Grainger. 'Yeoman' seems to have become, by degrees, a status-word without much reference to ancient forms of tenure, and, for the rest, an individual who was a manorial tenant, appearing, for example, at the Duke of Buccleuch's annual court at Dalton-in-Furness, might have added reason for deference rather than for independence of view. Meanwhile, the apparently steady disappearance of persons styling themselves yeomen, as indicated in directory entries during the nineteenth century, does not necessarily indicate a decimation of owner-occupiers, but may also suggest a change of emphasis in the use of a title. It is striking that contemporaries of weight, like Garnett, the historian of Westmorland agriculture, argued for the reduction of small owner-occupiers, citing their absorption into a great estate like Underley, but it is not at all clear that the 220 owners thus absorbed by Lord Bective were old-style yeomen, or indeed persons designated as such in directories.[30]

Nevertheless, the directories have their uses as rough indicators of possible trend, and as long as totals of persons within given categories are not taken literally, and the land-occupiers themselves are not defined rigorously, then we can still be impressed by the steady reduction in the appearances of the *word* yeoman, and the consistency shown in this diminution district by district in, for example, Westmorland and Furness. Since it is, on the whole, unlikely that the word itself, which was a clear indicator of proud status even in the twentieth century, dropped equally steadily out of usage, we have to conclude that a certain type of owner-occupier, above the mere smallholding class, was indeed tending to disappear (see Table 5.2).

Table 5.2   Westmorland and North Lonsdale; yeomen as a proportion of all persons given as farmers in directory lists[31]

	Separate parishes or town- ships	1829		% of yeo- men	1849			1885		
Westmorland		F	Y		F	Y	%	F	Y	%
East Ward	46	950	388	*40·8*	845	254	*30·0*	923	188	*20·3*
West Ward	29	531	223	*41·9*	467	124	*26·5*	489	91	*18·6*
Kendal Ward	40	853	250	*29·3*	787	147	*18·6*	831	87	*10·4*
Lonsdale Ward	14	250	55	*22·0*	252	38	*15·0*	265	17	*6·4*
Lancashire										
North Lonsdale	44	831	295	*35·4*	797	156	*19·8*	718	63	*8·8*

Although the 'yeoman' category defies the niceties of agrarian definition in this period, its apparent reduction certainly has some (as yet rather unclear) significance for local political and social leadership; and, if this is so, then a measure of agrarian independence evidently did not affect political behaviour, or independence or deference together, especially in Westmorland. If there was, meanwhile, to be any true 'independence', it would surely be more likely to be manifested by middle-class settlers from outside the area.

These elements were so weak in the mid-century that, as Professor F. M. L. Thompson has shown, the small rural gentry and middle class of Cumbria were making little impact, and, county magnates could have had difficulty in recommending suitable persons for the magistracy.[32] However, this situation was rapidly changing. It is likely that there was a problem in the first half of the century, for the number of magistrates for Cumberland increased from 94 in 1847 to 233 in 1901,[33] a proportion far out of direct relationship to population increase, and this evident increase of available persons mirrors the social transformation of the time and place. The classifications (used as a matter of convenience) in Professor Thompson's analysis of land-ownership in 1873[34] create certain difficulties when locally applied (see Table 5.3).

While Table 5.3 gives a sound enough impression of the local territory owned by the great magnates and established gentry, the classification designated

Table 5.3   Percentages of land owned by classes of landowners (1873)

	Great owners (3000–10 000 acres)	Squires (1000– 3000 acres)	Greater yeomen (300–1000 acres)	Lesser yeomen (100–300 acres)	Small proprietors (1–100 acres)
Cumberland	10	12	16	22	16
Westmorland	11	9	16	18	16
Lancs.	12	14	18	12	13
England	17	12·4	12	12·5	14

Unuseable waste land is excluded.

'Greater yeomen' in reality hides a growing and varied group of *bourgeois* settlers, many of whom were joining the magistracy. In fact, Westmorland's 'greater yeomen', even in 1873, were its lesser squires and comfortably-off settlers, as an analysis of the original return of landowners, subsequently related to the magistracy lists, indicates (Table 5.4).

Table 5.4   Landowners and the magistracy in Westmorland, *c.* 1873

	No. of land- owners	No. of whom Magistrates	Non- residents	Resident in Windermere	Resident in Kendal	Resident in Eden & Lune Valleys
Great owners (3000+ acres)	9	4	3	1	3	2
Squires (1000–3000 acres)	15	6	–	2	5	8
Lesser squires (500–1000 acres)	11	7	2	2	3	4
Totals	35	17	5	5	11	14

It should be borne in mind that even at this time, numbers of magistrates owned less than 500 acres, so that H. Gandy of Skirsdale Park, Penrith (appointed 1868) owned only 127 acres, Alfred Harris of Lunefield, Kirkby Lonsdale (1874) owned only 85, T. F. Fenwick, of Burrow Hall, Kirkby Lonsdale (1874), owned only 83 acres, and one of Westmorland's most influential figures, W. D. Crewdson, of Helme Lodge, Kendal, owned only 90 acres – worth, it may be added, £501, or three or four times the value of good agricultural land in the region. G. F. Braithwaite, a prominent manufacturer from the Kendal district appointed to the magistracy in 1874, owned only 50 acres, but his territory was worth £731.[35] The influence of urban expansion is here visible.

A further point is that not only were numbers of the new 'squirearchy' local men, but that these middle-class residents and magistrates were tending to cluster in salubrious or convenient areas, a point indicated in Table 5.5 (p. 118). For this reason, direct social control of much rural behaviour was unfeasible or unlikely, and we must here return to an earlier argument, that Conservative voting behaviour was not necessarily landowner- or leader-influenced, although the new settlers undoubtedly helped to maintain that vote in part. However, these *bourgeois* residents, growing more numerous, were not necessarily as Conservative as many of the farmers – and labourers – and in the election of October 1900, North Westmorland elected the Liberal hotelier of Windermere, Richard Rigg, as its parliamentary representative, with a substantial majority, while both North and South Westmorland fell to the Liberals in 1906. This being said, there can be little doubt that the great estates, and the older landed gentry, exerted considerable influence for Conservatism, but this was done not by some subtle intimidation, but by ceremonial, tradition and display, and the encouragement of a sense of togetherness. Tenants' dinners, rent day celebrations, annual shoots, coming-of-age parties, displays of benevolence at Christmas time, the encouragement of old traditions like Easter mumming plays and pace-egging, the gentlemanly patronage of games and sports – cricket transcended and strengthened deference at one and the same time – and the gracious giving of prizes for cottage economy at local horticultural society shows, all of these showed the older gentry and the established squires in a favourable light, and the regional newspaper press abounds with examples.

There is reason to think that even the richer elements who settled in southern Lakeland did not easily become part of the older gentry society, but here we must enter some caveats. Those who still maintained business and family connections in Lancashire or Yorkshire built up, as O. M. Westall has so convincingly shown, a social world of their own in districts like Windermere,[36] and, as Mr Westall puts it, they created their own retreat to Arcadia as well as their own patterns of amusement. Sir William Forwood was able to reign undisputed over the Royal Windermere Yacht Club, but the older gentry, like the Machell and Sandys families, provided leadership in the organisation of the Grasmere Sports, where the guests of honour would be the Earl and Countess of Lonsdale, Lord Henry Bentinck, Lord Muncaster and Lord Hothfield.[37] Even Sir William had to take a relatively minor place here, but he was not, like most of his own peers from the world of business and commerce, tied to local social duties to the same extent, and the settlers could build their own thoroughly satisfying social life. Something of the leisured and spacious nature of existence by Windermere is conveyed by the fine house that is now the National Park Centre, Brockhole, built by a Manchester businessman, G. H. Gaddum, between 1889 and 1903.[38]

There is probably no parallel with this Windermere *milieu* in other parts of Westmorland, where settlers were more isolated and the society less select, or simply more easily dominated by the established gentry families. We must also draw a distinction between these Lancashire and Yorkshire settlers and the home-grown or locally established businessmen of wealth and standing, who by degrees moved towards genuine county status, or who succeeded in developing an easy

115

relationship with the dominant or existing squirearchy, one strengthened by common business or administrative preoccupations. The Cropper family of Ellergreen, near Kendal, although Liberal (and Quaker in origin) were recognised as county gentry by both Burke and Walford before the end of the century, although it was well known that their standing rested largely on the paper mill at Burneside. The leading industrialists of West Cumberland were similarly fairly easily absorbed into local gentry circles, assisted by the relative weakness of the county gentry in the first place, and it is instructive, in this connection, to examine the list of guests at the coming of age celebration of the heir to Workington Hall and its estates, Edward Darcy Curwen, in 1885. These fell into three main categories; county, industrialists of eminence, and local minor *bourgeoisie*. The county were chosen without regard to politics, and were headed by Lord and Lady Lonsdale, making a roll-call of much of Cumberland – Brisco, Dykes, Howard, Hasell, Lawson, Senhouse, Spedding, Vane, Wyndham. With them was an admixture of leading industrialists, some of whom were already on their way to acceptance by Walford if not by Burke, like Sir James Bain, and others who were already accepted, like Lindow of Cleator and Ferguson of

15 An Edwardian shooting party at Mirehouse, the modest but charming country home of the Speddings, near Bassenthwaite.

116

Carlisle. Others were in a more indeterminate position, like John Stirling of Fairburn, the chief iron-ore mine operator in Cumberland (who died virtually a millionaire in the new century), and the ironmasters Kirk and Valentine, of Workington. The other guests were local citizenry, for the Curwens, middling great and fairly wealthy landowners, were lords of the manor of Workington, and took a dutiful interest in its civic affairs. The acid test of acceptance of the new *bourgeoisie* was, of course: were reciprocal invitations extended and duly accepted? The answer, in the case of at least a dozen of the most eminent guests, was almost certainly no; but this matter of acceptance and rejection calls for the fullest and most careful analysis, and must be one of the many serious questions raised by this book. A minority, like the Ainsworths, Bains and Lindows, were in process of full acceptance.

Rural county society, if we may judge from the entries in such sources as Burke and Walford, was in fact subject to a great deal of flux, and so strong is the impression of change that one must suspect an element of caprice in the listings of gentle families in Edward Walford's *County Families of the United Kingdom*. The 1868 edition of the latter misses out the Lutwidges of Holmrook, whose commercial fortune had been made a century before.[39] The fact remains that of 100 Cumberland families listed in 1868, by 1902 37 had disappeared, but 61 new ones had been added.[40] Many of these families were not deemed worthy of notice by Sir Bernard Burke in his *Landed Gentry*. In the case of Westmorland (which Sir Bernard also regarded very distantly), out of 55 families listed in 1868, 26 had disappeared 34 years later, but no fewer than 47 new ones had appeared.

We must, then, allowing for the uncertain criteria applied by Walford, allow for a very considerable turnover in both counties. A family, once settled in its substantial or comfortable residence, did not stay in the same place, or even stay in the county. Often its sojourn was short, as elderly moneyed people moved near the Lakes and their issue remained non-existent, or the house passed to relatives or other settlers. Nor must we assume that the settlers were all industrial or commercial *bourgeoisie*; the data given by Walford suggest that many of them were not, or had ceased to be so at least a generation before.

The most satisfying data indicative of the social changes that were taking place are the simple archaeological ones relative to large houses built and occupied, or in some cases abandoned. These do, interestingly enough, support the thesis that the rate of change or growth of residents was greater in Westmorland, with its competing moneyed settlers, than in Cumberland. Nor is this a matter of historical measurement only; it has innumerable subtle and other implications for social life, in that it relates to the ease or otherwise with which the newer settlers could hope to accommodate themselves to the communities in which they settled. Even a table of this kind, based on visible artefacts like houses, creates or involves complexities, in that minor gentry and other social leaders have to be recognised

117

and defined in their periods of occupation, and it can, of course, give no idea how rapidly ownership changed. The minor gentry can be recognised by directory designations like 'Esq.', 'J.P.' or 'C.C.', and the clergy, who were the main social leaders in many Cumbrian parishes, have to be left out, with the observation that vicarage-building or rebuilding was roughly as rapid as that of substantial houses in the same region. Again, the appearance of large houses in many townships was not so much a simple matter of augmentation, as one of replacement or repair — in an impressive list of cases, the former manor houses of numbers of Cumberland and Westmorland townships were lying empty, or, in a common phrase, were, in the mid-century, 'occupied by a farmer'. Cumberland examples occur at Nether Denton, Bowness-on-Solway, Hayton and Newton Arlosh, and, in Westmorland, at Hoff, Hilton, Asby Coatsforth and Asby Winderwath, Smardale, Wharton, Milburn, Ormside, Orton, Hartsop, Sockbridge and Cliburn. Table 5.5 then, is concerned with houses that were, for the most part, newly built or rebuilt in the second half of the century.

Table 5.5 Appearance of large houses in main districts of Cumbria in the second half of the nineteenth century

	Grasmere, Ambleside, Windermere		Kendal, S. Westmor- land & Lune Valley		Penrith, Appleby, Brough & E. Westmor- land		Carlisle and N. Solway Plain		Cockermouth district & W. Cumberland rural areas	
	1851	1905	1851	1905	1851	1905	1847	1901	1847	1901
Main seats	4	4	12	12	6	6	6	6	2	2
Other houses (minor & new gentry, excluding clergy)	17	31	29	55	30	50	20	33	19	30
Disappearance of house names (cases)	–	18	–	8	–	–	–	–	–	–
Cases of new houses (apparent)	–	14	–	26	–	20	–	13	–	11

Note:
The disappearance of house names in the Windermere area is undoubtedly explained, in part, by rebuilding or by conversion to hotel use.

As regards the Westmorland of 1851, it should be stressed that nearly half its substantial houses were within 8 miles of Ambleside, or within 4 miles of Kendal or Kirkby Lonsdale — that is to say, an area covering about a tenth of the county. Nor is this a matter of arid statistics for their own sake; the continuing popularity of such localities meant that the distribution of magistrates was decidedly uneven by the turn of the century, and seventeen of them lived in Ambleside, Windermere or Grasmere in 1905 — more justices than available policemen. The distribution of JPs was clearly much wider in the county of Cumberland. Meanwhile, Table 5.5 cannot pretend to indicate clearly the degrees or types of

16 A comfortable Victorian residence, Fell Foot near Newby Bridge, Windermere. This was the home of a succession of wealthy settlers before its demolition at the turn of the century.

social influence which were exerted by well-to-do people, if only because many of the latter were clustering in suburbs like Stanwix, just across the Eden from Carlisle, or Hensingham above Whitehaven, or the outskirts of Kendal or Workington. Sometimes the countryside itself was becoming settled by influential 'commuters', as in the case of the parish of Papcastle just outside Cockermouth, where a scattering of the substantial citizens of that town were undoubtedly enabled to create a satisfactorily neighboured environment. Social tone and social control are different considerations, however, and the control exerted by the magistracy, over localities as well as those brought before courts, calls for further examination.

In 1847, Cumberland had about 100 magistrates, counting those serving the borough of Carlisle, and, of these, we have to assume that the majority were active members of the bench. There was roughly 1 magistrate to 2000 of its total population, a ratio which had more than halved by 1901, when Cumberland had about 1 magistrate to 850 of population. Westmorland, in approximately the same half-century, was far better served, with roughly 1 : 870 in 1851, and a startling 1 : 400 in 1901. Although this averages out at about one 'leader' for every parish or major township, the magistrates were, as we have seen, concentrated in the more salubrious places.[41] These ratios contrast sharply with those for North Lonsdale, which suffered a desperate shortage of such officers during its period of rapid industrialisation after 1860, and, even in 1901, had a ratio of one magistrate to over 900 persons for the Hundred of North Lonsdale *outside* the borough of Barrow. Barrow had its own borough magistrates, 35 of them by 1909, but the concentration of population in and around the town was so great that the majority of North Lonsdale inhabitants lived there, and it had a ratio of one magistrate to over 1600 persons in the first decade of the new century. (The proportion is stated cautiously, because this figure is derived from the year 1909, when large numbers of magisterial appointments had been made in Barrow, and a figure for 1901 would show an even more sensational disparity.)[42]

Such imbalances undoubtedly arose from the social assumptions of the age. A leisured and wealthy person settling in Westmorland might be regarded as properly eligible for the bench, and be left with very little to do. Even in Furness and Cumberland, the majority of magistrates were members of the gentry or the professions, and the habit of using the services of fairly newly-arisen town councillors for this work, or even established industrialists, was by no means wholly the rule. In Cumberland, now widely industrialised, not more than one-fifth of the magistracy had direct industrial or commercial connections, although such persons were performing, after 1890, magisterial duties in the areas where they carried on business, like James Duffield, the managing executive of Cammells in Workington, or the brewer Thomas Iredale of the same town.

The County Councils, 1889–1914

The formation of County Councils, following the Local Government (County Councils) Act of 1888, is often supposed to have reduced, if not broken, the power of the magistracy. In the case of Cumbria, the enactment certainly did not 'break' the influence of the more influential magistrate landowners, and no fewer than 32 out of 39 committee chairmen of the Cumberland County Council (1889–1914), had experience as magistrates.[43] What the enactment *did* achieve was to bring about the wider participation of the industrial middle class in Cumberland county government, if not markedly in that of Westmorland.

Such involvement, too, was noticeable in Lancashire, where Sir John Hibbert, the first Chairman of the County Council there, who lived in Grange-over-Sands, was an active proponent of grassroots government, and was accompanied in his work by numbers of the new industrial gentry.[44] It should be said, however, that these were not strongly represented in the Hundred of Lonsdale. Meanwhile, the formation of district and parish councils in 1894 led to a new awareness of the potentialities of local government, in the region and nationally, and parish councils in particular were often seen as the plain man's answer to the domination of the squire. Although this soon proved to be an illusion, the earliest campaign for the election of Cumberland county councillors was marked by real excitement, resulting in the election of 37 Liberals, of whom 20 were from the west coast, 9 Liberal Unionists (of whom 2 were from the same area), and 33 Conservatives. There was, then, an industrial middle-class Liberal 'victory' of sorts, although 10 of the Conservatives were also from West Cumberland communities.[45] *The Cumberland Pacquet*[46] argued that the Tories had been defeated in the mining villages by the 'Sharp–McConvey–Parnellite–Primitive Methodist–radical combination troupe'. (McConvey was the leader of the Irish League and Andrew Sharp the leading local labour representative.) Yet, when elective county government commenced its work, one of the most prominent industrialist members, William Fletcher, could comment calmly on 'the absence of party spirit'[47] and it is apparent that the earlier local election brawls were far removed from what went on in the council chamber. It is significant that interest rapidly waned, and the conduct of county affairs soon resulted in uncontested elections. A delicate political balance was only occasionally shaken by serious issues, like that of education in 1902, and the social composition of the Cumberland council reflected a sort of deadlock, with (1889), 22 landowners, 13 yeomen and tenant farmers, 14 in commerce, 14 in mining, 1 in shipping, and 16 professional or retired persons. The then chairman was one of the county's great landowners, Henry Charles Howard of Greystoke, and no fewer than 12 persons in this category, or their heirs-apparent, stood for the County Council before 1914; of these 11 were elected and 5 became chairmen of committees.[48] The key posts remained in much the same hands up to that year, and the composition of the Council remained much the same also, with a slight increase in farmers, a slight decrease in landowners, a fairly stable trading and industrial group, and a marked increase in professional men.[49] Such analyses can give no idea of the personalities who subordinated themselves to the working of the cumbrous and tedious county administrations, and we should here add that some remarkable men played their parts – Francis Grainger, who has already received mention,[50] John Musgrave and William Fletcher, both wealthy middle-class politicians of high skill, and, not least, H. D. Rawnsley, the defender of the Lake District. There was a strong admixture of what would now be called community politicians, with representatives reflecting that kind of interest – like the Carlisle-centred group of J. R. Creighton, Miles McInnes, the Binnings and the Chance family, and William McGowan,[51] William Burnyeat, Alfred Hine, and J. S. Ainsworth representing the western mining district's Liberal interest. Not all industrialists were Liberal, and there was a west-coast brewing and Conservative interest in Col. F. R. Sewell and in Thomas Iredale, who represented Workington.

County Council politics became divorced from the involvements of the man in the street for a simple reason. As the *Whitehaven News* (then William McGowan's newspaper) put it in 1902, regarding the Cumberland council: 'Membership is a tax, both on the time and money of the councillor residing at a distance from Carlisle, so that as the years roll on the position (of councillor) is being gradually left to men of means and leisure.'[52] It may be taken as indicative that the Westmorland County Council was a body of the suggested character (i.e. run by 'men of wealth and leisure') from its commencement, and, out of 56 members, over 30 were identifiable as country gentlemen, while others were the agents of great landowners − Frederick Punchard for the Earl of Bective, William Little for the Earl of Lonsdale − who was himself a member for a few years (1892−5) − and F. M. T. Jones for the Flemings of Rydal.[53] Unlike Cumberland, Westmorland showed no excitement over the elections for the new body, and the *Westmorland Gazette*, a zealous organ of Toryism, saw little sense in contests between gentlemen.[54] There was, in both counties, a frequently direct connection between those who conducted county affairs in Quarter Sessions or Guardians, and the later aldermen and councillors. Westmorland's first chairman, James Cropper of Ellergreen, was described (1892) as having had 26 years' chairmanship of the Kendal Poor Law Union, and several of his colleagues had served in Quarter Sessions over similar periods. Meanwhile, the key position of Chairman of Finance went to substantial landowners in both counties − to G. W. Mounsey-Heysham in Cumberland and W. H. Wakefield in Westmorland. The appointments were appropriate; the families of Mounsey, Heysham and Wakefield had been, at an earlier stage, much concerned with local banking, in this instance the Carlisle City and District Bank, and in the case of the Wakefields, the Kendal Bank.[55] Finance could certainly cross barriers and knit regional relationships.

Control from outside the region

The County Councils, much as they might draw together men of weight from local towns and landed estates, had limited legal and other functions at this stage. The economic power that resided in the control of industrial development was, or could be, of much greater consequence, and this power could be wielded from afar. The Scottish influence upon West Cumberland ironmaking and banking is discussed in Chapter 2.[56] As we have seen, numerous Scottish-financed ironworks went into operation along the Cumbrian coastline, and, in a few instances, their principal capitalists or managers were drawn into local residence and thence into politics. Hence, when the Maryport Haematite Iron and Steel Co. ran into difficulties in 1883, Glasgow investors played a large part in rescuing and refloating it, and one of them, Rudolph Feldtmann, iron merchant and member of the Glasgow pig-iron ring, became sufficiently involved in local affairs to stand as a candidate for the Cumberland County Council in 1889. It was said of him that his firm had brought 'hundreds of thousands of pounds into West Cumberland, spent in ironmaking and therefore going direct into the pockets of the working classes'.[57] The directness could well have been questioned by an ironworker in the thrall of the two-shift system.

These remarks do not imply that Scottish involvement in local politics was extensive; but some industrialists from over the border left their mark, and James Baird, managing director of the re-formed Lonsdale Haematite Iron and Steel Co. of 1883, was a prime mover in forming the West Coast Ironmasters' Association in 1887,[58] and was a Whitehaven Town and Harbour Trustee. The influence of the Bain family in Harrington and, later, Whitehaven, has been noticed, and John Stirling of Fairburn, Muir of Ord, who owned the productive Montreal Mine at Cleator Moor, had a considerable interest in the development of that town and its institutions, whilst John F. Kirkconel, Scottish manager of the ironworks there in mid-Victorian years, played a great part in the running of the Cleator Moor Local Board.[59] In other words, imported technical and managerial staff might contribute more to local government and institutions than did the efforts of weightier capitalists and landowners; sometimes, it is true, representing their employers in that work, but sometimes transcending the watchdog role in the scope and force of their activity. Hence, when Charles Cammell and Co. of Dronfield (near Sheffield) founded the highly successful Derwent Works at Workington in 1882–3, the manager-organiser of the transfer of an entire works from Yorkshire to Cumberland, the self-made James Duffield, stayed in the area to make his mark in local government and good causes.[60] Yet another industrial agent and administrator, John Scurrah Randles of the Moss Bay ironworks, who began to play an important part in that firm in 1881, ended his career as an even more memorable Workington public figure. He was a man of Lincolnshire background, and a minister's son.[61]

As regards the Furness district, the story of the labours and impact of the remarkable H. W. Schneider has been sketched elsewhere,[62] and the impression could easily be given that the key industrial enterprises of the region were in general instigated by initial outsiders or by capitalists making decisions at a distance. Limited liability companies of the larger kind, which often encouraged such remote control, were slow to become rooted in Cumbria, and fewer than 100 have been traced (in the Joint Stock Company Records in the Public Record Office) for the region in the period 1856–77, although there were many more subsequently, thus strengthening somewhat the idea of outside economic influence. But such influence is by no means even a substantial part of the whole truth, and is one of those notions which can be shaped by definition, period and circumstances, in what was in reality a series of most complex economic stages.

123

The leading capitalists of Furness were all originally 'outsiders' in some sense, who became closely identified with their district, not least the influential Seventh Duke of Devonshire, and their activities did not, save for short periods, encourage incomers; their fundamental creation, the Furness Railway, remained an independent entity,[63] although the great firm of Vickers-Maxim solidified the naval shipbuilding interest in Barrow at the end of the century. Incomers, as was noted briefly in Chapter 2, played some part in the Victorian industries of Carlisle and Kendal, but so did indigenous personalities, not least local bankers and woollen manufacturers. Banking, a most interesting case, had moved out of largely local hands by the early twentieth century, as the Bank of Liverpool and (later) Midland interests pressed extensively into the south of the region, although the locally-inspired banks, especially in Cumberland, remained. Meanwhile it is largely true to say that the Scottish influence on Cumberland ironmaking was much weakened by 1900. The great railway companies could exert subtle and not so subtle forms of pressure upon regional development during middle and late Victorian decades. In some fundamental ways, such companies could dispose of more extensive and continued power or influence than any large landowner. The London and North-Western Railway controlled, by 1866, both the main Lancaster–Carlisle line and the rail connection through Keswick to the West Cumberland towns, as well as the linkage to the Furness Railway network; and, moreover, its stranglehold obliged the Midland Railway, another mammoth, to build the costly Settle and Carlisle line[64] as a means of approach to the border city (1871–6). However, Professor Pollard has remarked, writing primarily of West Cumberland, that 'the prosperity of the district was not much affected' by this growing dominance of the LNWR,[65] since that company had all it required in the way of good communications with iron mines, blast furnaces and coke supplies. The north-west corner of Cumberland, meanwhile, became the area of penetration by Scottish railway companies, and this is discussed by Dr Walton in Chapter 8. Elsewhere, the lines of Lakeland carried tourists as well as merchandise.

It was the pressure of railway rates that weighed heavily in the decision of Charles Cammell and Co. to move to Workington,[66] and, as regards lines of communication generally, it has already been seen that the export of iron ore – and its importation – could affect the economic history of the region considerably by influencing the prosperity of ports and railway lines. Where, and in what ways, did such prosperity lead towards political power? The latter seems to have emerged overtly only where a local or a sub-regional line, like the Furness Railway, was connected intimately and crucially with a complex pattern of local industries, and where the railway company wielded more power over them than they did over the company; and where, moreover, the organisation and *ambience* of the railway itself worked towards the loyalty and subjugation of employees, through its regular social observances.[67] A company dinner was apt to rank the chairman and managing director very close to royalty. Otherwise, such a line could stimulate regional or local antagonisms as well as loyalties, and Whitehaven traders were restively aware of their dependence, for some supplies of goods, upon the FR system, and it is highly likely that a press correspondent spoke for a wider business community in 1885: 'The Furness Railway favoured Barrow at the expense of Whitehaven'.[68] A similar theme, again expressing some jealousy of Furness interests, was later pursued by a Millom tradesman.[69] In other areas, railway company influence was either so generalised and remote as to seem beyond striking distance, even where the great companies provoked and irritated, or it was intensely localised, as in the instance of the North British Railway's development of Silloth, or that of the Maryport and Carlisle line's largely benign stimulus to its terminal port, coupled with the creation of a genial and almost familial atmosphere on the part of investors and staff by the avuncular chairman, Sir Wilfrid Lawson. Generally, the Cumberland lines and their chairman and managers did not dominate local economic life as did the companies that have been mentioned. There was no ineluctable rule which ordained that exceptionally well-placed landowners automatically wielded *force majeure* through railway systems, and the latter had to satisfy a complex of business interests to augment their own power. The Furness Railway was unusual in that it controlled an industrial empire.

Leadership in the towns

Cumbrian towns, especially after 1870, did not develop in the same way or at the same tempo. With the exception of Whitehaven, the larger towns tended to have certain leadership-characteristics in common, although the groups which wielded power often had very different historical backgrounds and tended to be composed of differing elements. Carlisle and Kendal had, by the mid-Victorian years, strongly established Whiggish or Liberal town leaderships with a long tradition of political independence; both had fought the Lowther influence in past generations, and both towns had time to build up a stable middle-class and trading element. Cockermouth, a former pocket borough of the Lowthers, had developed its own industrial and trading leadership after the formation of the town's local board in 1864, notwithstanding the manorial influence of Lord Leconfield, and was disfranchised in 1868 and made part of a wider division which included Workington. Thereafter both Cockermouth and Workington developed keen civic sense on the part of their board members and later councillors, not untinctured by a certain parochialism, and, perhaps inevitably, somewhat slow to develop at first. Workington had severe growth problems, especially in the 1870s, as did Barrow, but the latter town suffered from the lack of a strongly established middle-class element, and was virtually ruled by an industrial junta. Whitehaven's leadership became increasingly split between the supporters or nominees of the Earls of Lonsdale, and an independent trading and middle-class element, and it remained largely under the influence of the Lowther representatives until the 1880s, if only because the Earls were the major employers of labour there. The inner Lakeland towns were stimulated by the growing tourist trade to look to their basic amenities, but had to take what they could get in the form of responsible leadership – so that the formidable H. W. Schneider, the Barrow industrialist, dominated the Bowness Local Board for more than a decade after 1870, while the generality of these towns, like Keswick, Ambleside and Windermere, were led by a mixture of local gentry, hoteliers, traders, manufacturers, lawyers, schoolmasters and the like.[70]

As local government developed in complexity, so more such persons came into participation; but it should also be remembered that 'leadership' in such communities did not devolve purely upon board members or councillors, and church, chapel, charity and voluntary and recreational bodies threw up their own activists and officers who contributed to community life. The trade unionist and co-operator also made an increasing impact on local affairs, especially in fairly small industrial communities like Cleator Moor, but also in Barrow and Workington, which had flourishing trades councils by the 1890s, constituting small industrial parliaments in their own right. However, the labour movement as a political force made little impact until the new century, when, as will be noted, it was asserting its influence in Barrow, and to a lesser extent in the other larger towns.

It is instructive to trace the subtle shifts of power within towns. The following examples are indicative only, and the whole field calls for more comparative research, over and above the useful monographs on which these comments are based. To take the case of Kendal first; it, like Barrow, was ruled before the 1870s by a Liberal industrial élite, which the Tory *Westmorland Gazette* dubbed 'the family party'. The members of this 'family', who were in fact often interrelated by kinship, the Wilsons, Whitwells and Somervells, were major employers with a long record of industrial peace within their firms, and it was freely alleged (by the Tories) that these firms positively influenced Liberal voting by town workers. After 1872, this group was challenged by a group of small shopkeepers and small business and professional men, whose main policy plank was that of objection to expensive schemes of town drainage and sewerage.[71] Meanwhile, a number of Kendal's most influential figures tended to withdraw from the front line of town politics as, by degrees, they became assimilated into county society – a process which seems to have been accelerated in 1886 by a move to Liberal Unionism by both James Cropper and W. H. Wakefield.[72] However, the cavillings of a tradesman's council did not prevent the emergence of symbols of civic pride and even caring – public baths and washhouses (1884), a free library (1892), a market hall (1887), and the imposing town hall on Highgate, rebuilt into its present shape in 1893. Much of the town remained

17 Old Police Office Yard, Kendal, representing much of the pattern of the nineteenth-century town. Many of the yards were much more insanitary than this would suggest.

inbuilt and seamy behind the attractive main thoroughfares, and there were evil spots like Fellside, but change was in the air.

Much the same was happening in Carlisle. That town, too, had long had a traditionalist Whig leadership, and it remained, on the whole, Liberal in temper, with the important qualification that the Whiggism or Liberalism rested on deference, of a kind, to leading employers like the Dixons, Fergusons and Chances. But the Dixons had faded from the scene by closing decades of the century,[73] through financial loss[74] rather than through translation to county society, while the Fergusons carried on their influence into the new century, R. S. Ferguson and his son Spencer adding to local Tory weight.[75] The town council itself consisted (1895) of a small group of the established notables, including W. I. R. Crowder, J. R. Creighton and R. S. Ferguson and of a mass of small tradesmen and businessmen.[76] Rates in Carlisle were low, and the shopocracy remained determined to keep them so, until, in the 1890s, their resistance began to weaken — the town had already acquired a fine new market hall (1889), public baths (1884) and a fine library, museum and school of science at Tullie House (1893). These, as in Kendal, were significant but superficial embellishments, and when a real onslaught upon property appeared, in the civic interest, there was more resistance — the Lowther Street Improvement scheme (1895–6) led to a counter-attack by a group of tradesmen, mostly local Liberals, unsuccessful in the event.[77] The *Carlisle Journal* delivered a lecture very much in the newer spirit of the time:[78] 'They fancy that this policy tells with the electors. We think that they are grievously mistaken. Everybody knows that there is a false wasteful economy as well as of rash and extravagant expenditure.'

The provision of basic services, manifestations of so-called gas-and-water socialism, had long been established in most Cumbrian towns, as in others in England, by the end of the century. This was so not only in a major town like Carlisle, but was an especially noticeable factor in Workington, which had otherwise laboured under two inhibiting influences, its position as an old market centre, and an intense preoccupation with the harbour and its trade. Maryport and Whitehaven had this preoccupation in an even greater degree, and much mental energy that might have gone on town improvement was for long diverted into this primary concern. But Workington, stimulated by the iron industry, found itself growing ahead of the others in the 1870s, and was described by the *West Cumberland Times* (1875) as possessing 'the reputation of being the richest town of its size in the kingdom'.[79] Although it suffered heavily from trade fluctuations thereafter, and although its water supplies remained inadequate to the end of the century, it developed a strong business community and a marked civic sense, and was especially to the fore in the promotion of a public gas enterprise, having made a purchase of the local gas company as early as 1847.[80] It is true that the earlier gas supplies were said to be of a kind that prompted the 'use of candles and lamps',[81] this in 1872, but the town was well set on the route of civic trading by 1889, and the Gas Committee was selling gas cookers for domestic use (against the expected attacks of tradesmen on 'monopoly').[82] There was a great drive for street improvement after the town had acquired its charter of incorporation in 1887. However, the old Local Board had been somewhat dominated by H. F. Curwen, the lord of the manor, and the later much more contentious and lively meetings, fully reported in the press, indicate the large sense of public participation which sprang up in Workington. But, as a town which was strongly dependent upon iron and steel manufacture, it necessarily experienced sharp and visible social divisions (which enabled it to play a major part in the return of the extreme radical Sir Wilfrid Lawson to parliament), and the inner depths of Workington's social life remain to be explored.

Barrow, too, was a place of rulers and ruled in frequent confrontation, with few middling-group social graduations to act as buffer elements. Nevertheless, trading and business groups duly appeared, to give their services in a town council which became noticeably less servile to the Cavendish followers and 'Ramsdenites', as the old-generation councillors of the 1867 incorporation died off.[83] The town itself, meanwhile, was enabled to plan its streets (largely through the Duke of Devonshire's landownership, if not his guidance) in an especially spacious manner paralleled mainly by the north Cumberland resort of Silloth, and the Town Council systematically followed this generous spacing,[84] just as it caused a Town Hall of something approaching splendour (1887) to appear. The public library[85] was jealousy watched by Barrow councillors whose minds were as narrow as their streets were broad, and who debated whether the young might lay hands on books by Tim Bobbin, or dealing with evolution or surgery.[86] But, despite allegations of high rents, the town itself was well built and drained, and, by late Victorian and Edwardian standards, healthy.[87] Workington, by contrast, had less easily available building land, and its working-class terraces grew without large-scale planning, the New Yard area early creating problems. Carlisle, as we have seen, was fortunate in that it could develop the Denton Holme area west of the old city walls.[88]

Barrow and Whitehaven provide striking but contrasting examples of great landowner influence, exerted both positively and negatively. The seventh Duke of Devonshire, who was a leading figure in several dominant Furness industrial enterprises as well as a major landowner in Barrow itself, made little or no attempt to interfere with the town's local government beyond nominating its charter councillors in 1867.[89] Later, when the town's main industries were in increasingly desperate straits in the late 1870s and 1880s, the Duke lost great sums of money keeping them in operation,[90] and there can be no doubt about his sense of duty, and of obligation to those who were employed there. On the other hand, and in line with the conscientious Anglicanism of the Duke and his followers, much more money was expended on churches than on the care of the sick or injured, but this was one of the penalties of paternalism; a somewhat more open community, like Workington, could excel itself in campaigning for a hospital.[91]

Whitehaven had a long history of domination by the Lowthers, Earls of Lonsdale, and its story from 1859 to the close of the century is one of struggle to limit this influence on the part of the town's merchants, shipbuilders and tradesmen. The struggle was not merely against Lonsdale landownership, but against the inertia of tradition, in which paternalism and authoritarianism were intermixed. The Lowthers were direct employers of part of the Whitehaven population (in their coalmines), and were house-owners and political leaders or pressurisers at the same time, with a mansion in the town itself. In this instance, too, there is no parallel with Barrow, which was rarely visited by the Duke of Devonshire from Holker Hall. In Whitehaven there was a visible symbol of domination in the Lowther mansion, playing an important part even when it was unoccupied by the Earl, and, moreover, the Lowthers had had considerable control over the Whitehaven Town and Harbour Trustees since 1708, with direct nomination of 7 members out of 21 and marked influence over the remainder. This last was maintained until the 1850s and later: 'I do not like filling up the whole fourteen', remarked the Second Earl of Lonsdale to his private diary (1853).[92] But in 1859 a Town Bill placed greater control in the hands of elected trustees, by reducing the numbers of those nominated by the lord of the manor and instituting annual elections, and there had for some time been a conflict between two groups in the town, known as the Castle and the Town Parties.[93] After a long and fluctuating contest, in the course of which the Town Party enjoyed some incidental victories, but during which it was apparently much inhibited by the tendency of the colliers to support the Lowthers, the conflict was largely resolved by the appearance of an independent spirit on the part of organised Whitehaven labour in the 1880s, but also through the skill and resource of the rich and powerful solicitor John Musgrave, and Augustus Helder, the town's later M.P.[94] Musgrave led the Trustees stage by stage towards the incorporation of Whitehaven (1894), which had the effect of separating the administration of the town and harbour. By this time (1888) the operation of the Lowther-owned collieries had been leased to James Bain and Co., and any direct paternalism on the part of the Lowthers had less chance to show itself – the more so because Hugh Lowther, the 'Yellow' Earl, who came to the title in 1882, at first manifested little interest in the town and locality, although he became its first mayor in 1894–5.[95] By a striking paradox, his sporting and womanising exploits earned him more hero-worship than had been reaped by any of his predecessors,[96] this in spite of the Yellow Earl's initial lack of interest in the working of the collieries which helped to support his hunting activities with the Cottesmore.

Whitehaven's struggle for independence from the Castle was one which cut across party, but was also one in which autonomous middle-class elements played a considerable role – Musgrave, for example, was a local railway promoter as well as a country gentleman of sorts. Such powerful independent figures were lacking in Barrow, and were relatively few in Workington, and in both towns there was heavy emphasis on employers or employers' representatives. Shifts of power were only gradual in the Cumbrian towns, and their working out must be, in the future, a subject for the most careful analysis.

However, the word 'power' must be used with the most careful qualification in these analyses. Outright power struggles of any kind occurred only intermittently among the middle-class and property-owning groups, and the most naked conflicts occurred between the employers and the employed of the major industries of Cumberland, a subject discussed briefly in the next section. For the rest, the local governmental transformations of late nineteenth century Cumbria brought great numbers of minor property-owners into *participation* in decision-making of all kinds. This was not an unmixed blessing, for the tradesmen who played such a large part in vestries, local boards, and, in 1894, the urban district councils, were hardly dynamic leaders or improvers, and this was almost certainly the case in a town like Penrith. The fact remains that a small local industrialist like William Philipson, of the Briery bobbin mill, Keswick, could become a magistrate in that town by the turn of the century,[97] something which would have been impossible fifty years earlier, and scores of his fellows in other localities gained experience as Guardians, school board members, members of school attendance committees, rural district councils and parish councils. Generally speaking, wage-workers of any kind were almost totally absent from these bodies, which must have seemed to represent an alien culture, and the working-man's own culture – represented by co-operative and friendly societies, pigeon clubs, Primitive Methodist or Catholic congregations and the football teams of industrial towns and villages – is surveyed in Chapters 6 and 7. Any subtle shifts of influence in local government and affairs were often brought about by accidental or geographical factors; hence, a rural district council like that of Appleby was principally run by farmers and small landowners, whilst, by contrast, the RDC for Penrith was more noticeably endowed with major gentry or great landowners (like the Howards), and the similar bodies in southern and mid-Westmorland had more than their share of gentry settlers, as we should expect from localities which had such a heavy admixture of new magistrates. These bodies, lacking much initiative or originality of any kind, played their respective parts in administering a society which was becoming both more complex and more aware of certain needs and deficiencies; but the councils themselves had little dynamic, even in the towns, and local electoral politics, in district councils as well as county councils, were often at a low ebb when the new century came. Contentious issues seemed few, and only the 1902 Education Act readily fed the flames of controversy.

The working man's challenge

Before 1900, the working man had little or no direct political representation in Cumbria, with one or two salient exceptions; the region's most prominent trade unionist, Andrew Sharp, was a member of the Cumberland County Council, for example. Organised labour made little political impact until the new century, when the movement in Barrow left a record which provides material for an interesting case study. In the years immediately following 1900, the electoral politics of that town were marked by distinct apathy and uncontested elections, 'politics having been unknown in the Council',[98] and the candidatures themselves were 'lifeless efforts'. By 1909, however, it was noted that 'the Labour Party have sought, legitimately, for a larger representation of their class in the Council Chamber, and, as a consequence, the pulse of the electorate has been quickened . . . such is bound to be for the ultimate well-being of the town itself'.[99] In 1904–8, nearly every Barrow ward saw a contested election, a contrast with previous years, and in 1906 it was noticed that this was attributable to 'the efforts of the Labour Party'.[100] The era of the unchallenged rule of the businessman and the shopkeeper was at an end, and it will be proper, therefore, to conclude this chapter with a short section on the labour movement of the region's main towns. Before this, however, the trade unions and trades councils had laid the foundations of the political movement of the new century, and it will be well, then, also to examine the substantial roots from which the new tree sprang.

It is tempting to trace the habit of independent working-class expression far back to the regional Chartist movement, and assiduous research will probably show that there were personal ties and connections between some local leaders of the 1840s and those of the 1870s. Occasionally there are signs, at a superficial level, that such connections did indeed exist, and the chairman of a demonstration of miners at Ellenborough Moor in 1872, John Bell, used the doubtless significant turn of phrase 'let us try moral force'.[101] For the rest, the real work of building up a solidly structured labour movement commenced in coalmine and ironworks, and Andrew Sharp, the most memorable of Victorian trade unionists in Cumbria, began life in a local pit, 'thinking it a great blessing if he saw the sun on Sunday'.[102] However, radical sentiments are not an automatic product of coalmining and its milieu, as the case of Whitehaven shows, and, as is noted in Chapter 1 above,[103] the Chartist movement had manifested only a brief flickering in Whitehaven, but was more strongly developed in weaving or craft centres like Cockermouth, Carlisle, Kendal and even Wigton. What happened subsequently appears to have had little connection with the political demands of distressed weavers, but a great deal to do with the complex chemistry of industrial conditions in West Cumberland in the boom period of 1872–3, which brought an explosion of strikes fired by a potent mixture of overwork, accumulated wage demands, and rapid inflation of prices. This period saw the formation of two distinct coalmining unions in the area – a branch of Alexander MacDonald's National Association of Miners, based on the Aspatria district, and a West Cumberland organisation of the rival Amalgamated Association of Miners, which ceased to exist locally after 1875.[104] The former body, usually known as the West Cumberland Miners' Association (July, 1872) was supported by fellow-miners in South Durham and Yorkshire, and Andrew Sharp was already its full-time agent by 1875,[105] when it could count 1500 members out of 5000 miners in the coalfield. Sharp's own subsequent career shows that a body like this ultimately and inevitably sought political expression.

The early years of the Association were almost disastrous, as the industry faced slump conditions, Cumberland coal being in competition with coal from Scotland. Hence the union had to face repeated demands for wage reductions, and Sharp himself had much trouble with dissident lodges and angry critics, which elements were prone to resent the periodically unfavourable results of sliding scale agreements.[106] In 1880 the membership had shrunk to 1000,[107] and it will be seen that Sharp's struggles to support lodges in individual disputes were often fruitless. However, there was a period of recovery at the end of the century, and membership rose to 3259 in 1890 and 6326 twenty years later, rather more than half of all the miners employed in the Cumberland coalfield.[108]

Two points here require emphasis. First of all, the masters were themselves organised into the Cumberland Coal Owners' Association; and, secondly, the Whitehaven miners, for long in thrall to the Lowthers, kept aloof from the union until the middle and late 1880s. R. W. Moore reported in 1889 that 'the Miners' Union which was almost defunct at the time of the transfer of the collieries (in Whitehaven) has now become very strong. Nearly all the hands, both above and below ground are members of it'.[109]

The period 1889–94 was crucial in the history of Cumbrian labour. Nationally, the first of these years saw the growth of a new awareness as a result of the Great Dock Strike and the formation of general labour unions. In Cumbria, the blastfurnacemen were making strenuous attempts to organise local groups in Millom, Askam and Ulverston, and at other points in the west of the region, with help from the Blastfurnacemen's Association based on Middlesbrough; and the Askam Ironworks management, backed by its related firm in Millom, attempted a boycott of union members on the ground that unionism was a destructive importation by Cleveland competitors.[110] The ironworkers of the coastal towns were already embittered by the grinding two-shift system, experiments with the more humane triple-shift arrangement having already shown an alternative to be possible, and the iron towns of Millom and Askam found themselves plunged into a four-month strike during the early part of 1889. During this time, the strikers were sustained and regularly visited by the West Cumberland secretary of the Association, Patrick Walls, who supported his national secretary, Snow, in the negotiations[111] – and Walls, too, was to become one of the most notable labour leaders in the region. The strikers were unable to hold out indefinitely, under police pressure and the threat of evictions, and they had to leave the district as non-union men came in, but the general point had been made. The two-shift system was abandoned within the next few years (and in principle, in the following year, 1890),[112] and, by then, Walls was District Secretary of the Association for Cumberland and Lancashire, and he later turned to political organisation for labour.

The iron-ore miners were not solidly organised until the turn of the century, and this aspect of regional trade union history serves to point the moral that union organisation was often transient, and that it frequently reflected the temporary efforts of scores of unknown men to form local branches or associations. There were repeated attempts to achieve such ends, taking place notably in Furness in the 1860s and 1870s, but marked especially by the formation of the Dalton and District United Workmen's Association in 1882. This last body appears to have been helped by the Cumberland Miners' Association.[113] Andrew Sharp was prominent in carrying the message to Dalton,[114] and four years later he was still striving to unite the iron miners of Cleator Moor, Egremont and Dalton,[115] and was telling the local haematite iron miners that 'they had no freedom, and were even worse (off) than the dock labourers in London' – an interesting comment on the atmosphere of late 1889.[116] It is clear from his comments that the Dalton Association was then well established,[117] and this likelihood is confirmed by the appearance of John Myers, the Dalton Secretary, in West Cumberland in 1890. The latter explained that the Dalton body was a federated group within the Cumberland Miners' Association, and contrasted 'the condition of the iron miners with that of the colliers'.[118] The type of appeal used is interesting, and we must infer that Sharp had been successful in achieving a measure of unification on the west coast,[119] if not in creating an effective single miners' union in both coal and iron.

By the turn of the century, numbers of iron-miners were indeed solidly organised alongside the colliers, and 2860 of the former, mainly from the Cleator, Egremont and Frizington areas, were led by James Flynn working in association with Sharp and the coalminers.[120] However, this was barely half the number of iron-miners in the coastal districts as shown in the Census of 1901, and it appears that Flynn was in process of forming a distinct body, the National Iron Ore Miners' Association, and by 1910 there were two separate iron-mining unions in the area – Flynn's organisation and another one, the Cumberland Iron Ore Miners' and Kindred Trades Association, led by the dynamic T. Gavan Duffy, who had entered the district about 1907. The latter organisation was based on Moor Row, and was more militant than Flynn's body, becoming identified with the rising Labour Party in its own area.[121] Flynn pressed for workers' representation on more socially received bodies; 'good work could be done on local boards', he said, 'in seeing that the working men got fair play, and on the Boards of Guardians'.[122] Flynn had in fact entered the County Council in 1898, as a Liberal, and, from a comfortable villa in Hensingham, continued to represent Cleator (South) until the outbreak of war.[123] In company with Sharp, he succeeded in making the image of trade unionism – of the kind based on coaldust and skin-dyeing haematite – respectable in county administrative circles, and his achievement was to make the lowly haematite miners into beings to be recognised organisationally by the employers. As he boasted in 1902, 'today every employer is compelled to recognise our association'.[124] The two leaders followed a now familiar form of evolution into establishment status, and it was not difficult for Duffy to gain a large following by pursuing a more militant line, to the extent that Flynn's organisation was, by 1914, virtually supplanted as a negotiating force in the ironfield.[125]

The history of the iron-ore miners, like the history of their industry, has not been satisfactorily set down at the time of writing, and these few remarks can provide little substitute for the detailed survey that is needed. It is often said, meanwhile, that the study of local history is in part a search for the uniqueness of communities and situations. While iron-mining was not unique to Cumberland and Furness, its social developments have some striking characteristics, and perhaps the most remarkable achievement of the ironfield towns and villages of the region was that of producing a consumer co-operative movement unparalleled in the small-town *milieux* of northern England. Again, a superficial view might assume some connection with the Owenite societies set up by idealistic weavers in Kendal or Carlisle,[126] or, perhaps more pertinently, with the famous farming co-operative set up at Blennerhassett in West Cumberland (1861–6) by William Lawson of Brayton, the brother of the Sir Wilfrid who appears in this chapter.[127] It is true that the balance sheet of the Cleator Moor Co-operative Society (1857) was held up by Lawson as an example to be followed in the Solway Plain villages,[128] but the Cleator Moor, Millom and Dalton societies, all strikingly successful in their respective ways, were based on iron-miners' communities, and were commenced by such workers.[129] Consumer co-operation is briefly examined in Chapter 7, as an aspect of regional and community culture, and so cannot be dealt with fully in a chapter concerned with types of power, organisation and leadership. However, the co-operative movement was also associated, sometimes vaguely, with a wider labour movement, and so it has its place here. And, whilst the membership figures and exploits of the Cleator Moor society make memorable reading to the student of co-operation (it had well over a dozen late Victorian branches, as a small-town and district society, and was one of the largest in the north of England at that time), a more detached view of its strength in terms of social influence gives a less flattering picture. When, in 1885, the President of the Cleator Moor Society, Edward Pritchard, 'pitman', stood for election to the local board of that town, he was the only candidate not to be elected out of five standing, while at the top of the poll were a local mines manager, and the manager of a nearby colliery.[130] Pritchard himself was a member of a firmly entrenched 'establishment' in his own society, one which ran into a stormy period some four years later,[131] and working-class leaders of this kind often came to hang on to institutional office for its own sake. The Cleator Moor and other societies had far too much of a bent for practical operation to have much time for social idealism. Meanwhile, an overwhelmingly working-class community could still put employers at the head of its affairs.

In other industrial localities, the labour movement was more effective. Patrick Walls, whose office was in Workington, had been moving towards the formation of a Cumberland Labour Electoral Association during 1891, and early in the following year its manifesto was published in *The Carlisle Journal*.[132] Both Walls and Alfred Baines were elected to the Workington Town Council in the November of the same year, and Baines, who promoted the Labour Club in the town, and acted as its full-time secretary, was made a local alderman by the turn of the century. Walls had hoped to form a 'non-political' association (i.e. one not anchored to the Liberal Party), and in 1892 Labour candidates for the County Council were put up, all unsuccessfully, for Aspatria (where 49 per cent of the votes were won), Brigham, Cleator, Egremont, Moresby and Workington. In 1901, however, Walls himself was elected to the County Council for the Seaton division,[133] there to join Andrew Sharp, who was, by that time, representing Workington Rural District Division. It is also clear that these men had their own special 'constituencies', and Walls became, about this time, general secretary of the National Federation of Blastfurnacemen, which (1904) had an office in Workington, with 6246 members.[134] Of this number, 2109 furnacemen were working in Cumberland and Furness (1902), and it is clear that Walls and his colleagues had succeeded in unionising a very large number of their Cumbrian fellows. Andrew Sharp reigned over a considerably greater body of coalminers, 5641 in 1902, organised in six groups of lodges, of which, strikingly enough, Whitehaven was by that time the strongest, with 1743 district members in three lodges.[135] Not only this; a massive miners' demonstration, with a dozen brass bands, marched through that long-suffering town in the July of 1902, its echoes seeming to lay the ghosts of the past, as Robert Smillie made ready to address the multitude.[136] In fact, the laying was less easy than might appear, and Whitehaven workmen had little success in electing Labour candidates to their council until 1904, when a miners' agent and socialist, John Hanlon, was successful as a representative of the Newtown Ward,[137] where the Earls of Lonsdales miners' houses were to be found. This, perhaps, was the true end of that particular chapter, although the town's Independent Labour Party afterwards registered an effect, even promoting the election of a Lib–Lab MP, Richardson.[138]

Barrow was to attain a much more spectacular success in the 1906 general election, with the victory of the region's first Labour member of parliament, Charles Duncan. Yet this was the culmination of years of effort; the year 1892 brought the formation of the Independent Labour Party in Barrow,[139] which was in turn built upon a long-established and virile trade union movement, partially united through a trades council formed in 1871.[140] This body had about 600 affiliated members in 1883, but no fewer than 2873 subscribing members, representing 21 affiliated union branches, in 1896.[141] This rapid growth in membership, which had its roots in the general labour unions, coincided with more labour-inspired activity at the council polls in the early 1890s – commencing with a victory in Hindpool Ward in 1892. However, when Pete Curran, of the Gasworkers' and General Labourers' Union, stood for Barrow in the parliamentary election of 1895, he gained scarcely 7 per cent of the votes cast, a clear indication of the specialised or minority nature of trades unionism at that instant, or of its lack of connection with clearly formulated left-wing opinion. Nevertheless, Barrow, like other regional towns, was experiencing an intellectual ferment of sorts during the 1890s (an ILP branch had appeared, too, in Carlisle[142]), and, after repeated visits by notables like Hardie, Blatchford, Tillett and Mann, the trades council and the ILP branch together formed a Labour Representative Committee (1898), and five years later the latter appointed a fulltime official and secretary, Arthur Peters.[143] The upswing of the Labour vote at this time was both a national and a local phenomenon, and the Taff Vale decision of 1901 encouraged trade unionists to vote for Labour candidates. Barrow, in any case, was a relatively class-conscious town, and was well-organised, and Duncan's victory, with over 60 per cent of the votes cast, probably represented an amalgamation of minority socialist opinion and the existing working-class Liberal vote. The significant event locally was the formation of a branch of the newly-fledged Labour Party, which had, by 1908, drafted a 'Municipal Programme Manifesto', to project the views of local socialists including the small group on the Town Council. The party had, as we have seen, revitalised local election contests.

Even in Barrow, the employer and the tradesman were still in control in 1914, and it would be mere pretence to suggest that the labour movement was more than a challenge, armed with the teeth of the occasional effective strike and the power to campaign in working-class districts of a few towns. Its detailed development is well worth a study in depth, and its significance lies in the ever-deepening contrast between town and country *mores* and attitudes, but also in the variations of its rate of development as between towns, and in the subtler nuances of the character of the movements themselves. After a lapse in 1906, the regional countryside moved towards the Conservative stance that it has since taken, and the industrial towns, likewise, developed the more or less permanent state of varying but marked allegiance to Labour that has been a feature of the twentieth century. Yet how deep do political attitudes, based on reason rather than habit, in fact go? There are plenty of problems to engage the researcher into political stances at the regional level.

137

The training of the human being: formal institutions, 1830–1914

In Chapter 5 an attempt was made to examine the parts played by leading personalities, individually and in groups, in influencing or even coercing their fellows. The great majority of Cumbrians, who were sometimes thus influenced, were not of course inert or passive; they, too, often had deep-seated social and political attitudes, and they, too, took critical decisions which sometimes affected their entire lives and those of their families. Mostly, however, they received orders, and less often gave them, except to their wives and children. To use a phrase common in that age, they 'knew their place' in society, and in turn recognised the positions of persons who were considered superior to themselves. Such attitudes, whether genuinely deferential or not – and the nineteenth century nurtured increasing numbers of critical-minded people – were of course deeply instilled into the young, not only by informal means in the family or other circle, but through formal institutions like schools and religious bodies. This chapter is concerned with such institutions.

Formal if basic education was not only a significant force in Cumbrian society; it was evidently given a high valuation by large numbers of people who made up that society, and was provided more extensively than in most other parts of England. The claim relative to this high valuation must rest upon the total numbers of people, studied comparatively at successive stages, who could sign marriage registers. It will be clear enough that in any individual case the ability to form certain letters may simply disguise virtual illiteracy. In very large groups, however, consistent trends appear, district by district and county by county, and it is evident that these are not statistically meaningless, even though they may well over-estimate by 5 or 10 per cent the numbers of people who were genuinely literate. As was observed in Chapter 1 (see Table 1.1), Cumberland and Westmorland stood high in the county lists of persons who could sign the registers (1839–45), and the two counties maintained significantly high positions during the century. To put it another way, their numbers of analphabetics, or illiterates, declined, and did so with striking steadiness in the rural areas. This in turn points to a deeper reality, an extensive and effective provision of schools and teachers *pro rata* of the youthful population over a long period. We must therefore examine any evidence which appears to have bearing on the case.

As we shall see, there is no doubt whatsoever that both schools and teachers were relatively numerous in both counties, even though we know little enough about the quality of the education provided; indeed, there is much room for research in this field. The regional Anglican church, which of course had a deep interest in education as a means of extending its influence, seems also to have been subjected to long-term popular pressures which came from outside its normal spheres of operation, and to internal economic pressures represented by the neediness or even poverty of its own clergy. It is likely that the popular interest in schooling had a very utilitarian and materialistic foundation indeed. In remote, poor or pastoral areas, which do not offer easy avenues to employment for younger sons, but which are within reach of economically more developed regions, a premium is placed upon any form of education which appears to offer a means of escape or advancement. Much of the educational history of Scotland can be interpreted, however impressionistically, within these terms of reference; and Cumbria lay upon the border of that country and was, conceivably, subject to similar influences. As regards pressures within the local Anglican church, which provided many of the schoolmasters of parish schools, there can be no possible doubt that these teaching clergymen were ill-paid. In 1835, the average Anglican stipend in England and Wales was £285, but in the Diocese of Carlisle it was a mere £175.[1] Not surprisingly, many of the Lakeland clergy were pluralists, responsible for several parishes covering large districts, and were accordingly obliged to employ curates who were paid very meagre sums indeed. Both incumbents and curates were often forced to teach school to augment their incomes. Nor did the situation alter during the greater part of the century, and in 1872 the newly inducted Bishop of Carlisle, Harvey Goodwin, was to hear that there were still fell parishes which had no resident clergy 'because of the smallness of the stipends'. Nor is it surprising that the Anglican church attendances (1851) in Cumberland and, less seriously in Westmorland were among the poorest in England when taken as percentages of county populations; parishes were large and churches difficult to reach[2]

The internal economy of the church was not the only factor with an immediate bearing upon educational provision at any one period, since many regional schools were of the endowed or of the private variety, some offering grammar school training and others including commercial subjects like accounting. There are few reliable sources of information on the private academies which multiplied in the towns. On the other hand, we should not under-rate the socialising effect of the village school. Hence Robert Anderson, the Cumbrian folk-poet, ended his school career at 10 years of age, but his editor, Sanderson, implied that by that age a good foundation could be laid, and most Cumberland peasants could, *c.* 1820, 'read, write and cast accounts', although this editor also stressed that they were 'good *Bible scholars*'.[3] It is reasonable to conclude that the church influence was pervasive but not imposed; it met a demand, and filled a vacuum through the work of its curates, and the region could, moreover, provide a more advanced education for the sons of farmers and yeomen through its network of local grammar schools,[4] which were partially controlled by men of that type. Where middle-class and trading elements burgeoned, or where farmers sought to give their daughters refined accomplishments and manners, private schools accordingly tried to meet more specialised demands, usually in the main country towns, with money-making in mind.[5] This, however, is what one would expect, and the town 'academies', reacting to market forces, do not in themselves help us to explain the apparent high literacy of the region. The towns also provided Schools of Industry, as in Kendal, Carlisle, Cockermouth and Workington in the earlier nineteenth century,[6] whilst the Census of Education performed during the 1851 Census enumeration shows a fairly wide distribution of Sunday Schools in the region, and these are possibly of more weight in helping to explain the extensiveness of basic literacy before the establishment of school boards. But the force of this contributory factor is difficult to assess.

When Cumbria's apparent educational performance is considered, we must bear in mind that its schools worked in a predominantly rural setting, and school provision in rural areas at the end of the 1850s was almost invariably superior to that of the industrialising counties: it is worth noticing, for example, that Westmorland was one of the three English counties with the highest proportion of public week-day scholars to total population (*c* 1858), and in this form of achievement it was accompanied by the agriculturally dissimilar counties of Wiltshire and Oxfordshire.[7] Otherwise, it might very well be concluded that children in a pastoral district, with fewer field tasks to perform, would in any case be more likely to be sent to school, but, as our brief study of regional agriculture indicates (Chapter 3), much arable farming was being pursued in the Lake Counties until the 1860s or later, and child field-gangs were certainly used in our area in that decade.[8] Our point here must be that rural social organisation and *attitudes* had a great deal to do with the nature of local education, but forms of farm work might have far less to do with the case. Against this, the swing to pastoral farming within Cumbria after the 1860s may have helped rural education, but the argument here would rest on decidedly shaky foundations, for the local farmer came to rely even more on the labour of his sons and daughters – and we find the *Agricultural Gazette* of 24 November 1879 claiming that Furness farmers in remoter situations were keeping their boys from school for haymaking and grain harvests. This, however, became atypical, as some further evidence will show, and our case must be that general attitudes and traditions transcended more specific economic changes and requirements.

The ratio of Westmorland schoolteachers to those individuals denominated 'scholars' in the 1851 census, and again in that of 1871, was 1 : 29. These figures, although the roughest of indicators in any precise statistical sense, suggest an extraordinarily generous provision which cannot take into account the part-time work performed by clergy, Sunday school volunteers or even parents. The corresponding Cumberland ratios were 1 :33 and 1 : 36, although the day school proportion of teachers to scholars (as calculated from the 1851 Census breakdown of types of school[9]), was 1 : 26 in the latter county, again a generous ratio. As might be expected from the Census data, then, the rural districts were the most literate or the least analphabetic, and, as is shown in Table 6.1, Longtown, Penrith and the East Ward of Westmorland registration districts, followed by Wigton and the West Ward of Westmorland, had the most striking records in the middle years of the century. Any 'explanations', for what they are worth, and as far as they can be inferred from the 1851 school statistics,[10] vary from district to district; hence, Longtown, a thinly populated border area with a strong endowed school tradition, had nearly half its day scholars in schools of this kind. Here we have one aspect of a kaleidoscope of educational traditions, one which suggests a strong connection with the Scottish type of educational aspiration, and a lack of direct relevance to Anglican influence as such. The endowed school influence, too, was strong in Penrith district, but additional background denominational support came largely from the Methodists of the middle Eden Valley rather than from the Anglicans. In the Wigton district, on the other hand, the Anglican day school and Sunday school influence was far more noticeable, whilst the two Westmorland wards, East and West, combined a heavy saturation of endowed and grammar schools with a strong population of Anglican Sunday scholars. We must here lay stress once more on two points; the Anglican educationalists did not share the apparently utilitarian attitude to schooling of many of their parishioners, which in turn caused the latter to make use of whatever educational or religious institution offered itself. As Canon J. S. Simpson of Kirkby Stephen put it in 1866:[11] 'Children's education is a great deal more than mere reading, writing and casting of accounts. I think the formation of character is a great thing.'

A more tangible achievement in both Cumberland and Westmorland was, as we have noted, that of leading the English counties in apparent literacy during much of the last century, and Westmorland and some rural parts of Cumberland were well in the van long after civil registration had taken effect. Eventually, by 1890, little Westmorland had overtaken even the metropolis in reducing its ostensible illiterates almost to vanishing point. But the picture is not one of continuous, Whiggish regional progress. There are signs that industrialisation halted the onward march in some coastal districts, although it cannot be claimed that urbanism as such did so. Just as London could exhibit remarkably high levels

141

of letter skills, so towns like Kendal and Carlisle, despite many incidental difficulties of school organisation, were able to achieve some improvements.

In Table 6.1, the registration districts of Cumberland and Westmorland are combined together and also grouped in terms of type of economico-social influence, to demonstrate the alphabetism of each in percentages of marriage signatures.[12]

Table 6.1 Alphabetism in Cumberland and Westmorland, 1855–9 and 1872–6

Primarily rural districts	1855–9 Marriages	% signing		1872–6 Marriages	% signing	
		Males	Females		Males	Females
Longtown	180	93·4	81·2	216	94·9	89·1
Penrith	676	92·1	72·9	815	92·1	79·9
Westmorland East	446	91·5	84·1	529	91·7	88·5
Wigton	635	89·3	78·5	771	92·1	86·3
Westmorland West	215	83·8	80·5	240	93·8	92·5
Total/mean	2152	90·4	80·5	2571	92·4	89·2
Affected by rural mining						
Alston	145	78·7	44·8	179	91·6	79·3
Brampton	242	88·9	73·6	341	88·9	73·6
Bootle	206	82·6	79·2	391	83·4	78·9
Total/mean	593	84·2	68·5	911	89·4	82·3
Urban centres affected by light industry						
Kendal	1250	82·4	76·6	1423	90·7	87·4
Carlisle	1376	87·0	65·0	2098	90·1	74·7
Total/mean	2626	84·8	70·7	3521	90·4	79·9
Districts affected by coal and iron manufacture						
Whitehaven	446	79·6	74·1	2498	76·7	68·2
Cockermouth	1329	78·7	67·7	2086	83·8	74·4
Total/mean	1775	78·9	71·9	4584	79·9	71·0
England (means)		72·0	60·9		82·4	75·7

It should be stressed that the very considerable educational development suggested by this table covers a period before the Education Act of 1870 had had any time to take effect. Indeed, the rural localities seem to have reached a plateau of achievement as regards male letter-skills, and the following twenty years (to the 1890s) saw massive regional improvement in the 'alphabetism' of girls or brides. The generally high standards of the region were of course known, and it was remarked of the Lake Counties, in 1868, that 'the proportion of educated adults in the rural districts is probably greater than in any county of England, although the amount of education may be but moderate'. Whether the butter of education was thinly spread or not, these data show conclusively that distinct gains were being made.[13] It should be stressed, wherever very detailed correlations between school provision and literacy are being sought at the local level, that increased provision by churches or other agencies at any given times and in very specific localities did not in itself produce clear or automatic effects upon apparent literacy levels; some investigations relative to Furness, pursued by Mr T. G. Goodwin, have demonstrated the dangers of such linkages, because there was, first of all, much movement between localities in the years between schooling and marriage, and, secondly, the acquisition of basic skills could sometimes be effected in the most haphazard manner.[14] But over large districts or regions, much clearer and more reliable trends are usually discernible, and there is little doubt that church agencies increased their efforts in these mid-century decades, and that those efforts had some palpable, and in a broad sense, measurable effects, contributing to the changes shown in Table 6.1.

There was still much to do, however. An Education Committee for the Diocese of Carlisle was set up in 1854, and the secretary of this committee sketched a grimly revealing picture of the region's more defective schools, widely scattered and lacking any sets of texts beyond the Bible itself, with 'a few hacked and badly placed desks, tattered lesson cards and broken slates'.[15] It remains true that something of a transformation was brought about in, for example, Furness, the country parts of which had acquired writing as well as reading skills,[16] although it is clear that this was not the work of the Anglican body, the National Society, alone.[17] In Cumberland as a whole, the National Society's day schools and the British Schools (for the nonconformists) catered for 28 per cent of the pupil total (1851), and in Westmorland, 25 per cent. However, Anglican control of Sunday schools was generally much more extensive, especially in Westmorland, but even there the Methodists had much influence in the upper Eden Valley.

The 1870 Education Act laid down that every child had to be provided with an elementary school place, and, in areas where existing voluntary schools were unable to meet this need, local ratepayers had to form an elected school board, supported out of rates. It was meant, in W. E. Forster's words, to 'fill the gaps'. In the previous decades, the building of National and other schools had been considerable in Cumbria; whereas there had been 33 National and British Schools in Cumberland in 1851, there were 69 two decades later, out of 159 grant-aided schools altogether.[18] There were, in addition, 37 other Anglican schools there, whilst Westmorland education tended to be dominated by the latter.[19] However, it would be wrong to give the impression that in Cumbria generally, even at this stage, the church had done more than fill holes in the road, for a mass of endowed and, to a lesser extent, private schools together played an important part. The grassroots urge to provide basic instruction remained. This conclusion is in some wise supported by Cumberland's record in the provision of school boards, in pursuance of the 1870 Act, whereby a very clear majority of the Cumberland boards were founded or formed by the desire of ratepayers (64 per cent) between 1870 and 1895, instead of being formed under the compulsion of the Education Department – and, in this sense, the county came high in the list of

English and Welsh counties.[20] Westmorland had a slightly better record than the English and Welsh average in the same respect,[21] but its opinion-formers plainly resented the Education Act by virtue of the county's previous achievements.

It may be significant that a noticeable willingness to form school boards was manifested in two areas of the Lake Counties – the Solway plainland, which was thickly dotted with public and private schools, but which suffered from the consequences of rapid industrial growth, and in the Eden Valley, where nonconformity was strongest in relation to population.[22] The region's earliest boards, following those pioneering bodies appearing in Kendal (1871) and Carlisle (1872), were in the areas described.[23] In Longtown district, which had long given most impressive evidence of high literacy in the region, the HMI for the area gave a glowing report of progress, suggesting that the locality had been almost bereft of schools previously.[24] In reality (as the Inspector elsewhere acknowledged), the greatest deficiency had been in the west coast industrial belt.[25]

This last consideration, too, was acknowledged by the Bishop of Carlisle (1876), if in a somewhat back-handed manner;[26]

> though my advice to the clergy has ever been to avoid the introduction of school boards as much as possible, on the ground of the inferiority of religious teaching which is inseparable from a school board school . . . still I cannot and dare not utterly reprobate school boards . . . One complaint frequently is that a village or town spring up under the influence of a company or of a rich man, and the moral and spiritual interests of the village or town are left to any one or no one to look after. So far as elementary education is concerned the law now steps in and says this shall not be; and I bless the law which says so.

Quite plainly the Bishop was referring to an extreme case, that of Barrow-in-Furness and district. A board had been formed in that town in 1872, and had found a shortfall of 3000 places,[27] and, as Mr Goodwin has shown, the apparent literacy level of the entire sub-region was adversely affected by the headlong industrialisation within it.[28] But the prelate was wrong in assuming that major industrialists were – in the region itself – especial offenders. The great magnates who ruled Barrow were ready enough to support church and other schools,[29] and the villains of the educational piece were more likely to be small-town tradesmen, who, having supported private schools for their own children, were apt, as in Ulverston, to become complacent. It remains true that the school boards of industrial Furness has to be established under the pressure of the law.[30]

The National Schools, with other voluntary establishments, and the school boards, did in fact sometimes rise to the challenge of rapidly growing centres. The post-1870 dispensation provided a good, tri-departmental school in the coalmining locality of Dearham, where accommodation had been seriously lacking before,[31] and in Carlisle there was marked improvement in the schools provided, with the qualification that 'comparatively few children of the ragged classes seemed to be present, and it is not easy to see how they are to be brought in'.[32] Nevertheless, both Carlisle and Kendal had some success, by 1875, in improving school attendance,[33] and the problem of attendance was one which was to beset the school boards of the region, especially in rural areas, for many years thereafter. Whitehaven, meanwhile, remained a black spot – as late as 1889, the *Cumberland Pacquet* was able to assert that 'there are a very large number of children in Whitehaven who never go to school at all, and at present there is no adequate machinery to get hold of them'[34] – and the town remained without a school board, the threat of the formation of a board causing the churches to hold the educational reins even tighter, a point freely admitted by the Bishop.[35] It was not until 1903 that the newly formed Whitehaven Education Committee took over the church schools in the interest of more general supervision.[36] In other towns, like Barrow and Carlisle, the school boards had much to their credit by the closing years of the century,[37] and Barrow in particular founded a higher-grade school (1880) which was in some respects a pattern for the region.[38]

Complexities of educational administration, and the religious animosities which seemed inseparable from the proceedings of most urban school boards,[39] now tended to overlay the ingrained indigenous tradition of large parts of Cumbria; and the old village or small-town interest in basic education, with minor landowners and farmers watching the welfare of their sons through a board of trustees or vestry, now gave way to the ostensibly democratic rule of a board of five or seven members, usually the former, elected by the public. Cumbrian board divisions tended to be small, and the boards themselves were often dominated by forceful public persons, ministers, managers or tradesmen, although sometimes a workman, as at Egremont, might be elected (1889), to justify his position strongly – 'as working men, we are rising to a sense of our duties and our responsibilities in respect of the comforts and edification of our children'.[40] The curricula within schools in town and country were being, by very slow degrees, enriched from the bare minimum of mental fare which had been characteristic of the education of too many children of an earlier generation outside the better grammar schools. The *Whitehaven News*, passing judgement on the more elaborate education system of 1885, felt that although the operations of the school boards had been 'costly' and cumbrous, they had at least drawn attention to the need for education. Weakly children were, however, being driven to the limit of their strength 'in order that the government grant may be kept up'. The same newspaper returned to the attack a few years later, claiming undue cramming in some board schools, and there were indeed schoolboys' strikes in Carlisle and Dearham in 1889.[41] This agitation, however, was a hangover from a national controversy over the consequences of payment by results,[42] and was an example of the *Whitehaven New*'s willingness to truckle mildly to the church schools and authorities.

Far more important was the work of getting pupils to school, and, outside black spots like Whitehaven, the worst problems of irregular school attendance occurred where small farmers were numerous or where industries like shellfish-gathering called for the use of the very young,[43] as in the Flookburgh area. The story of the battle for school attendance is a long and complex one and it was not until 1880 that such attendance became clearly and totally compulsory through the so-called Mundella Act.[44] During the following decade, prosecutions began to shower on coal and iron miners and labourers, who had to pay 5s. each for proven infringements of the law where their children were concerned;[45] but close investigation would probably show that the law was much more effective in the towns. Nevertheless, some figures published by the Kendal Rural School Attendance Committee[46] show, in so far as they are truthful, that percentage average attendances in some rural districts of Westmorland were notably higher than the national average – the latter was 76.41 per cent in 1885,[47] whereas the figure was well over 80 in the Ambleside, Grayrigg, Milnthorpe and Kirkby Lonsdale districts (1884). Westmorland's educational reputation was not achieved without solid work, although there were clearly blemishes.

What of the educational ladder of which so much has been made? Both endowed grammar schools and a mass of private schools remained into the new century – 31 of the former were in existence in 1894 in Cumberland, and no fewer than 36 in Westmorland, many of them with totally inadequate endowments.[48] Some, like the Wigton Grammar School,[49] were rescued by benefactors, and few could have had much impact – only seven within Cumberland were recognised as worthy of development by the new Cumberland Education Committee in 1903.[50] Yet the disappearance of the older foundations (the once-famous Hawkshead Grammar School ceased to operate as such in 1909) symbolised a culture, rurally rooted, which was passing.

The school boards, too, were soon passing at the insistence of the Balfour Education Act of 1902. The boards had their vigorous and predictable defenders, mainly among the west-coast Liberals,[51] led by William McGowan, but the nonconformists, although greatly augmented in strength since the early Victorian age, were still not numerous enough to register more than a forcible token resistance.[52] Before more than a few months had passed, the leading Liberals and nonconformists were taking their places on the Cumberland County Council's new Education Committee – Andrew Sharp, H. D. Rawnsley, Francis Grainger, with Miles McInnes of Carlisle as the chairman.[53] The period of change-over to the new local government system, which critics saw as a threat to the democratic control formerly represented by the school boards, also affords an insight into the balance of educational interests in both Cumberland and Westmorland – in the former county, the numbers of pupils, rather over 15 000 in each case, were almost equally split between former board (now 'council') schools, and voluntary or church schools, which were more numerous (167 as against 91 council schools), and which were also, accordingly, smaller. It is a matter of some interest that up to 1914, the numbers of Cumberland voluntary schools decreased slightly, and that the numbers of council schools increased equally slightly.[54]

However, this is not the place for a history of educational administration in the period. The two main Lake Counties, unlike Lancashire, left much initiative to school managers, and did not experiment with area administrative systems of any weight[55] – in this matter, it seems that they were instinctively reacting to local opinion. Local, especially rural, involvement in education remained real, and the rural districts manifested exceptionally good school attendance figures, reaching nearly 90 per cent in the Eastern Division of Cumberland (1905), embracing localities like Alston, Brampton and Aspatria.[56] Before the outbreak of war, the entire county was aspiring to this high level of attendance, the industrial districts having offered rather more problems than the rural.[57] Westmorland's children were equally firmly directed to school.

In this respect, then, the weight of past tradition was still felt. But, in view of what is said in a subsequent section of this chapter, it should be stressed that the self-directing, self-improving element among the common people of industrial Cumbria failed to develop between about 1870 and 1914. One basic reason will become evident. The staple industries of coal- and iron-mining did not lend themselves to the types of skilled craft training which could be fostered in the evening technical class, but, over and beyond this, the paternalism of local government committees and employers combined tended to create its own resistance. Yet again, the region's reaction to the Technical Instruction Act of 1889, which attempted to rationalise that field of education in face of continental competition (and to do so as cheaply as possible), was not vigorously followed through, even in the provision of evening classes.

The region's County Councils did, of course, form and maintain technical instruction committees following the Act, and the press made frequent and usually uncritical references to their efforts, but much of the real truth about Cumberland evening school education emerged in a Board of Education report of 1906.[58] In Carlisle and Whitehaven, the teaching premises were unsatisfactory, and in the former, the engineering instruction was inadequate; in Maryport, there were 'no courses of study adapted to the practical needs of the students'; in Cleator Moor and Cockermouth, fewer than 2 per cent of the population attended evening classes; and in the general sphere of mining education, out of every thousand coalminers in Cumberland, only 7.8 attended classes, and out of every thousand ore-miners, only 4.6.[59] This is not to say, however, that non-vocational and semi-vocational classes did not fulfil a certain social purpose, especially in country districts. Indeed, a bad reason for going to evening instruction is better than no reason at all, and as the Board's inspector found:[60]

147

'Miners and quarrymen are seldom at home during their leisure time, and the circumstances of the cottages – bad lights and a crowded room common to all – are not conducive to study. They go to school because it is a well-lighted, well-warmed club, and they have company to and from it.'

Nevertheless, evening continuation schools did a little to augment the basic education of those who had left school a considerable time before, despite great wastage and repetition of earlier work.

Meanwhile, we may ask what opportunities were offered by the new dispensation, which had been lacking in the rurally based system of a century or more before. The county authorities shared responsibility for 'higher' education (i.e. secondary grammar schools) with major local education authorities like Carlisle, Workington and Whitehaven, but were themselves responsible for giving grant-aid to established grammar schools at Carlisle, Keswick and Penrith, and to the two Wigton schools, now combined as the Nelson Thomlinson School. In addition, in the few years before 1914, the county authority created its own secondary (grammar) schools at Alston, Brampton, Carlisle (girls), Whitehaven, Millom, Penrith and Workington. In all there were 1506 scholars at these establishments in 1912–13, out of a total Cumberland school population of 30 250,[61] which means that if we allow for variations in age-ranges, fewer than 5 per cent of all pupils were occupying the road to personal and social advancement offered by a grammar school education. It is doubtful, then, if the newer administration offered many more very marked advantages to the young, when compared with the traditional but popularly supported 'system' of a century earlier.

As regards the less fortunate elementary schools pupils, it seems that Cumberland, soon after the passing of the 1902 Act, had average classes of 45 pupils per adult teacher. It is an ironic twist of circumstance that the economic decline of the industrial west of the region had the effect (1913) of reducing this figure to 29,[62] one not far removed from the likely size of the average regional village school class of a century before. The spiritual fare received in the new century, and the teaching skills offered, were of course a different matter.

How far had the basic educational and formal training given by early Victorian regional agencies conditioned the minds of labourers, industrial workers or potential migrants? Social statisticians of that age, expressing their thoughts in publications like the *Journal of the (Royal) Statistical Society*, sought eagerly for correlations between high apparent literacy and low crime rates, and the example of the Lake Counties certainly appeared to support any case they might concoct. Much of the rural region was apparently free from serious crime or even misdemeanours,[63] but an ostensible unwillingness to commit acts of larceny was balanced by the remarkably high bastardy rates noticed in Chapter 4 above. It would appear that robbery of virtue was little regarded, and the Anglican church reacted hardly at all to the latter, being unwillingly involved in debate only by the passionate evangelism of George Moore.[64] Then, again, the inevitably religiously inclined teaching which prevailed in most schools, and not only in the Anglican ones, might have been expected to have some effect on church attendance. Westmorland provides an interesting test case; the Upper Eden valley apart, it was overwhelmingly Anglican, with two-thirds of all sittings (1851) in that category, but its Anglican seats were only 45 per cent full on Census Sunday morning in that year. Since the Anglican sittings themselves catered for 42.5 per cent of the Westmorland population, it is clear that well under a quarter of the latter had been steered towards the Church of England, although a substantial margin was provided by the Wesleyans, catering, in sittings, for 14.6 per cent of the population – and even these were barely over half-full on that particular morning.[65] Since the vast majority of children had had some schooling, and hence some religious indoctrination, these figures are hardly impressive, although it remains true that at least 11 000 Westmerians attended the services of the established church on this date, and a maximum of over 15 000 if we assume that others attended once only in the afternoon or evening.

Nor can it be assumed that both passionate evangelism and religious bigotry did not flourish in parts of the region. The Methodist missionary work of the mid-century bore visible fruit in a variety of circumstances, as in Glenridding, where the lead-mining proprietors backed it, or in the Pennine lead villages,[66] or where there was a distant vacuum left by the Anglican church.[67] In other areas, the church could be merely stultifying and oppressive; Harriet Martineau, who had strong Unitarian prejudices, wrote to Lord Morpeth from Ambleside to claim (1848):[68]

> If a poor man (in one case, a reformed drunkard) goes to the chapel, he is threatened with being turned out of his cottage. His landlord – a mighty gentleman, would rather see him reeling in the road, and nominally belonging to the church than soberly attending the chapel (now Wesleyan). These gentry are utterly hopeless; inane, stupid, talking solemnly of Puseyism, and blind to the plainest duties of their position.

It is clear not only that the nonconformists faced powerful foes, but equally clear, as was noted in the last chapter, that the established clergy represented a minor gentry or ruling group in several scores of Cumbrian parishes. This may well be reflected in Mannix and Whellan's 1847 *Directory* list of 'Gentleman's Seats and C.' for Cumberland, where out of 301 residences listed, 77 were rectories, parsonages or simply gentlemen's houses occupied by clergy, a total of rather over 25 per cent. In a number of the more populous parishes (Whitehaven, Carlisle, Aspatria, Cockermouth, Harrington, Distington, Alston, Dovenby, Penrith, Maryport and some smaller places), an incumbent was also one of the local magistrates, the church playing a considerable role on the bench in the mid-1840s. In some cases, the influence of the great territorial magnates, the Lowthers was exerted through their control of livings – thirty in West

18 Decoration for an unidentified celebration at the church of St James, Whitehaven, in
1865. One of the finest Georgian interiors in the north of England is here obscured
by tasteless hangings which must have appealed to Victorian parishioners.

Cumberland (1872), and eight in Westmorland.[69] This, however, doubtless
merely encouraged a conformist outlook on the part of incumbents, and may not
have weakened church influence as such; in 1872, too, the vicars of all three
Lowther-provided churches in Whitehaven attacked the notion of appropriated
pews, supported, it is true, by Bishop Goodwin,[70] and the Anglican church was
at this time clearly struggling for working-class support in industrial settings.

Whitehaven and other coastal towns not only saw much diversity of sects and

150

religious groups during the last thirty years of the century, but were also given to a Protestant bigotry much sharpened by the existence of a Catholic challenge in the vicinity. It should be stressed that the Cleator Moor Catholics were (1872) willing to demonstrate publicly for Home Rule,[71] and there was an almost inevitable reaction to this seemingly alien challenge; in the same year, an Orange demonstration of 400 to 500 persons could be held in Workington,[72] and two of Whitehaven's leading clergy, the Rev. F. W. Wicks and Canon Dalton, took the chair at Orange Protestant meetings,[73] despite the threat to the peace which had been represented by the recently 'martyred' anti-Catholic demagogue William Murphy.[74] Nor was such extreme feeling confined to the Anglican element, and the Rev. Joseph Burns of the Presbyterian Church, Whitehaven (d. 1885) was a noted anti-papist polemicist.[75]

Religious fervour, then, could receive a powerful stimulus if linked to existing political prejudices and grievances, and it is often argued that Anglican schooling, combined with anti-Irish feeling, led to a form of Tory Protestantism common among Lancashire or northern working men after the 1860s. Yet, whilst Whitehaven may well have manifested an extreme case of this in the 1870s and earlier, a religious census taken in that town in November, 1881 showed the

19 A symbol of rural Methodism in nineteenth-century Westmorland; Ravenstonedale Wesleyan Chapel.

combined Anglican churches receiving fewer than 30 per cent of all possible religious attenders on a Sunday in that month, whilst on an admittedly wet Sunday in December, 1902, the proportion had fallen to barely 20 per cent.[76] Yet, in 1851, Whitehaven registration district had had the largest absolute numbers of Anglican Sunday scholars of any district in Cumbria, and, proportionately, greater numbers than had Cockermouth or Carlisle.[77] A tentative conclusion here must be that religious indoctination had, in many cases, little long-term effect, and the latter was of course much watered down after the 1870 Education Act. Schools and schooling had a more immediately practical purpose, whatever their religious basis, than the merely theological, and this fact was tacitly recognised throughout Cumbrian society.

The Anglican church remained the prime religious organisation in rural Cumbria, but one of the most striking features of town life was, as has been noted, the increasing variety of religious organisations of all kinds. Many of the latter were narrowly respectable, inward-looking and totally sectarian in their commitments, and the truth of this contention can, in some measure, be tested by the reception accorded to the Salvation Army, which took its evangelism into the open much as the Old Dissent had done, and which met with determined official and legal resistance in Workington,[78] even though it could count as many as 200 tea-party followers in Millom in 1889.[79] The fact remains that its indoor attendances in Whitehaven, Maryport, Cockermouth and Keswick were tiny in 1902, and throughout West Cumberland, in both town and country, the religious census of 1902 showed the 'respectable' nonconformists to be in the ascendancy on a decidedly wet December Sunday that was in itself a test of the solidity of faith.[80] The Wesleyans nearly everywhere enjoyed a stable following, sometimes challenging that of the parish churches (as in the Egremont district), although in Egremont, Cleator Moor and Frizington, the Catholics were by far the most powerful group. The Congregationalists were firmly established in the industrial belt and also in the Cumberland market towns like Cockermouth, Keswick and Wigton,[81] whilst the Primitive Methodists had a tight organisation, with twelve centres in the Maryport Circuit alone in 1889,[82] and were showing a modest but by no means contemptible numerical impact in the smaller western towns in 1902.

This wet December Sunday, however, revealed that church and chapel attendances, when taken as a percentage of population, fell so far below those of 1851 as to suggest that religion was simply not a major force even in this pre-1914 age of predominant respectability. It undoubtedly worked its influence throughout the educational system in a very limited, formalistic and even superficial way, providing a bare structure of belief without much underlying thought, and it may well be a fallacy to suppose that the undeniably massive impact of the First World War on religious belief represented a clear historical break. There was possibly a weakening of impulse before the holocaust, even though Anglican confirmations continued to increase nationally between 1900 and 1911.

As has been implied, there was a growth in the *variety* of religious observance and expression, and this is true of the regional countryside as well as the towns. In Kendal, there had been a multiplicity of denominations from the eighteenth century onward,[83] but, as regards the Westmorland countryside, it is noteworthy that Wesleyan Methodism was, by the early years of the twentieth century, no longer largely confined to the Eden Valley, but had spread to places as diverse as Burton-in-Kendal, Barbon and Bampton, whilst it had long been established in industrial or transport centres like Staveley, Patterdale (Glenridding) and Tebay.[84] The tourist towns, like Windermere, manifested a noticeable variety of religious provision, but this no doubt reflected the width of the sectarian interests of the settlers in these places. Indeed, the tourist and residential communities, with their relatively high proportion of educated incomers with leadership-proclivities, displayed not only a considerable selection of religious groups, but a striking assortment of voluntary bodies of all kinds;[85] political and debating societies, mechanics' institutes, book clubs and similar associations. We should beware of assuming that such areas of settlement represented a broader or more traditional form of community culture within the region. This chapter, as will be clear, has been concerned entirely with those formal, official or specialised institutions concerned directly with the nurture and training of people within society; and the culture of communities, reflected in the pursuits and recreations of mature people, was in reality far more complex than is depicted here, and it embraced not only education for toil or achievement, but the multifarious uses of leisure. This culture is examined in the following chapter.

CHAPTER SEVEN 🐚

The culture of communities

The last chapter was concerned with the ways in which members of regional communities, especially the young, were trained, or given elementary or moral education, through formal institutions like schools or religious organisations. By contrast, this chapter is devoted to a survey of cultural changes, and to those traditions, customs and forms of recreation, self-education and self-organisation (on the part, for example, of small groups of industrial and other workers) in many hundreds of voluntary associations at the local level. Some of these customs and organisations owed their existence to ideas and practices transmitted from previous generations, and many were outgrowths of new movements, ranging from particular aspects of trade unionism to cycling. Plainly, this complex of activities, which we can only describe as a developing culture, or a set of cultures based on given communities and groups, changed considerably during the nineteenth century as urban influences penetrated the countryside through the printed and written word and through human contact. But the change was even more fundamental than this would imply, and was made more momentous by the growth of town and industrial populations, by the movement of people from country to town, and by the development of a far from homogeneous middle class which nevertheless controlled or influenced the means of information (the 'media' of present-day parlance), then largely represented by the newspaper press.

Clearly, the older rural traditions and customs were subjected to continual erosion, sometimes indirect and insidious, sometimes direct and powerful, even though, by a paradox, consciousness of regional popular and literary culture (a topic touched upon towards the end of Chapter 1) was enhanced as never before. Yet, to put the case in crudely practical terms, a dialect writer or folk-poet had to have his work accepted by polite society, much as was Robert Burns's experience, before it had much hope of acquiring wide currency. Hence, the self-conscious regionalism which was propagated by educated Cumbrians, aided by literature and the press, was a dual culture which increasingly became weakened at its roots, and which eventually degenerated into the romantic nostalgia of the uprooted but prosperous native, represented by the Cumberland and Westmorland Societies of the early twentieth century. Whilst a fascinating monograph could be written on this subject, an illustrative example may add clarification.

The most famous of all Cumbrian ballads was written by John Woodcock Graves in 1829, the work of a man who was far from being an unlettered peasant, but who was also a friend of John Peel and who was deeply and passionately involved in the local fox-hunting which was, and remained, an immovably solid part of popular sport and tradition. Some thirty years later, the song was printed by a Carlisle bookseller, Coward, but it made its resounding and effective début before a polite gathering, that of the Cumberland Benevolent Association in London in 1869.[1] Two points may here be noticed: the song was successfully received by an educated group of Cumbrians who were detached from their local soil, and who were on that very account inclined to feel a nostalgic patriotism; and, to complete the picture, many of these émigrés were the products of the local grammar schools who had sought their fortunes elsewhere. One may contrast Graves's not entirely accidental success (and even his tune, that of the Scottish rant, *Bonnie Annie*, was not original) with the bitter struggles of the Cockermouth poacher-poet, John Denwood (1845–96), the weaver's son and radical, who had to arrange for the printing of his own verses. These, like the products of numerous working-class writers of that age, imitated received forms for the most part, but came to life when they flared into social protest or turned to dialect.[2]

Yet it remains true that even Denwood found an outlet for many individual lyrics in the Cumbrian press of his time,[3] even if he had no consistent patronage, and the newspapers, secure in their allegiance to established conventions and political norms, also opened certain avenues to radical or unconventional thought and expression (as we saw in Chapter 4), and immensely widened, socially rather than ideologically, many areas of discourse. John Denwood's own lifetime saw some massive transformations in the uses of literacy and the printed word, and it is a sad thought that he was only to acquire fame posthumously and through his own descendants. We can measure the scale of this transformation through further examples. When our period opened, there were but six newspapers in the region, with circulations of a few hundreds or thousands apiece (see pp. 2 and 16 above and Appendix 2). Between 1860 and the end of the century, there was a remarkable extension of these means of information, brought about not only by the removal of stamp and other duties on the press, but also by greater literacy, increasing populations and, not least, by the agency of the railways. During these years, the newspapers themselves changed. They ceased to be mainly scissors-and-paste collectors of national news, with a mere central section of local snippets, and became much more vividly detailed reflectors of many aspects of local life. Inevitably, there was selection and sometimes distortion, but there was also a density of information that has never been equalled, and a willingness to report a great area of working-class activity. Inevitably, too, middle-class culture, assumptions and folk-lore, and their partial concomitants in the imitative culture of the respectable working-class, were delineated there on an ever-increasing scale, and there can be little doubt that the press helped to mould attitudes, and to present many prominent people in the images they most liked to see. But neither editors nor readers were mere makers or receivers of impressions, and there was controversy, criticism and interplay, not only of a formal political kind. In matters of local tradition and anthropology, the newspapers have to be searched, and treated, with care; but viewed with strict objectivity as purveyors of attitudes, they are irreplaceable sources.

Of 152 separate Cumbrian newspapers traced by Mr F. Barnes and the late Mr J. L. Hobbs, 90 belong to the period 1860 to 1900[4] (although, indeed, many remained extant for a few months or years only) and a solid core of wide-circulation newspapers has remained; the *Whitehaven News* (1852), the *West Cumberland Times* (1874), the *Cumberland and Westmorland Herald* (originally the *Penrith Herald* of 1860), the *Barrow News* (1881), and the remarkable and perennial little *Keswick Reminder* (1897), have all survived from that age, together with the indestructible *Westmorland Gazette* (1819). By the 1880s, total circulations, district by district, reached into the tens of thousands, and it is probable that at least half the adult population were regular and assiduous newspaper readers. Moreover, newspapers reached into the dales hamlets, and the whole region became aware of itself as never before. However, the weekly newspaper was adapted to the rhythm of rural and semi-rural life; daily newspapers, like the *Barrow, Furness and North-Western Daily Times* of May, 1871, a product of Barrow enterprise, had a far more difficult time of it,[5] and the *Cumberland Evening News* (1910) was the first successful venture in that *genre*.

Local and regional cultural attitudes are spread out for us to examine in these Victorian newspaper sheets; but of what did they consist? And what is likely to be missing? Perhaps the most important single tendency to become visible is a changing attitude to the use of leisure, as it became more available to the masses. The institutions connected with Saturday afternoon leisure, mainly sporting, proliferated, but there appears a noticeable sub-stratum of respectable working-class self-help, self-teaching and self-organising activities and groups — friendly and benefit societies, trade unions (not usually covered unless there was a local strike or crisis, or until trades councils became fully recognised), co-operative societies, and mutual improvement, political, religious and musical groups. The culture they represented was essentially an urban one, and was propagated as such by editors like Francis Leach of the *Barrow Times*, who suggested that the Ulverston hiring fair might be dispensed with, if that market town was to take its place amidst the dynamic places of the regional seaboard.[6] The regional press increasingly used rural correspondents, but they, again, dealt with town-type voluntary associations or minor items during the second half of the century, and the newspapers dealt less often with rural and agricultural problems as such. More subtly, the press reflected a culture which spread out to assimilate country pastimes and sports, just as the railways which carried the weekly papers also tended to draw rural people into town for shopping or amusements. Beneath the display of leisure activity was a serious imbalance, which ignored much in rural life, and, in the towns, much in the lives of the non-reading, drinking, pub-singing and less respectable working class.

The press did not create a new culture; it merely reflected and transmitted cultural activities and ideas at several levels. But it was, nevertheless, the primer and educator of the observant working man, encouraging him in his pursuits, but sometimes leaving behind indicators which reveal to the historian how thinly spread some aspects of this auto-didact working-class culture really were. It is unsurprising to find the adherents of the Lorton Working Men's Mutual Improvement Society (1872) described as 'respectable'[7] flax and brewery workers in the main, and such bodies were never a large part of the mass. Nor should the contributions of the mechanics' institute and reading room movements be overstated. Most of the main Cumbrian towns, and some smaller ones, like Brampton, Ambleside and Milnthorpe[8] had such institutions between 1830 and 1889. In 1851, when the press was still heavily taxed (but accessible in reading rooms) and regional literacy was notably widespread, the total Cumberland membership of reading rooms amounted to some 4.6 per cent of all adult males over 20 years, whilst the proportion for Westmorland was even more insignificant.[9] These bodies represented a failure to impose an urban middle-class culture on the masses, but were, in the Cumbrian instance, further weakened in several ways, in that ironworkers' hours were long and their labour heavy, and in that spontaneous reading habits were not greatly furthered in the case of local children, who had few books for their own edification,[10] and few opportunities to attend evening classes when they were older.[11] The institutes themselves, in failing to provide an effective alternative, were eroded by more overtly political clubs and movements, which had the good sense to provide, for example, billiards for their members.[12] The Maryport Mechanics' Institute collapsed in attempting to keep pace with this kind of demand,[13] whilst the Whitehaven Mechanics' Institute, second in the region only to that of Carlisle, 'might justly have been called a Tradesman's Club' (1885).[14] Nor, unfortunately, were the regional institutes saved by the evolution into technical colleges which became commonplace elsewhere in England, and in 1885, when technical instruction was a national issue, the *Whitehaven News* remarked that the local institutes, 'as such, have long since had their day'.[15]

The university extension movement, drawing lecturers from Oxford and Cambridge, made little impact in the Cumberland coastal area,[16] and only limited progress elsewhere,[17] although Barrow was the most successful pioneering locality (1881), the achievement in this case owing much to the efforts of a local scientific and antiquarian society which still exists, the Barrow Naturalists' Field Club (1876).[18] It is here that we come to one of the mainsprings of local cultural endeavour, the self-educating business- and professional man in the rapidly changing urban surroundings of the time, whose interests were partly scientific and derived from the newer industries, but whose interest in the countryside and in the past was often awakened by his uneasy consciousness of over-rapid transformation by bricks and mortar. At the same time, he was frequently aware of his lack of a university education, a mark of culture the absence of which often did not seem to square with his achievements and standing in other directions. It is significant that the scientific and 'literary' societies of the region flourished most markedly in the period of exceptionally rapid industrial growth, the 1870s, and at or near the main points of that growth, like Barrow and Workington. The Cumberland Association for the Advancement of Literature and Science was formed in February 1876, and had, in its turn, grown out of the Whitehaven Scientific Association, the Keswick Literary and Philosophical Society, and the Workington Scientific Association.[19] Isaac Fletcher, Liberal MP for Cockermouth, industrialist and intellectual, G. J. Snelus of Workington, one of the leading industrial metallurgists in Britain, James Baird the ironmaster, and Dr I'Anson, Tory paternalist and doer of good works in Whitehaven, were amongst the instigators. The Association was fairly rapidly joined by the literary and philosophical societies in Cockermouth, Maryport, Longtown, Carlisle and Ambleside, all in 1877–8, and by that time the main body had become the Cumberland and Westmorland Association, and was a movement spreading across the region, Brampton, Windermere and Silloth joining later. By 1878, there were 1100 regional members, and by 1885, 1290, although by 1892 the Association was about to fade[20] – a hypothetical but plausible reason being the growing absorption of the more willing organisers in developing local government and in increasing numbers of voluntary associations. Meanwhile, another organisation, already well received by county gentry society and totally concerned with a receding or distant past, had in effect taken its place, and had certainly appropriated some intellectual members.

The instigators of the Cumberland and Westmorland Antiquarian and Archaeological Society (1866) were not leading county gentry, although its prime mover, Canon J. S. Simpson of Kirkby Stephen, was an outspoken magistrate, and his first secretary, the Rev. A. F. Curwen of Harrington was another formidable clerical and public figure. It was a distinguishing feature of this learned society that many of its leading members or contributors were gentry and clergy who had, as a matter of course, university educations, and some were scholars of genuine eminence. To that extent, they represented a 'mandarin' culture that had little time for scientific and industrial topics, even though leading industrialists of growing social standing (like Sir James Ramsden of Barrow) joined readily enough, to take their places at the side of such scholars as Canon C. W. Bardsley (who joined in 1880), H. S. Cowper (1886), W. G. Collingwood and J. F. Curwen (1887), and T. Alcock-Beck (1889).[21] Their activities, too, like those of the workmen or the businessmen, presupposed allocations of leisure, and the scholars of that age seem to have had very great areas of leisure indeed — far more than was available to any other members of the communities of the region. It will be noticed, meanwhile, that the Antiquarian and Archaeological Society, like the Cumberland and Westmorland Association, saw the region as a unity, and that it laid claim to the study of Furness without any argument. It saw the Cumbrian land-mass as its intellectual province, and such a historical fact has a striking relevance to debates about the validity of 'regions' as suitable areas for historical study. Cumbria had become an intellectual region as well as a physical one.

Nevertheless, it may be significant that the Antiquarian and Archaeological Society, which has contributed signally to prehistoric, Roman and architectural studies in the Lake Counties, has produced very little of value in the area of the study of folk-life and folk-culture, including that of modern and recent history — and it is to this that we must now turn.

Education and religion, providing the formal training of the young in Victorian terms, can in practice be related to our much wider and all-embracing concept of local culture, covering customs, traditions and recreations at a variety of social levels. Even education, as was implied in the last chapter, could be given a certain impetus and direction by popular pressures. In other words, the collective inclination of local communities could utilise an existing formal institution for some purpose which fitted more appropriately to local needs, and we shall do well to examine this idea a little more closely. Meanwhile, there can be little doubt that the half-century before 1914 saw the disappearance of much in Cumbrian rural culture and tradition, although remnants of it survived well into the present century, and witnessed its partial replacement by systems of activities which were more urbanised and more continuously organised. An immense range of spare-time pursuits became available to the local man, if not to the local woman, and eventually both sexes were also enabled to seek relatively passive or inert forms of amusement in the early cinema, or the reading of light fiction on a large scale. Indeed, there was a growing emphasis on amusement rather than vigorous or skilled activity, if only for the reason that organised mass sport requires space, money and equipment. However, despite the drawing power of drinking and gambling, it remains true that the closing decades of the century saw other developments in community life which were unprecedented. One straightforward example will give a measure of the distance that was travelled, in some such respects, during Victoria's reign; the free-for-all brawl between villages, represented by an annual football match, was supplanted by the organised football league covering a large part of the region, but made up of a score of local clubs. Such examples can be multiplied.

Education, as has already been indicated, came under the control not merely of a regional or a local committee, but moved decisively into the sphere of state tutelage. In this sense, one very fundamental expression of local culture was virtually destroyed. There can be no doubt about Cumbrian popular involvement in village education; as Sanderson made clear in his essay on 'The Character, Manners and Customs of the Peasantry of Cumberland' (1820), the schoolmaster in a given parish, who was often the curate or vicar, might receive *whittlegait*, the right to eat a meal provided by each of 'those (who) sent children to his school',[22] and the master was thus directly maintained by these practical acts of approval. It will also be in place to draw attention to the groups of local trustees, farmers and yeomen, who partially controlled the smaller grammar schools of the region.[23] The church, which influenced the teaching in innumerable schools, was in turn utilised by popular sentiment and action. Part of the basic education of a Cumbrian peasant or rural worker took the form of musical training at the hands of parish clerk or choirmaster, and according to Sanderson's artless account, musical exercises in church were often followed by a ball or celebration at the village ale-house – 'a practice so offensive to every pious and religious mind', lamented this author, '(is one that) cannot certainly be too soon abolished'.[24] As will be seen, the concept of local culture here envisaged is derived, inductively, from known village activity; the church, schooling, musical training and the ale-house come together in a unity. A recent authority, Malcolmson, indicates that such cultural traditions of the older English rural society were being rapidly eroded by the middle of the century,[25] but it is clear that this was not a sudden process, especially in the remoter north, where the most destructive agency probably was the large-scale rural depopulation (1851–81) that has already been described.

The dancing which often accompanied social drinking involved both skill and pride of achievement, demanding training from itinerant dancing-masters who catered for the poorer peasantry as well as for the more socially aspirant groups.[26] The urge to expression in this way was immensely powerful: 'dancing', went on Sanderson, 'has so many advocates among the lower, as well as among the higher classes of the community, that to censure it would probably be to incur the charge of puritanical austerity'.[27] Physical prowess was at a premium, and a champion dancer would make a point of touching the roof beams with his head, whilst the *merry neets* of the age and region, which embraced cards as well as dancing, drinking and music, were usually ale-house assemblies held around the Christmas period. Sanderson connected them with the night-courting that was a feature of the sexual life of the region,[28] and so they may well have been related indirectly to the high illegitimacy rates mentioned in Chapter 4.[29] Here, however, one must exercise caution, for popular amusements were under heavy and puritanical criticism from evangelical and other groups in the first half of the century. What

160

is certain is that the dance celebrations remained, as did the training by instructors, and both were cemented into the calendar by the twice-yearly occurrence of hiring fairs at Whitsuntide and Martinmas, when farm servants ended their terms of employment by taking a holiday. Tremenheere, reporting in 1868, remarked that dancing was a 'universal accomplishment', and even the poorest labourer paid his pence to the dancing master, the farm girls dressing themselves in 'a white muslin dress, white kid boots and gloves, and with a wreath of artificial flowers on (the) head'.[30]

As Sanderson and other writers imply, terminology and customs varied from place to place. The phrase *merry neet* – still understood and sometimes used in present-day Cumbria – could cover a multitude of activities, including what were called, in northern and eastern Cumberland, *snap neets* and *taffy neets*, involving respectively the consumption of biscuits or toffee, and sometimes *kurn suppers*, the harvest feasts,[31] which must have declined as the region moved from arable to pasture farming from the 1860s. A summer barn dance was known as an *upshot*,[32] whilst an *auld wife hake* could take the form of a more sedate social assembly, according to the status of the people who patronised it – one such gathering held at Winster in 1870 provided tea and currant cakes as well as a 'merry dance'.[33] Polite pressures produced other forms of words over time, and the word 'assembly' was used for local balls until a fairly late date, as at the Lowwood Hotel near Ambleside or the Derby Arms at Witherslack, both in 1848.[34] The dances given out as part of the entertainment on these occasions were pursued by a multitude during the century – 'Highland schottische, square dances, quadrilles and lancers', said the grandmother of Mr Melvyn Bragg, Elizabeth Armstrong, 'And you know the lads went with great big boots in those days'.[35] Terminology changed, but the reality remained, and it is amusing to find a reporter for the *Whitehaven News* (1914)[36] self-consciously using the expression 'merry evening' for what was in fact a 'potato-pot supper and smoking concert' at the White Bull Hotel, Cleator Moor. The 'tatie-pie supper' is itself part of Cumbrian folk-tradition.

It will be noticed that much of Cumbrian folk-culture devolved on the ale-house, inn or public house, although connections with the church and with church festivals remained. Sports, too, were held at or near drinking places throughout the nineteenth century, especially the lesser wrestling meetings or bowls tournaments, and this was a feature of local recreation that did not change with the onset of heavy industry. In other respects, community recreation and culture changed vastly during the century, and it is the purpose of this chapter to trace the main transformations. Traditional local folk-culture can be said to have had three main aspects, not in themselves mutually exclusive, but exhibiting different stresses: outlets, observances and skills.

Outlets could be called for by the isolation and privations of much of hill farming existence, and meant a release, sometimes violent, from supervision and discipline, and mass football contests or inter-village fights served this purpose admirably. A Methodist missionary (1848) was horrified to discover an annual contest between the males of Matterdale and Patterdale in which the participants fought it out 'in a state of frenzy and nudity'.[37] The local lead-mining company at Glenridding, keenly Methodist, doubtless extinguished the practice rapidly enough, and, according to Sanderson, religious elements had earlier won a battle against Sabbath sports in Cumberland.[38] Remarkably, and despite a similar form of religious attack,[39] the famous Workington Easter football contests between the 'uppeys' and 'downeys' survived, to last until the time of writing, just as similar town football matches (like that at Ashbourne in Derbyshire) have remained as annual spectacles. The Workington contest, which could attract 5000 spectators, many of them brought by special train (1875),[40] has been seen as a variant or development of the 'Lord of Misrule' type of outlet; but whatever its anthropological origins, it is quite clear that an inter-village custom emerged as a battle between occupational groups, miners and sailors. Whellan, writing in c. 1860, remarked that the occasion was one in which 'all disagreements during the past year (were) put off into this night to settle'.[41] No better description of the form and purpose of an outlet could be given. Drunken affrays may have continued to serve the same purpose in urban society.

Observances were related mainly to seasonal festivals, and were still in some instances church-based or in other respects institutional; but they might also acquire, in some instances, an economic foundation during the period of post-mediaeval history. Hence Candlemas, long detached from its original religious significance, was the time for settling farming debts, and became a ceremony marked by the drinking of spirits – 'on that day, it is unpleasant for ladies to be abroad', wrote Miss Martineau[42] rather primly but very sensibly. Easter was the time for pace-egging and mummers' plays as well as the straightforward church festival, but again, post-mediaeval history may have brought a divergence, and Sullivan[43] has traced the mummers' play, now resuscitated by such groups as the Furness Morris Men, to the miracle and mystery plays of the middle ages, even though Lord Nelson and Boney managed to appear amongst its performers. Whitsuntide brought sports as well as fairs and hirings, and Martinmas, too, acquired an economic foundation as the start of the winter hiring term. Some observances were, by the nineteenth century, religiously based but almost wholly local, like the rushbearing at Ambleside, Grasmere or Warcop, whereas others were based on the economic needs of the farming tenant throughout the region, like the *boon plough*, which entailed the lending of men and plough teams to a new neighbour around Easter, when a tenancy began. This custom persisted into the twentieth century as shortages of farmworkers became more keenly felt,[44] and the same can be said about the reciprocative or neighbourly sheep-shearing. Nevertheless, by the 1870s, the changes sweeping the region and its countryside were felt to be putting even the most solidly-based customs in danger, and in

1872 the *Whitehaven News* was commenting, incorrectly, that 'the Cumberland sheepshearings of the reciprocative system are now things of the past: the shrill whistle of the steam engine having "put out of court" many of the old-fashioned practices'.[45] Yet this form of fear was not wholly without justification, for the maintenance of rituals which had no obvious economic *raison d'être*, and which depended upon the stability and the oral culture of dales populations, was a vastly different matter. 'Bidding', the calling of neighbours to a birth, a marriage or a funeral, is touched upon in Sanderson's remarks on Cumberland folk-culture,[46] but a lifetime later, in 1889, the mother of the Vicar of Nether Wasdale had to request specially that the custom be maintained in the event of her own funeral.[47] Such a special request, and the apparent need for it, must give rise to the suspicion that some of the older practices had all but totally disappeared, although the mummers' plays, which young people enjoyed performing as a means of collecting money and pace-eggs, lasted longer.

As we saw earlier,[48] the system of hiring farm servants at twice-yearly fairs attracted the dislike of some farmers, landowners and clerics, who criticised their timing and also their supposed 'immorality'. Just as the reapers' gatherings at Dalton-in-Furness, before 1850, had drawn evangelical condemnation,[49] so H. F. Curwen (1872) was 'pained and shocked to see the behaviour of some of the farm servants'[50] at Cockermouth hiring fair. There is no doubt that the latter occasion was full-blooded and popular, with its fat boy, waxworks and drawing-room circus, its booths, dice-men and merry-go-rounds, and its shooting galleries, lemonade and gingerbread,[51] mostly innocent enough, but all inducements to spend money, or to meet and treat the opposite sex.

Such an occasion as a major fair could of course provide outlets, but also the opportunity to exercise *skills*, like dancing, which took the mind away from work. Next, we must remember the skills rooted in physical strength and speed, like wrestling or running, or those based on work practices, like ploughing, all of which received encouragement as sports meetings drew in greater audiences, and agricultural societies and their shows multiplied after the 1830s.[52] Many of these skills, like the more carefully cultivated athletic ones, were restricted to very limited groups, and so they tended to draw in the non-participating or unskilled spectator. Long before the days of mass-attended football matches, huge crowds assembled to see wrestling at the Flan, Ulverston,[53] and elsewhere, and this most characteristic of all Cumbrian sports was well organised early in the nineteenth century.[54] It provides a reminder that mass spectator-sport is not in itself a product of industrialism, but that the railway system could greatly assist the growth of audiences. Spectator-sports are sometimes directly associated with gambling or betting, but even though horse-racing, which could be marked by local observance, as at Cartmel, Carlisle or Whitehaven, never struck deep roots regionally, cock-fighting and then hound-trailing supplied lively substitutes. 'Cocking' was submerged under official banning and disapproval, after thriving until the 1830s, and was then largely supplanted by the much more humane sport of hound-trailing.[55] The latter, like Lakeland fox-hunting, was not at bottom a gentry-dominated pursuit, although fox-hunting went through a phase, especially in the northern lowlands, whereby mounted gentry groups took part in the hunts, especially in the earlier nineteenth century. It is important to remember that John Peel spent much of his time mounted, even though the participants of today cover considerable distances on foot and (let the truth be told) in motor vehicles. Lord Lonsdale organised his own private hound-trails after 1900, and the Cumberland and Westmorland Hound Trailing Association of that age tended to be ruled by local notables.

In what ways did the newer industrial or urban world bring about changes in the uses of the Cumbrian's leisure time? There can be no doubt that the latter increased in quantity, generally speaking, after the 1870s, and that this increase in leisure coincides with the rise of organised football, cricket and other major sports and minor pursuits on a much larger scale than hitherto. This rise was not only a concomitant of greater leisure, but of the willingness of landowners and industrial firms to supply or lend playing fields for regular use, and also of the development of public education, and of the ability of individuals and groups to organise their affairs. At the same time, the rurally-based sports, which might call for the annual use of a field or ground only, continued with vigour, just as village skills and crafts were pursued with vitality, encouraged by agricultural or horticultural societies. Indeed, there was often more direct or active participation in the relatively small-group activities of the village and the countryside than there was in the more widely organised sports of the urban world, which tended to rely more and more on the admission money paid by the casual spectator. People in semi-urban and rural places, in short, were often forced by circumstances to create their own amusements, and this pressure has continued to within living memory; Mr Melvyn Bragg, after interviewing country people from the Solway Plain, has observed that the phrase ' "People had to make their own pleasures then" was a litany, word for word, from all the older people I spoke to.'[56] The urban world, however, for all its more forbidding aspects, offered a wealth of opportunity for the man or woman able to take advantage of it.

This chapter is not restricted to sports, or to skills, outlets and observances falling within that general field. As we have suggested, community culture has to be seen more widely than this, and in the towns, some activities which had hitherto been dominated by the local church became secularised and more widely diffused, music-making providing a salient example. Technology, partly that of Adolph Saxe, produced the cheap brass instrument in the 1840s, and the consequent bands were a marked feature of mid-Victorian urban recreation. By the late 1860s, a Great Northern Brass Band contest was established in

Workington, bringing in bands from as far afield as Barrow and Langholm.[57] It is very noticeable that numbers of those taking part were works bands, like the Derwent Tinplate Works Brass Band, although some were supplied by the volunteer movement (which had grown in the sixties, as a mid-Victorian Home Guard), or even bodies like the Orange Protestants in Whitehaven. By 1875 there were contests in both Workington and Whitehaven,[58] and it is important to remember that this was the decade of the August Bank Holiday, inaugurated by Sir John Lubbock (1871), and by degrees Bank Holiday Monday became the time when the bandsman could display his skill. During the 1880s, Barrow became the major band contest centre of the region, attracting competitors from

20 Ambleside town band in 1893.

Workington,[59] but also such formidable contestants as the Black Dyke Mills and Besses o' th' Barn bands. The players, too, tested their skills on Meyerbeer, Beethoven or Weber, and it does not do to disparage the musical attainment to which steelworkers or mill operatives aspired. However, the bands had a ceremonial significance nearly everywhere, and they played or acted for communities at different levels, colliery, steelworks, town, industrial village or regiment. Inland towns like Ambleside and residential centres like Grange-over-Sands acquired their town bands by the turn of the century, but such activities were, of course, most keenly supported in the industrial setting.

With instrumental music-making went choral singing. When Barrow was still a tiny industrial village (1850) it had been able to produce an audience for the Ulverston Philharmonic Society to listen to choruses from the *Messiah*,[60] and it is hardly surprising that Barrow itself was able to set up a Choral Society in 1873.[61] Indeed, when the Workington Brass Band Contest fell into desuetude at the end of the 1870s, it was replaced by a famous festival, covering a much wider range of skills and instruments and originated by the manager of the Barepot (Seaton) tinplate works, William Ivander Griffiths,[62] whose Welsh employees, like some of the Cornish miners, injected enthusiasm for song into new and receptive areas. After such a revelation, the well-known story of the Mary Wakefield Festival (1885), with its Westmorland and Kendal connections, comes as a mild anti-climax,[63] even though this occasion came to play an outstanding part in its own area's choral and musical history. The towns continued with their own sturdy endeavours, and Carlisle's Musical Festival, largely choral in inspiration, was commenced in 1895.[64] By the opening of the new century, such gatherings, or the Workington or Dalton-in-Furness eisteddfods, were indicators of popular talent and demand in an urban setting. They gave hundreds of people something to which they could aspire, and it should be stressed that the churches and chapels continued to play a part in the encouragement of concerts and choral performances, as did scores of voluntary organisations. Indeed, there were innumerable tributaries leading to audiences and achievements – the mid-Victorian penny readings which were so popular as a means of raising money for good causes provide an excellent example – and the newspaper press, which would give prominence to any public performance, however limited in skills, played its part in stimulating private ambitions, just as it was an essential stimulator of sporting reputations.

Many of the region's urban workers did not, in fact, enter into individual or collective musical or sporting activity, and after the 1870s their lives were likely to be centred on the now more strictly controlled public house, where, in any case, trade unions and friendly societies, as well as glee-clubs and pigeon societies, regularly met. But the man who felt that he could not afford sporting equipment, or club fees, was enabled to see a new world of exciting partisanship portrayed in the newspapers, and most urban males had at least one afternoon free to be spectators if not doers. For most of the working class, participatory sport was out of the question, for the simple reason that the team sports required too much space, even though dozens of Cumbrian towns or substantial villages had a cricket and football ground by the end of the century. The railways, too, brought greater mobility in pursuit of new scenes as well as games, as did the 'safety bicycle' of the 1880s. Nevertheless, it is necessary to make careful reservations about both the scope and the following of the main sports, which we now describe in greater detail.

Cricket led the way, during the nineteenth century, as a region-wide ground-using game, and the Kendal Cricket Club was formed as early as 1836, whilst

21 The public house as emporium of spirits and palace of delights; the Golden Lion Hotel, Botchergate, Carlisle as seen about 1900.

there were clubs at Carlisle and Maryport by 1848, cricket having been played in Carlisle in 1827.[65] The Kendal Football Club, pursuing a form of rugby, was not formed until 1871.[66] The Kendal cricketers were playing those of Carlisle in 1851,[67] and the Carlisle Club, with its intimate ground by the Eden, soon afterwards gave hospitality to the greatest of Victorian cricket figures, playing All-England teams on several occasions. Tom Hayward appeared at Kendal in 1864,[68] and Carlisle played 'Eleven of All England' at home in 1850, including George Parr, Alfred Mynn and John Wisden.[69] Meanwhile, cricket slowly broadened its popular appeal, and after the 1860s, no longer depended on employer tolerance, on persons with some kind of prolonged leisure and on members of the gentry, for basic support; it rapidly struck root in the industrial world, assisted, it is true, by the patronage of such benefactors as Lords Lonsdale and Leconfield, the former providing the fine sports ground at Castle Meadows, Whitehaven,[70] and the latter assisting the Egremont Cricket Club.[71] By the 1870s, Cumberland was playing county-level games, and even met the MCC[72]

167

yet the game's position was never wholly secure, and it is extraordinary that in 1885 lawn tennis was seen by seasoned local cricketers as a rival game which could have caused cricket's 'decline in popularity'.[73] Small sums of money only were taken at the ground in entrance payments,[74] and it is clear that this sedate game could never hope to win the hearts of the masses as did the two forms of football. The ever-informative Lamplugh correspondent of the *Whitehaven News* (1889) threw a beam of light into social reality when he pointed out that not only did the mining settlements of Kirkland and Arlecdon have difficulty in raising more than weak cricket teams, but there was also 'scarcely a suitable pitch to be obtained'.[75] Much depended on both situation and occupation, and cricket was slow to bring labourers and miners into its thrall, especially in the wind-blown western foothills.

Yet cricket, like football, received much stimulus from local industry and from the railways – league clubs appeared within reach of the main railway lines, and were especially numerous in the western districts at the end of the century – and it could draw strength from the small community or social unit, ethnic, occupational or industrial. In the 1870s, as Dr Wood has pointed out, the Cornish miners of Moor Row were able to field a cricket team,[76] just as, in the Kendal district, 'in 1858 and the following years the Carpet Works, the Mechanics' Institute and Messrs Braithwaite and Co.'s Clubs became powers in the land'.[77] It was football, however, which drew out the real sporting potential of the urban centres, and here the years after 1870 seem to be crucial.

The Carlisle Football Club was founded in 1870, and, as we have seen, the Kendal Club in 1871,[78] and the original game in each case seems to have been rugby, the Kendal games being of the 15-a-side kind. As in the case of cricket, the contests were often organised passably high in the social scale, and were then emulated at lower levels, if only because the originally available grounds belonged to colleges or major landowners; hence, grounds belonging to Heversham Grammar School, Sedbergh School and Windermere College were amongst those most used outside Kendal itself in the Westmorland of the 1870s.[79] However, by 1886 'every village and every works had their teams' in that county,[80] and it may well be significant that in industrial Cumberland, popularisation of both forms of football, rugby and association, proceeded even more rapidly.

The Football Association, designed to regularise 'soccer', had been formed as early as 1863, and the extreme north was at first slow to organise it on a large scale. Rugby, meanwhile, had its own code fixed by the formation of the Rugby Union in 1871, and, in this instance, there was a swifter reaction from Cumbria. The Rugby clubs in the coastal area inaugurated a silver challenge cup competition in 1882, and by 1888, Cumberland had reached a standing which brought it a national representative on the committee of the Rugby Union.[81] Westmorland also had its county Rugby Club, formed in 1886,[82] and association football did not catch on rapidly in that county until the first few years of the new century.[83] Meanwhile, Cumberland had been forging ahead, and in 1884 the Cumberland Football Association was formed in Wigton, and five years later, as many as 36 teams were fielded in that county on Saturdays,[84] when there had been four clubs three years earlier.[85] It should be stressed, however, that both football codes remained popular amongst the masses, the Cumberland Cup competition, for association football, being inaugurated in 1885–6, only three to four years after the rugby equivalent in that county, and it was remarked, significantly, in 1889 that 'Football notes are now appearing weekly in the *Whitehaven Free Press, Workington News* and *Maryport News*',[86] so that of the several hundred young males who turned out on the field, thousands of images and impressions reached the wider male public. The *Whitehaven News* correspondent from Lamplugh had a most revealing comment to make in that year:[87]

> (With) the end of the football season . . . lovers of both the dribbling and the carrying game will have to reserve their enthusiasm for another season. It is rather remarkable that both challenge cups – which are contested for annually in the county – should be won so often and successively by the players from two towns so similar in many respects as Workington and Millom. Both towns are situated on the coast, and are great centres of the iron industry.

A few years later (1893), the rugby organisations of Lancashire and Yorkshire were torn away from the less industrialised areas further south by a controversy over payment for time off work for important matches, and so the Northern Union, which also embraced Cumbria, appeared. This later became the Rugby League, and, although it has not been possible to pursue its regional development for the purposes of the present study, it is very noticeable that rugby in West Cumberland was, by the year of the Great War, split between 15-a-side games, and 13-a-side games, and that the Northern Union had its adherents.[88] Whether the split temporarily weakened the game is not clear; what is plain enough is that 'soccer' could draw many hundreds of spectators even in the case of local contests, as in the case of a match (1914) between Moresby Parks and Frizington Athletic.[89] Thereafter the two main forms of football co-existed, the Rugby League teams of the future eventually reaching high peaks of excellence in Barrow and Workington, but association football calling in much greater mass participation.

By 1900, organised sport had reached every level of local society, and the great rural sports, wrestling and hound-trailing, were firmly controlled by the Cumberland and Westmorland Wrestling Association and the Hound Trailing Association respectively. Even the nurture of young wrestlers was more institutionalised, and by 1914, wrestling 'academies' were appearing in villages, and Bootle's reading room had been converted into one.[90] The Wrestling

Association (1913–14) was responsible for 216 registered and affiliated meetings, some of them in Scotland,[91] and the high state of organisation and supervision of both wrestling and trailing, a far cry from the locally-organised and custom-guided sports of a century before, was probably underpinned by the increasing popularity, but also respectability, of the famous Grasmere Sports, with its aristocratic and gentry patronage. It was there that the great champions Steadman, Lowden, Kennedy and Hexham Clarke made their most memorable appearances.[92] The Hound Trailing Association, which controlled some 61 fixtures in Cumberland alone in 1914,[93] even tried to legislate against the noisy demonstrations to draw on hounds to the finishing line, thereby threatening to split the Association.[94] It may be significant that many of the trails were on weekdays; as in the case of fox-hunting, rural people often managed to find time to spare.

However, it would be a mistake to pose some kind of urban–rural distinction of a rigid kind. The Moor Row Old Brass Band (1914) organised a hound trail for charity,[95] and it is clear that ore miners could be enthusiastic trail supporters. On the other hand, industrial workers were running whippet clubs at places like Egremont and Wath Brow at the outbreak of war.[96] Meanwhile, the calendar of sporting or holiday observances became more flexible, so that Whitsuntide brought local sports, embracing athletics as well as wrestling, at only a few places, e.g. in Furness, and different types of body, like friendly societies or brass band organisations, might hold them at any convenient time in high summer. As we have seen, the August Bank Holiday brought brass-band contests, but it also encouraged a host of open-air activities; pageants, outings, and above all, walking and cycling in the Lake District as members of industrial communities discovered their own heritage. For the socially aspirant, lawn tennis and badminton not only provided a meeting ground, but also mixed the sexes, and by the end of the Victorian age, Cumbria had fashionable or attractive golf courses at Walney and Seascale, good enough to bring visits from professionals like Harry Vardon or Sandy Herd, but meant to cater for players 'many of whom desire to visit links at a distance from their home courses'.[97] In other words, thought was being given to the needs of the well-to-do visitor, although golf has never been a wholly select pastime in industrial Cumbria, and in that it follows the Scottish tradition.

All of the sports so far touched upon involved some measure of high organisation as well as active participation in greater or lesser degree. There are, it is clear, many other aspects of popular culture which require attention (which will duly be given, it is to be hoped, in further studies or monographs), and what has been described here is the sporting activity of the rural daytime or the urban Saturday afternoon. The culture of the Sabbath, and of the weekday evening, were alike of great importance. Hence, if we continue to refer to only one aspect of local social activity, that of the sports club, then it would often have its social evenings and foregathering places, and, by the end of the century, this was no longer necessarily a public house, even in the villages. The reason is a simple one; urban growth created not only terraces and shops, but church and chapel meeting rooms, temperance halls and co-operative buildings, political clubs, reading rooms, mechanics' institutes, drill halls, theatres, assembly rooms, libraries and restaurants. The trend away from the public house – which remained of great importance as a meeting place – was not simply the work of the temperance movement alone. There was more alternative space available. Hence, in 1857, fourteen out of seventeen Kendal friendly society branches met in known and stated public houses.[98] Even then, however, there was a temperance hall in that town, and similar edifices were appearing in Kirkby Stephen, Orton and Warcop.[99] By *c.* 1905, no fewer than two-thirds of Kendal's 1739 friendly society members met *outside* public houses, chiefly at the Albion Chambers or the Dolphin Cocoa Rooms.[100] It is equally indicative that the Oddfellows' branches in Furness villages rarely held their regular business meetings in inns in the new century, despite their membership of a far from teetotal body; hence, the Penny Bridge branch (1905) met in the Co-operative Hall, that for Broughton in the Wesleyan Schoolroom, that for Dalton in the Board School, and that for Cartmel in Shaftesbury House. At Bootle, a schoolroom was brought into use.[101] Against this, Barrow's eleven branches of the Ancient Order of Foresters met generally in public houses, as did the four Free Gardeners' branches, and the Buffaloes' six. Equally unsurprisingly, the 31 Barrow and district temperance friendly society branches, temples or tents met commonly in mission rooms, but also in Methodist or Baptist schoolrooms.[102] Such linkages are of course more than accidental, and one movement encouraged or helped the other.

Nor had the more drink-oriented societies necessarily moved far from the church and public house, and the Whitsuntide parades which had been a feature of the friendly society movement throughout the century were still resplendent affairs in the 1880s, as repeated newspaper reports show.[103] At Coniston, 200 friendly society members marched to church, with the obligatory band and regalia (1885), and filled three hotels in the village when taking their annual dinner.[104] It is clear that a majority of married adult males, in these times and localities, belonged to such social security organisations. In a town like Workington, the societies' parade, a fine affair with ten bands and eight or nine branches or orders taking part, took place not at Whitsuntide but on the August Bank Holiday by the 1880s.

There are, indeed, signs that the older rituals were breaking down even in that decade. In Ulverston in 1885, it was noted that 'the people proceeded either by rail or road to popular places of holiday resort ... this year only two benefit societies paraded', one of them a temperance body; and the Methodists had taken over in Millom,[105] if only temporarily. These ceremonials were finally undermined by the National Insurance Act of 1911, and it was reported from Millom (1914) that 'in recent years there has been a great falling off in ...

interest' in the parades.[106] The war undoubtedly completed the work of destruction, even though the interest in ritual had been profound; the volunteer companies, never very strong in actual numbers, had also provided the spectacle that people enjoyed. Meanwhile, the Post Office Savings Bank, and the growth of penny-a-week insurance collections, had earlier played their part in limiting the social 'reach' of the friendly society movement.[107]

The work of these voluntary self-help movements was not restricted to the provision of sickness or other benefits, and consumer protection was fostered by the co-operative movement. The business or routine meetings of co-operators were, in sum, far more fully reported in the press than were those of trade union branches, which received maximum publicity only at times of industrial conflict. It is clear, however that co-operation was marked by two distinguishing characteristics, one of which was its close affinity to *industrial* communities of fairly homogeneous nature or small size, and the other its fruitfulness as a field of largely independent working-class endeavour − this even though local societies often received initial employer encouragement. Hence, small but workable societies appeared in modest industrial communities like Langdale (gunpowder making), Shap (granite quarrying), Staveley (bobbin turning), Tebay (railway operation) and at Naworth Colliery in the small border coalfield to the north-east. As was pointed out in Chapter 5, the iron-ore mining societies led the way in spectacular fashion, but their leaders, through administrative detachment or puritanical or religious bias, came to be rather unrepresentative of large bodies of the workpeople in particular areas. In turn, however, the latter felt themselves to be deeply involved in the economic fortunes of the societies, in which much working-class savings money was invested, and crowded and excited half-yearly meetings came to be commonplace at Cleator Moor, Millom and Dalton, representing a community participation which reached its height in the 1880s, but which waned thereafter.[108] Subsequently the societies, especially in the larger towns, became relatively more static administrative and retailing institutions with only a limited social impact and power of growth, even though societies like that of Dalton-in-Furness kept some of their idealism and encouraged book culture through a co-operative library and reading room. Village societies, as in Sawrey or Kirkby-in-Furness, showed great tenacity and remained very much a part of local life, but were generally guided by dominant individuals or small groups. (See also Appendix 9.)

These societies represented Victorian voluntary working-class enterprises and associations at their highest peak of achievement, involving skilful planning and organisation. It is very difficult to estimate how many people took part in voluntary 'organisational' activity, sporting, 'cultural', mutual-aid or religious, for in every organisation there were people who merely attended or stayed on the fringes. It is reasonably clear that whilst the numbers of voluntary organisations increased in every town and village, the working masses of the region were also tending to split into two groups, the small minority of 'activists' in every sphere, and the large majority made up of passive spenders of leisure. The spectator of games, the passive concert-goer, the inert reader of fiction, and, in the new century, the absorber of cinematographic fantasies, were together elements which were made noticeable by the sheer scale of provision for their needs. This characterisation, of course, implies no moral judgement, for people were only too happy to have escape or relaxation from working conditions that were still arduous. Many younger people were able to follow physically vigorous pursuits in urban areas which were nearly always close to the countryside or the sea.

We must remember, too, that friendly societies, trade unions, temperance, or religious bodies were more than capable of providing their own amusements. There was still much self-help in entertainment, made feasible by the greatly increased accommodation for concerts as well as meetings. Hence, Cleator village used its Lecture Room for light entertainments (1889),[109] and Cleator Moor its Market Hall for similar purposes.[110] A West Cumberland Amateur Dramatic Society was in being in the same year,[111] perhaps an unsurprising fact, but at the same time Aspatria, with a population of less than 3000, had an Amateur Orchestral Society with well-patronised concerts.[112] We must also remember that in 1891 both counties had only a tiny scattering of persons, 114 in all, classed as musicians, actors or amongst those organising shows or exhibitions as given in the census occupation tables, making one such individual to well over 3000 of the population. Any contact with professional performers was decidedly transient or confined to the major urban centres. Yet, where there was physical contact with urban gatherings whereby standards of amateur performance and skill could be exhibited and maintained, the results could be remarkable indeed. In the Carlisle Musical Festival, already mentioned, children from day-school choirs competed with members of girls' friendly society choirs from a dozen town and suburban places; vocal quartets came in from Penrith and Wigton, and village church and chapel choirs from Scotby and Greystoke, or Aspatria and Wigton.[113] It is also abundantly clear from the reports of the Cumberland Musical Festival at Workington, that the Anglican churches (and nonconformist chapels and mission rooms) continued to contribute heavily to the mainstream of musical culture.[114] Almost any formal institution for the maintenance of religious observance and doctrine might branch out into a variety of activities, taking its children or adults into the countryside, or in some way stimulating the passion for 'mutual improvement' which appeared in scores of study groups throughout the region.[115]

With religious or group activity went charitable endeavour. In Carlisle, for the New Year of 1903, the Caldewgate Wesleyan Band of Hope contrived to give a treat to 'waifs and strays'; in the same week Appleby's leading citizens, with the mayor and aldermen present, gave a tea for older inhabitants, and a further tea for inmates of St. Anne's Hospital in that town, whilst remote Hutton-in-the-Forest could actually organise a dance in its reading room in aid of Carlisle Infirmary[116] – an interesting commentary on the dependence of a distant parish community on a major town medical service. Keswick, too, managed to organise an old folks' dinner, and Cockermouth an old folks' supper.[117] It can be argued that these charitable gestures bore little relevance to the underlying problem of poverty and social inadequacy which was formally dealt with by the Poor Law authorities, and it is true that this problem, affecting mainly orphans, widows, the sick and the elderly, was an intractable one (but not by any means unusually so in Cumberland and Westmorland[118]) which remained firmly in the area of social pathology. Mere surface attempts to lighten the lot of the elderly or the workhouse inmates are not, however, to be dismissed as hypocrisy on the part of the comfortably off, for they stretched through a variety of groups and social strata, and are not, in any case, wholly unconnected with the slow humanisation of the Poor Law itself. These gestures of charity often symbolised the concern of a village, a suburb or a town for those old or sick persons it knew or could see. Poor Law Guardians frequently knew little about the lives and trials of their charges, which were represented by scarcely more than entries in minute books.

During much of the nineteenth century, it is certain that the cultural, social and religious attitudes and observances of the remoter villages and parishes changed little. As we have seen, certain old-established customs may have disappeared when they had no economic justification, or when the tide of out-migration disturbed the transmission of such customs from one generation to another. The imposition of state tutelage in education must have come into conflict with existing educational tradition, or at least caused the latter to fall into quiescence. The rural self-help tradition in amusement and recreation remained into the twentieth century, and in this sense, the countryside and the urban world went their separate ways even more noticeably, as spectator-type or semi-passive amusement became much more easily available. It remains true, nevertheless, that the recreations and activities of the towns could continue to unfold in their variety; all was not loss.

But the significant changes are clearly indicated in the 1911 census and its occupational lists. There were then 550 Cumberland and Westmorland persons engaged in professional work as musicians, singers, actors, performers or showmen, a fivefold increase over the 1891 count, and one which is to be measured against a virtually static total population. This remarkable growth of the entertainments industry, which was reflected in every field of activity mentioned, but especially in the variety theatre and the development of the cinema, inevitably had its repercussions for thousands of people. Yet, allowing for the technological developments of the electrical industry and the cinematograph, much of it had its roots in earlier tradition – the variety stage had partly evolved from the earlier, frequently public-house-based music hall. Such a development can be traced in Whitehaven, where the Shakespeare Hotel in Roper Street produced a music hall in the 1860s, and where the Royal Standard Inn developed a music hall as an extension of its premises two decades later.[119] Otherwise, variety and music hall provision is not to be explained in terms of edifice, for existing buildings were frequently used for multiple purposes, like the St George's Hall at Kendal (1880), which was in use as a theatre at the end of the century. Barrow, in the 1870s, acquired three new centres of popular entertainment — the Amphitheatre, the Royal Alhambra (later the Royalty) and the Star Music Hall on Forshaw Street, later the Tivoli, which started life as a 'free and easy', another main source of the Victorian Music Hall proper.[120] The Barrow Tivoli came into its own during the golden age of this form of amusement (the 1890s), and attracted performers like Dan Leno and Vesta Tilley. Carlisle's efforts to promote such entertainments for the masses seem to have been less successful,[121] but the legitimate theatre had a more durable existence there, and Her Majesty's Theatre (1874) alone survived the century. Yet it must again be stressed that when the history of the region's entertainments comes to be adequately surveyed, it will certainly be found to be dangerous to write it in terms of permanent buildings like those of theatres. Russell's Theatre of Varieties, using an all-too-collapsible structure which fell on its audience in Maryport in 1889, is known to have visited Penrith besides that town,[122] whereas Penrith does not seem to have had a theatre building at all, but put on performances of varying kinds in the George Assembly Rooms and in its Market Hall.[123]

The 'legitimate' theatre of course continued to operate, with varying degrees of success, in all the main towns throughout our period, although it should be remembered that it was subject to disapproval from the more puritan religious groups on the one hand, and the competition of music halls on the other. The manager of the theatre in Workington (1879) protested that he was obliged to 'pander to a depraved taste or be ruined'.[124] But all was not mere earthiness or knockabout, and in 1889 the Whitehaven Theatre Royal was able to present *Don Giovanni, The Bohemian Girl, The Yeomen of the Guard* and *The Mikado* in quick succession, and to attract special trains from Cleator, Egremont and Frizington.[125] Its precise degrees of appeal and influences are, like so many topics in these pages, worthy of closer examination, and, as has been suggested already, the urban professionals and urban performances set standards for amateurs to utilise as best they might. Many of the latter were quick to learn.

Even so, theirs was activity for people who could make, do and organise, and who had some kind of talent, and there remained a submerged multitude whose clothes, hands, tastes, ungainliness and lack of education disqualified them from public performance or even background help. The building of cinemas, like the public house free-and-easies, came as a blessing to this inarticulate mass, and proceeded rapidly in late Edwardian Cumbria, after 'magic lantern' displays had accustomed thousands to the screen, and after moving picture shows (post-1900) had been contrived in music halls and variety theatres as one part of an evening's

175

entertainment. In 1909, if the *Barrow and District Yearbook* does not mislead, there was no permanent cinema in Furness; by the outbreak of war there were several such buildings. Kelly's *Directory of Cumberland and Westmorland* for 1914 reveals in the region of a score of 'cinematographs' in the two counties; indeed, the purpose-built edifices of that age, like the fabric of the Kendal Cinema on Sandes Avenue, sometimes remain to fascinate the social archaeologist. The title 'Picture Palace' was becoming accepted; Frizington had one, as did Millom, whilst Windermere had its Picturedrome. Cultural history was itself moving like a speeded-up cinema film.

This is a cultural sketch of a few broad strokes; it has, inevitably, little depth. There has been little mention of the volunteer movement of Victorian times, and the manly militarism inculcated by the 'Yellow' Lord Lonsdale and his admirers, leading *inter alia* to social pressures on middle-class professional men to dress up as soldiers; and, of course, little real exploration of the indoor amusements which the more educated people pursued, both men and women. We have been concerned with the generality of people, and the interests and activities which were part of their leisure lives. If we take Dalton-in-Furness as typical of a small western industrial town, it had, in 1909, two political clubs, nine sports clubs, and seventeen or eighteen clubs, societies and guilds concerned with matters ranging from music to horticulture and poultry-keeping, as well as eight friendly societies, a masonic lodge, and, of course, a mass of religious activity, as well as its outstanding co-operative society. Its shop window of enjoyments, groups and movements had, if we may judge from directories, increased in size immeasurably in sixty years. It was small enough to be a 'know-everybody' town, and had roots in the neighbouring countryside. Much the same could have been said of a dozen small Cumbrian towns, with the important qualification that the ones which had experienced industrial growth were those, generally speaking, with the most to offer. Yet there was, to counterbalance these gains, an insecurity of existence, especially in Low Furness, and a harsh sub-structure of experience for many Cumbrians. The fortunate and the unfortunate alike were not to be left to cultivate their gardens, and too many were to be dragged away from horticulture to die amid rats and mud. Their names still stare inscrutably from war memorials.

The tourist trade and the holiday industry

So far, we have tended to concentrate on the general social and industrial development of the region and on the problems of an agrarian society still dominated by the small farmer. Over a wide area of the central fells, however, new influences for change were already appearing in the early nineteenth century, as tourists began to make their presence felt and to make a modest contribution to the economy not only of the market towns, but also of many of the outlying farmsteads. On parts of the coast, too, the seaside holiday habit was beginning to transform sleepy tracts of shoreline into emergent resorts by the mid-century. Growth was, admittedly, steady rather than spectacular. Here were no mushroom resorts, no Blackpool, Southend or even Bournemouth.[1] Lakeland holidays remained a minority taste, and relatively few people seem to have depended on the visiting season for their livelihood. But the tourist trade came to make a real, if usually unobtrusive, contribution to the regional economy. It was, however, perhaps more important to the visitors than to the locals, for Lakeland attracted an educated and often influential élite among the holidaymaking public, many of whom concerned themselves deeply about the attributes they valued in its scenery and *ambience*. Beyond the region's boundaries, Cumbria's fame rests largely on the scenic beauties and literary associations of the inner lakes and fells; and this important consideration gives a study of its tourist trade much more significance than would be warranted by its place in the local economy.[2]

The eighteenth-century craze for spas and sea-bathing made little impact on Cumbria. Communications were rudimentary and uncomfortable, and the mineral waters and coastline had little of distinction to attract outsiders. The region was short of resident gentry and commercial men of substance, and those who could afford the time and expense of a visit to a watering-place were likely to venture further afield. But the gentry and substantial farmers of Cumbria, with a leavening of tradesmen and professionals from the towns, did provide enough custom to sustain a handful of watering-places in the eighteenth and early nineteenth century. The most important of these were Allonby and Gilsland, each of which was already flourishing in a small way by the mid-eighteenth century, and neither of which had developed very far by the eve of the railway age. Allonby was the sea-bathing resort of the gentry and farmers of north Cumberland, with a sprinkling of Carlisle lawyers and merchants and a fair showing of the more prosperous clergy. But the brief holiday season made little impact on the village's economy. Most of the inhabitants depended on agriculture, fishing and linen or calico weaving for their living, and amenities for the visitors were few. The opening of baths and an indoor promenade in 1836 was greeted with great enthusiasm, but it marked the high point of Allonby's popularity, and it never attained more than a local importance.[3] Gilsland, the region's oldest-established spa, was dominated by a single hotel, and for all the efforts of the Mounsey family to develop it, the number of visitors rarely ran to more than a hundred even at the height of the season. The clientèle had never been exclusive, and by the 1870s the farmers and yeomanry of Cumberland and Northumberland were being joined by 'the comely daughters of Newcastle and Carlisle shopkeepers out on their brief holiday'.[4] The very limited development of Allonby and Gilsland is indicative of the lack of stimulus within Cumbria for the development of health and pleasure resorts on the orthodox national pattern.

During the first half of the nineteenth century, as health resorts multiplied and grew rapidly further south, Cumbria acquired one small new commercial spa. This was Shap Wells, close to the main Carlisle turnpike road across the bleak fells between Kendal and Penrith. Here, the Earl of Lonsdale had a hotel built in the 1830s, with seventy beds and a bathhouse; but in spite of the eminence of the promoter, the new spa failed to grow any further, and a critic remarked that its visitors were hardly superior to those at Gilsland.[5]

On the eve of the railway age, Cumbria had no other spa or bathing-place of consequence, although there was sea-bathing to a limited extent at Rampside in Furness, at Skinburness on the Solway, and at Maryport.[6] The great tide of investment in the fashion for taking the waters and bathing in the sea had passed Cumbria by in the eighteenth and early nineteenth century, and her early Victorian health resorts were stunted in their growth, limited in their amenities, and parochial in their clientèle.

In sharp contrast, the main growth area in the Cumbrian tourist trade was Lakeland, where Bowness and Ambleside on Windermere, and Keswick on Derwentwater, were already emerging as centres of a visiting industry based less on the pursuit of physical health than on the intellectual, moral and spiritual benefits to be derived from the contemplation of lake and mountain scenery. The vogue for appreciating the picturesque and later the sublime and awe-inspiring features of landscape had been disseminated through the moneyed, leisured and educated ranks in the late eighteenth century, and by the 1830s the pull of fashion had long been drawing its devotees to Scotland and Snowdonia as well as

178

Lakeland, guide-books in hand, in search of the approved views, experiences and intellectual and emotional reactions. The growing reputation of the Lake Poets helped to ensure that the Lake District attracted a disproportionate number of these wealthy travellers.[7]

By the 1830s, the tourist trade was well established in the three main urban centres, and its expansion was accelerating as turnpike improvements, faster and safer coach and posting services, and steamers to Whitehaven and Bardsea made the approaches easier; and the reduced cost, in time as well as money, enabled the growing professional and commercial middle classes to participate increasingly. In the early 1840s the opening up of additional steamer routes to Barrow and Ulverston or Bardsea, in connection with the rapidly expanding Lancashire railway network, gave a further impetus to this process, and foreshadowed the imminent arrival of the railways themselves.[8]

Under these favourable influences, Keswick and Ambleside saw their populations expand at twice and nearly three times the rate for Cumbria as a whole between 1831 and 1841, and Bowness was not far behind.[9] The taking of the 1841 Census in June, two months later than usual, seems not to have distorted these figures, for the season was not yet under way; and in the absence of significant evidence for growth in other aspects of the local economies, the tourist trade, with its multiplier effects in retailing, transport and services, seems likely to have had a considerable influence on this trend.[10]

It is difficult, however, to demonstrate an extensive tourist influence in a positive way at this stage. The season was almost confined to July and August, and it is clear that relatively few people specialised in catering for the visitors. Before the railways, accommodation was largely hotel-centred, especially in the Windermere resorts, where a handful of substantial hostelries took most of the custom, and also did well out of the hire and maintenance of horses and carriages. The 1829 directory provides no lists of lodging-house keepers for these resorts, although it indicates that private lodgings were available. The June census of 1841 is no more helpful. At Keswick, admittedly, lodgings for visitors seem to have been more important to the local economy, with twenty landladies listed in 1829 and ten in the 1841 Census, which always under-records the numbers engaged in this elusive trade. But the hotels, with their armies of servants, clearly dominated this aspect of the tourist trade in terms of employment as well as visitor numbers.[11]

The listed places of accommodation, together with the circulating libraries, bookshops, museums, exhibitions, drapers and milliners, the guides, mineralists and boatmen, form the tip of an iceberg of uncertain size. Keswick, with eight 'guides and boatmen' and six mineralists, two of whom doubled up as Aeolian harp manufacturers, offered more competitors to provide a wider range of tourist services than its southern rivals; but we cannot assess the importance of those who catered for the visitors in some way during the season, but derived most of their

179

income from other sources, and were listed in the sources under their more regular occupations. Tourism lends itself to integration in this way into an existing economy, especially when, as in this case, that economy was not working to capacity; and this prevents us from assessing the contribution of the visiting season to the growth of Keswick, Ambleside and Bowness in any definite way. All the circumstantial evidence, however, suggests that it was already considerable and increasing.

By the 1830s, indeed, the rudiments of a tourist trade were becoming established even in the remoter western dales, as the more determined pursuers of romantic and sublime scenery pressed on beyond the range of even the sturdiest and most stable carriage. Few visitors seem to have approached Lakeland by the Whitehaven route, but at Strands in Wasdale and Calder Bridge on the coastal plain, hoteliers were already accustomed to dealing with parties of adventurous tourists who had struggled over the east-to-west passes, which were negotiable only on foot or horseback. Where carriages from the tourist centres were able to penetrate, special provision for visitors might run to a 'commodious inn', as at Crummock Water, where boats were provided to visit Scale Force or Buttermere.[12] But these were the outposts of a trade which was still concentrated in and around the three main urban centres.

The arrival of railways in Lakeland intensified the influences for growth. The opening of the Lancaster and Carlisle line brought tourists to within a few miles of Pooley Bridge, at the head of Ullswater; but the creation of a new railhead at Windermere by the opening of the branch from Kendal in 1847 made a far greater impact on the tourist trade. Within a few years, the centre of gravity of the industry had shifted south from Keswick, which had been growing rapidly since the late eighteenth century, to the Windermere resorts; and it was not until the late nineteenth century that Keswick, with a railway of its own, began to make up the lost ground. The crude population trends in the Lakeland resorts during the Victorian years can be found in Table 2.2.[13]

The bare bones of the story are clear enough. The main benefits of the first railway to penetrate Lakeland proper came, predictably, close to the railhead, and after a decade and a half of rapid growth Bowness, combined with the new settlement of Windermere which had grown up around the station, had overtaken Keswick as the most populous of the tourist centres. Ambleside, served by coach and steamer from the railway terminus, felt the pressure of demand more sluggishly, and grew by fits and starts, steadily falling behind its southern rival despite its excellent position as a touring centre. While this mid-Victorian activity was afoot, Keswick stagnated, and the arrival of the railway in 1864 had relatively little immediate impact. It was not until the last quarter of the century that the town began to grow consistently at a faster rate than the Windermere resorts. Meanwhile, a certain amount of tourist-based growth was taking place outside the established towns, especially in the mid-Victorian years around

Grasmere. In the Patterdale and Coniston areas, too, the tourist trade brought new building, although here the population trends were confused by the fortunes of the lead and copper mines, which fluctuated in Patterdale and declined steadily in Coniston, where as many as 43% of household heads had been copper miners in 1851.[14]

But the population figures in themselves tell only a small part of the story, and we ought to compare the experiences of the resorts in a little more depth, to try to establish what was distinctive about particular places, and what was common to Lakeland as a whole.

The railway affected Windermere in three significant ways. It attracted commuters, summer residents and the semi-retired, mainly from the Lancashire

22 The Old England Hotel at Bowness, from a steel engraving of c. 1875.

industrial towns, and especially from Manchester; and the demand for substantial residences for these people stimulated the building trades, while the large gardens which prevailed provided further work for local people, and the demand for retailing and personal services increased.[15] Secondly, it brought increasing numbers of the established kind of long-stay visitor, and made the resort more accessible to the less prosperous sectors of the middle classes. Thirdly, it enabled working-class excursionists to make the long journey from the industrial centres for the first time.[16] Let us examine these points a little further.

The presence of commuters and the semi-retired in large numbers made Windermere unique among the tourist centres of Lakeland proper. They exercised a strong influence on local government throughout the second half of the nineteenth century, and their contribution to the economy was considerable. Moreover, their recreational pursuits added to the resort's attractions, as the regular regattas of the Windermere Yacht Club entertained the less opulent with spectacular display. The building of yachts and steam launches, indeed, was already a significant employer of local labour by the early 1870s.[17] Even their 'numerous villas lying buried in their shrubberies' could be seen as enhancing the beauty of Bowness, forming 'an agreeable contrast to the bare monotonous rows we are accustomed to find in too many of our watering-places'.[18] Even in the 1880s, there was room for disagreement about this; but on the whole the proprietors of the 'villas and gentry houses', which accounted for one-sixth of Bowness' inhabitants in 1885, made the lakeside more attractive to most of its visitors, while they provided a lot of employment for the locals.[19]

The middle-class visitor, in various guises, remained the mainstay of Windermere's tourist economy. The growing importance of the lower levels of the middle classes, the superior clerks, middling tradesmen and lesser professionals, was expressed in a rapid increase in the number of private lodging-

23 Keswick: purpose-built boarding houses for the less affluent among the middle-class visitors of the late Victorian years.

houses listed in the local directories, although the hotels retained a considerable proportion of the total visiting public. They dominated at mid-century, when the new Windermere Hotel at the terminus added its considerable capacity to the existing hostelries in Bowness; and the numbers were later augmented by the conversion of some of the larger residences. Even in 1885, when the surveyor found 63 'lodging-houses' in Bowness alone, the eight hotels there still provided 40% of the sleeping accommodation, although the proportion at the top of the hill in Windermere itself would probably have been smaller. But the high-class market seems to have remained buoyant in the town.[20]

The expansion in lodging-house keeping was, however, marked, especially in the later nineteenth century, when the unreliable lists in the directories suggest that Windermere may have overtaken Ambleside and Keswick in its ability to cater at this level of the market. The number of landladies listed rose from 12 in 1849 to 32 in 1869, 88 in 1885 and 100 in 1894, and many more houses must have offered accommodation at the height of the season.[21] The number of staying visitors increased in step with this trend; Bowness seems to have doubled its

24 The lake steamer *Swift* at Bowness Bay, Windermere. An inter-war photograph by J. Hardman.

maximum total from about 750 in 1879 to 1500 in 1900, while Windermere's grew more slowly from about 500 in 1885.[22] This was a very limited tourist season in comparison with the great popular resorts of the Lancashire and Yorkshire coasts, and we shall see that Windermere's Lakeland rivals probably fared rather better for most of the century; but these were visitors of reasonable means, and they put a disproportionate amount into the local economy.

This could not be said of the working-class excursionists, although they, too, had their influence. As soon as the railway opened, day excursions were run from the Lancashire towns, especially at Whitsuntide, when the number of trippers might run to several thousand. By the 1870s, some working-class visitors were coming for the weekend, and the cottagers of Bowness began to offer cheap lodgings as well as hot water for the visitors to brew their tea.[23] Numbers were never spectacularly large, but in Whit week and increasingly on July and August Saturdays the trains and steamers might bring 10 000 trippers into the town, and the limited promenading space at Bowness Bay could make for uncomfortable overcrowding in the area around the lake. The excursionists came mainly from the great industrial centres of Lancashire and the West Riding of Yorkshire, with a fair representation from the North-Eastern mining and shipbuilding district by the 1880s, and with an increasingly passenger-conscious Furness Railway bringing growing numbers from Barrow and West Cumberland via its Lakeside branch and the steamers at the turn of the century.[24]

The middle-class visiting public and wealthy residents might have been expected to view these incursions with distaste, but the trippers seem to have been unusually well-behaved, and a little judicious regulation from the local authorities was sufficient to maintain order and decorum to most people's satisfaction. The trippers mixed with the other visitors at Bowness Bay, where they used the rapidly-growing fleet of pleasure boats (a dozen craft in the 1840s, rising to nearly 300 at the turn of the century) alongside their betters; but the occasional market they provided left little scope for street vendors or specialised commercial entertainment, beyond the occasional itinerant band or performing dog show.[25] There was no migration of fairground entertainment from the manufacturing towns, as there was at the Lancashire coast resorts, and occasional fears about tripper misbehaviour turned out to be largely groundless. This was partly due to the nature of the excursionists themselves, for Windermere, as a morally safe and 'improving' venue, seems to have attracted more than its fair share of Sunday School and employers' outings. Deference and good order predominated, and even outside the ranks of the 'respectable' working man, it could be argued in 1892 that 'the very presence of the better class of visitors . . . has a wonderfully subduing effect upon the rougher element'.[26] From time to time, problems did arise: Jarrow trippers might disturb the peace of the bay and splash the 'fanciful boating costumes' of the more affluent, or tipsy adolescent Sunday School trippers, bored at the end of a long day devoid of conventional amusements, might raid the gardens on the road to the station for laburnums; but these were isolated incidents, largely confined to Whitsuntide.[27] In any case, the wealthy residents and 'better-class' visitors had the resources to escape from the occasional proximity of their social inferiors by taking refuge in hotels or private grounds, or by moving away from the immediate vicinity of the railway and steamer terminals, beyond which few excursionists penetrated.[28] All these safety-valves meant that, although Windermere's economy as a resort was more mixed than those of its Lakeland rivals, there was no serious conflict between wealthy residents, 'better-class' visitors and the excursionist interest, at least until the eve of the First World War.[29]

Ambleside is a less complicated case. Although it was served by steamers and coaches which connected with the trains, its residential development was limited by the difficulty of regular commuting to the industrial centres, and the excursionist presence was likewise less noticeable than at Windermere. Michael Taylor, a hotelier who had recently moved to Ambleside from Blackpool, provided a revealing comparison between the Lancashire resort and his new home in 1887: he found 'a far larger number of educated gentry (in Ambleside), and a far larger proportion of the middle class, but the lower class we see less of . . . unless they have a taste for the beauties of our district, and receive culture therefrom, they do not come twice'.[30] At Waterhead, where the steamers called, there were stalls and pleasure boats to cater for the tripper, but he seems to have made little impact on the town's economy.[31]

The strength of Ambleside and nearby Grasmere, indeed, lay almost entirely in the solid middle-class holiday market, although Ambleside's hotels might attract their quota of titled visitors.[32] Mid-Victorian Ambleside, indeed, had more lodging-houses listed than either of its rivals, although slow growth in the 1870s and after lost the town its brief primacy in this respect.[33] Even in 1876, however, a Quarter Sessions return suggested that Ambleside still specialised in accommodation to a greater extent than Windermere. The town's visitor population was estimated at 2000 at the season's height, nearly twice that of Windermere, whose resident population was, in turn, twice that of Ambleside. Grasmere, indeed, was credited with more visitors than Bowness and nearly as many as Windermere as a whole, with a resident population of 800 as against nearly 4000.[34] In each case, no doubt, and especially at Grasmere, the number of accommodation units was augmented by the common practice of letting villas for the season. It is clear that by the 1870s, even if Ambleside and Grasmere did not provide the greatest concentrations of visitors in Lakeland, they were certainly more heavily dependent on the middle-class family tourist trade than Windermere or Keswick.[35] As Ambleside's old manufacturing and commercial functions stagnated or declined in the later nineteenth century, the dependence of the local economy on tourists and building became steadily more pronounced, and on the eve of the First World War these related activities had long been the

25 A scene in Edwardian Ambleside with holiday coaches in view.

major sources of income and employment in the town.[36]

Ambleside never got its railway, despite the efforts of its inhabitants at various points in the later nineteenth century, and this inconvenience clearly retarded its growth for most of this period, as the expansion of the Lakeland tourist market came to depend increasingly on the growing band of middle-class visitors who were holidaymakers first, sightseers second and devotees of romantic mountain solitude hardly at all. The importance of good transport links is further emphasised by the case of Keswick, which was relieved from mid-Victorian stagnation by the arrival of the Cockermouth, Keswick and Penrith line in 1864.

We have seen that Keswick in the 1830s and 1840s had more urban amenities to offer to the tourist than its rivals. As well as a wide range of services, there was Crosthwaite's museum, which attracted up to a thousand people to sign the visitors' book in a good year; and there were exhibitions, theatrical performances and concerts at the Town Hall. By 1850, the facilities had been augmented by a 'splendid pavilion', with space for 2000 people and scope for the holding of

---

26 Rational recreations for opulent visitors: a handbill advertising Crosthwaite's Museum, Keswick, in 1842.

186

The Quadrant, Telescope, and Weathercock,

A LITTLE BELOW THE MIDDLE OF THE

TOWN OF KESWICK.

JUNE 9th, 1842.

CROSTHWAITE'S CELEBRATED

MUSEUM.

DANIEL CROSTHWAITE,

(Son of the late PETER CROSTHWAITE, Establisher of the Museum at Keswick, in the Year 1780; formerly a Naval Commander in the East Indies; Surveyor and Seller of the Maps of the Lakes in Cumberland, Westmorland, and Lancashire, attestations of the accuracy of which are given under able hands, and may be seen at the Museum,)

With much gratitude, returns his most grateful thanks to the Nobility, Gentry, and others, for the great encouragement which he has received; and from his unremitting attention in procuring every desirable addition to his Collection of CURIOSITIES, he hopes to merit their future favours and attention.

THE MUSEUM

Consists of rare CURIOSITIES, both of Art & Nature, viz.:--Antiquities, Coins, Medals, Arms, Petrefactions, Fossils, Minerals, Quadrupeds, Birds, Insects, Fishes, Serpents, Shells, Grottos, and many Models and Useful Inventions, &c., &c., &c., contained in five rooms. Two New Zealand Chieftains' Heads in excellent preservation. The Geology, Minerology, and Botany of Cumberland. A number of Trophical and other Fossil Plants; also various Antiquities; as Roman, Celtic, and Ancient British Armour, Battle Axes, Swords, Spears, and other Weapons; all found in Cumberland.

MUSICAL STONES.

The First Set of Musical Stones ever found,

Were discovered by the late Mr. P. CROSTHWAITE, June 11th, 1785, and consist of sixteen regular notes, upon which a number of tunes on the natural key can be heard at the Museum.

Admittance to Ladies and Gentlemen, 1s. each; Servants, 6d. each; and open from Seven in the Morning until Ten in the Evening; or at any other time if particularly requested.

His Maps ars engraved by the best Artists, and every addition thought necessary has been added, viz. :—the Sounding of the different Lakes in Fathoms, contigious Roads, West's finest Stations for Prospects, with many others of the Author's own choice, all distinctly marked out. The Maps are sold at the Museum, at 9s. per set, bound; and 8s. per set unbound. The Æolian Harps of his late Father's Invention, at 7s. each. Otley's, Baine's, Wordsworth's, Ford's, and Scott's Guide to the Lakes. Minerals, Fossils, Spars, and Shells. Also Sells the best improved hard and other kinds of Black Lead Pencils, &c., all of which he sells on reasonable terms.

Westall's, Farington's, and other Views of the Lakes.

D. C. has on Sale, on the most reasonable terms, (being the latest new discoveries in Cumberland,) Blue Calamine and Phosphate of Lead, the Calsite of Barytes, the Murio Phosphate of Lead, the Blue Carbonate of Lead, Arseniate of Lead, the Tabular Crystals of the Sulphuret of Iron, and the Slip Shift in Shistos, which defines the Mining System the best of any thing that has been discovered, and all the other scarce Minerals the produce of Cumberland; either in Collections or single Specimens.

He has also lately collected the Geological or Rock Specimens, which he sells in sets to his numerous Visitors.

☞ *The Museum continues to be exhibited in the same house where his late Father and himself have resided for the last Fifty-eight Years.*

Catalogues of the Curiosities are sold at the Museum.

equestrian performances.[37] In 1836, the prosperity of the season drew in a gang of eight or ten prostitutes from the West Cumberland coastal towns, to cater for the more determinedly pleasure-seeking of the visitors.[38] Keswick was the resort of the élite of Lakeland visitors, with Oxford and Cambridge reading-parties already strongly in evidence; and its hotels accommodated a good sprinkling of the nobility and gentry.[39]

Keswick kept this élite patronage, and its slow mid-Victorian growth was due to its inability to compete for the expanding middle-class market. The railway did not change matters overnight. Unlike the Windermere line, it was never intended to live by tourist traffic alone. Although Keswick's tourist trade enabled it to be described in 1862 as the greatest surviving coaching centre in a nation already dominated by the railways, with 22 coaches in and out daily during the summer,[40] the railway promoters found the prospect of through coke traffic from Durham to West Cumberland much more attractive. The railway was keen to encourage visitor traffic in its earliest years, before the mineral traffic was properly under way, but despite the directors' involvement in accommodation through the opening of the substantial Keswick Hotel in 1869, Keswick's needs soon ceased to bulk large on their list of priorities.[41]

The railway company's lack of interest helps to explain the limited nature of the changes in Keswick's late Victorian tourist trade, especially by comparison with Windermere; but the greater length of the journey from London and the main population centres, and the lack of through carriage facilities, also played their part. The residential and excursionist sectors of the town's economy were stunted in their growth. Some villa development did take place, but it could cater only for those who sought a secluded retirement, for regular commuting was out of the question. Excursionists, admittedly, were rather more in evidence. Most of them came from West Cumberland, Durham and Carlisle, areas which developed the excursion habit much later than the Lancashire textile towns which dominated the Windermere traffic; and their numbers, even at Whitsuntide, could rarely stand comparison with Windermere on a busy holiday. The trippers never made a major contribution to the town's economy, although plenty of restaurant proprietors and petty tradesmen would have liked to see more of them. As at Windermere, problems of disorder and incompatible holiday styles never became a major issue, despite complaints about the awkward tendency of the excursionist and 'better-class' holiday seasons to reach a peak together in August.[42]

As its woollen industry declined into extinction, Keswick became increasingly dependent on its tourists; and even the pencil industry which continued to grow

---

27 The commercial exploitation of scenery: an advertisement for Stock Ghyll falls, Ambleside, 1885.

STOCK GHYLL WATER FALLS.

VISITORS

Are respectfully informed, that the above Falls, and the lovely Grounds surrounding, together with a Safe and Easy Descent to

The FOOT OF THE FALLS

Can be reached, **ONLY** by the

UPPER FOOTPATH THROUGH Nelly Close Wood.

A Refreshment "Shelter," has been erected. Teas and Provisions are provided, at reasonable charges.

Bathing is permitted, Under the Falls,

Between 6 and 9 a.m., and after 7-30 p.m.—Towelling provided.

With the object of securing the Comfort and Safety of Visitors, and of keeping **The Shelters, Railings, Seats, Rustic Bridges,** and **Fences in Repair,** the Owner of Stock Ghyll Grounds, has Reduced the Charge to

ONE PENNY

FOR EACH PERSON.

THIS PAYMENT includes a Free Passage over " THE **PRIVATE** OCCUPATION ROAD " called " THE GROVE ROAD," from the Entrance Gate, close to the Stable Yard of " **The Salutation Hotel**," to **The FOOT OF THE FALLS,** and Return.

N.B.—Visitors, desiring to **extend** their Mountain Walks, **after Visiting the Falls,** have Colonel Rhodes' permission to proceed further up " The Grove Road," to " **The Grove Farm,**" (about One Mile). They can return to Ambleside, by the same **Private** Road, or by " The Kirkstone-Pass Road," a pleasant round of about Three Miles.— **Milking Time is at about 5 p.m.**

Rothay Holme,
Ambleside,
July 27th, 1885.

G. RHODES (COLONEL),
Owner of the Grove Estate.

throughout the period probably depended heavily on the purchases of visitors. The 'better-class' visitor became the mainstay of the local economy, to nearly as great an extent as in Ambleside. Lodging-houses proliferated alongside the hotels, and Keswick gained from its position as natural touring centre for the northern lakes. As Baddeley's *Guide* put it at the turn of the century, 'Except for a few nights at one or more of the comfortable inns which stand in Borrowdale and on the margins of the wild Western lakes, it is Keswick or nowhere.'[43] The coming of the railway had confirmed Keswick's position as the natural exploration centre for a wide area, and this ensured a healthy demand for the large number of horse-drawn conveyances operated by the local hoteliers.

Despite this advantage, which contrasted with the stiff competition between the resorts further south, Keswick did little to cater for visitors within its own boundaries. It remained parasitic on the surrounding scenery, and late Victorian guide book writers had to admit that the town itself was dull. Between 1852 and 1883, informed contemporaries thought that the number of visitors in a season increased from 8–15 000 to 40–50 000; but the latter figure was still thought to be a plausible estimate in 1912.[44] This was hardly spectacular growth, and it reflected an unwillingness to invest in advertising or amenities. The visitor trade was thought to be self-selecting and unresponsive to new initiatives, and the Queen of the Lakes Pavilion, opened in 1894 to dispense refreshments and the occasional entertainment to excursionists, was the only major new attraction of the post-railway period. The $28\frac{1}{2}$ acres of Fitz Park also enhanced the town's late-Victorian amenities, but Keswick generally rested content with steady but unspectacular growth based on its unchallenged role as the accommodation and communications centre for north Lakeland.[45]

Outside Keswick and its immediate neighbourhood, little tourist penetration of the rural economy took place in this area. Wastwater and Ennerdale, in particular, remained little more frequented than they had been in the 1830s, for the difficulties of the terrain put them beyond the reach of a day excursion from Keswick, except for the most determined.[46] Wastwater had added little to its accommodation by 1868, when William Ritson's farm-house offered 'clean and comfortable' lodgings at Wasdale Head for ten or twelve people at a time; the rest had to carry on down the valley to Strands.[47] Even thirty years on, when climbing was well-established as a summer sport in the area, the only rival to Ritson's farmhouse, now the Wasdale Head Hotel, was a single 'temperance inn'.[48] The Sty Head Pass track from Borrowdale, where the Keswick coaches penetrated, over to Wastwater might now be 'traversed in summer daily by scores of tourists of both sexes', on ponies or on foot, but little provision was made for them at the Wastwater end. Most visitors to the lake came by the less spectacular but more comfortable carriage roads from the West Cumberland seaside resorts.[49]

Ennerdale was similarly remote, and the few climbers and anglers who chose

190

to stay there put little pressure on limited resources. The Anglers' Inn, a speculation by one of the local landowners, was enlarged in the mid-1860s, but in the absence of a railway up the valley it remained the only substantial hostelry in the area.[50] Like Wastwater, Ennerdale was visited mainly from the West Coast, but not only by the leisured and genteel; 'the *canaille* of Cleator Moor, Frizington and all the district around' were also finding their way there on foot by the 1880s, at least on popular holidays in the nearby mining and iron-working district.[51]

These western lakes were unique in their continuing isolation from the main tourist centres. Even the cyclists who were filling the Lakeland roads in the late-Victorian and Edwardian summers, and giving a further stimulus to the farmhouse tea and lodging trades, found them hard to reach, for all the passes except Hardknott were described as 'unrideable' by Baddeley in 1913, and the only direct through route to the west 'admits of machines being taken over it chiefly by pushing'.[52] Here, as almost everywhere, some effort was being made to cater for the tourist; but away from the main resorts, the impact on the rural economy was still very limited even in Edwardian times.

Where the coaches ran from Keswick, Ambleside or Windermere, admittedly, secondary nuclei of tourist development were becoming apparent by the turn of the century. Buttermere could support three hotels by 1901, although the only other regular accommodation was provided by a joiner and two farmers who let apartments.[53] Higher up the scale came Ullswater, where there were three hotels, a temperance hotel and 'numerous lodging-houses', fed by the lake steamer and regular coaches from the Keswick and Windermere areas; and Coniston, which benefited more than most from the Furness Railway's rich and varied menu of circular tours in the 1890s, had accumulated five 'refreshment rooms' and fourteen lodging-houses to supplement its two hotels. In both places, railway access was too inconvenient to make a significant direct impact on the tourist trade, but carriages, steamers and the ubiquitous bicycle allowed considerable development in the late nineteenth century.[54]

At the turn of the century, too, a widespread rejection of commercialised resorts was leading people of all classes, who enjoyed relaxation in a peaceful country setting, to colonise rural villages for holidays and short breaks. The bicycle and later the motor-car assisted in the development of this trend, which was as marked in Cumbria as in other parts of the country, as unpretentious villages outside the Lake District proper found themselves catering for holidaymakers. By 1899 Brampton, east of Carlisle, was already establishing a summer season based on its rural attractions and historic associations, with all the available accommodation booked up in advance for August and early September. Even more surprisingly, the remote market town and old lead-mining centre of Alston, high in the rather featureless fells of East Cumberland, was turning visitors away at August Bank Holiday.[55] At the south-eastern fringe of Cumbria, too, the attractively-situated market town of Kirkby Lonsdale was rapidly emerging as a pleasure resort for 'well-to-do persons from all parts of England', and for some discriminating Americans.[56]

The inland tourist trade was thus spreading its influence throughout the Lake District and its fringes even before the coming of the motor-car; but the great majority of Lakeland visitors continued to base themselves in the three major resorts, with Grasmere easily the most important of the secondary centres. As places to stay rather than points on a daily itinerary, Buttermere, Wasdale Head or Coniston were the preserves for the most part of the more specialised or purist of Lakeland's increasingly diversified visiting publics: climbers, anglers and seekers after peace and contemplation in the manner of Wordsworth or Ruskin. The towns were given over largely to sightseers with limited time and carefully-prepared itineraries drawn from any of several popular guide-books, such as those produced by Baddeley, Jenkinson, Black's or Ward Lock. All this activity generated traffic, and the resulting problems of highway maintenance were already apparent in the 1880s, even in Borrowdale; but most of the income went to the towns, and especially to the hoteliers who ran the stage-coach services, as well as providing the most lucrative accommodation and catering. By the late 1880s, a major hotelier like Michael Taylor of the Queen's and Salutation Hotels in Ambleside might run six four-in-hand coaches and keep eighty horses in the summer. He had his counterparts in other towns, and these were the men who did really well out of the tourist trade, generating considerable seasonal employment in the process.[57]

All this was beginning to change in the early twentieth century, as the car and the charabanc brought a new style of holidaymaking; but the Lakeland holidaymaker had always been mobile, and the resorts had long been accustomed to the problems of catering for short, unpredictable visits. The major resorts kept their pre-eminence, and it may be useful, after having spent some time in looking at the differences between them, if we look at the attributes they had in common, and venture a few general statements about the characteristics of the Lakeland tourist resorts in this period.

In the first place, we can point to the persisting dominance of the 'better-class' visitor, staying for two or three weeks or more in hotel, lodging-house or rented villa, and drawn from the expanding ranks of commerce, industry and the professions, especially the academic, literary and religious worlds. A top-dressing of titles and gentry remained throughout the period, but the prosperous middle classes continued to be the mainstay of the tourist economy, in spite of the excursion train and later the bicycle. Judging by the visitors' lists in the local press, too, the Lakeland resorts had much in common in the geographical origins of their visitors. Industrial Lancashire bulked large everywhere, with about 40 per cent of the visitors in the later nineteenth century; and London was also important, with over 10 per cent of the visitors everywhere and up to 20 per cent in Keswick. The accidents of railway and commercial alignment also brought a fair number from the North-East, again especially in Keswick, but Yorkshire was very poorly represented. The importance of academics and the affluent retired was brought out by a noticeable presence from Oxbridge and a variety of residential resorts, both inland and coastal; and foreign visitors were growing in importance in the late nineteenth century, especially from the United States.[58] The Lakeland resorts, despite the importance of Lancashire and other parts of the industrial north in supplying visitors, had an unusually wide and varied catchment area, and this seems to have provided increasingly effective insulation from the regional trade cycles which affected such resorts as Morecambe.[59] Bad trade might still make a bad season in the mid-Victorian years, admittedly, but bad weather was a much more persistent and dangerous enemy. This leads us to consider a further common feature of the Lakeland resorts: their continuing dependence on outdoor, natural attractions, and the lack of an organised entertainment industry on any significant scale.

Lakeland's visiting public provided an unpromising market for commercial amusement. Sightseeing, walking and contemplation provided their staple fare, with rowing and fishing on the lakes, and later climbing, providing more specialised diversions. The hotels offered dancing and company in the evenings, and most of the visitors seem to have desired little more. Persistent rain might precipitate a lot of premature departures, but most visitors were unlikely to be consoled by the offer of indoor entertainment. Even if the market had looked more promising, however, there were logistical problems. Given the relatively small numbers of visitors, and their tendency to be spread over quite a wide area, the difficulty in raising an audience was much greater than in the generally compact and concentrated Victorian seaside resort. Capital was hard to come by, too, especially as those locals who were most plentifully endowed with it were likely to see commercial entertainment as a threat to residential amenity or to existing vested interests. Moreover, the summer season was even shorter than in most resorts, and though it was being extended a little from its July and August base in the late nineteenth century, when week-end visitors were beginning to appear even at Easter, there was still a very limited time in which to generate an adequate return on capital, especially when a sophisticated and demanding audience had to be wooed. It is not surprising that schemes for Winter Gardens and the like came to nothing, and that commercial entertainment remained *ad hoc* and occasional. In contrast with many seaside resorts, moreover, local government hesitated to step in where private enterprise feared to tread, and the entertainment industry as such made very little headway. Even the occasional provision of a town's band, maintained partly by subscription, had a flavour of daring extravagance about it, and Windermere's burgesses begrudged the spending of a mere £300 on a new pavilion and promenade in 1892.[60]

Occasional sporting events, largely organised by the local gentry, provided the only regular highlights in the entertainment calendar during the season. Regattas, athletic sports and wrestling in the Cumberland and Westmorland style all featured regularly at the resorts, and the high point of the year in this respect came to be the Grasmere Sports in mid-August. This event developed rapidly from the first of the regular meetings in 1865, and by 1873 it was already attracting a thousand or more spectators. Three years later, with four times the patronage, it could be seen as a 'tolerably select' gathering, 'the most brilliant outdoor reunion in the Lake District.' The Earl of Bective and members of the Lowther family were regularly prominent, and the wrestling, fell racing and hound trailing ensured the event a central place in the local calendar. Baddeley, at the turn of the century, described it as 'the "Derby Day" of the district'.[61]

The Grasmere sports were capable of attracting a good attendance even in the rain;[62] but this only emphasises the lack of artificial all-weather amusements. In all the resorts, there was little attempt to go beyond the natural attractions of the area, which were seen as being entirely sufficient for the needs of the visitors. Investment went into accommodation, and into the improvement of transport facilities so that the visitors could tour a round of well-publicised beauty spots with ease and in comfort. The hoteliers, as befitted those with an interest in improvement and the resources to pursue it, took the lead in this respect, and their voluntary organisations were also responsible for the first concerted efforts to advertise the delights of Lakeland to the wider world in the 1870s. Local government, by contrast, made little impact in these important areas throughout the period; the Local Boards of Health confined their activities almost entirely, and not always very effectively, to paving, lighting and sewering. When invited to go beyond the basics in the interests of the tourist trade, they baulked; in 1880, for instance, Grasmere Local Board declined an invitation to repair the main Windermere–Keswick road over Dunmail Raise, as 'they do not consider the road sufficiently dangerous as to warrant any expenditure on it'.[63]

The hoteliers, with some patronage from local gentry and an increasing amount of help from the lesser tradesmen in the resorts, made strenuous efforts to improve communications in the late nineteenth century. Apparently prompted by a suggestion from Cook's, the travel agents, in 1876, they formed themselves into an English Lake District Association, ELDA, whose objectives involved the maintenance and improvement of roads and footpaths, and the provision of outdoor amenities without impairing the natural beauty of the area.[64] In 1879 this body amalgamated with the Lake District Advertising Association, formed in the previous year, which promoted the hotels of its subscribers in *Punch* and other periodicals, and distributed pamphlets and other literature to such promising outlets as the passenger ships of the White Star Line.[65]

Although ELDA devoted some of its resources to signposts, shelters, bridges and the keeping open of footpaths, road improvements and advertising were its main preoccupations. The committee canvassed a series of schemes for new carriage roads throughout the Lake District, but the regular favourite was Hardknott Pass, which was improved at considerable expense in the early 1880s. The result was less than satisfactory to the promoters, for in 1891 it had to be admitted that the road 'is certainly not the success that was anticipated . . . for three-quarters of the distance there is no public conveyance, and it is thought that the experiment of instituting one might be tried with advantage'.[66] There was no stampede to fill the gap in communication across this very difficult terrain, and the failure of the Hardknott scheme to widen the hoteliers' repertoire of coach excursions was not encouraging for subsequent ambitious but unsuccessful schemes for opening out difficult corners of Lakeland.[67]

ELDA was not much more effective at first in agitating for the proper upkeep of the existing roads, many of which had been dis-turnpiked by the 1870s and thrown back on the local surveyors of highways. As traffic increased, some hoteliers were driven to repairing the roads out of their own pockets, and seeking recompense from the Association; this happened in Newlands on the Buttermere road in 1882, for instance.[68] But a steady flow of funds into road improvement must have brought some reward for the Association's efforts, and the powers of the new County Councils were beginning to make matters easier by the 1890s.

Advertising was the other main element in the Association's budget, with nearly £150 being made available as early as 1881. The aim was to increase the flow of 'better-class' visitors on the established pattern, especially from the south of England, the United States and the Continent.[69] The railways supplemented the Association's efforts with their own propaganda, although the Cockermouth, Keswick and Penrith was always decidedly parsimonious towards Keswick.[70]

Keswick was not only left out in the cold by its railway company; it also reaped little benefit from the activities of ELDA. Only one of the thirteen members of the Association's first committee came from Keswick, and the Windermere resorts continued to dominate its activities. Not surprisingly, the advertising material was heavily slanted towards southern Lakeland, and this reduced the level of Keswick participation still further. By 1891 there was only a solitary Keswick hotelier on the subscription list, and there was little improvement thereafter. Keswick's own advertising campaign did not really get under way until the early twentieth century, when a local Improvement Association was started with the backing of the Urban District Council.[71]

Perhaps because it was significantly more difficult of access than its southern rivals, Keswick does appear less than enterprising in its approach to the tourist industry in the later nineteenth century. Some of the local townspeople certainly thought so, and agitated in the 1880s for an attempt to diversify the holiday economy by attracting a lower and more numerous class of visitor.[72] But when we compare the Lakeland tourist resorts with seaside resorts of a similar size and clientèle, we find little difference in the scope of the artificial attractions on offer. The natural attractions might differ in kind, but they remained the basis of the appeal of each kind of resort. Despite the local variations, moreover, the Lakeland resorts had a great deal in common in their social and economic structure, and in the manner in which they catered for an unusually discriminating clientèle.

But there is more to the tourist trade in Victorian Cumbria than the inland resorts. On a smaller scale, the belated growth of the region's seaside resorts for most of the second half of the nineteenth century was more dynamic than that of the Lakeland tourist centres. The seaside resorts remained small, admittedly, and it is impossible to disentangle their population statistics from the surrounding rural areas. Even in 1901, indeed, no Cumbrian seaside resort had yet reached a population of 2000 in its own right. But Grange and Silloth, in particular, grew rapidly in the mid-Victorian years, and St Bees and Seascale experienced sharp surges of expansion which were not subsequently sustained. The Cumbrian seaside probably attracted fewer visitors than the Lakes and, Silloth and Allonby apart, its resorts were partly dependent on the scenic attractions of Lakeland; but the development of these little bathing-places deserves some attention.

Several years before the coming of the railways, some of the possibilities for watering-place promotion on the fringes of Lakeland were becoming apparent to far-sighted property-owners. In 1833 an attempt was made to develop Harrington, soon to be disfigured by mining and a variety of industrial activities, as an inexpensive sea-bathing resort; and two years later efforts were made to promote Cartlane, near the present Grange-over-Sands, as a watering-place with ready access to Windermere and Coniston Water.[73] These schemes were still-born, but it is significant that the established attractions of Lakeland were already being used to stimulate resort growth on the Cumbrian coast.

But it was the railways that brought Cumbria's new seaside resorts into being. At Silloth and Seascale, indeed, they owned the land on which the crucial early development took place; and at Grange the Furness Railway was responsible for the large hotel which really marked the beginning of resort expansion, and for the gasworks which offered an essential amenity at an early stage.[74] Only at St Bees was the railway not an active participant in the emergence of a new resort, and only here did development languish, after a promising start in the immediate aftermath of the opening of the line. The railways passed Allonby by, and its population declined steadily through the second half of the nineteenth century; but its ageing inhabitants seem to have been content with their genteel isolation. They did not encourage new building, and it is doubtful whether the coming of a branch line would have prodded them into life. Allonby survived the mid-Victorian vogue for Silloth, and continued to cater for the farmers and gentry of North Cumberland as it had done for over a century. Its economy changed little, and the village prospered little; as the Vicar remarked in 1899, 'The break-up of old ships was not a very lucrative industry; the herring fishery did not often yield productive results, and the summer season was not long enough to enable them to rook the visitors as they should like to do.'[75] A sedate continuity was all the resort achieved or, apparently, sought.

Allonby's lethargy was exceptional, as was its dependence on the surrounding countryside for most of its visitors.[76] Its Solway Firth neighbour, Silloth, was also exceptional, but for different reasons. It, too, owed little to the relatively distant charms of Lakeland, but it came to depend much more heavily on Carlisle and southern Scotland for its visiting public. It was, moreover, entirely a railway creation, and for many years its fortunes depended almost completely on the attitude of the company which effectively owned it. Unlike all the other Cumbrian resorts except Seascale, a similar railway promotion, it was a planned town, and its gridiron plan and formal terraces gave it a distinctive physical appearance.

Silloth grew up as part of a plan to give Carlisle a new outlet to the sea, free from the silting and tidal problems of the existing harbour at Port Carlisle, at the head of the Solway Firth, which had been connected to the city by a canal since 1823.[77] The dominant trading interests in Carlisle sought emancipation from the existing railway companies, and they were prepared to spend heavily on a railway which might be unremunerative in itself, but which would, it was hoped, bring considerable benefits to the city's trade. In 1853, the Port Carlisle canal was converted into a railway, but the port's competitive disadvantages remained, and in 1856 an extension to Silloth, 21 miles from Carlisle, was completed.[78]

Silloth was intended to prosper, and to bring prosperity to Carlisle, as a commercial port for ocean-going vessels; but until the necessary docks could be opened, traffic receipts were low enough to cause severe financial problems, for the railway had been built through sparsely populated countryside to terminate in a wilderness of sand-dunes. In the early years, some of the directors had to dip deeply into their own pockets to save the line from insolvency. Salvation was sought through the development of a sea-bathing traffic, a possibility which had at first received little attention. Under the pressing circumstances, however, Silloth's potential as a watering-place soon grew to dominate over all other considerations. In September, 1855, the Silloth Bay Railway acquired 46 acres of Blitterlees Common, close to the terminus; and two years later a further 160 acres had been added.[79] By 1861, a full-scale planned town was taking shape on railway land, and the company had built a hotel and lodging-houses as well as laying out streets and sewers, and providing a gasworks.[80]

In doing all this, the company had exceeded its powers; but it had also created what was to become the largest and most specialised seaside resort in Victorian Cumbria. When the North British Railway took over the line in 1862, it publicised the attractions of Silloth for invalids and 'better-class' holidaymakers all along its new route from Edinburgh to Carlisle, and throughout the Scottish Lowlands; and the result was several years of mid-Victorian prosperity based on visitors from Scotland and the Borders as well as Carlisle itself.[81] By 1869,

197

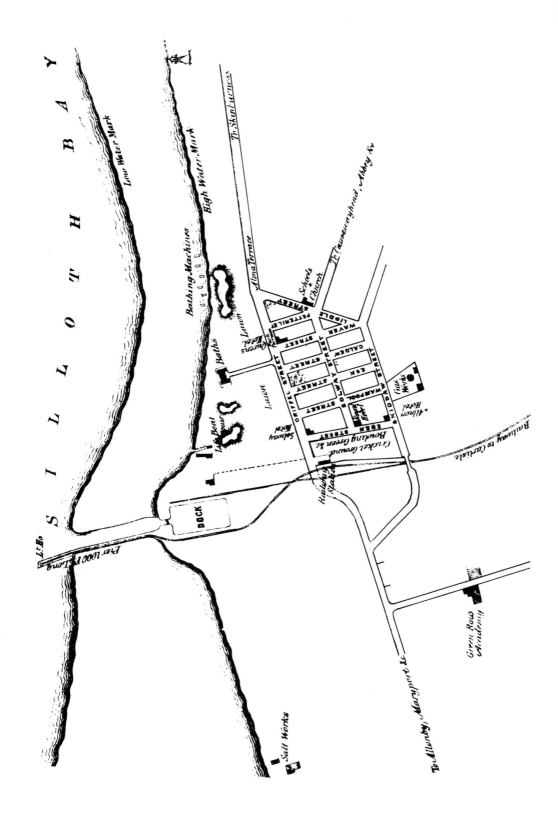

Silloth's roll-call of lodging-house keepers stood comparison with the three largest Lakeland tourist resorts, and the growth of its holiday season had already left the other Cumbrian coast resorts far behind.[82]

Subsequently, Silloth entered a phase of stagnation and depression, as the North British was riven by financial crisis and found itself unable or unwilling to look after the town's most basic needs.[83] The town also suffered from the rural preoccupations of its local government, for it formed only a small and indigestible part of the area and population covered by the Holme Cultram Local Board after 1863. In the late 1870s and early 1880s a crisis occurred when neither the railway nor the Local Board was prepared to maintain the town's sewers, and Silloth's public health, amenities and visitor numbers all suffered from this neglect.[84] But this was the low point of Silloth's Victorian career, and by the turn of the century, after the Local Board had accepted responsibility for the town's sanitary needs, it was again flourishing modestly as a specialised resort catering mainly for the middle classes of the border counties, with a growing working-class presence from Carlisle making itself felt during the city's race week.[85] The industrial workers of West Cumberland, too, were at last beginning to find their way to Silloth by excursion train, and by 1901 the town ranked as Cumbria's premier resort, at least as measured in units of accommodation, for the 117 lodging-houses listed in Bulmer's *Directory* put it ahead of Windermere and Keswick, and far ahead of any seaside rival.[86] The dock was often busy with shipping, but the resort activities continued to dominate the local economy.

It will be clear that Silloth's growth, like Allonby's stagnation, had little to do with the proximity of Lakeland.[87] They were, and remained, small provincial resorts of a kind familiar in other parts of the country. Further south, matters were rather different. The West Cumberland industrial towns, with their concentration on mining and heavy industry, and their limited middle-class presence, were slow to generate any significant demand for specialised sea-bathing resorts.[88] The impetus for development of this kind, such as it was, came from outside; and the emergent resorts of St Bees, Seascale and Grange depended for much of their custom on the well-off inhabitants of a wide range of mainly northern industrial towns, who sought to combine a family sea-bathing holiday with the occasional excursion to the more accessible parts of Lakeland.

West Cumberland had never been popular as a gateway to the Lakes, despite the relative cheapness of the Whitehaven steamer service even in railway days.[89] Attempts were sometimes made to remedy this, and as late as 1856 the new

28 Silloth as envisaged by the Carlisle and Silloth Bay Railway: this plan was reproduced in the *Silloth Gazette* in 1860, when the resort was just beginning to take shape.

Whitehaven Railway Hotel sought the patronage of the 'Nobility and families visiting Cumberland and the Lakes' for its numerous apartments 'with extensive sea views'.[90] But Whitehaven, not surprisingly, did not commend itself as a tourist centre, and it was the nearby village of St Bees, just south of the coastal coalfield, which benefited in the early stages from the arrival of the railway in 1847, limited though it was by the lack of a through route to the south until ten years later.

With its pretty little bay, its interesting ecclesiastical history and its theological college, St Bees had a lot to offer to the speculator aiming at the respectable middle-class family holiday market; and its comfortable access to Ennerdale and Wasdale was an important bonus. The approach of the railway from Whitehaven in 1847 brought a hotel company into being, and many villagers were soon offering apartments in July and August. There was a short, sharp boom in the late 1840s, when most of the visitors originated from West Cumberland, but the presence of families from the London area, Liverpool, Birmingham, Leeds, Bradford and even Barbados and Calcutta indicated that there was potentially a national market for this novel combination of sea-bathing and lake tourism.[91]

Although St Bees found its way into mid-Victorian guide books as the approved starting point for visits to Ennerdale and even Wastwater,[92] it never built on its promising start to any significant extent, and the season stagnated. There was no expansion in amenities or accommodation after the 1850s, and the rise of Seascale a few miles to the south, with advantages of its own, ensured that the increased demand for seaside holidays in the late nineteenth century passed St Bees by.[93]

Seascale came into being as an embryo resort at about the same time as St Bees; but despite the virtues of a good beach and proximity to Eskdale and Wasdale, there was little development until the Furness Railway took the resort in hand in 1870, purchasing a tract of cheap land close to the station with a view to creating a planned watering-place on quite an ambitious scale.[94] The grand design was never achieved, but by the end of the century, assisted by the provision of a golf links and other sporting facilities, Seascale consisted of seventy or so houses, about half of which took in visitors during the July and August season. In 1891, the high point of the season in mid-August found 89 family parties accommodated in 39 apartment houses. A minority of these came from Cumbria, and very few indeed from Barrow or West Cumberland. This was the middle-class family holiday in the full glory of its prosperity, servants and all, with a strong bias towards the Church, medicine and the universities, and a leavening of mercantile and industrial leaders from the manufacturing towns of Lancashire and Yorkshire. Always, however, a sprinkling of visitors came from further afield: Bournemouth, Salisbury, Merthyr Tydfil, New Zealand, Canada, Bombay. This might have been a visitors' list from Keswick or Windermere, and it was on this part of the Cumbrian coast that the spin-off effect of central

Lakeland became an effective generator of family holidays in late Victorian times.[95]

Despite Seascale's advantages, its remoteness prevented the Furness Railway from securing to it even the limited degree of success achieved by Silloth, where an informal census in 1882, at the height of the crisis over the sewers, found 953 visitors staying over a Saturday night at the height of the season, and up to 2000 day-trippers might appear at Race Week or in August.[96] But even Seascale's holiday season was looked upon with envy elsewhere on the coast. At St Bees, local tradesmen resented the favours lavished upon Seascale by the Furness Railway, and complained that the decline of the local season was due to the company's failure to 'take even an ordinary business interest' in the town.[97] At Haverigg, near Millom, the fishermen and traders wondered what was so special about Seascale, and resolved to form a committee to spend 'a few shillings . . . on advertising the place' in the belief that 'several people . . . would come to Haverigg for a holiday if they could find proper accommodation'.[98] The Furness Railway may have failed to turn Seascale into a second Eastbourne, but it certainly succeeded in channelling the limited demand for West Cumberland holidays into its own resort, leaving intending competitors frustrated and bewildered.

At the southern edge of the Lake District, Grange-over-Sands offered yet another contrasting experience. Like Seascale and St Bees, it clearly gained by its proximity to romantic scenery, but, under the wing of the Furness Railway and in response to the impetus provided by its first hotel company, it became a retirement centre and weekend retreat for Lancashire and West Riding industrialists and their widows. Without the sandy beaches and lively sea of West Cumberland and the Solway, Grange did not develop to the same extent as a family holiday resort, and its clientèle seems to have drawn its wealth more directly from trade and commerce than did Seascale's visitors. Grange, indeed, had only 300 visitors at the height of the season in 1893, although it kept a significant residue of winter visitors. Once Grange had come within second-home range of the industrial districts, a conspiracy of topography and wider geographical considerations, abetted by an interested railway company and the early formation of a local élite which saw no future in excursionists, mapped out the resort's future.[99] As it developed, Grange had more in common with residential Windermere than with the rest of the Cumbrian seaside resorts, with the exception of its smaller neighbour Arnside, which shared similar characteristics.[100]

We are now in a position to draw the threads together, and to try to look at the Cumbrian tourist trade as a whole. It is clear that growth was steady rather than spectacular, and that the seaside holiday, in particular, was slow to make an impact on the region. About 4 per cent of the population of England and Wales lived in seaside resorts at the turn of the century, but in Cumbria the proportion was less than 1.5 per cent, and the Lakeland resorts housed nearly twice as many residents as the seaside watering-places.[101] The social tone of the region's resorts was generally elevated, but the numbers of residents and visitors were relatively few.

Part of the explanation for this lies in the limited and specialised market for the resorts' services throughout the period. A region whose economy was based largely on agriculture, whose urban middle classes were generally thin on the ground and not noted for their prosperity, and whose industrial labour force was largely employed in arduous jobs associated with heavy drinking and frequent casual holidays, was not likely to generate rapid resort development. Most of the demand came from outside the region, and in almost all cases it was channelled into Cumbria because of the fame of Lakeland scenery and its literary associations. The Cumbrian resorts attracted a mixture of landed and moneyed wealth, of intelligentsia as well as aristocracy and plutocracy. Only Silloth, Windermere and (to a lesser extent) Keswick drew a significant working-class presence, and the resorts were cushioned by distance and by their lack of artificial attractions from the emerging centres of effective working-class demand in the Lancashire and West Riding textile districts.

Transport innovation, and especially railways, played an important part in canalising demand and localising its impact. This was more obvious on the coast than inland. In Lakeland, the railways created no new resorts as such, although the settlement pattern of Windermere was radically altered by the siting of the station above the lake.[102] Rather, they confirmed the pre-eminence of the established tourist centres, and gave an extra impetus to their growth by adding to the social and geographical range of the visiting public. On the coast, the railways not only opened out new resorts; they also invested in them, and favoured their chosen sites with cheap amenities, advertising and special traffic arrangements. Largely as a result, Silloth, Seascale and Grange achieved relative prosperity, while Allonby and St Bees languished. In this relatively remote area, with lines hugging the coastline and opening out a wide range of options to resort developers, the influence of railway policy in this sphere was unusually great. It was certainly stronger than that of land-ownership or local government, which have been stressed in explaining the differences between the Lancashire resorts.[103] Given the structure of demand, there was never any real doubt, even in Windermere, that it paid best to cater for the 'better classes'. Villa development and a restrictive approach to excursionists obviously provided the most promising way forward, and the doubts and conflicts over what kind of visitor was most desirable, so important close to the industrial centres, never posed serious problems in Cumbria. The late-Victorian excursionist lobby in Keswick and Windermere made some noise but little headway.

The main area of conflict in the Cumbrian tourist trade, indeed, concerned the relationship between tourism and the wider economy of Lakeland, although it was entwined with the thorny problem of what kind of visitor was desirable. How far would the exploitation of the region's natural resources, which were attracting increasing attention from outsiders, threaten the established tourist industry by detracting from the beauty and solitude on which it fed? Would the transport improvements associated with plans for mining and other developments help or hinder the economy of central Lakeland? How far should the influential outsiders who had become attached to the special qualities of the area be allowed to intervene in defence of the amenities they enjoyed? These were difficult questions, and they retain a great deal of contemporary relevance. We shall examine them in the next chapter.

The defence of Lakeland

As the growth of tourism made the Lakeland fells better known to wealthy and influential outsiders, pressure for development of various kinds began to mount. Tourist demand itself brought hotels and lodging-houses, usually in a gaunt and prickly Victorian Gothic, and it generated transport improvements; while aspiring businessmen began to buy building plots and small estates for weekend retreats and county residences. Even on a limited scale, some of these developments were already making an impact on the landscape close to the tourist centres in the early nineteenth century, and the ostentatious intrusiveness of some of the larger houses, and the ornamental planting associated with them, began to worry lovers of unspoiled Lakeland scenery. The coming of the railway, first to Windermere, then to Keswick, increased the pressure for what to some was improvement, to others desecration, but it was not until the last quarter of the nineteenth century that serious conflicts began to be engendered. By this time, a rapidly developing interest was being taken by entrepreneurs of various kinds in the natural resources of the Lake District. Proposals for railway extension threatened to bring large numbers of holidaymakers and excursionists into the remote solitudes of the inner fells; but a much greater danger was seen to lie in the proposals for new or vastly expanded mining and quarrying activities which invariably accompanied the railway schemes and were, indeed, essential if lines involving expensive engineering works and heavy operating costs were ever to provide an adequate return on investment. The growing manufacturing centres not only threatened the existing character of Lakeland by the recreational needs of their crowds of pent-up citizens, and by the industrial speculations of their capitalists; they also had an urgent need for the most basic commodity of all, water for their homes and factories, and the region's lakes offered a tempting potential source of supply, at some cost to the natural beauty of the exploited places. Urban businessmen in search of second homes, too, would be given added encouragement by railway extension to extend the building of villa residences which already gave a suburban air to quite a wide area around Windermere, in particular, by the 1880s. As threats of this kind proliferated in the later nineteenth century, and their scale increased, opposition mounted, and a powerful preservationist lobby emerged, to win some surprising battles at a time when orthodox ideas were not, at least initially, sympathetic to interference on non-economic or 'sentimental' grounds with the pursuit of profit and the free operation of market forces. In examining the rise of the Lakeland conservation movement, we shall shed further light on the economic development of the area; but, more importantly, we shall also show how the peculiar qualities of the Lake District, and its power to inspire passionate admiration among influential people, helped to bring about a significant change in attitudes and expectations among some of the higher strata of English society.

Wordsworth was the chief prophet of the conservation movement, although the sentiments expressed in his *Guide to the Lakes* and his subsequent letters to the *Morning Chronicle* on the consequences of a railway invasion of central Lakeland did not gain widespread acceptance until the last quarter of the nineteenth century, when Ruskin added his own considerable moral weight to the campaign against the forces his predecessor had feared. In the very widely-read *Guide to the Lakes*, first published anonymously in 1810, Wordsworth's strictures were directed mainly at the new leisured residents who built villas and planted ornamental gardens and woodland in a manner out of keeping with the subtle colouring and natural harmony of the surroundings. He also had hard words for landowners who planted regimented forests of larch and fir instead of self-sown native trees, but his main concern was to educate the taste of residents and tourists into preferring 'the perception of the fine gradations by which in nature one thing passes away into another' to 'the perception of order, regularity and contrivance' crudely expressed in 'formality and harsh contrast'. New houses and gardens, he urged, should be self-effacing, built of local materials, and calculated to blend into the scenery rather than aspiring to dominate it. He pointed out the inconsistency of those who 'were so eager to change the face of that country, whose native attractions, by the act of erecting their habitations in it, they have so emphatically acknowledged', and he concluded by urging the legitimacy of his intervention on the grounds that 'persons of pure taste throughout the whole island . . . by their visits (often repeated) to the Lakes . . . testify that they deem the district a sort of national property, in which every man has a right and interest who has an eye to perceive and a heart to enjoy'.[1]

In 1844, Wordsworth's famous letters to the *Morning Chronicle* in opposition to the extension of railways into the heart of the Lake District introduced further themes which were later to prove important. In his head-on attack on ' "Utilitarianism", serving as a mask for cupidity and gambling speculations', he based his central argument on the defence of the 'moral sentiments and intellectual pleasures of a high order' which were nourished among a select but important few by the experience of a tranquil and unspoiled Lakeland. He also drew attention to the private rights of those proprietors whose amenities would be damaged by a railway, but this, a more effective argument in the contemporary climate of opinion, was secondary to the overriding moral outrage.[2]

We have considered Wordsworth's position at some length because so many of his ideas anticipate those of his successors in the later nineteenth century. Although his views made little immediate impact, running as they did directly counter to the prevailing currents of political economy, they were to provide a ready-made battery of arguments, sanctified by the literary fame of their author, for use when the intellectual tide began to turn in face of new threats of increasing magnitude late in the century, and as part of a more general retreat from the cruder doctrines of laissez-faire.

Until then, however, the consensus generally ran against Wordsworth. In the late eighteenth century the ornamental gardening indulged in by the owners of islands on Windermere and Derwentwater had its admirers, and in 1830 Edward Baines' successful *Companion to the Lakes* praised the 'mixture of rustic simplicity and irregularity with cultivated taste' which prevailed in Bowness, and the 'handsome mansions, which heighten the natural beauty of the scenery'. The cult of the picturesque died hard. Nor did Baines share Wordsworth's aversion for plantations, as he described with evident approval 'the solemn forest of larch and fir with which the hills are mantled'. Baines' influential little book also reminds us that quarries could be brought within the canons of romantic beauty as sublime and awe-inspiring; at the Thrang Crag quarry in Langdale, for instance, 'We . . . admired with awe its enormous masses of slate-rock, threatening to entomb the spectator by a hideous fall.'[3]

Through the early and mid-Victorian years, a more prosaic spirit of improvement gained ground, and Harriet Martineau's praise for the railways and the changes they brought in their wake is symptomatic of a general enthusiasm for Gothick villas and urban expansion.[4] Wordsworth's campaigns against railways in Lakeland and steamers on Windermere drew support almost entirely from entrenched vested interests, and the Windermere railway stopped short of the lake largely because it would have been prohibitively expensive to proceed further.[5] When the Cockermouth, Keswick and Penrith line, which passed close to Skiddaw and along the shore of Bassenthwaite Lake, came before Parliament in 1861, the only opposition came from a local landowner who was anxious to secure a clause ensuring an adequate passenger service for his estate.[6] Mid-Victorian tolerance of commercial and residential development can be further illustrated from later guide-books; Black's of 1868, for instance, on Windermere: 'Numerous villas and cottages, gleaming amid the woods, impart an aspect of domestic beauty, which further contributes to enhance the character of the landscape.'[7] The existence of mines and quarries was merely noted in passing, and the Glenridding lead mines in Patterdale were regarded as an added attraction on the climb of Helvellyn: 'The whole of the ore-crushing, washing and smelting processes can be inspected. The mines . . . overlook the works, and command a fine view of Patterdale.'[8] At this stage, there was little or no public dissent from the consensus that villa residences and mineral extraction were the inevitable concomitants of 'progress'; indeed, they were often regarded as positively enhancing the tourist's enjoyment of the Lake District.

By 1891, another influential guide-book could describe the Glenridding mines as 'the one blot on Patterdale's otherwise perfect loveliness';[9] and this change in the prescribed reaction to the industrial exploitation of Lakeland reflected the development since the mid-1870s of an entrenched opposition to the further despoliation of the lakes and inner fells. Wordsworth's precepts were revived and taken up by an active and well-connected band of educated residents and visitors, with Ruskin as figurehead and Canon Rawnsley, a prolific author of somewhat lesser merit, emerging as the most conspicuous campaigner and organiser. The advocates of further development, whether for tourism, minerals or water supplies, remained strong and confident, with a great deal of support among the locals wherever new jobs and extra visitors could be promised at little material cost; but their opponents were able to claim some surprising victories at an early stage.

An identifiable conservationist movement emerged in 1876, although it was several years before a permanent organisation was formed to safeguard the peace and natural beauty of Lakeland from a growing volume and variety of threats. But there was a steady flow of resources and commitment into a series of campaigns against particular proposals from 1876 onwards; and it was the revival of a scheme to extend the Windermere branch railway into the heart of central Lakeland, to Ambleside and on to Keswick, that first caused conservationists to stand up and identify themselves. They had passively tolerated a piecemeal and limited expansion of housing and quarries; but the new railway posed the threat of commercial development on a new and altogether more disruptive scale. At this very time, moreover, the growing Lancashire conurbations were beginning to envisage Lakeland as a potential supplier of water, and the engineers of Liverpool and Manchester were already taking a long and covetous look at Ullswater, Haweswater and even Windermere, despite its pollution problems. At this stage, however, the railway seemed the more immediate danger.[10]

The leading part in the campaign against railway extension was taken by Robert Somervell, a Kendal manufacturer resident in Windermere. With help from Ruskin and from articulate supporters in Ambleside and Grasmere, he sought to arouse public opinion by writing to the daily and periodical press; and he issued a pamphlet, *A protest against the extension of railways in the Lake District*, with a substantial and powerful preface by Ruskin himself. Somervell's own arguments consciously echoed those of Wordsworth, although he pointed out that the defenders of Lakeland accepted the present level of access and development, excursionists included. There was no desire to return to complete exclusiveness, to conserve inner Lakeland solely for the wealthy and leisured; but there was already adequate means of access for those in every rank who could appreciate the area's special qualities. He pointed out 'the folly of destroying the charm of the district, on the pretence of bringing people under its influence' – a fundamental paradox of tourism in remote areas – and he argued that Lakeland should be preserved from the 'defilement and destruction' wrought by the untrammelled pursuit of material prosperity. Ruskin was more abrasive, suggesting that the scenery was already accessible to those working men who saved their money rather than spending it on drink, and fearing pollution and despoliation on a grand scale. All the railway would achieve would be to 'open taverns and skittle grounds around Grasmere, which will soon, then, be nothing but a pool of drainage, with a beach of broken ginger-beer bottles'. All this would destroy the sturdy honesty and independence of a virtuous peasantry, without improving the minds and morals of those disqualified by a deprived urban background from benefiting from a fleeting visit to the fells.[11]

Most of the moral arguments against economic development and increased accessibility were thus already being marshalled at this early stage, when the future Canon Rawnsley was still a slum curate in Bristol.[12] As in subsequent campaigns, however, although the defenders of Lakeland made explicit their assumption that there were higher goals than economic prosperity, they were always willing to appeal to the baser natures of those who would not be swayed by what opponents derided as mere sentiment. R. T. Farquhar of Grasmere, in a letter to the *Times* early in 1876, put an economic case against railway expansion. The new railway would bring increased population in its wake, polluting the rivers and lakes; it would open out no profitable new fields for mining speculation, especially as there were plenty of alternative sources of slate; it would upset the well-managed local stage-coach system, drive away the 'best customers' of the 'better sort of innkeepers', and undermine the living standards of the labourer as the needs of tourists and villa residents forced up prices.[13]

The resistance was thus conducted on two levels, the moral and the economic. The former approach was a little ahead of its time, as press reactions made clear. The *Westmorland Gazette* accepted Ruskin's sincerity, but likened him to Don Quixote in stressing his opposition to the spirit of the age. It accused the railway's opponents of promoting 'a sort of aesthetic Enclosure Bill of their own, which would fence around the rugged majesty of Skiddaw . . . for the benefit of men of taste', and it argued that the project could not be condemned if the Lakes were only to be preserved inviolate for 'this select company'. The conflict was seen as pitting 'the material interests of trade and capital against the immaterial enjoyments of the few'; and the *Gazette* came down firmly on the side of the former.[14] The *Daily News* went the same way, complaining at the attempt to protect 'sentiment at the cost of the material prosperity of individuals, and . . . of the country . . . in most cases the ordinary laws of economy must have their way'.[15] Even these discouraging responses were not unequivocal, for each recognised, by implication, that there might be a limit to the permissible level of exploitation; but there was little comfort for Somervell and Ruskin here.

Economic considerations, however, came to the rescue before the proposed line was brought before parliament. Traffic projections were discouraging, and estimated costs were high. The scheme was laid aside, although the conservationist opposition had little or nothing to do with the outcome. The next crisis, however, was not far distant; and this time an organised campaign took resistance into Parliament, securing significant concessions in dealing with a new intruder.

As Manchester's demand for water had grown rapidly in the mid-Victorian years, trebling between 1851 and 1864 and continuing apace thereafter, warnings began to be sounded about the long-term inadequacy of the existing Longdendale reservoir, and the need to go further afield in search of a sufficient source of supply. Several possible sites were inspected, and in 1876 a special Waterworks Sub-committee came down in favour of Thirlmere, a remote and unspoiled lake which figured prominently in the writings of the Lake Poets and remained inaccessible to that vast majority of visitors who were unable or unwilling to go far beyond the railheads and the main carriage roads.[16]

It took a year for an opposition movement to emerge. The local landowners resisted Manchester Corporation's blandishments, and preliminary land purchases accumulated slowly. There was, indeed, widespread opposition among the dalesmen, tempered by disbelief in the practicability of the scheme. In the autumn of 1877, however, it became known that the Corporation intended to go to Parliament for power to construct a reservoir and supply pipeline; and its plans were found to involve a great increase in the size of the lake, with a considerable alteration in the character of the scenery. This indication that Manchester was in earnest, and that its plans appeared to involve the disfigurement of the natural beauty of the lake, provoked the formation of a Thirlmere Defence Association.

The defence of Thirlmere was orchestrated within the Lake District. Robert Somervell was the secretary, and the Bishop of Carlisle provided important rhetorical support. John Harward, who saw the amenities of his Hollens Estate at Grasmere threatened by the Corporation's proposed aqueduct, was prominent enough to be described by the scheme's historian as the 'chief promoter' of the opposition, but there was plenty of disinterested involvement. From September onwards, as the controversy was fully ventilated in the national press, influential outside support began to accumulate. Octavia Hill brought the Commons Preservation Society into the fray, and the Defence Association's committee came to include Ruskin and Carlyle as well as a string of professors and several noblemen with extensive Lakeland holdings.[17]

This time, most of the national press supported the conservationists. Manchester's need for water was generally admitted, but it was argued that less controversial alternatives were available, and Manchester did its case no good by proposing to cut its local rates by selling Thirlmere water to other nearby towns, and by bombastic pronouncements to the effect that its engineers could construct an embankment and lay out surroundings which would actually improve on nature. The *Saturday Review*, described by Manchester's Alderman Grave as 'the usual organ of the sentimentalists', came out strongly against the scheme; but so did the *Times* and the *Spectator*, the *Standard* and the *Pall Mall Gazette*, and even the *British Architect and Northern Engineer*.

Punch versified to good effect:

We trust no earthwork of creative Cash
Nature to mend, no Engineer would thank
For banking Thirlmere to a monster tank.
A hideous foreshore, graced with Cockney grots,
Straight roads, squared slopes! These are not boons but blots.
Nay, canny Cottonopolis, your plan,
Though by your Bishop blest, *Punch* grieves to ban.
Your water-wants you must supply elsewhere,
And for your greed of cash, that's not our care.
Nor will we spoil our lakes to sluice your City,
Or please a Vandal Water-works Committee.

The *Daily News* held out on Manchester's side, but it stressed that the locals had a right to watch over the preservation of the 'natural beauties of the scenery'. The overall tone of élite press opinion was unremittingly hostile; and the justification for this revulsion of feeling was perhaps best expressed by the *Times*:

> For great masses of our countrymen it becomes every year more difficult to get any recreation which is really refreshing. Some few spaces are left to us in England . . . where the weariness of daily toil can find the healthiest refreshment, and among these the hills and meres of Cumberland and Westmorland hold perhaps the highest place. They are the very lungs of the crowded cities of the North; they are to many an artisan the one opportunity of tasting purer and more elevating pleasures than the conditions of his daily life render possible to him. It is in the name of Utility rightly understood rather than of Beauty only, in the interest not of aesthetic *dilettanti* but of hard-worked men of business and toilworn hands, that the Bishop of Carlisle pleads in our columns this morning for a reprieve for Thirlmere.[18]

The defence of Lakeland was thus harnessed to doctrines of utility in a way which cannot have given complete satisfaction to the more outspoken of the defenders; but the *Times'* formulation, and others like it, gave the Thirlmere opposition respectability in the eyes of orthodox opinion. This may help to explain the extent of Parliamentary support for the Defence Association when Manchester's Bill was introduced early in 1878, and the course of the debate on the second reading which was initiated by two of the Cumberland MPs in February.

The arguments against the Bill again mingled the practical and the principled. The opposition argued that Manchester's need for water was neither so pressing nor so great as had been urged; that the Thirlmere scheme was really a gigantic speculation with the ratepayers' money, depending for its success on the sale of water to the surrounding Lancashire towns; and that the possibility of alternative sources of supply, less damaging to solitude and scenery, had not been properly considered. But the 'sentimental' arguments were also strongly urged. E. S. Howard, one of the MPs for East Cumberland, put the opposition view of the aesthetic impact of the scheme:

> The Lake and its surroundings are, in fact, to be converted into an extensive people's park, with a serpentine containing two artificial islands in the middle, and a great broad path all round. But there are some people who, after all, prefer Thirlmere as it is — small, wild and inaccessible. We have been taunted with being sentimentalists and enthusiasts; but I do not see anything wicked in that.[19]

Manchester and its supporters were clearly impressed by the strength of the opposition. They did not think it safe to stop at labelling the Defence Association as mere sentimentalists attempting to obstruct the attainment of a public good. They preferred to do battle with the conservationists on their own ground, arguing that the works would be carefully landscaped and that fears that the rise and fall of the water level would leave unsightly mud-banks were entirely unfounded. Indeed, Isaac Fletcher, MP for Cockermouth, achieved a palpable hit with the objectors' own weapons when he urged that the Bill, which would empower the Corporation to acquire a considerable expanse of catchment area, would 'reclaim 11,000 or 12,000 acres of the most beautiful part of Cumberland from the incursions of those aesthetic gentlemen who come down surveying the district and building Gothic villas upon the shores of this beautiful lake'.[20] It is true that the creeping invasion of Lakeland by the speculative builder of villa residences was not yet being treated as a problem by a defence movement whose members were largely denizens of or regular visitors to such houses; and this enabled Manchester to present itself as the guardian of rural amenities rather than their destroyer.

The crucial intervention came from W. E. Forster of Education Act fame. He stressed that, 'The scenery of the Lakes is a public interest . . . We have in this part of England some of the most beautiful scenery in the world, and it is the object of the House of Commons and of the country to preserve it'.[21] He took up a point made by two earlier speakers, and urged that the Bill be considered by a special committee rather than the usual form of Select Committee. The standard practice was for evidence on private bills to be admissible only from those whose property was likely to be directly affected. Instead, the Thirlmere enquiry should

211

allow all those who were interested in the area, even solely from the standpoint of preserving its natural beauty, to present their views. This proposal was accepted, and it was to form an important precedent when similarly contentious measures subsequently came before Parliament.

These widened terms of reference enabled the Defence Association to present its case directly, rather than trying to make its views known under the guise of protecting the property of one or other of the landowners. Despite these favourable conditions, however, the verdict went against the Association, after a long and costly hearing. The Commons committee declared itself convinced that Manchester needed water from Thirlmere, and that the embankment and aqueduct could be constructed, and the lake enlarged, without impairing the natural beauty of the area. Certain changes in the Bill were made, which did not affect the Lake District; but they were deemed sufficient to prevent the Bill from proceeding further in the 1878 session. Manchester was irritated but undaunted; and when the Bill was reintroduced in 1879, it proved impossible to marshal the opposition forces for a second costly struggle. Harward of the Hollens Estate had been bought out, and Manchester's propaganda had convinced the farmers and tradesmen that the labour force engaged on the works would bring them several years of prosperity. The Defence Association had won some important battles, but by March 1879, when the new Bill entered Parliament practically unopposed, it was clear that it had lost the war.[22]

The Thirlmere defeat was an important watershed. The physical impact of it did not become apparent until 1885, when work on the embankment began; and the strength of the opposition had helped to ensure that the work was carried out with such scrupulous care that Canon Rawnsley, a fervent opponent, felt able to offer prayers and sonnets at the opening ceremony in 1894.[23] The defence of Thirlmere set the pattern for future defensive actions, but the failure of such a well-supported campaign showed that the time was ripe for a tactical reappraisal. When it became clear in the early 1880s that Thirlmere and the Windermere–Keswick railway scheme were only the first of a series of threats to the seclusion of inner Lakeland, the opponents of development responded by forming themselves into a permanent watchdog organisation, the Lake District Defence Society.

The society came into being in response to a proposed railway line from Braithwaite, near Keswick, to serve slate quarries on the Buttermere side of Honister Pass. This was the heart of Lakeland solitude, in spite of existing quarry workings, and its seclusion was passionately defended by lovers of the mountain fastnesses. At first, opponents of the railway tried to work through the English Lake District Association, but this body soon came out in favour of the line on the grounds that it would improve access for visitors to a remote area without seriously damaging its attractions. By this time, in the spring of 1883, the committee which formed the core of the Lake District Defence Society was already beginning to organise, with Canon Rawnsley of Crosthwaite, near Keswick, taking a prominent part alongside W. H. Hills of Ambleside, the shoe manufacturer Gordon Somervell and several other industrialists and academics with first or second homes in Lakeland.[24]

The Braithwaite and Buttermere Railway was an ideal opponent for conservationists. It would have disturbed the serenity of a district particularly rich in scenic beauty and literary associations, and the only beneficiaries appeared to be a syndicate of quarry owners, probably acting at the behest of Lord Leconfield, who owned the mineral rights. There was a possibility of excursion traffic, but the intentions of the promoters were uncertain in this respect. There were plenty of alternative sources for roofing slate, and the scheme could be presented as the unnecessary destruction of a national shrine, motivated by mere greed. The opposition benefited from current controversies about speculative railway proposals in Epping Forest, and some well-placed letters by Rawnsley and his allies generated a sustained campaign against the railway in most of the national and provincial press, from the *Times* and *Spectator* downwards. Again, commercial motives for opposition were advanced alongside the aesthetic and spiritual, as J. B. Baddeley, the guide-book writer, pointed out the threat to the Keswick hoteliers' stage-coach traffic if the line were to carry passengers. Keswick opinion, indeed, was firmly opposed to the line, and the *Westmorland Gazette* joined the campaign on this particular issue. National petitions were organised, with the Universities and public schools featuring prominently on the lists, and witnesses were marshalled for an expected Parliamentary hearing. Landowners on the route were also mobilised in opposition, and the Commons Preservation Society weighed in with money and influence. It was Thirlmere all over again, with two crucial differences: the opposition case had much more general support, with fewer reservations or doubts, and the quarrymen were much weaker opponents than Manchester Corporation.[25]

In the event, the railway promoters withdrew their bill. Various reasons were adduced, but the opposition committee was happy to believe that the quarry interest had retreated from an expensive contest in face of an outraged public opinion.[26] But no sooner had one threat been defeated than another began to arouse alarm, as mining interests pressed for a line to the head of Ennerdale Water. Again, Rawnsley and his allies mobilised the local landowners, and the promoters encountered stiff resistance in Parliament. In July, 1883, the Ennerdale Railway Bill passed its second reading by a mere seven votes, and it was agreed that the select committee to consider the Bill should enquire into the impact of the railway on the scenery through which it passed. This set an important precedent, confirming that the decision to allow the consideration of general environmental implications in the Thirlmere case could be applied under similar circumstances elsewhere; and the railway promoters withdrew, realising that they stood little chance of success.[27]

These were significant victories; but it was clear to the defenders of Lakeland that the schemes of 1883 were not just isolated episodes, and that the pressure for development of various kinds in central Lakeland was bound to continue. The Ennerdale scheme, indeed, reappeared unsuccessfully in 1884. *Ad hoc* committees to counter individual threats were by their nature inefficient, and Rawnsley, in particular, seems not to have been the best of managers. At one point the opposition committee had as many as eight secretaries, with no proper control over expenditure, and there were long arguments over the division of responsibility for various payments after the battle had been won.[28]

The need for a properly-constituted permanent society, to maintain a watching brief and to organise fund-raising and resistance wherever necessary, was increasingly apparent. Canon Rawnsley introduced the idea to the Wordsworth Society in the spring of 1883, and the Lake District Defence Society was formed. This was to be a national movement for the protection of Lakeland against threats to its peculiar character and attributes; as Rawnsley suggested, 'The inhabitants of the dales, who have their world of beauty "too much with them late and soon", are not the safest guardians of their lovely homes'.[29] Such sentiments brought an angry response from the *Whitehaven News*, mouthpiece of the West Cumberland industrial interest, which described Rawnsley and his allies as 'cheap aesthetes' and 'noisy sentimentalists', and endorsed John Musgrave's attacks on 'the Cockney sentimentalism that seeks to prohibit land and property owners ... from participating in railway advantages and conveniences'. Cumberland people, it was urged, could look after their own interests without interference from outsiders who put the protection of scenery before the livelihoods of the locals.[30]

An examination of the membership of the Lake District Defence Society in the 1880s suggests, not surprisingly, that it was indeed dominated by outsiders, mainly drawn from the ranks of the professional and intellectual élites, but with a strong leavening of serious-minded industrialists. Of nearly 600 people on the list, fewer than 10 per cent were based in Cumbria. More than a quarter lived in London and the Home Counties, and a further quarter came from Lancashire, the vast majority from the Manchester area. Yorkshire and the North-East were as strongly represented as Cumbria, and there were 35 names from Oxford and Cambridge alongside a dozen Americans, mainly from colleges on the East Coast. There were 40 professors, 60 clergy and 34 masters from public schools, 18 of whom were at Charterhouse; but Eton, Harrow and Winchester were also represented, as were the headmasters of Rugby and Uppingham. Literature and the arts were well in evidence, as befitted a list drawn up partly by recruitment from the Wordsworth Society; but Manchester merchants and Leeds industrialists were also well to the fore. Personal connections of the moving spirits of the society had much to do with this membership pattern, but a formidable body of influence, expertise and capital was potentially available to the society.[31]

The society's preoccupations, and the social composition of its membership, left it vulnerable to accusations of élitism, but Hills and others were at pains to repudiate this. The Lakes were to be preserved for all, including the 'toiling masses'; they were a possession of the whole British people, a 'national health and recreation ground', for artisans, after all, had a particular need for the 'refining influence' of the Lakes.[32] In fact, however, there seems to have been a consensus that the full appreciation of the Lakes was only for the educated mind. Professor Campbell Fraser described the district as 'Nature's own English university in the age of great cities'.[33] The self-educated artisan was welcome, but he would have to have the thrift and strength to beat his own path beyond the railheads.

Lakeland was being defended, then, against the frivolous and irresponsible tripper rather than the respectable working man; and it was being protected from industrial despoliation arising from quarrying or the indiscriminate abstraction of water. In all these respects, the pressure on Lakeland continued to be felt during the late nineteenth and early twentieth centuries. How did its defenders fare?

Although there was no shortage of causes for concern, especially transport innovation proposals which would render remote parts of Lakeland more accessible to the tripper, the Lake District Defence Society suffered no major defeats between the mid-1880s and the First World War. Indeed, by the early twentieth century it was largely dormant as an organisation, although its leading members remained alert to all threats to Lakeland's amenities. New railway schemes came to nothing, although a renewed attempt to extend the Windermere branch line to Ambleside attracted a lot of local support and reached Parliament in 1887. It was opposed on aesthetic grounds, but failed because of its financial shortcomings, and the opposition of the London and North Western Railway may well have had more to do with the result than the resistance put up by the Lake District Defence Society.[34] Despite the favourable precedents in 1883–4, indeed, it was probably fortunate for the conservationists that they did not have to encounter a determined attempt on central Lakeland by a major railway company; but the traffic projections proved not to be sufficiently attractive, and capital was in short supply during the most dangerous years. In mining, quarrying and water supply, too, powerful opponents were no longer forthcoming. Quarrying was sometimes controversial in the Grasmere and Keswick areas, but operations were usually desultory, involving small extensions to existing works, and many landowners were responsive to informal pressure from their neighbours.[35] Manchester's appetite for water was sated for the time being, and Liverpool found Wales an easier and less controversial source of supply; so apart from the unobtrusive works required by the small Cumbrian towns, the only major incursion was threatened in 1889, when conflict arose over the alleged needs of Barrow's Haematite Steel Company. The Company, acting in concert with Barrow Corporation, sought to abstract water from the River Duddon, famous as the subject of a Wordsworth sonnet sequence; and it became clear that the river would sometimes be left dry as a result. The Bill was opposed in Parliament, however, and a Commons committee found the need for extra water not proven.[36]

Roads provoked more frequent controversies, and here the interests of the Defence Society came into frequent conflict with those of the English Lake District Association, especially when the new County Councils were empowered to allocate money from the rates towards the repair and even the construction of important roads. All of the Lakeland passes were argued over at different times, but the longest-running and most important controversy centred on the proposed new road over Sty Head Pass, which came before Cumberland County Council in 1895, and was still a live issue on the eve of the First World War. The plan was to replace the existing track from Seathwaite in Borrowdale over to Wasdale Head by a metalled road, opening it out to carriages, cyclists and motor-cars, cutting the distance from Keswick to Wastwater from 56 miles to a mere 17, and bringing the coastal resorts into much closer touch with central Lakeland.[37] A scheme had been considered by a leading Keswick hotelier in 1889, but it was not until the Whitehaven lawyer, industrialist and railway promoter John Musgrave began buying land on either side of the pass, and conceived the desire to open out his Wasdale holdings for development, that serious proposals were put forward in a sustained manner.[38]

Musgrave was eager to see the road made, but he was not so keen to pay for it himself, and for several years he lobbied assiduously to raise subscription lists and to obtain assistance from the County Council. The county surveyor, G. J. Bell, was a devoted ally, and persistently urged Musgrave to take the initiative; and several of the staunchest former opponents of the Buttermere railway could see little harm in the road plan. Early in 1897 a meeting at Keswick brought promises of over £850 in subscriptions, and R. D. Marshall, the major local landowner and an important opponent of the railway, was prepared to match Musgrave's offer of £250. J. B. Baddeley promised £10, and the English Lake District Association offered £100 to encourage the scheme.[39]

Despite the loss of some useful former supporters, the defenders of Lakeland rallied their forces. Canon Rawnsley was particularly assiduous in his attacks on the road plan, pointing out that any public money invested would merely provide undue private benefits for Musgrave, and that the scheme, which involved new hotels at Sty Head and Seascale, would bring competition for the existing accommodation industry without any compensating benefits.[40] As usual, the practical arguments probably carried more weight than the concomitant appeals for the preservation of mountain solitudes, and it is significant that Keswick's hoteliers were most unwilling to subscribe towards the road. In any case, Rawnsley and his allies were able to deploy considerable strategic influence by lobbying leading members of the County Council. Despite Musgrave's own ability to mobilise support in county politics, his scheme never came to fruition.[41]

Musgrave's failure, however, was a lucky escape for the conservationists. Public opinion might have been harder to sway than in the more clear-cut conflicts of the 1880s, and a younger and more single-minded opponent might well have gone ahead and made the road himself, without seeking County Council aid. It would have been difficult to counter the point of view represented by the *West Cumberland Times*, which pointed out in 1897 that hardly 1 per cent of Lakeland's visitors at present saw the magnificent views from Sty Head, and disparaged the few who would 'make wry faces because their haunts of solitude are now to be discovered for the delight and admiration of the many'.[42] The cyclists and the emergent motoring lobby were strongly behind the road-builders, and this time there were no parliamentary safeguards. As it happened, however, the opposition was able to harness a combination of inertia and vested interests, and the full power of the development lobby, as in several other cases, was not brought to bear.

Even on the existing roads, the invasion of Lakeland by the motor-car was already provoking complaints of noise, dust and excessive speed in the Edwardian years; and the defenders of Lakeland were powerless to stem this creeping intrusion. There were further threats from modern technology, some of which were more vulnerable to resistance on the established pattern. In 1912, however, a protest committee and a petition of ten thousand signatures failed to secure the banishment of seaplanes from Lake Windermere, as the Urban District Council came down in favour of a new attraction while denouncing outside interference in the town's affairs, and the Rector of Bowness leased his glebeland for what Canon Rawnsley called 'two gigantic factory sheds or hangars'.[43] Telephone lines, too, were a problem, and in 1905, for instance, pressure was applied to the relevant company to refrain from displaying its poles along the skyline of White Moss Fell at Grasmere.[44] Underground cables were, of course, more expensive, and these skirmishes foreshadowed the great battles over electricity pylons in the inter-war years. The comfort, convenience and commercial interests of the locals were coming into increasingly frequent conflict with the special characteristics of inner Lakeland.

By this time, the active members of the Lake District Defence Society were working on two levels. Where a serious and immediate threat could be discerned, protest letters, petitions and appeals to government bodies were employed, as in the 1880s. In dealing with gradual and insidious encroachments, like the proliferation of roadside advertisements, the conservationists used their contacts in county and central government to push for legislation or to persuade landowners to bring pressure to bear on offending tenants. This quiet mode of acting behind the scenes was to become increasingly important between the wars, especially in dealing with such bodies as the Central Electricity Generating Board and the Forestry Commission; and on the whole, the conservationists achieved a reasonable degree of success in holding back the tide of mass invasion and commercial exploitation before the First World War, although their inability to come to terms with the motor car and the charabanc was already becoming apparent.

Not all of the conservationists' activities were negative and restrictive. In two ways, at least, a positive contribution was made in this period towards the wider enjoyment of Lakeland, as well as the protection of its amenities. Rawnsley and many of his allies were deeply involved in campaigns to protect rights of way in Lakeland, and in the preservation for the public of beauty spots and monuments through the work of the National Trust. Moreover, Rawnsley himself, during his spell as Chairman of the county highway committee, seems to have favoured road improvements when they were unobtrusive and useful to the locals, and he even battled against local landowners for the extension of the telegraph up Borrowdale, provided that it went underground.[45]

Footpath closures were becoming increasingly frequent in mid-Victorian Lakeland, especially around the more accessible lakes, as land-owners complained of damage and depredations by the growing number of excursionists. The Lake District Defence Society conducted a quiet campaign of persuasion and negotiation in opposition to closures, and it was assisted by national societies for the preservation of footpaths and commons. Occasionally, the sudden closure of a treasured route provoked bitter conflict, as at Ambleside and Keswick in the mid-1880s; and in the latter case Canon Rawnsley, as an active president of the revived local Footpath Preservation Society, found himself embarrassed by the generalised attacks on landowners which were advanced by some of his supporters. Landowners were essential allies on various issues, and had to be conciliated by Lakeland's defenders; but in spite of this constraint on their behaviour, it seems clear that the society and its allies had a genuine commitment to maintaining the right of access to the fells and lake shores for all those who were prepared to make the effort to reach them.[46]

The same inner circle of conservationists was also prominent in the formation of the National Trust in 1894–5, and by 1914 important areas of the shore at Derwentwater and Ullswater, which were visibly vulnerable to the speculative builder, had been acquired for preservation and public enjoyment in their natural state. By the early twentieth century the National Trust was also taking on some of the watchdog functions of the Lake District Defence Society, especially in campaigning against an electric tramway from Bowness to Ambleside; but its main role, again, was to safeguard and extend rights of public access to the most attractive parts of Lakeland while preserving the peace and natural beauty of the area.[47]

All this activity reveals the extent to which the defence of Lakeland, though organised largely by local residents and property-owners, was capable of attracting national support, especially among an educated élite. The Oxford and

Cambridge reading parties had done their work well. All the great causes, from the Thirlmere campaign to the Keswick rights of way dispute and the Windermere seaplane controversy, depended on petitions and financial contributions from visitors and occasional residents, as well as the support of a widening range of newspapers and periodicals; and the degree of commitment shown to the preservation of landscape and solitude provides a remarkable indication of the unique character of Lakeland's visiting public and the ways in which it appealed to them. It was in Lakeland that some of the earliest challenges were made to the rights of Victorian property-owners to develop their land as they saw fit, and it was in the anti-railway campaigns of the 1870s and 1880s that widespread acceptance came to be accorded to the principle that under certain circumstances the intangible benefits of solitude and scenery should come before the opportunity to make a profit. It was at this time and in this context, indeed, that the concept of a National Park was first enunciated.[48] The Lake District had not only become a tourist centre of importance; it had also become a forcing-house for new ideas about the proper relationship between man, property, morality and the environment. The issues posed by the pressure to open out and develop central Lakeland played a significant part in the retreat from laissez-faire economic doctrines in the later nineteenth century, and it is here, perhaps, that Cumbria made its most significant impact on the history of the nation at large.

The twentieth century: variations on a theme

The world of the twentieth-century Lake Counties was, like all our modern worlds, at the mercy of changing technology and fortuitously moving economic trends. The intimate details of its regional history await full exploration, and an initial purpose of this final chapter is to trace the more palpable roots running from the contemporary region into nineteenth century soil.

The nineteenth century produced Faraday, Clerk Maxwell, Benz and Daimler, standing for electricity and the internal combustion engine, which were to condition the lives and destinies of innumerable people who followed in the new century. The man who first effectively utilised the concept of the atom in chemistry, John Dalton, was born at Eaglesfield in West Cumberland and it is a bizarre and (to many) a sinister paradox that the massive complex of Calder Hall and Windscale, with its other-wordly dome and towers like minarets of a new religion, should stand only a few miles from his birthplace. It may be significant that Mr Norman Nicholson, who is most certainly not associated with the cruder forms of partisanship, should have expressed himself on this subject with a force equal to that of Wordsworth on railways, and with an eloquence that almost certainly transcends that of the Poet Laureate:[1]

> The toadstool towers infest the shore:
> Stink-horns that propagate and spore
> Wherever the wind blows.
> Scafell looks down from the bracken band,
> And sees hell in a grain of sand,
> And feels the canker itch between his toes.

Yet, even though the great electrical inventions pointed, however obliquely, to atomic energy and its use, many associated aspects of electrical and engineering technology, and of the chemistry which John Dalton had helped to foster, came along both to rescue West Cumbrian industry from the almost scything depressions that tormented it in the third and fourth decades of the new century, and also, too often, to make its men redundant. It is yet another paradox that the same vast complex of technology has, in recent decades, offered hope in the form of science-based industries, and has yet produced the cheap and almost universally used motor car to carry people into the most beautiful recesses of the Lake District, not along discreetly hidden tracks, long absorbed into the landscape, and not to known and organised points of dispersal and departure – like Windermere, Lakeside, or Keswick railway stations – but to any grass verge which takes their fancy, or to any converted farmhouse or barn which can no longer contribute its traditional ways of work and life to the fabric of a local community.

Thus far, then, the theme of this chapter, like the underlying theme of the book as a whole, must appear to be that amorphous and ill-defined topic, 'the influence of technology', especially if we include not only the effects of major inventions, but also those of changing skills and techniques in man-management, community organisation and environmental protection. It is suggested, however, that the theme lies even deeper than this. It embraces not only the transport (and enforced migration) of human beings and of materials and energy, whether in the form of coal, water, or electricity, but also the movement of ideas and the application of semantic and administrative influences, coercive and persuasive, through multiplying governmental functions and organisations. Seen in this sense, Cumbria has become, quite simply, more clearly part of a nation than ever before, with an industrial strip offering special problems to the civil servants and elected rulers of that nation, and a recreational function and use to anybody who can travel quickly enough or far enough along its motorways.

Within the terms of its own microcosm and self-consciousness, it had become two apparently separate economic worlds long before the end of the nineteenth century, and the local awareness of fundamental change and the accompanying loss of tradition and stability, together with the tendency of its natives to diffuse themselves throughout Britain and the world, led to an almost desperate sense of nostalgia on the part of more educated or migrant groups. Even this desire to re-create the old Cumbrian traditions and sense of fraternity owed much to improved communications by rail, steamship, telegraph, telephone and newspaper. The historian must always find fascination in the *timing* of a movement amidst a broader social scene, and there was a marked resurgence of Cumberland and Westmorland society gatherings in the main British and some overseas cities between 1904 and 1914. Chapter 1 draws attention to the growing regional consciousness of Cumberland and Westmorland people, and Chapter 7 suggests that the two counties were drawing together, in the later nineteenth century, through their cultural or historical organisations. Gatherings of people from each had met in London from the eighteenth century,[2] and it is hardly surprising to find that a Cumberland and Westmorland Association had existed in London from about 1904; the important difference being that the two

221

counties were now associated in one body, which had branches in Newcastle, Glasgow, Manchester, Birmingham, Liverpool and Wigan, with overseas groups in Vancouver, Calgary, Winnipeg, Toronto, Cape Town, Johannesburg and Melbourne. The Glasgow gathering existed to 'promote loyalty and patriotism in the minds of the coming generation of Cumbrians and Westmerians', which suggests that it existed consciously to protect regional awareness and tradition. Out of some 4286 Cumberland and Westmorland people in London in 1911, some 500 belonged to their London Association, and a member explained why he found such an organisation attractive: 'they who had in their younger days the terrible loneliness of knowing no one in a big city appreciated the advantages that Associations such as these (gave) to those fresh from the countryside'. There were, of course, society rituals; the singing of *John Peel*, and a heavy emphasis on Wordsworth and Lakeland,[3] as well as some concern with mutual welfare, and it is of course clear that the nationally received image of the Lakes countryside was one which stimulated Cumbrians themselves. It only remains to add that such regional clubs and societies have remained common in larger cities throughout the present century, and that their history and origins are well worth attention. They are more likely to relate to regions from which out-migration has been heavy, but they point to a pride in geographical, social, cultural and family background which purely local historians are unlikely to be able to interpret. At the time of writing (Summer 1980) it has become clear that the remaining societies, victims of greatly improved road communications, are in a state of serious decline.

There is more than mere nostalgia in the complex of attitudes represented; many Cumbrians, after all, have been virtually forced by economic circumstances to leave their native territory, and there is a real sadness in this sense of an all-but-lost inheritance, one which explains the steady outflow of local newspapers and magazines to all parts of Britain and the world even today. Its impact is portrayed in cold population statistics, and it is to these, and to the economic realities beneath them, that we must now turn.

The population of Cumberland and Westmorland, taking both counties together, decreased in absolute terms between 1891 and 1911, increased slightly in the war years, and decreased yet again between 1921 and 1939. Indeed, it is a startling fact that the total population of the two counties was less in 1939 than in 1891. Both wars brought increases of population. Between 1951 and 1961, too, there was a measure of recovery, but the rate of increase in that decade was still below the national average.[4] These broad indications of population movement conceal a complex story, which must here be rendered into the crudest of simplicities. One major factor was the partial decline of West Cumberland industry, which became especially evident between 1921 and 1931, when the Workington and Whitehaven sub-regions alone lost some 10 000 persons.[5]

There was a similar fall of population in industrial Furness, and this general loss in what may be called the industrial belt of Cumbria was evidently a consequence of the joint operation of two types of movement; a low rate of natural increase of population (i.e. excess of births over deaths), and heavy loss by migration.[6] As we have seen, this general drain of people was common in Cumbria throughout the middle and late nineteenth century, and it was especially noticeable in the rural areas up to 1911. By a bizarre working of circumstances, large parts of mid-twentieth-century rural southern Cumbria no longer suffer from net population loss — the result of the two types of movement, or force, described — even though natural increase throughout the region tends to be low in national terms. This is partly because southern Lakeland has attracted large numbers of retired settlers, but, more generally, because the continued loss of numbers of people in the more youthful age-groups has had its effects, during the last few decades. Yet it should also be stressed that the coastal region as a whole has shown some encouraging, if not spectacular, tendencies to total increase of population since the Second War and up to the 1960s, as a consequence of limited but significant industrial development. The story has no ineluctably unhappy ending. We must bear in mind that all population and economic histories are to be seen relatively one to the other, and that Cumberland and Westmorland populations have increased *in toto* at one-half the rate of England and Wales since 1801.[7]

This fact of continual population loss can be comparatively studied in data given by Saville.[8] The stark facts of post-1920 economic change in West Cumberland can be summarised in few words; increasing exhaustion of local reserves of both coal and iron, the development of newer methods of steelmaking which rendered those of Cumberland largely obsolete, and world economic conditions combined to bring about a deterioration of the industrial structure of the coastal belt. Ironworks, ore mines and collieries closed one after the other, and little appeared to take their place, leaving, in the early 1930s, roughly half the working population unemployed.[9] Hence, Maryport had no fewer than 61.2 per cent of its insured population unemployed in 1934, and Cleator Moor was 'partially derelict', although Workington, Whitehaven and Harrington, and, much of the time, Barrow-in-Furness, were never in such a desperate state.[10] It was dependence on a few insecure industries which made for demoralisation or loss of population.

What had led to this unhappy state of affairs? First of all, iron and steel provided the foundation of the then existing economic system, principally because the local coal could be fed into Cumberland coke-ovens and then into furnaces.[11] The decline, however, did not take place suddenly, and even before 1914, there was demolition of blast furnaces at Cleator Moor, Distington, Harrington, Maryport, Askam and Carnforth.[12] This left ironmaking at Workington, Barrow, Millom and Ulverston, with the first three remaining productive centres until the middle of the new century. Meanwhile, there were important technological as well as structural changes in the industry. The challenge of 'basic' iron and steel, which could employ phosphoric and low-quality ores throughout Europe, undoubtedly led to the steady erosion of the Cumberland iron industry.[13] Also, the 'acid' pig produced by the latter had important uses in naval armaments, and especially in the manufacture of armour plating, and this fact threatened the coastal steelworks after the end of the First War. Again, the acid, Bessemer or non-phosphoric pig and steel of the region was also more expensive than the basic product, and hence sales plummetted more easily during years of recession.[14] Finally, the capacity of furnaces and their output per man increased markedly, as three major industrial units operated in a state of intense competition and also of rationalisation.[15] Fewer men were needed; large numbers became unemployed as large outputs were maintained. The output per man in the haematite ore mines was also greatly increased by mechanical methods, including power drilling,[16] with similar results – Frizington was described as the most derelict-seeming town of all.[17]

The staple industries of the western belt were under the control, during the 1920s, of a tiny handful of major firms. The largest single controlling influence appeared when the Workington Iron and Steel Company became a member of the United Steel Companies Limited in 1919, the latter representing Sheffield

29 Setting up the winding engine of a West Cumberland iron ore mine *c.* 1900; the foundations of these installations can still sometimes be traced.

steelmakers seeking to secure control over their raw materials.[18] This organisation came to own Cumberland blast furnaces, steelworks, collieries, coke-ovens, iron ore mines and limestone quarries.[19] A highly integrated vertical productive unit, it invested in a large dock in Workington in 1927, thus virtually destroying Maryport as a port, and it also made Workington the most stably functioning town of the western seaboard during the following decades. The United Steel establishment there concentrated on the production of steel rails, which has remained its staple – with British Steel Corporation policy support – until the present day.[20] The other major companies of the 1920s and 1930s fared less well in the light of later history. The Barrow Haematite Steel Company tended to struggle through the inter-war years, until overtaken by nationalisation in wartime, although it, too, had a large interest in Cumberland coal-mining,[21] and owned haematite mines in Furness. The third major company, the Millom and Askam Haematite Co., which made merchant pig, was likewise an iron-mine, colliery and coke-oven owner in Cumberland.[22] The striking Victorian multiplication of firms, assisted by Scottish influence, now had no parallel except in that vital decisions continued to be taken outside the region; and this topic of external control is one that always repays further study.

The west of the region demonstrated some remarkable contrasts in the fortunes of its industries. The Furness haematite mining industry, although subject, like that of Cumberland, to the more general competition of imported, phosphoric or low-grade ores, experienced a decline in output much more rapid than that of its neighbouring county, and it is clear that this was a consequence of the more rapid exhaustion of ore deposits.[23] By 1931, the ore industry of Furness was negligible,[24] whereas in Cumberland, in the previous year, output was more than ten times greater,[25] and well over 2000 men were still employed in the mines near Egremont and Cleator Moor. This remarkable industry still maintains a tenuous existence near the former town, and only the closure of the great Hodbarrow Mine at Millom in 1968 really reduced it to negligible proportions – although it is worth noticing that despite high skills in technical organisation, Hodbarrow's output declined steadily between 1931 and 1968.[26] The virtual destruction of this major branch of mining also destroyed a way of life, one which is slipping into the mists of history with few records.[27] Nor is this surprising, for many of its miners migrated to other areas, and accordingly relatively few of their families remain to tell a tale to the oral historian.[28]

Cumberland's coal industry, which still clings doggedly to life in Whitehaven's Haig Pit, resisted decline much more strenuously, and was the leading major employer of labour in the entire region (after agriculture) through-out the 1920s. Even when the writing was on the wall, it maintained annual outputs in excess of a million tons between 1931 and 1958, falling fractionally short in 1945 only.[29] Indeed, the decline of the Cumberland industry was less than that in Britain as a whole during the 1920s, and the demands of local furnaces, allied to a persistent Irish export trade which accounted for between a quarter and a third of all local coal produced, kept output high. Yet, even in the later 1920s, there was unemployment in the local coal industry, an apparent result of immobility of the workforce in local communities, and the inability of the industry to absorb young workers into underground tasks.[30] Subsequent nationalisation was accompanied by steady closures of the smaller and less economically viable pits, and it was fortunate indeed that during the 1930s, the formation of the Cumberland Development Council (1935), consisting of representatives of industry, trade unions and local authorities, was already seeking to attract new industries into the area. Cumberland was declared a Development Area, and the west coast district a 'Special' Area, but the results were not at first spectacular, and a second 'industrial revolution' in the area was slow to appear. War came as a stimulative agency, with the planting of a Royal Ordnance Factory at Sellafield.

Perhaps the most serious erosion of nineteenth-century industries had taken place in Furness, with the loss of district iron furnaces (but not steel manufacture in Barrow), railway works, jute manufacture, salt works, ropeworks, cattle importation and oil refineries.[31] Barrow shipbuilding remained, but was plagued by industrial disputes and periods of acute unemployment, as in 1922 and 1933.[32] Reference to social tensions is here highly necessary, and those which had beset West Cumberland and Furness in 1871–2 were in some respects reproduced just as acutely during the First War and subsequently – the story of West Cumberland food riots in wartime has only recently been revealed by A. J. Coles,[33] and that of the unemployed workers' demonstrations in Barrow district (1922) has also received some attention.[34] It is an irony that the unemployment of this period was instrumental in creating valuable social amenities in Barrow,[35] and no less an irony that despite the grim unemployment that marked the west-coast industrial districts of the early 1930s, there were improvements in the provision of services, housing and employment before the outbreak of war. This is, of course, a subject that calls for detailed analysis, but available figures for Furness are indicative.[36] As for the social conflicts of the age, there can be little doubt that these had deep roots not only in deprivation of the right to work, but in much enhanced social expectations, some of them connected with the harrowing experiences of wartime. Carlisle, too, was affected by the marks of wartime conditions, but its state-administered liquor supply scheme (1916), born of attempts to control the drinking of nearby munitions workers,[37] was for long the most memorable and valued monument to that age. Carlisle, and to a lesser extent Kendal, had much more diversified industrial bases than did the west-coast towns, and the former town retained, during the inter-war and post-war periods, its textile industry,[38] supported by food processing, engineering and the general provision of services.[39]

The mention of Carlisle naturally leads to the subject of the predominant role played by railway transport in the history of the region. Carlisle's position as a centre of communications aided the tendency to diversity of its industries, and the railways, as we have seen, played a vital part in the early Victorian development of the coastal industries and in the spread of tourism. On the other hand, when recessions and then structural unemployment began to harass the heavy industry of the west, railway and port traffic necessarily suffered. But the matter went deeper than this; the Furness and the Cumberland industrialist was far from many sources of supply and far from his markets, with a very limited population within the immediate reach of, say, 30 or so miles' radius,[40] and the western side of the region remained isolated, to the twentieth-century rail traveller and then to the visitor by road. This inescapable problem was made evident, early in the new century, by the construction of Heysham Harbour by the Midland Railway in 1902–4, and that company, in consequence, chose to control its own traffic to Ireland and the Isle of Man without concerning itself with the Furness Railway at all.[41] Barrow, as a port, had already suffered a long period of decline,[42] and it was remarkable that the Furness Railway, like the Maryport and Carlisle, and the Cockermouth, Keswick and Penrith lines, remained independent until the regrouping of January 1923, the Maryport line continuing to pay passable dividends until the last.[43] But, with the sole exception of Workington, the Cumbrian ports either remained static or languished in the inter-war years, Maryport suffering disastrously, and Barrow falling under the control of the London, Midland and Scottish Railway (1923), which already owned Fleetwood and Heysham harbours, and had no interest in the development of Barrow docks.[44] For the rest, the region's western side was left with a deeply localised railway system.

Again, technology intervened, this time in the form of the motor vehicle, and, more especially, the motor omnibus. The coastal economic recovery of the later 1930s had, in the view of Mr David Joy, helped to give Cumbrian railways 'two decades of stability'.[45] Already in 1922 the Westmorland County Council's Main Roads Committee was noting that 'Road Transport is at present showing signs of very vigorous life. A motor omnibus service was started during the Easter holidays between Kendal and Bowness'.[46] Comparative data show that road traffic did not build up rapidly in Cumbria during the 1920s,[47] but yet another specimen of handwriting was already on the wall. As one would expect, the more populous areas attracted the most regular bus services, but Cumberland railway stations were often far from village nuclei, and by the end of the 1920s, bus competition was becoming severe. In 1931 and 1935, wholesale withdrawal of railway passenger services took place on the Cleator and Workington line, and that from Cleator Moor to Marron Junction, followed in the latter year by stoppage of such traffic on the Whitehaven–Egremont–Sellafield route.[48] In the central Lake District, the story was otherwise; from the 1890s, Alfred Aslett of the Furness Railway had resolutely pursued a policy of tourist attraction, and the

227

later LMS régime did nothing to reverse this approach between the wars. Yet, even in the 1930s, there was an increase of motor traffic shown in the central Lakes area at selected census points in 1931 and 1935, the average numbers of vehicles per day rising in case after case between 50 and 80 per cent,[49] figures entirely in line with the economic improvement of those years.

Another major historical factor may here be introduced, that of central and local and other major organisational pressures on the industrial and environmental policies of the region. Just as Cumberland had been classified as a Development Area, and West Cumberland a Special Area, after a Ministry of Labour investigation (1933–4),[50] so Ministry of Transport policy, bearing down on complacent or responsive county councils, now encouraged more or less continuous road improvement by means of its grant-aid system; and the already militant Friends of the Lake District, formed in 1934, felt bound to protest in 1938 at the interference with secluded and charming country roads in the interest of traffic speed and convenience.[51] The Friends were more prescient than they knew, for a long-term centrally inspired policy was taking shape, and appears as a force profoundly detrimental to the more peaceful appreciation of Lakeland. Writing of the later inter-war years, the late B. L. Thompson remarked: 'Before the war our roads were a turmoil all the long summer; the Windermere–Keswick road was never really quiet except at night'.[52] Even he never envisaged that a county council might accept the latter as a suitable route for heavy lorries – so deeply do attitudes become engrained.

Two other types of force, profoundly related to supposed or estimated community need, and once again born of changes in technology allied to massive administrative organisations, were those of electricity and water supply. The internal combustion engine, after all, is a by-product of the age of electricity, notwithstanding its use of petroleum fuel, and the making of electricity demanded large quantities of coal, a consideration moving to the advantage of the Cumberland coalmining industry. Between 1920 and 1931, the consumption of electrical power in industry in Cumberland and Furness increased threefold, and the coal, instead of being distributed widely by sometimes costly or wasteful rail transport, was merely sent to main generating stations in Carlisle and Barrow.[53] This was by no means a sudden or a unilateral technological development, and the Lake District had inaugurated its electrical 'revolution' by the already traditional use of water power;[54] Keswick was certainly one of the earliest towns to establish a substantial hydro-electric plant in Britain (1890), on the site of a former water-powered woollen mill,[55] and it was a pointer to the future that the new plant supplied local premises by means of overhead wires, which in turn gave rise to complaints about danger and unsightliness.[56] In 1892, the bobbin-making firm of R. H. Fell of Troutbeck Bridge thought of using their surplus water power to make electricity, and it was used to supply four major hotels, including the Old England at Bowness-on-Windermere,[57] just as W. Wilson of the

Keswick Hotel had been interested in the new form of lighting and energy.[58] Historically, then, the earliest uses of electricity, like the earliest tappings of local lakes for water supply, were inspired by natives, a fact which is sometimes overlooked in conservationist controversies. In 1894, the Windermere and District Electrical Supply Company was formed, ultimately, in the inter-war years, to supply Windermere, Ulverston, Grange and Kendal.[59] The main regional sources of supply, however, rapidly became Carlisle and Barrow (Whitehaven's early experiments representing a sorry story of mis-management and parsimony[60]), and Barrow's early electrical generating station (1899) ultimately came to supply Ulverston, Grange, Cark, Millom and South Cumberland, and was transferred to the British Electricity Authority in 1948.[61] These rather prosaic details are of crucial importance, for without these firms, and the National Grid with which they became associated in the 1920s and 1930s, no further major phase of industrial or even agricultural development would have been possible in the mid-century. However, one could deal with local firms and local men; but the Central Electricity Board, formed in 1926, was responsible for a national pattern of distribution through the Grid, and as a dedicated local electrical engineer, Mr W. E. Swale, has remarked, 'soon stately transmission towers and sweeping power lines added a new feature to the rural landscape'.[62] No doubt; but although a pylon is a remarkable piece of structural engineering, its intrusion into the countryside is equivalent to the scrawling of a Picasso sketch across a Constable painting. The Friends of the Lake District reacted accordingly, and in 1937 they successfully fought a CEB scheme to take pylons over Scout Scar near Kendal. In the same year they had a much more difficult battle to prevent the infliction of lines of pylons upon Borrowdale, and, in the following year, overhead lines along the side of Bassenthwaite.[63] There were echoes of the great Victorian campaigns against railway intrusions, but, in this instance, there was a fundamental difference, in that campaigners were fighting not 'Mr Moon and his North-Westerns', impertinent but recognisable railway functionaries, but massive central organisations of seemingly faceless men.[64] When such great amorphous bodies were associated with a scientific élite, using an impenetrable expertise in face of public pressure, as was to happen during the second half of the century, campaigns of amateurs were no longer equal to the realities of the age, and straightforward victories against mighty organisations became less and less probable.

It was fortunate indeed, therefore, that the combined pressures of a host of conservationist organisations (and not simply the Friends of the Lake District and the National Trust) were able to take advantage of a slowly changing climate of opinion in high circles, and to bring about the acceptance and creation of the idea of National Parks. But this campaign, extending through the 1920s, 1930s and 1940s, was never fundamentally successful in resisting the tapping of lakes and the creation of reservoirs for the use of great towns or industries. This struggle, like that against heavy lorries, still goes on, but it was a unifying factor in bringing conservationist bodies together.

The Forestry Commission had much the same effect. This governmental body so alarmed conservationists between the wars that the Council for the Preservation of Rural England, through informal committee discussions, actually succeeded in limiting Commission activities in the central Lake District,[65] thereby controlling the multiple disharmonies in the scenery which the straight-line planting of single species had introduced. This battle, too, strengthened the idea of a National Park, already discussed at some length by Abercrombie in his study, *A Cumbrian Regional Planning Scheme* (1932),[66] and by the 1930s it was already clear that the CPRE, National Trust, Rural Community Councils, the Commons, Open Spaces and Footpaths Preservation Society, the Society for the Promotion of Nature Reserves, and at least two bodies which preceded the Friends of the Lake District[67] were already moving in the same direction. Concern for the Lake District continued to have national impact, and the idea of National Parks became an accepted part of government thinking in the 1940s, especially after the publication of the Report of the Scott Committee on Land Utilisation in Rural Areas (1942), and the Dower and Hobhouse Reports (1945 and 1947), clarified official views in this respect, just at a time when the 1947 Town and Country Planning Act was introducing a general control of aspects of the environment which had never hitherto existed. Hence, when the Lake District Planning Board was formed in 1951, with the function of supervising the new Lake District National Park, one of nine set up during the 1950s, it was certainly the most significant historically. It also overlapped into the territory of no fewer than three county councils, Cumberland, Westmorland and Lancashire, all with full planning powers.

The new Planning Board, in common with its equivalent authorities in Snowdonia, the Peaks, Exmoor, Dartmoor and so on, was not only concerned with the preservation of scenery to be enjoyed by urban multitudes; it was an educator, a controller of building, and, increasingly, a diplomat dealing with a multitude of official and private agencies. The earlier reports relating to its activities suggest the role of a very well-meaning Canute standing firmly before a flood of water and electricity schemes put forward by powerful statutory and other authorities, and facing continual problems posed by equally powerful public transport bodies, not least British Railways, and bus companies which liked traffic but which were not interested in the remoter farming communities which the Planning Board had under its moral wing.[68] Meanwhile, the privately owned motor-car posed not only problems of parking disposal and litter, but was increasingly dragging behind it caravans and even motor boats. The indigenous inhabitants of the Lake District, the farmers and villagers, were receiving income from the growing influx of tourists, and were in some measure protected by the National Park's Warden Service and footpath control; but some of them bitterly resented controls on building or other enterprise, and more so because the Planning Board was obliged to make exception for those who wished to build holiday accommodation.[69]

Non-elected, but consisting of highly responsible appointees, the Board seemed to resemble one of the remote statutory bodies which created many of its own problems. It found increasingly, in common with the independent conservationist bodies, that the Lake District was not an island, detached from the rest of humanity and the political nation, but was a living entity with continuing problems, many created from outside. Its own hamlets still often suffered from depopulation and consolidation of farms, and the industries of the region were still far too concentrated in the main towns and on the coastal belt. As development bodies fought to safeguard the economic future of West Cumberland, so the question of rail and then road access continually bulked large – should traffic continue to approach the west coast from the coastal route via Furness, or cross the heart of the Lake District and the National Park? The conservationists of late Victorian times felt that they had scored a victory in preventing the railway from passing Windermere; the motor lorry made this a hollow victory, and ground its way almost unchecked through Ambleside and by Grasmere. Nor were all the indigenous residents of the Lake District convinced that the environmentalists and planners were facing up to the right problems, or had found the right answers. It has long been fairly plain that these will only be propounded and solved by a study of Cumbria as a whole in its relation to national social and technological developments.

The motor vehicle remained an increasingly large influence. If we take the average daily traffic figures at a key census point on the A591 route, Dunmail Raise, the following comparative figures emerge. Averages can, of course, be misleading, and recent surveys show that figures of this order might double at certain times in the year, with June–October as the peak months:[70]

Number of vehicles per day

1935	1938	1954	1974
1999	2294	2552	3871

It is worth noticing that these annual average daily flows did not keep up proportionately with the increases in national private car ownership during the same approximate span of years, and that even after the opening of the M6 motorway, the heaviest periods of invasion of the Lake District have occupied a comparatively short season only. Moreover, many vehicles on the A591, the Kendal–Keswick highway, merely passed through on their way to the west coast. The heaviest burden, in tonnages of traffic at least, has been thrust on to the direct M6 – west coast link road, the A66, which has superseded the railway link from Penrith into West Cumberland. Not surprisingly, it has become increasingly clear to the heirs of the Victorian conservationists that the railways were essential to the economic life of the region, and, as such, were relatively harmless to the environment. What was feared and hated by Ruskin was increasingly regarded as an attraction (as in the case of the privately run lines in Eskdale and at Haverthwaite), and the progressive destruction of the Cumbrian railway network has created constant problems for the Lake District Planning Board. Visitors (who, it is true, would probably prefer to use cars anyway) have had little encouragement to use rail transport as a *convenient* mode of travel in the area; and the destruction of local lines has affected the rural population.

The beginning of the end for the more intimate railway nerve-pattern of Cumbria came in 1958, with the closure of the century-old line from Foxfield to Coniston. That this caused inconvenience for rural residents cannot be disputed, and the bus services provided no adequate substitute.[71] Meanwhile, the main west-coast approach railway route from Penrith to Cockermouth was said to be losing £150 000 a year, having been deprived of much of its coke traffic, and almost immediately afterwards the Beeching microscope had it under examination, together with (significantly) the high-altitude line which had brought coke from Durham via Stainmore towards Penrith, and the railway from Ulverston to Lakeside. The Planning Board protested at the proposed closures (1960), but afterwards permitted the Stainmore line to fall under the axe without protest.[72] However, it was also, within the same short period, approving the idea of the M6 motorway along the edge of the National Park,[73] and felt itself (1963) unable to oppose the closure of the section of railway from Keswick to Cockermouth,[74] although it was willing to regard Keswick itself as a major railhead from Penrith,[75] and in the following year it lodged a formal objection to the Ministry of Transport against the closure of the Ulverston–Lakeside line.[76] But the Board was throughout ambivalent in its attitude to motor traffic, and tried morally to get the best of all possible worlds, stating in 1962 that it did not wish to 'discourage visiting motorists, even if such an exercise were practicable, but they hope(d) that the Lancaster–Penrith motorway (would) be so planned as to drain away from the internal roads, traffic . . . using those roads solely as through routes'.[77] But it recognised, nevertheless, that it would have to undertake a continuing programme of road improvement within the National Park itself, even though its aim was not to create 'high-speed motor routes'.[78]

In the intervening years, the policies of road improvement, as affecting the A590, A591, A595 and A66 main road routes through the region, have continued to apply. There has been especially keen pressure to improve the A590, which gives access both to Furness and to West Cumberland for vehicles leaving the M6 motorway, and which must still be regarded as one of the most twisting and unsatisfactory trunk routes in England. The needs of West Cumberland and Furness have, beyond question, kept the West Cumbrian coastal railway line in being, but the isolation of those two areas from markets and supplies is still keenly felt, notwithstanding serious efforts to broaden their respective industrial bases.

30 The main route over Shap; the M6 motorway at the side of Joseph Locke's Lancaster and Carlisle Railway route.

General transport policies on the part of powerful agencies like British Rail and the Ministry of Transport, or the regional sections of the National Bus Company, have had innumerable minor contradictory aspects and consequences which regional local governmental bodies have been unable to counteract or withstand.

The movement of goods, or even people, by road or rail is properly thought to signify important economic activity, and it will here be in place to consider, briefly, the economic development of the Lake Counties in the middle decades of this century. The motor car, representing a vast development of mobility on the part of the common man, must conceivably have brought considerable economic benefits not merely to the National Park area of Cumbria, but to the region as a whole, and it will be in order to test the truth of this proposition. Tourism has certainly been a growth industry, and as long as people have money in their pockets, and petrol is available, then it will surely develop. However, the matter is not as simple as this would imply; tourism creates costs as well as benefits, and the income from it – difficult to measure in fact – is most certainly finite. It is significant that the *Structure Plan Report for Cumbria* (1976), produced by the Cumbria County Council and the Lake District Special Planning Board, carries – besides a decidedly detached and critical survey of this subject – a terse subject-

233

heading, 'The problem of recreational traffic'.[79] Whilst the report has seen little evidence of real congestion on the roads of the region, it draws attention to the great increase of traffic consequent upon the opening of the M6, and to possible hazards of the environment. Much of this traffic adds little to the total income of the region, if only because the tourist accommodation available has been surprisingly limited. There were, for example, 520 hotels and boarding-houses in Cumberland and Westmorland in 1964, as compared with 880 in Morecambe and Heysham, and no fewer than 4064 in Blackpool.[80] The Cumbrian hotels and boarding-houses could accommodate, between them, under 11 000 persons, although, at roughly the same period (the early 1960s), 27 000 to 33 000 persons at one time, Whitsuntide, were enjoying caravan and camping holidays in addition to those within buildings.[81] Counting all kinds of accommodation, it was concluded that as many as 66 000 persons at one time might find holiday space in Cumberland and Westmorland in the early 1960s. Hence, for a whole year, in c. 1960, Fulcher and Taylor estimated that 668 000 persons spent holidays in Cumberland and Westmorland, spending £10.7 million.[82]

What increment of wealth to the tourist parts of the region does such an annual seasonal influx represent? Capstick estimated (1972) that total visitor spending in the (then) Westmorland Lakes must reach at least £3 million per annum – and, as she points out, a figure of this order is no more than the wage bill of a factory employing 2000 workers at the 1971 national average male industrial wage of £30 per week.[83] It remains true that such tourist spending has a multiplier-effect (the concept of the multiplier being that for every £1.00 spent in a defined area the ultimate increase in the income of the population of that area will be greater than £1.00 by a factor of more than 1.0), but it does not follow that the multiplier in the Lakes area proper has been a high one, since many goods are imported from outside it, and, indeed, Capstick has estimated it as 'very low', and as being of the order of 1.2,[84] as compared with 1.3 for Devon and Cornwall,[85] and 1.34 in Gwynedd (1974).[86] A somewhat more satisfactory approach might seem to be that of asking how many extra jobs, over time, tourism creates, but here the interpretation of employment exchange data is fraught with difficulties, and it is hard to 'disentangle' tourist-related occupations from others. It is clear, however, that the main concentration of such jobs is in the Keswick exchange area (1963), with 50 per cent of jobs in tourist-related industries, compared with 52 per cent in Blackpool and 54 per cent in Morecambe (these are such occupations as those connected with transport, distribution, hotels and catering, entertainment and related services); in general, the Keswick and Kendal districts, which together took in much of the central Lake District, had a far high proportion of such jobs than the other fourteen employment exchange districts in Cumberland and Westmorland (1963).[87] Unfortunately, much of such work is apt to be seasonal employment.[88] As regards the whole of Cumbria, one estimate (1972) gave the total number of jobs created by tourism as 12 000 and another as 23 000,[89] and it is clear that much depends upon definition, seasonality and concepts of the contribution of part-time labour, including that of farmers' wives. Such widely varying figures are plainly of little value in themselves and we must conclude by remarking that measured in general economic terms, the accretions of income to the region from tourism are useful, but not impressive or startling.

Agriculture has developed increasingly close links with tourism, in a twofold sense; it supplies dairy products to the tourists, and its farmhouses provide bed and breakfast and other accommodation. Indeed, it may be significant that the multiplier-effect of bed and breakfast establishments is thought to be higher than that of other forms of tourist accommodation,[90] and observation indicates that such farmhouse provision is now becoming widespread beyond the bounds of the National Park proper. It is, however, Ministry of Agriculture policy to encourage ancillary sources of income for hill farmers in marginal areas.[91] Nor should this be taken to underestimate the importance of farming in the Cumbrian economy, which is still, with a much-diminished labour force, the most important and productive industry in the region, and equally we should not underestimate the difficulties of the hill farmers. As Capstick points out,[92] there is no evidence whatever that tourism has enabled small hill farms in the Lakes area to survive better than elsewhere in the region because of their tourist income. A purely economic study of the Lake Counties would give tourism a considerably smaller space than it has received in this volume, and it is other considerations – social, cultural, recreational – which lead the historian to dwell on Lakeland's more conventional image. If we over-stress tourism purely and simply, then the discussions relative to transport systems, means and costs become misleading. Passable roads and restored railways are needed not for tourists, but for economic survival, and the farmer, ordering feeding stuffs and sending his sheep to the coastal marshes, needs them even more than the visitor. And, as is admitted on all hands by the more enlightened conservationists, it is traditional Lakeland farming which has shaped the landscape, and which gives the latter its memorable character. The planner or moneyed settler may feel himself cursed by increasing floods of private motor cars, but the farmer has reached the stage whereby he cannot do without motor transport, and the rural resident is increasingly dependent upon it. This, however, brings us to the topic of the quality of rural life, touched upon in a later section.

During the course of a century – say from 1870 to 1970 – Cumbrian agriculture altered surprisingly little in character. The emphasis on pasture has remained, with cattle (for both meat and dairying) and sheep increasing markedly in numbers during the century. Westmorland has retained its emphasis on sheep, and dairying has remained a mainstay in the lower Cumbrian territories, whilst in the upland areas of the region there has been an especially large increase in beef cows, 'reflecting the impact of the Hill Cow Subsidy'.[93] Between 1866 and

1963 the livestock of the region have more than doubled, with sheep merely doing so, and cattle in Cumberland registering a threefold increase.[94] This has been achieved with a diminishing farm labour force, and a decrease of holdings in Westmorland (up to 1963), but an increase of farmholdings in Cumberland by virtue of the existence of numbers of part-time, town-related holdings in the latter county. Generally, the plainland farms of the region have remained prosperous during the middle years of the present century, and, even during the inter-war depression periods, it is significant that Cumberland farms were able to react beneficially to local town demand, and (whilst reducing their arable acreages still more) add to their numbers of sheep and cattle.[95]

The numbers of persons occupied in agriculture in the two counties in 1911 came to a grand total of 18 687, whereas in 1963 the total numbers of farmers and farm workers (full- and part-time) in the same area was 14 115. It is not clear how far these two totals are directly comparable and the numbers of farming families, judging by the totals of holdings, have not dropped in like proportion; the loss has been in hired labour.[96] Taking all relevant factors into account, therefore, there can be little doubt that Cumbrian agriculture has increased its productivity in remarkable fashion. Cumbria is still more largely an agricultural region than most other parts of England and Wales,[97] and its farms play a far more crucial part in its economy than any other single industry, including, of course, tourism. This is not to deny that some of its hill farms offer profound economic problems, and that numbers would cease to exist as viable propositions without subsidy support[98] – and this is a matter not merely of economics, but of the stability and social health of entire rural communities.

Social health (which is not synonymous with hygiene) does not, of course, depend wholly upon technology, which may be a precondition of innumerable forms of historical development in the modern world, but is not their final determinant. Nevertheless, the Cumbrian countryside remained short of those basic amenities produced by technology until the fourth decade of the twentieth century, and in 1926 it was commonly the case that fewer than half the houses in the rural parishes of High Furness had piped water supplies. By 1943, however, nearly all of the same houses had such a supply.[99] In North Westmorland (1967) over 90 per cent of the rural housing was similarly equipped, and 'all nucleated settlements and most farms (had) electricity'.[100] serving both the quality of life and the efficiency of farming. Sewage disposal offered some technical problems, and led to the concentration of some housing,[101] thereby affecting the quality of social life in another sphere. The real problems of the remoter Cumbrian countryside, however, lay deeper than this by the middle decades of the present century. The smaller settlements, both diffused and nucleated, had lost any diversity in employments during the previous hundred years, and farm amalgamations, varying from parish to parish but otherwise a very real factor in the hill areas,[102] were driving some families away and were, at the same time,

236

bringing in scatterings of second-home purchasers and commuters to purchase vacant farm buildings and cottages,[103] and by their bidding to inflate house prices in local markets. Young couples and families were thereby permanently lost from local communities, a process assisted or followed by the closure of village schools, and, where depopulation was heavy,[104] as in the Pennine fringe, the deeper central dales and the Bewcastle Fells, church parishes were amalgamated as well as farmholdings, so that social meeting points were weakened. The incomers and commuters – as members of the clergy often complain – add too little to communal life, and, whatever the objective truth of such assessments, the researches of, for example, Capstick have shown that the smaller centres of settlement often lack social institutions and recreations.[105] It becomes fairly clear, therefore, that the quality of life of the deeper Cumbrian countryside has not become indisputably augmented during the period covered by this book; improved, perhaps, for the comfortable settlers, but not always for the remaining indigenous inhabitants.

The nature of this paradox is well brought out by average income and earnings statistics. Hence, the average *net* income level of Westmorland was higher than that of the UK in 1949, 1954 and 1959, whereas *employment* income was considerably lower[106] – in other words, there was plenty of money accruing to inhabitants from invested savings, but the earnings of those actually working were low, almost certainly a result of the relatively low wages paid in catering or non-union establishments. Nor was this the end of the list of disadvantages in Cumbrian rural life. The age-structure of large areas of Lakeland was distorted before and during the 1960s by the large numbers of 'well-breeched' settlers (so much so that annual deaths exceeded births by a considerable margin, in, for example, the Keswick area[107]), and this inevitably placed a heavier burden on the health services. The same services, during the last decade, have certainly not become more accessible to the less affluent people of the remoter countryside,[108] and it is startling to discover that the numbers of general practitioners available to residents of 450 square miles of North Westmorland (c. 1970) have become reduced since the early years of this century.[109] At the same time, one must remember that nurses and health visitors have become more numerous in a declining population during the same period, and especially since 1947, although the more serious hospital cases still have to travel from the upper Eden valley to Carlisle or Darlington.[110]

Planners and politicians, well aware of the threats to the continuity and stability of local rural society, have sought to diversify available employment in the country areas by the encouragement of small industries, to be concentrated in suitable small-town centres of population. But, even where government policy has provided Industrial Development Certificates or Board of Trade grants, the more general concern of governments, and the more effective political pressures within the region itself, have been pointed towards the direction of industry into

West Cumberland[111] and Furness. There has even been locally voiced suspicion that the pressure has been unfairly exerted,[112] if only because West Cumberland has experienced unemployment 'consistently above the national and regional levels'. The planning of the region, in other words, has (in this instance) suffered from the lack of an overriding authority, or a group of truly harmonised authorities, which might have been able to keep town and country problems within both interrelationship and perspective. Opinion, too, has been formed primarily in the major centres of population, and the two major towns outside the western coastal districts (Carlisle and Kendal) have, despite the existence of incidental problems in Carlisle, enjoyed the advantages of fairly balanced and stable economies; in the case of Carlisle, based upon public administration, transport, food processing and engineering, and in Kendal area, footwear, carpets, knitwear, paper, printing and light engineering.[113] It is an interesting sociological observation that the county government of the region has become (since 1974) more firmly based on these two towns; not a point which would have recommended itself to the West Coast industrialist Liberals of ninety years ago.

Even if much of rural Furness can feel a persisting cultural and even economic affinity with the remainder of modern Cumbria, its industrial heart, Barrow and district, has shown that the experiences of the last fifty years have given the latter a sense of isolation, and the resultant antagonisms emerge in county politics. The former West Cumberland has long had this sense of being a world apart, now much strengthened by its history of endeavour to safeguard its own industrial future. The formation of the Cumberland Development Council,[114] mentioned above, was in fact a piece of officially-supported local enterprise, working in association with the Commissioner for the West Cumberland Special Area, which led to the creation of a Development Company (1937) to provide factory space for new industries.[115] The latter was an institution which was rendered all the more urgent by the decline of the local coal industry following the Second War. Although the war itself had given a stimulus to local employment, especially through the establishment of the Royal Ordnance Factory at Sellafield, between 1945 and 1961 the National Coal Board was obliged to close no fewer than seven out of twelve remaining mines in the area, chiefly by virtue of the working out of economic seams, reducing the labour force within the industry there from about 6000 to 4000.[116] Steel production and heavy engineering, however, remained firmly established in Workington, which nevertheless (like Maryport) had a smaller population in 1961 than it had in 1921. The efforts of the Development Council and Company, working in association with the Board of Trade, and gaining from the propaganda efforts of individuals in local government and industry, succeeded in drawing, sometimes temporarily, nearly 90 enterprises, mainly small, into West Cumberland between 1933 and 1961.[117] These were frequently accommodated on industrial estates, especially in

Workington and Maryport. It is now customary to give much of the credit for this achievement to the former trade unionist J. J. (Jack) Adams, later Lord Adams of Ennerdale, but he was of course aided by local industrialists and other personages who gave their services free to the Development Council, (which became the Cumberland Industrial Association in 1975), and he was further helped by the arrival of a number of gifted migrants from central Europe, some of them fugitives from Hitler, and all of them able to develop some branch of high technology or industrial science. Just as the mid-nineteenth century had brought Scots and other enterprise and capital into the heavy industries of the coastal area, so these later settlers were instrumental in bringing about a minor industrial revolution in the same territory – Sekers from Hungary (1937) to produce high quality silk and rayon fabrics, and, most notably, Schon and Marzillier, with their development of a major sulphuric acid plant at Whitehaven from a relatively small experiment in making firelighters, together with a new plastics plant at Maryport (1940), started by 'refugees from Europe',[118] and Bata Shoes, set up on the Solway trading estate by the same town.[119] The sulphuric acid firm, Marchon, found that it could make its product from anhydrite mined directly beneath the Whitehaven coastal site. In Furness, the establishment of a major pharmaceutical industry near Ulverston was giving high hopes, which have since been realised, in 1948,[120] and there is today little doubt that the west of the region owes much to science-based industry of this kind, just as the developed paper and cellophane industries of the Barrow district have helped to broaden its perilously narrow ship-building base, depending very largely upon defence contracts.

The combined efforts of these industries and their sponsors have never been quite enough to reduce the unemployment figures of the western areas to the national average levels, and small industries have often found the typically scattered former mining community or village an unsatisfactory place from which to draw labour.[121] Likewise, the region's lack of a general reservoir of skilled and highly adaptable labour has been a serious disadvantage, despite Board of Trade grants and a variety of inducements to the establishment of advance factories on prepared sites in the area. The poor provision of technical education in the region, in the earlier part of the twentieth century, was remarked upon in Chapter 6,[122] and it is perhaps significant that Ulverston's major pharmaceutical plant has, at the time of writing, and a lifetime later, opened an Apprentice Training School costing more than £100 000.[123] The other disadvantages faced by local industry have become obvious; many do not interrelate or complement each other (so that, for example, local steel is not generally used in making local metal goods or castings), and most have markets or suppliers at a considerable distance from the region.[124] Most worrying of all to the local or regional planner is the consideration that the ultimate control of many local industries lies outside the region – in some cases far outside, as in the case of Marchon (Albright and

Wilsons), which is now (1979) under the control of Tenneco Inc., a US-based company.[125] Even in 1948, it was noticeable that smaller enterprises of the western seaboard were controlled from other parts of the country, Messrs Bata from a parent factory at Tilbury, and High Duty Alloys, Workington, from Slough.[126] The thorough surveys of ownership and control would doubtless throw much light on the true nature of regional economic decision-making; nor is it true that the large enterprise is inevitably likely to be part of a multinational combine. Small firms in the countryside are equally likely to be externally directed, or closed down.

If privately controlled industry can create local problems, so, clearly, can central government operating through powerful agencies, and this tendency may create compound dangers in the case of Cumbria's most significant new industry of all, that of atomic energy. The story of the plant opened at Calder Hall in 1947 is well known; from 1952 this plant was engaged, as a matter of key defence policy, in producing plutonium for the weapons programme, and was, in conjunction with the nearby Windscale complex, feeding electricity into the CEGB grid. A recent scheme for reprocessing spent fuels from overseas reactors, propounded by British Nuclear Fuels Ltd (1975–6), led to vigorous protest and to the protracted public enquiry, conducted by Mr Justice Parker, at Whitehaven (1977). National atomic energy bodies and conservationists were locked in struggle during the enquiry, and it became reasonably clear to many observers that any decisions taken by local authorities, although procedurally proper and legalistically necessary, were likely to be unduly influenced by central government, by fears of unemployment, or by the *force majeure* in persuasion of a professional élite in both private and public nuclear energy agencies. Yet disquiet has existed in western Cumbria since 1957, when a fire in an overheated reactor plant and chimney polluted a local countryside, and led to the composition of Mr Nicholson's passionately eloquent poem, quoted at the beginning of this chapter. The question now is whether decisions affecting the large-scale storage of dangerous radioactive waste, and its transport through the region, can be in any way influenced by local inhabitants, including those who earn a living in nuclear power installations. It should be added that the employment provided by the latter will probably not solve western Cumbria's other economic problems,[127] in any foreseeable sense. It is also becoming clearer that technology is not in itself our master; its bureaucratic agencies may be.

The general problem of powerful, sometimes interlocking and sometimes conflicting local and national planning and controlling agencies, touching regional life at innumerable points, is one which is largely of the twentieth century. Chapter 5 dealt with those who stood at genuine centres of power within Victorian Cumbria itself, who acted inside the framework of national government and national movements, but who were very much men of influence within their own territory. That age has now gone. The student of power-

240

wielding and decision-making has to look at large organisations, operating at both national and local levels, and at a mass of greater and smaller pressure-groups attempting to influence these organisations. The Victorian attempts to defend the Lake District represented a rehearsal of what was to take place in infinitely more complex circumstances. Nor can the conservationist merely look devotedly at scenery and forget human beings; he must think of petrol fumes, geological storage of fissile materials, pollution in general, and leukemia. All responsible persons, meanwhile, must see that the historian of the future has enough material to understand the complexities and the problems of our present society, and to ensure that our archives are as full as possible.

That society has, in the twentieth century, changed with increasing rapidity. Nevertheless, the historian now has one great advantage; he can learn from his elders of all types and social groups, using the invention of the tape-recorder to advantage[128] in an effort to understand the true nature of the experiences undergone by entire groups of workpeople and professional men and women, by housewives and by children, and so make up for the lack of intimate information from other sources. We may even, by astute questioning, and by looking beyond the inscrutable entries in minute books, find out how vital decisions affecting our fellow-citizens or forbears came to be made. We may learn more about that elusive concept, the quality of life, than Victorian blue books and reports normally permit us to learn; and we may discover what our parents and grandparents really saw as important in their own lives and opinions. Even the copiously informative Victorian press does not tell us this.

The definitive history of twentieth-century Cumbria has yet to be written, as we are ourselves making history in our respective minor ways — a difficult and dangerous process. Yet the challenge remains.

APPENDIX 1   Labourers, agricultural and other, as a proportion of all males, Cumbrian wards, 1831

Ward	Agri-cultural Labourers	Non-agri-cultural Labourers	Remarks
Cumberland			
Allerdale Above Derwent	10·79	8·17	Coal & iron area
Allerdale Below Derwent	14·18	3·36	N.W. Solway plain
Cumberland Ward	15·19	3·92	Lower Eden valley
Eskdale Ward	14·86	4·40	N & E of Carlisle
Leath Ward	11·02	11·18	Includes lead areas
City of Carlisle	2·68	8·71	
Westmorland			
East Ward	13·42	4·96	N.E. Foothills
Kendal Ward	14·25	3·77	Kent valley area
Lonsdale Ward	14·59	3·26	Lune Valley
West Ward	18·86	3·30	N.W. Foothills
Kendal Town	1·58	5·90	

This use of ratios of broadly indicated categories of employment to totals of males in given divisions gives crude but indicative results. The data are given in the published Census of 1831, and indicate how limited 'industrialisation' was in Cumbria in that year.

APPENDIX 2   Estimated newspaper circulations in Cumberland and Westmorland, 1837, 1841, 1845

	Issued Stamps 1837	Est. Weekly Circn	Issued Stamps 1841	Est. Weekly Circn	Issued Stamps 1845	Est. Weekly Circn
Carlisle Journal	97 700	1879	115 000	2216	147 000	2837
Carlisle Patriot	28 404	546	50 000	962	38 000	731
Cumberland Pacquet	36 500	702	–	–	50 000	962
Whitehaven Herald	37 100	713	38 000	731	35 000	673
Kendal Mercury	40 300	775	41 500	798	54 500	1048
Westmorland Gazette	20 000	385	33 000	635	31 000	596

Source: *Appendix to Report from Select Committee on Newspaper Stamps, B.P.P.*, 1851, xvii, 546ff.

APPENDIX 3 Occupations of persons employed, as given in Census returns

(i) County of Cumberland

	1851				1871			
	M	F	T	%(a)	M	F	T	%(a)
Food and drink	3116	940	4056	4·14	3387	1001	4388	4·18
Services	509	–	509	0·51	1303	28	1331	1·26
Shipbuilding	672	–	672	0·68	712	13	725	0·69
Building	4480	–	4480	4·57	5063	6	5069	4·83
Cloth manufacture	6028	9211	15239	15·56	2585	3488	6073	5·72
Clothes and shoes	4087	5064	9151	9·34	4240	4289	8529	8·13
Workers in metals								
Iron manufacture	216	–	216 ⎫		2310	–	2310 ⎫	
Iron mining	369	–	369 ⎪		3771	–	3771 ⎪	
Blacksmiths	1298	–	1298 ⎬ 3·26		1387	–	1387 ⎬ 9·24	
General workers in metals	747	–	747 ⎪		868	–	868 ⎪	
Engineers	235	18	253 ⎭		1359	–	1359 ⎭	
Horses and horse transport	852	27	879	0·89	1490	13	1503	1·43
Coal	3721	83	3804	3·88	5016	183	5199	4·95
Glass, pottery, chemicals	504	169	673	0·68	281	84	365	0·34
Sea and boatmen	1925	23	1948	1·98	1744	2	1746	1·66
Agriculture	18399	5227	23566	24·07	21673	2588	24261	23·12
Government service	204	9	213	0·21	308	41	349	0·33
Labourers (unclassified)	1964	158	2122	2·15	3578	280	3858	3·67
Lead mining	1840	–	1840	1·87	1082	–	1082	1·03
Teachers	456	478	934	0·95	419	650	1069	1·01
Domestic servants	633	7330	13663	13·95	615	13631	14246	13·58
Railway service	877	–	877	0·89	3299	4	3303	3·14
Quarrymen	235	–	235	0·23	385	–	385	0·36
Wood and timber workers	1211	54	1265	1·29	550	12	562	0·53
Others occupied	3969	359	4328	10·39	5632	1448	7080	6·74
Total occupations			97921				102738	
Total population (all ages)			195492				220253	

Notes:
(a) Percentage of all persons of all ages given as occupied.
Source: Occupational tables in the published Census volumes. There were numerous changes of classification in the period covered.

	1891				1911			
	M	F	T	%(a)	M	F	T	%(a)
Food and drink	3621	1678	5299	5·14	4332	2687	7019	6·72
Services	1369	251	1660	1·62	1718	445	2163	2·07
Shipbuilding	362	–	362	0·35	174	–	174	0·16
Building	5604	10	5614	5·45	5510	4	5514	5·27
Cloth manufacture	1719	1785	3504	3·40	1367	1986	3353	3·21
Clothes and shoes	3656	5080	8736	8·48	2898	4492	7390	7·07
Workers in metals								
Iron manufacture	4011	4	4015 ⎫		3693	–	3693 ⎫	
Iron mining	4609	4	4613 ⎬		4849	–	4849 ⎬	
Blacksmiths	1486	1	1487 ⎬ 12·46		1238	–	1238 ⎬ 13·53	
General workers in metals	744	68	812 ⎬		371	–	371 ⎬	
Engineering	1868	42	1912 ⎭		3946	15	3961 ⎭	
Horses and horse transport	2108	14	2129	2·06	2086	4	2090	2·00
Coal	7513	173	7686	7·45	9808	314	10122	9·69
Glass, pottery, chemicals	273	32	285	0·27	80	1	81	0·07
Sea and boatmen	1545	–	1545	1·50	543	1	544	0·52
Agriculture	13556	1251	14807	14·37	12710	819	13529	12·15
Government service	494	105	599	0·58	772	267	1039	0·99
Labourers (unclassified)	5972	64	6036	5·86	1851	–	1851	1·77
Lead mining	517	–	517	0·50	439	–	439	0·42
Teachers	563	1252	1815	1·76	612	1536	2148	2·05
Domestic servants	521	15410	15931	15·46	933	10701	11434	10·94
Railway service	4232	7	4239	4·16	4452	26	4478	4·28
Quarrymen	779	–	779	0·75	933	2	935	0·89
Wood and timber workers	503	5	508	0·49	635	15	650	0·52
Others occupied			8117	5·03			17358	15·51
Total occupations			103007				104445	
Total population (all ages)			266549				265756	

Notes:
(a) Percentage of all persons over ten years of age given as occupied.
Source: Occupational tables in the published Census volumes. There were numerous changes in classification of occupations during the period covered. For this reason, for example, general labourers diminished in numbers after 1891. See also the comments on the Westmorland tables, p. 247.

(ii) County of Westmorland

	1851		1871	
		%(a)		%(a)
Food and drink	1251	4·83	1329	4·67
Services	174	0·67	257	0·90
Building	1412	5·46	2045	7·18
Cloth manufacture	2169	8·38	1357	4·77
Clothes and shoes	2580	9·97	2754	9·68
Workers in metals	575	2·20	1088	3·82
Horses and horse transport	313	1·21	593	2·08
Coal (b)	102	0·39	93	0·32
Glass, pottery, chemicals	111	0·42	276	0·97
Sea and boatmen	30	0·09	55	0·19
Agriculture	9313	36·01	7694	27·05
Lead mining	317	1·22	226	0·79
Government service	56	0·21	111	0·39
Labourers (unclassified)	685	2·65	439	1·54
Teachers	318	1·22	396	1·39
Domestic servants	3048	11·78	4696	16·51
Railway service	164	0·63	1913	6·72
Quarrymen	44	0·17	201	0·70
Wood and timber workers	865	3·34	284	0·99
Others occupied	2317	8·96	2594	9·11
Total occupations	25856		28443	
Total population (all ages)	58387		65130	

Notes:

(a) Percentage of all persons of all ages given as occupied.

(b) Coal services primarily.

Source: Occupational tables in the published Census volumes. There were numerous changes in classification of occupations during the period covered.

	1891(a)				1911(a)			
	M	F	T	%(b)	M	F	T	%(b)
Food and drink	824	346	1170	4·42	1010	801	1811	6·12
Services	336	89	425	1·60	544	55	699	2·36
Building	1655	5	1660	6·28	1822	2	1824	6·16
Cloth manufacture	149	602	751	2·86	349	368	717	2·42
Clothes and shoes	1136	1378	2514	9·50	1028	1203	2231	7·53
Workers in metals	789	28	817	3·09	702	39	741	2·50
Horses and horse transport	753	20	773	2·92	831(d)	4	835	2·82
Coal (c)	82	–	82	0·31	48	–	48	0·16
Glass, pottery, chemicals	75	8	83	0·31	23	11	34	0·15
Sea and boatmen	56	1	56	0·20	35	1	36	0·12
Agriculture	5976	318	6294	23·80	4917	241	5158	17·42
Lead mining	151	1	151	0·57	116	–	116	0·39
Government service	147	48	195	0·73	249	74	323	1·09
Labourers (unclassified)	1800	6	1806	6·83	815	–	815	2·75
Teachers	157	308	465	1·76	163	445	608	2·05
Domestic servants	248	4845	5093	19·26	136	4904	5230	17·66
Railway service	994	4	998	3·77	965	5	970	3·27
Quarrymen	248	–	248	0·93	332	–	332	1·12
Wood and timber workers	440	10	450	1·70	464	14	458	1·54
Others occupied (d)			2420	9·15			6629	22·39
Total occupations			26440				29602	
Total population (all ages)			66215				63575	

Notes:

(a) Both male and female totals are here given by way of illustrating the tendency of woman employment to fall in a number of main industries. Other than this, there was not a fall; in 1911 many women are included under 'Others occupied', and numbers of new female occupations appear in dress, food and drink, paper and stationery, laundry and other domestic workers, sick nurses and invalid attendants, and even post office and commercial clerks. A form of social revolution was in fact in progress.

(b) Percentage of persons of over 10 years given as occupied.

(c) Coal services in the main.

(d) This figure now included some motor transport.

Source: Occupational tables in the published Census volumes. There were numerous changes in classification of occupations during the period covered. For this reason, for example, general labourers diminished in numbers after 1891.

247

(iii) Occupations in Barrow, Carlisle and Whitehaven compared; males and females of 20 years and over (1871)

	Carlisle		Whitehaven		Barrow	
	Total	%	Total	%	Total	%
Gentry, annuitants	172	1·54	129	2·15	17	0·25
Services	557	5·00	374	6·23	141	2·04
Food and drink	873	7·84	470	7·83	377	5·40
Building	669	6·00	372	6·20	700	10·15
Cloth manufacture	2286	20·52	52	0·86	30	0·40
Clothes and shoes	902	8·10	658	10·97	420	6·08
Workers in metal	762	6·84	304	5·06	1369	19·84
Horses and horse transport	273	2·45	92	1·53	79	1·14
Shipbuilding	3	0·04	165	2·75	84	1·21
Coal	15	0·13	700	11·67	16	0·23
The sea and boatmen	18	0·16	528	8·80	373	5·36
Agriculture	406	3·64	123	2·05	117	1·69
Government service	68	0·61	56	0·93	6	0·08
Labourers (unclassified)	625	5·61	399	6·65	1977	28·68
Teachers	108	0·96	43	0·71	34	0·49
Domestic service	1313	11·74	657	10·95	293	4·24
Railway servants	822	7·38	143	2·38	267	3·87
Quarrymen	2	0·01	41	0·68	–	–
Wood and timber	90	0·60	65	1·08	57	0·82
Glass, pottery, chemicals	45	0·40	98	1·63	92	1·33
Others occupied	1126	10·11	528	8·60	542	7·85
Female non-activity rate		55·95		66·33		76·68

Some points to note:

Carlisle was of course a great railway and textile centre (mainly the latter), and even Barrow, the HQ of the Furness Railway, had far fewer railwaymen in proportion. Note, in Barrow's case, the lack of teachers and servants, and the great proportion of 'non-active' women (i.e. those not working out of the home). The building trades, in a rapidly expanding town, are very strongly represented in Barrow's case.

Barrow's famous shipyard on the Island had not really commenced at this time, and shipbuilding was restricted to a few smaller firms. Note the great number of general or unclassified labourers that heavy industry brought in.

Many of Whitehaven's coalminers lived outside the town boundary.

APPENDIX 4 Farming occupations in Cumberland and Westmorland, 1851–1911

Cumberland	1851	1861	1871	1881	1891	1911
Land proprietors	1323	1097	1113(a)	–	–	–
Farmer, grazier	5266	5556	5410	5156	5309	5179
Farmers' kin male (b)	3318	2909	2131	2486	2427	2976
Farmers' kin, female (b)	3142	2453	2282	–	–	(2169)
Farmers' wives	3575	3460	3630	–	–	
Agricultural labourers (day or outdoor)	8286	7674	5176	9638	8358	6402
Farm servants (indoor)	7870	5976	5836			
Westmorland						
Land proprietors	483	439	485(a)	–	–	–
Farmer, grazier	2439	2719	2695	2589	2590	2418
Farmers' kin, male (b)	1410	1239	976	1130	991	1253
Farmers' kin, female (b)	1189	905	904	–	–	(1059)
Farmers' wives	1780	1839	1889	–	–	–
Agricultural labourers (day or outdoor)	2461	2353	1451	3136	2733	2126
Farm servants (indoor)	3057	2191	2228			

Notes:

Persons 10 years and upwards as given in successive censuses, both sexes added together unless otherwise stated.

(a) The 1871 Census pointed out that 'land proprietors' often appeared under other occupations.

(b) Farmers' kin included 'son, brother, grandson, nephew', or 'daughter, granddaughter, sister, niece'. 'Wives' were given separately up to 1871. In 1911 these categories were simply given as 'sons, daughters or other relatives assisting in the work of the farm'.

APPENDIX 5   Comparative agricultural returns for Cumberland and Westmorland

	Cumberland				Westmorland			
	1867	*1899*	*1900*	*1963* (rounded)	*1867*	*1899*	*1900*	*1963* (rounded)
Arable land	273 760	239 681	237 336 ⎫		55 584	42 334	41 853 ⎫	
Wheat	22 856	3 578	3 174 ⎪		1 889	177	169 ⎪	
Barley	11 511	2 350	1 988 ⎪		2 932	897	794 ⎪	
Oats	72 046	73 918	73 030 ⎪		16 977	15 387	14 995 ⎪	
Potatoes	11 498	9 232	8 863 ⎬ 490 000		1 771	1 501	1 440 ⎬ 207 000	
Turnips & Swedes	34 690	31 454	30 419 ⎪		8 493	6 778	6 377 ⎪	
Mangolds	442	1 521	2 221 ⎪		93	524	858 ⎪	
Permanent pasture	241 612	342 403	344 428 ⎭		166 366	205 905	206 360 ⎭	
Animals								
Cattle	104 184	149 313	148 399	301 000	50 653	68 146	67 608	122 000
Sheep	525 064	594 820	580 618	741 000	328 328	380 900	374 453	532 000
Pigs	35 386	22 781	18 816	30 000	6 466	4 695	4 274	10 000

Source: Given by Bainbridge in *CW*2, xliv, 1944, 92; based on the official statistics of the Ministry of Agriculture and Fisheries.

APPENDIX 6   The Cumbrian farmworker's life cycle. Distribution of numbers of males in age-groups by occupation; farm (indoor) servants and farm labourers

		Age, years (1851)								
	5–9	*15–19*	*25–34*	*45–54*	*65–74*	*85–*
		10–14	*20–24*	*35–44*	*55–64*	*75–84*
Westmorland										
Farm servants (1854)	2	160	686	448	301	96	80	63	15	3	–
Farm labourers (2 240)	–	42	149	192	481	445	363	295	202	62	9
Cumberland										
Farm servants (4 890)	2	393	1698	1218	795	325	241	152	53	12	1
Farm labourers (6 250)	7	106	327	468	1288	1288	1104	931	557	211	24

This is of course a static picture of a continuing process; the skew of the series of groups to left and right respectively indicates a process of transfer from one to the other. The sharpest point of transfer is in the 25–34 age group, when farm servants got married and became day labourers.

Source: *Census of 1851*, Occupations of the People, Northern Counties, Table 13, 67.

251

APPENDIX 7 The upper part of the landed power structure in Cumberland and Westmorland, 1873

Great landowners in 1873–4	Cumberland		Westmorland	
	Acreage	*Value*	*Acreage*	*Value*
The Earl of Lonsdale, Lowther Castle	28 228	42 818	39 229	27 141
Sir F. U. Graham, Netherby	25 270	26 696	–	–
Earl of Carlisle, Castle Howard	47 730	16 850	–	–
Sir H. J. Tufton, Appleby Castle	–	–	16 094	11 772
Henry Howard, Greystoke Castle	13 008	6 778	–	–
Marquis of Headfort, Underley	–	–	12 851	13 466
Lord Leconfield, Cockermouth Castle	11 147	6 742	–	–
Hon Mary Howard, Milnthorpe	–	–	8 868	4 649
Sir R. C. Musgrave, Eden Hall	7 515	7 537	3 097	2 173
Sir Henry Vane, Hutton Hall	7 174	5 082	–	–
Wm Wilson, Rigmaden	–	–	8 690	7 989
Sir Wilfrid Lawson, Brayton	7 388	8 439	–	–
Geo. E. Wilson, Dallam Tower	–	–	7 630	8 523
E. S. Curwen, Workington Hall	6 011	9 351	–	–
John E. Hasell, Dalemain	1 434	1 977	3 407	1 651
W. H. Wakefield, Sedgwick House	–	–	5 584	7 949

Source: *Return of Owners of Land*, BPP, 1874, lxxii, Pt I; Pt II, 484ff.

APPENDIX 8 Housing accommodation and overcrowding in Cumbrian sanitary districts, urban or rural (1891)

	People living more than two to a room (%)	Percentage of total housing stock with (rooms)				
		One	Two	Three	Four	More than four
1. 'Inbuilt' towns and their nearby districts						
Carlisle–Urban	33·9	9·0	25·8	14·5	20·2	30·5
Brampton–Rural	22·3	2·9	25·4	14·6	12·2	44·9
Longtown – Rural	28·0	4·5	30·7	17·9	11·3	35·6
Wigton – Urban	16·1	3·8	15·8	14·9	21·5	49·0
Cockermouth – Urban	18·6	0·9	12·9	21·2	17·2	47·8
Kendal – Urban	13·3	0·3	7·5	17·3	18·6	52·3
Whitehaven – Urban	33·4	3·9	16·3	27·1	13·4	38·3
Maryport – Urban	23·5	1·5	14·8	25·1	14·6	44·0
2. The new industrial towns						
Workington – Urban	16·2	0·4	6·6	11·8	28·8	52·4
Barrow – Borough	13·5	1·5	12·9	9·5	9·9	66·2
Millom – Urban	4·9	0·2	4·0	3·5	8·8	83·5
Cleator Moor – Urban	19·6	0·1	2·4	11·2	36·5	50·2
3. Rural areas						
Wigton – Rural	9·1	0·2	6·5	10·9	21·8	60·6
Kendal – Rural	5·5	·01	2·7	8·0	16·7	72·6
Bootle – Rural	4·2	0·4	2·5	5·4	14·0	77·7
4. Lakeland residential areas						
West Ward (W'land) – Rural	5·7	0·6	4·7	7·6	4·1	83·0
Keswick – Urban	9·3	0·4	5·1	15·7	15·9	62·9
Windermere – Urban	1·5	0·7	3·3	2·4	12·6	81·0
Bowness – Urban	7·4	0·3	2·8	7·0	20·6	69·3

Source: *Census of 1891*, Accts. and Papers, 1893–4, cv, 1025ff (Table 6, Total Tenements and Tenements with Less than Five Rooms).

APPENDIX 9 Comparative annual records of co-operative retail societies in Cumberland and Furness, 1875 and 1886

	1875		1886	
	Members	Annual (cash) sales (£)	Members	Annual (cash) sales (£)
Iron-ore mining societies				
Cleator Moor	1 840	80 912	3 592	109 734
Dalton-in-Furness	1 787(a)	15 807(a)	2 880	71 184
Millom (Holborn Hill)	341	11 413	1 007	25 118
Egremont Industrial	515	2 452	810	17 528
Ulverston & Swarthmoor	n.s.	n.s.	1 405	31 725
Other centres of heavy industry				
Workington District	324	7 686	413	6 983
Workington Beehive	–	–	144	2 510
Maryport Industrial	515	12 731	1 300	36 695
Wyndham Row, Maryport	113	4 146	67	2 005
Parton	61	1 871	–	–
Whitehaven	–	–	146	2 567
Barrow-in-Furness (1872)	399	n.s.	1 675	32 132
Great and Little Broughton	86	1 763	–	–
Naworth Colliery	–	–	686	18 943
Lead mining				
Nenthead Industrial	88	2 278	92	516
Alston Industrial	212	3 577	266	3 794
Carlisle district				
South End (Carlisle)	1 423	54 202	2 713	87 533
Dalston Industrial	140	4 184	244	5 182
Upperby	58	2 693	87	2 278
Warwick Bridge Industrial	157	6 527	122	5 010
Small market towns (examples)				
Wigton	n.s.	n.s.	285	5 924
Longtown	144	3 125	314	7 559

Notes:

(a) 1873 figures.

The primacy of the west-coast iron-ore mining societies is shown very clearly here. Westmorland, too, had its seven or eight societies, of which only Kendal, with 1402 members in 1886, had over 250 members in that year. Of the small Westmorland bodies, all except Windermere were in small centres of industry, like Langdale (with its gunpowder works), Shap (with its granite works), Staveley (bobbins) and Tebay (a railway centre).

Sources: *Co-operative Wholesale Societies Annual for 1888*; 370ff; *CWS Annual for 1897*, 528ff.

LIST OF ABBREVIATIONS

B.Her   *The Barrow Herald and Furness Advertiser*, published 10 January 1863 to 8 August 1914. At the British Museum Newspaper Library (1863–) and Barrow Public Library (1868–).

BJ   C. M. L. Bouch and G. P. Jones, *A Short Economic and Social History of the Lake Counties, 1500–1830* (Manchester, 1961).

B.News   *Barrow (Weekly) News and Dalton Chronicle*, 1 January 1881 to 17 March 1883, contd. as *Barrow News*, 20 March 1883 to date.

BPP   *British Parliamentary Papers.*

Bulmer Cumb. 1884   T. Bulmer and Co., *History, Topography and Directory of Cumberland* (West Cumberland volume only, n.d. but *c.* 1884)

Bulmer Cumb. 1901   T. Bulmer and Co., *History, Topography and Directory of Cumberland* (Preston, 1901).

Bulmer West. 1905   T. Bulmer and Co., *History, Topography and Directory of Westmorland* (Preston, n.d. but *c.* 1905).

C.Jnl.   *Carlisle Journal* newspaper, October 1798 to June 1873; *Carlisle Daily Journal*, June–December 1873; then again *Carlisle Journal*, January 1874 to date.

C.Pacq.   *Cumberland Pacquet*–newspaper, 20 October 1774 to 25 March 1915. At Tullie House Library, Carlisle, and the British Museum Newspaper Library.

CRO Carlisle   The Record Office for Cumbria, the Castle, Carlisle.

CRO Kendal   The Record Office (formerly for Westmorland), County Hall, Kendal.

CW2   *Transactions of the Cumberland and Westmorland Antiquarian and Archaeological Society*, New Series.

CW Tract S.   Tract Series of the foregoing.

EHR   *Economic History Review.*

ELV   *English Lakes Visitor and Keswick Guardian*, 26 May 1877 to 31 December 1910. At the British Museum Newspaper Library.

JRAS   *Journal of the Royal Agricultural Society.*

K.Chron.   *Westmorland Advertiser and Kendal Chronicle*, 1811 to 26 April 1834. At Kendal Public Library.

Kelly 1897   *Kelly's Directory of Cumberland* (London, 1897).

K. Merc.   *Kendal Mercury and Northern Advertiser*, January 1841 to 2 April 1880, contd. as *Kendal Mercury & Times*, April 1880 to 18 July 1913.

MW 1847   *Mannix and Whellan's Directory of Cumberland for 1847* (Beverley, 1847).

PRO   Public Record Office.

P&P   C. M. L. Bouch, *Prelates and People of the Lake Counties* (Kendal, 1948).

PW   W. Parson and W. White, *History, Directory and Gazetteer of the Counties of Cumberland and Westmorland with that Part of the Lake District in Lancashire* etc. (Leeds, 1829).

VCH Cumb.   *Victoria County History of Cumberland*, vol. II.

WCT   *West Cumberland Times*, 21 March 1874 to date. At the British Museum Newspaper Library.

LIST OF ABBREVIATIONS

WG   *Westmorland Gazette*, 23 May 1818 to date. At Kendal Public Library.
WN   *Whitehaven News*, July 1852 to date. At Whitehaven Public Library.

Where not so stated, it may be taken that more or less complete sets of local newspapers are at the British Museum Newspaper Library.

NOTES 🌊

Preface

(1) A. E. Smailes, *North England* (1960), vol. 2, 294.

(2) R. N. Thompson, 'The New Poor Law in Cumberland and Westmorland, 1834–1871.' (Ph.D. thesis, University of Newcastle, 1976).

Chapter one
The Lake Counties, 1830–51: the changing face of the region

(1) *PW*, 62.

(2) *PW*, 58–9.

(3) Ernest de Sélincourt (ed.), *Wordsworth's Guide to the Lakes* (Oxford, reprint of 1970), 90.

(4) Mary Moorman, *William Wordsworth: Early Years* (Oxford, 1965), 156–64.

(5) *BJ*, 345.

(6) L. A. Williams, *Road Transport in Cumbria in the Nineteenth Century* (London, 1975), esp. 110–13, 203–6.

(7) *BJ*, 317.

(8) J. D. Marshall, 'Kendal in the late seventeenth and eighteenth centuries', *CW2*, lxxv, 1975, esp. 211–18.

(9) See the suggestive settlement examination documents in the CRO Kendal, WPC/8, relating to the late eighteenth and early nineteenth centuries. These trace the movements of labourers employer by employer.

(10) William Dickinson, 'On the farming of Cumberland', *JRAS*, xiii, 1852, 219–20.

(11) *K. Chron.*, 17 September 1831.

(12) Royal Commission on the State of the Irish Poor in Great Britain, *BPP*, 1836, xxxiv, Appendix on Individual Towns; the entry on Whitehaven gives its Irish population as about 400.

(13) Dickinson, 262.

(14) A. R. B. Haldane, *The Drove Roads of Scotland* (London and Edinburgh, 1952), esp. 207–20. Brough Hill Fair, the great barometer of trade, varied in its fortunes: in 1828 it was 'never remembered to be larger' (*WG*, 4 October 1828), but in 1830 'uncommonly flat, dull and heavy' (*WG*, 2 October 1830). See also Dickinson, 260–62.

(15) T. H. Bainbridge, 'Land utilisation in Cumbria in the mid-nineteenth century as revealed by a study of the tithe returns', *CW2*, xliii, 1943, esp. 87–92; see also the Corn Rent maps and schedules (i.e. tithe documents) at the CRO, Kendal. The percentages are calculated from acreages given by Bainbridge; the fell districts mentioned in the text included Borrowdale, Over Derwent, Underskiddaw, St John's Castlerigg, Buttermere, and Shap and its townships.

(16) E. Hughes, (ed.), *The Diaries and Correspondence of James Losh, Vol. I, 1811–23*, Surtees Soc., vol. 171 (1956), 140.

(17) Dickinson, 289; for Westmorland, F. W. Garnett, *Westmorland Agriculture, 1800–1900* (Kendal, 1912), 75–8; for further data on Cumberland, W. E. Tate, 'Cumberland enclosure acts and awards', *CW2*, xliii, 1943, esp. 186ff, and the fuller if provisional index issued by the

CRO Kendal; B. C. Jones, *Cumberland Enclosure Awards* (n.d.).

(18) Stockdale, *Annals of Cartmel* (Ulverston and London, 1872), 329ff; R. W. Dickson, *General View of the Agriculture of Lancashire* (London, 1815), 290ff; enclosure papers in Lancashire CRO, Preston, DDCa/22, and miscellaneous documents, including Minute Books of the Cartmel Enclosure Commissioners (from 25 July 1796).

(19) *BPP*, 1833, v, QQ. 6588ff.

(20) *Ibid.*, Q. 6671.

(21) *Ibid.*, Q. 6656.

(22) This is an estimate derived from the 1851 census schedules; however, it relates primarily to larger farms, and does not take casual or family labour into account. In fact, farms of 70 or 80 acres could employ two farm servants if there were no sons at home. The census totals (for persons in occupations) strongly support the typicality of this last example, for 1831 and 1851.

(23) See *BJ*, 339; for more detailed data, p. 270 below, note (21).

(24) Question 36 of 'Answers to rural queries' (circulated by the Poor Law Commission of 1831–4), in *Reports on the Administration and Operation of the Poor Laws*, Appendix B.1 (1834). This source (Question 2), also indicates how much arable and other land was employed in given parishes, and the data handsomely support the deductions from the tithe schedules.

(25) Blamire's evidence to Select Committee on Agriculture, *BPP*, 1833, v, Q. 6665.

(26) *Ibid.*, Q. 6649.

(27) *Ibid.*, Q. 6613.

(28) *Ibid.*, QQ. 6611–13.

(29) See below, p. 58.

(30) See E. J. T. Collins, 'The diffusion of the threshing machine in Britain', *Tools and Tillage*, ii, 1972, esp. 17.

(31) The 1831 Census purported to discover that the County of Cumberland had 6456 'occupiers', and in 1828 the same county was reckoned to have some 700 000 acres of farmland (*PW*, 57), giving just over 100 acres to each occupier. The later census schedules show that most farms were smaller than this; this theme is developed in Chapter 3 below, esp. at p. 000, relating also to Westmorland. Nearly half of the 1831 Cumberland occupiers did not employ wage-labour at all, suggesting a heavy reliance upon family labour – but a proportion of between two and three labourers to each of the rest, who did employ such workers. In 1851 the proportion working without hired labour was higher.

(32) W. B. Kendall, 'History of Salthouse', *Proceedings of the Barrow Naturalists' Field Club*, vi (NS), 1948, 35–6. Mr Kendall painted a convincing picture of the mixture of the archaic and progressive on local farms; one farm used the threshing machine (1830), but two more used the flail until the 1850s. The author made absolutely clear that the period of advance was in the late 1840s and 1850s.

(33) See the diary in CRO Carlisle, DX 74/5.

(34) Dickinson, 241, found 306 threshing machines in use in Cumberland in 1849. It is fairly clear that these were mostly of recent adoption.

(35) There had been attempts to drain by tiles long before 1820; by 1829, 800 000 of the latter were made annually in the region. By the end of 1851, however, the number of tiles and pipes made in Cumberland alone was over 275 million. See *PW*, 59; Dickinson, 284–5, 289.

(36) See answers to questions 6, 8, 10, 12 and 13 in 'Answers to rural queries' (see note (24) above). Few Cumberland and Westmorland parishes would go beyond 'very few' or 'seldom any' unemployed in 1832. Blamire (see note (25), Q. 6690) thought that there was 'some' unemployment among cottagers in winter, while the *Annual Reports of the Poor Law Commissioners* after 1836 indicate little able-bodied unemployment, but a considerable residue

of socially incompetent or elderly paupers, in Cumberland and Westmorland.

(37) For local effects of railway-building, J. D. Marshall, *Furness and the Industrial Revolution* (Barrow, 1958), 142. This has to be seen in combination with other factors, as is made clear in the reference cited.

(38) R. Price Williams in *Journal of the (Royal) Statistical Society*, xliii, 1880, Table E, 482–3.

(39) *Annual Reports of the Registrar-General, passim* (giving data from 1839); the very high rates of *local* increase are exemplified in Marshall, 235–6.

(40) *Wordsworth's Guide*, 60.

(41) It is clear that many smaller occupiers are missed by the directories, which are a guide mainly to the established farmers and yeomen. This should be borne in mind in examining *BJ*, 335.

(42) Land tax lists at the CRO Carlisle, filed under QRP, and the same for Westmorland (1773, 1793, 1809, 1811, 1823 and 1830) at the CRO Kendal. The later specimens (early nineteenth century) suggest a decline of owner-occupiers valued at £3 or less, but a multiplication of small owner-occupied properties in growing towns and villages.

(43) Blamire (see note (25)) Q. 6697.

(44) *BJ*, 335.

(45) MS. calculations kindly given to the authors by the late Professor Jones. The highest proportions of all were in Leath Ward (i.e. of the county of Cumberland) namely the countryside near Penrith and the eastern borders, and Allerdale Above Derwent namely the western coastal fringe. Yet it is here that the yeomen disappeared most rapidly afterwards, although it is also fair to say that they were most tenacious in isolated places like Eskdale and Wasdale Head. See directories *MW 1847*, *Bulmer Cumb. 1884*, *Bulmer Cumb. 1901*.

(46) See pp. 111–14 below, Chapter 5.

(47) J. W. Pringle, Appendix to *First Report from Commissioners of the Poor Laws*, Report on Cumberland and Westmorland, pub. 21 February 1834, 310Aff.

(48) See Appendix 1.

(49) See The published *Census of 1831*, vol. 1, BPP, 1833, xxxvi, 97, note (*n*), which is illuminating on the increase of population in Carlisle, 1821–31, ascribed partly to manufactures, and partly to 'the influx of Irish and Scotch Labourers, who gains employment in the Mills and in making the Railroad'. Even the population of Hayton (note, p. 92) had its influx of railway labourers.

(50) W. W. Tomlinson, *History of the North Eastern Railway* (London, 1915), 198.

(51) *MW 1847*, 147.

(52) *MW 1847*, 146.

(53) R. N. Thompson, 'The New Poor Law in Cumberland and Westmorland, 1934–71.' (Ph.D. thesis, University of Newcastle, 1976), 62–77, 124–8, 148–54 and *passim*.

(54) Calculated from the census enumerators' books.

(55) *MW 1847*, 290.

(56) David W. Twiss, 'The Demographic and Social Structure of Kendal, 1790–1850.' (M.A. Dissertation, University of Lancaster, 1971), 25–6.

(57) When London policemen were brought in, aided by special constables, to put down the Cockermouth Chartists in August 1839, all those arrested were handloom weavers: information by courtesy of Mr C. J. O'Neill; see also June C. F. Barnes, 'The trade union and radical activities of the Carlisle handloom weavers', *CW2*, lxxviii, 1978, 149–61.

(58) Information by courtesy of Mr O'Neill, and Dr Oliver Wood (for information on the Whitehaven strikes).

(59) J. D. Marshall and C. A. Dyhouse, 'Social Transition in Kendal and Westmorland, *c.* 1760–1860', *Northern History*, xii, 1976, 152–3.

(60) *Census of 1831*, vol. 2, BPP, 1833, xxxvii, Summary Table, 688–9.

(61) Marshall and Dyhouse, 154; Twiss, 25–6, analysis of the census schedules for Kendal,

1851.

(62) *Census of 1831*, vol. 2, *BPP*, 1833, xxxvii, Summary Table, 688–9.

(63) *PW*, 722ff.

(64) *WG*, 11 March 1848.

(65) *K. Chron.*, 8 October 1831.

(66) The towns or centres with some degree or kind of industrial infrastructure were Carlisle, Whitehaven, Kendal, Cockermouth, Keswick, Workington, Alston, Maryport, Penrith, Wigton, Brampton, Kirkby Stephen, Egremont, Caldbeck, Milnthorpe, Longtown and Harrington. The remaining centres were Brough, Ambleside, Appleby, Bootle, Dalston, Shap, Burton, Kirkby Lonsdale, Cartmel, Bampton, Broughton-in-Furness, Ravenstonedale (Town Angle), Kirkoswald, Hesket Newmarket, St Bees, Allonby and Ravenglass. The 'industries' included hat-making (as in Brampton) and sail-making and shipbuilding (as in Maryport). Small workshop and craft industries were very common. The industrial village of Staveley could of course be added to this list.

(67) *PW*, 681–5.

(68) See *PW*, 640.

(69) Lancashire CRO, DD Pd/26/342.

(70) Microfilms of the 1851 Census schedules for Westmorland, at the Kendal and Westmorland Library, Kendal.

(71) *Census of 1861* (pub. volume), Birthplaces, Numbers and Distribution of the Population, *BPP*, 1862, l, 661. The totals given here may be modified by an actual count in the enumerators' books or schedules; but they are not likely to be wildly inaccurate.

(72) T. Sanderson (ed.), *The Poetical Works of Robert Anderson* (2 vols., Carlisle, 1820). Robert Anderson died in 1833.

(73) See the introductory notes in E. R. and Marley Denwood, *Oor Mak O' Toak* (Carlisle, 1946), esp. 14ff.

(74) See *8th Report of the Registrar-General* (1849), 35, 68. See also p. 142, Chapter 6.

(75) J. Nicolson and R. Burn, *The History and Antiquities of the Counties of Westmorland and Cumberland* (2 vols., London, 1777); W. Hutchinson, *History of the County of Cumberland and Some Places Adjacent* (2 vols., Carlisle, 1794).

(76) William Green, *Guide to the Lakes* (2 vols. 1819).

(77) Rev. J. Hodgson, *Topographical and Historical Description of the County of Westmorland* (London and Kendal, n.d., but *c.* 1817); also John Gough, *Manners and Customs of Westmorland* etc., (Kendal, 1827; first printed in *K.Chron.* 1812).

(78) *PW, passim.*

(79) See Appendix 2.

(80) The doings of the Westmorland Society are regularly reported in *WG* throughout much of the nineteenth century.

Chapter two
The economy of the region, 1830–1914.

(1) Relative densities are shown (1891) in *Census of 1891*, vol. 4, General Report, *BPP* 1893, cvi, 120, Table 31. See also A. L. Bowley, 'Rural population in England and Wales', *Journal of the Royal Statistical Society*, lxxvii, Part vi (May 1914), App. III.

(2) Population figures and distributions calculated, in this instance, from the 1851 census enumerators' schedules, PRO, HO/107/2440.

(3) For a general conspectus of mining and quarrying in the central mountains of Cumbria at this period, see J. D. Marshall and M. Davies-Shiel, *The Industrial Archaeology of the Lake Counties* (2nd edn, Beckermet, 1977), 135–60.

(4) *Census of 1891*, vol. 3, Condition of the People etc., *BPP*, 1893, cvi, 482, Table 9.

(5) See Samuel Smiles, *The Life of George Moore, Merchant and Philanthropist* (London, 1884); for Joseph Crossfield and Sons Ltd, A. E. Musson, *Enterprise in Soap and Chemicals* (Manchester, 1965); for a biography of Clement (1779–1844), see *Bulmer West. 1905*, 94–6; for Isaac Dobson of Patterdale, see B. Palin Dobson, *The Story of the Evolution of the Spinning Machine* (Manchester, 2nd. edn 1910), 108ff; for the Brocklebank family, D. Hay, *Whitehaven* (Whitehaven, 1966), 69, although the Liverpool connection is eloquently dealt with by Orchard, *Liverpool's Legion of Honour* (Liverpool, 1889), s.v.; for T. H. Ismay, effective founder of the Cunard White Star Line, *WN* 26 September 1889. The list could be greatly lengthened by the use of press biographies of the latter kind.

(6) See A. D. Harvey, 'The regional distribution of incomes in England and Wales, 1803', *The Local Historian*, 13, No. 6, 332–8, citing *BPP*, 1812–13, xii, *passim*.

(7) *Census of 1831*, *BPP*, 1833, xxxvi, 284 and *passim*.

(8) See 'Return relative to parliamentary constituencies', *BPP*, 1882, lii, 398–409, for income tax particulars. Much wealth, as can be expected, was concentrated in the town constituencies, and the returns for landed wealth were unexceptional.

(9) The truth of this probable underestimate may be tested against other calculations; e.g. at the time of the 1861 Census, no fewer than 23 068 Westmorland people, out of a total county population of 60 810, were found to be living in other counties; see Tremenheere's comment as reported in *WG* 8 January 1870. For later population movements, see the independent judgements, covering the later part of our period, in Jewkes and Winterbottom, *An Industrial Survey of Cumberland and Furness* (Manchester, 1933), 56–7. See also Chapter 4, p. 68 and note 3.

(10) The substantial main area of Carlisle is held, for these calculations, as being covered by the parishes of St Mary's and St Cuthbert's.

(11) See T. H. Bainbridge, 'Cumberland population movements', *Geographical Journal*, 108, 1946, esp. 82, and *passim*.

(12) *Census of 1891*, vol. 4, General Report, *BPP*, 1893, cvi, 122, Table 31.

(13) *Ibid*.

(14) Calculations from *Census of Great Britain 1851*, Population Tables, Part I, vol. 2, Occupations of the People, *BPP*, 1852–3, lxxxvi, 768ff and 775; *Census of England and Wales 1911*, vol. 10, Occupations and Industries, Part I, *BPP*, 1913, lxxviii, 152 and 289. The difficulties encountered in the use of successive sets of census calculations are of course well known, and have to be overcome by general grouping designed to avoid snags caused by changes in names of occupations. In this case, workers on farms, in woods and in occupations directly connected with agriculture (like gamekeepers) have been counted, but not fishermen. For the general analysis of related data, see Appendix 3(i). Some of the problems are discussed by D. J. Rowe, 'Occupations in Northumberland and Durham, 1851–1911', *Northern History*, viii, 1973, esp. 120–29. I am grateful to Dr Rowe for his advice and guidance; he is not of course responsible for any gaucheries in the calculations given here.

(15) The number of female domestic servants in the UK rose to 1·7 million in 1891, but fell to 1·6 million in 1901, and did not recover thereafter. Between 5 and 10 per cent of non-agricultural servants were male during the sixty or so years discussed here.

(16) Rowe, 129ff, appended tables. The proportion of 'Domestic servants' was close to the Cumbrian level in Northumberland, with its larger agricultural sector, and the parallel with the two Cumbrian counties is striking when Durham is taken into account.

(17) It is instructive to compare *PW*, 394 (showing a wide variety of Wigton industries with textiles predominant in 1829) with *MW 1847*, 495, which shows the textile trade collapsing in the 1840s. The reference is to the Population Tables of the Census of 1851, notes.

(18) Kenneth Smith, *Carlisle* (Clapham, 1970), 50–51. See note (22) below.

(19) See Jewkes and Winterbottom, 65–6.

(20) See *Census of 1871*, Accts and Papers, Part II, *BPP*, 1872, lxvi, 510; 'The increase of population in the townships of Kendal and Kirkland is attributed to the extension of a shoe manufactory.' Robert Miller Somervell had established his firm in the town in 1842.

(21) Marshall and Davies-Shiel, 94ff. This is one of those cases where ground evidence suggests that census data (which are not infallible, especially in the published form) may well underestimate certain occupations at given times.

(22) For Warwick Bridge, see D. J. W. Mawson, 'Langthwaite Cotton Mill', *CW2*, lxxvi, 1976, 168–9, which shows that the Dixon partnership, after suffering from the American Civil War, became bankrupt on their own petition in 1872.

(23) Jewkes and Winterbottom, 65–6.

(24) Smith, 50–51.

(25) Enumerators' schedules, Census of 1861, HO RG 9/3962 (for Over and Nether Staveley).

(26) Evidence of J. E. White, Children's Employment Commission, *BPP* 1865, xx, 246ff.

(27) The evidence for the use of 'Scholars' as part-time bobbin workers is clinched in the MS. School Log Book of Joseph Martindale of Staveley, 6 January 1868, at CRO Kendal.

(28) See, for example, the MS. Day Book of the Horrax Bobbin Mill, CRO Kendal, for 1839–46, which shows customers at Manchester, Salford, Preston, Oldham, Lancaster and Huddersfield.

(29) J. Somervell, 'Industries of south Lakeland', *Transactions of the Newcomen Society*, xviii, 1937–8, 242. Newspaper file research and site recording has confirmed this picture of decline. Bobbin mills were also especially subject to fire hazards.

(30) Data regarding Messrs Fell in early trade catalogues; for Messrs Gilbert Gilkes and Gordon by courtesy of the late Lord Wilson of High Wray. Messrs Fell supplied bobbin-making machines to Russia in the early years of this century, and Messrs Gilkes have also an international connection. See also Paul N. Wilson, 'Canal Head, Kendal', *CW2*, lxvii, 1968, 132–50.

(31) Somervell, *passim*.

(32) Paul N. Wilson, 'The gunpowder mills of Westmorland and Furness', *Transactions of the Newcomen Society*, xxxvi, 1964–5, esp. 47, and ICI, *The History of Nobel's Explosives Company Ltd.*, vol. 1 (1939 reprint), 175ff.

(33) Regional press, *passim*, especially that of Westmorland (e.g. *WG*) and Furness. As Lord Wilson argued, the comparative mortality figures in the industry were not outstanding (Wilson, 'Gunpowder mills', 47).

(34) *Ibid.*

(35) MS. Business Papers of the Greenside Mining Co., Record Office, Kendal, General Account Book, 'Acct. of Lead and Silver Raised Within the Glencoine Boundary', 1838–76, and succeeding entries, which show that output went up appreciably near the end of the century, more than doubling by the 1880s. See also T. Sopwith, *Transactions of the North of England Mining and Mechanical Engineers*, 1863–4, 199; Postlethwaite, *Mines and Mining in the Lake District* (2nd edn 1976), 126, which give correct data.

(36) See C. J. Hunt, *The Lead Miners of the Northern Pennines* (Manchester, 1970), 249, which remarks, correctly, that the collapse was in the closing decades of the century. There is no sign of it in Sopwith's production figures for the period 1845–62, (Sopwith, 199). More generally, there were striking variations of production as between Lakeland mines, which depended on chance as much as on markets; see also J. Lawson, 'Statistics of mineral production in the Pennines: Part 2, Westmorland and the Lake District', *Memoirs of the Northern Caves and Mines Research Society*, 2, No. 2, August 1972, 44–52.

(37) Information by courtesy of Mr E. G. Holland.

(38) The FR's major change of heart came with the appointment of Mr Alfred Aslett as its general

manager in 1895. The stronger policy towards the encouragement of tourism is vividly described in W. McG. Gradon, *The Furness Railway, Its Rise and Development, 1846–1923* (Altrincham, 1946), 56.

(39) Rowe, 120–29.

(40) Lancaster and Wattleworth, *The Iron and Steel Industry of West Cumberland: An Historical Survey* (Workington, 1977), 97ff; J. Marshall, *Furness and the Industrial Revolution* (Barrow, 1958), 356, but also trade directories, *passim.*, and Leach, *Barrow, Its Rise and Progress* (Barrow, 1872), *passim.* Whitehaven and district also had foundries, and engineering works like that at Lowca. There were small foundries at Maryport.

(41) Much light is thrown upon this subject by a comparison of *The Annual Report of the Chief Inspector of Factories and Workshops* (C–8561, HMSO, 1896), 154–5, and the Census of 1891. Gratitude is expressed to Dr P. R. Mounfield for an analysis and survey based on these sources, which deliberately excluded the extractive industries.

(42) Marshall, *Furness*, esp. 398–9. This is one of those instances where national and international politics, reflected in the Naval Defence Act 1889, had a profound bearing on the history of the Furness sub-region. In 1891, Barrow had 2558 persons working in the category 'Ships and Boats'.

(43) Much can be learned about local trades and industries from the very comprehensive directories for the region, especially those of Kelly and Bulmer for the late Victorian period. These are not always literally accurate for a given year, as the census records may claim to be, but they are remarkably revealing. For Barrow's wagon works, Marshall, *Furness*, 345–6. Local railways of course made or serviced their own rolling stock, but the main companies certainly did not attempt, for example, to turn Carlisle (LNWR-fashion) into a second Crewe by installing a large locomotive works.

(44) For Barrow, Marshall, *Furness, passim*; for Silloth, J. K. Walton, 'Railways and resort development in Victorian England', *Northern History*, xv, 1979, esp. 199ff.; for Seascale, Marshall, *Old Lakeland*, 184–95.

(45) E.g. Gradon, *Furness Railway*; Jack Simmons, *The Maryport and Carlisle Railway* (St Albans, 1947); J. Melville and J. L. Hobbs, *Early Railway History in Furness* (CW Tract S., xiii, Kendal, 1951); W. McG. Gradon, *A History of the Cockermouth, Keswick and Penrith Railway* (Altrincham, 1948); S. Pollard, 'North-west coast railway politics in the eighteen-sixties', *CW2*, lii, 160–77; D. Joy, *Main Line Over Shap* (Clapham, 1967); D. Joy, *Cumbrian Coast Railways* (Clapham, 1968).

(46) D. Hay, *Whitehaven*, 45; A. Harris, 'The Tindale Fell Waggonway', *CW2*, lxxii, 1972, 229ff.

(47) *C. Jnl.*, 23 June 1838.

(48) Peter Dixon, Carlisle's leading textile manufacturer, did however remark that 'the greatest assistance had come from Newcastle', *ibid.*

(49) See D. J. W. Mawson, 'The canal that never was; the story of the proposed Newcastle/Maryport canal, 1794–1797', *CW2*, lxxv, 300ff, and esp. 311; J. Simmons, *The Maryport and Carlisle Railway*, esp. 4–5.

(50) W. T. Jackman, *History of Transportation in Modern Britian* (2nd edn, London, 1961), 542–3.

(51) Melville and Hobbs, 4–5, is valuable on this subject.

(52) See also Gradon, *Furness Railway*, 12–13.

(53) MS. Diary Notebooks of the Second Earl of Lonsdale, at the Record Office, Carlisle, D/Lons, vol. 28, entry for 8 August 1839; 'From the cursory view of Whitehaven it looked flourishing active & busy & I hope its trade is prosperous.'

(54) *C.Jnl.*, 15 February 1845; see also Simmons, 9.

(55) *C. Pacq.*, 23 March 1847; George Stephenson, engineer of the line, was present at the

opening dinner. As will be evident, Lord Lonsdale had by this time experienced a change of heart, a point well made by J. T. Ward, 'Some West Cumberland landowners and industry', *Industrial Archaeology*, vol. 9, No. 4, Nov. 1972, 347–8. The surviving volumes of his diary, and his letters, D/Lons/L, 1848–50 (correspondence with his estate steward, Joseph Benn) suggest a primary interest in his landed estate, and make little or no reference to George Stephenson's work and campaigns.

(56) At Chatsworth House, Cavendish family archives; the Earl became 7th Duke of Devonshire in 1858. For his concerns, see Marshall, *Furness*, 174–5. The Earl's diary entries in February, August and September, 1842, are especially revealing.

(57) See *WG*, 16 September, 30 September, 14 October, 11 and 18 November, 1837.

(58) See the lively account in D. Joy, *Main Line Over Shap*, 11–25, and *WG* for the period, *passim*.

(59) The cost calculations are crude but indicative, and based on initial capitals divided by known mileage. The cost of other Cumbrian lines was roughly one-half to two-thirds the amount of the figures given here, and by national standards (where roughly £20 000 a mile was common), they were cheaply made. Much appreciation is expressed to Mr A. W. H. Pearsall for his advice and guidance.

(60) See Joy, *Main Line Over Shap*, 21. There are scattered but vigilant references in the Second Earl's diary and letters to railway affairs on the east of his territory, but he was concerned primarily with their possible effect on his land.

(61) Information by courtesy of Mr David Joy, to whom gratitude is also expressed for more general advice.

(62) Joy, *Main Line Over Shap*, 21.

(63) Melville and Hobbs, 53.

(64) It was reported that this line had 'many' shareholders living in Kendal; *C.Jnl.*, 30 April 1847. For a report of its directors' and the line's activities, *WG*, 26 July 1851.

(65) It should be remembered that the Earl was an ageing man during this period. Nevertheless, he did struggle to take an interest in the affairs of the Whitehaven and Furness Junction; see his MS. Diary Notebooks, cited, vol. 36, esp. 17 August 1855.

(66) For this line, see John Linton, *A Handbook of the Whitehaven and Furness Railway* (London and Whitehaven, 1852).

(67) For the Furness line's record, *Board of Trade Annual Returns for Railway Traffic*, s.v. Furness Railway; half-yearly annual reports in *Ulverston Advertiser* and *WG*, *passim*.

(68) Gradon, *Furness Railway*, 68.

(69) R. Hunt (ed.) *Mineral Statistics of the United Kingdom*, *1856*, 57–8. These figures are to be seen as indicators, and their literal accuracy has been questioned; see note (152) below.

(70) Select Committee on Manufactures, 1833, Q. 10,207 *et seq.*; *VCH Cumb.*, ii, 385.

(71) Marshall, *Furness*, 202–3, 212.

(72) *VCH Cumb.*, ii, 386.

(73) Sir H. Bessemer, *Autobiography* (London, 1905), 176–7, 180, 187.

(74) Gradon, *History of the Cockermouth, Keswick and Penrith Railway*, 2. The line was opened for mineral traffic on 4 November 1864.

(75) A. Harris, *Cumberland Iron: the Story of Hodbarrow Mine 1855–1968* (Truro, 1970), esp. 27–30 and App., 177; *Mineral Statistics of the United Kingdom*, *passim*.

(76) Harris, *Cumberland Iron*, 49.

(77) At the Cumbria County Record sub-office, Barrow-in-Furness; it should be added that Dr Harris's book provides excellent guidance through this great collection.

(78) For the ironworks, *Ulverston Advertiser*, 20 October 1859; for subsequent developments, MS. Diary of the 7th Duke of Devonshire, 29 December 1863, 15 January, 14 March, 9 August, 21 September 1864; *B. Her.*, 22 April, 27 May 1865.

(79) Register of Joint Stock Companies, PRO Kew, file of Barrow Haematite Steel Co. The original capital was £500 000.

(80) Select Committee on Rating of Mines, *BPP*, 1857, 122ff for Schneider's evidence on Cornish investment.

(81) Harris, *Cumberland Iron*, 26.

(82) Lancaster and Wattleworth, *Iron and Steel Industry of West Cumberland*, 50–51, 137–8.

(83) Duncan Burn, *The Economic History of Steelmaking* (Cambridge, 2nd edn, 1961), esp. 11ff.

(84) See Lancaster and Wattleworth, 38–9, for examples of furnace types.

(85) Harris, *Cumberland Iron* 19ff.

(86) Harris, *Cumberland Iron* 18ff.

(87) Snelus did not, however join the company until 1872; some of its enterprise was undoubtedly owed to Isaac Fletcher of the Cockermouth, Keswick and Penrith Railway directorate, who became chairman. He was a *savant* of unusual ability. For the bare facts, see Lancaster and Wattleworth, 48–50.

(88) B. *Times*, 20 November 1869.

(89) O. Wood, 'The Development of the Coal, Iron and Shipbuilding Industries of West Cumberland, 1750–1914.' (Ph.D. thesis, University of London, 1952), 274–6; Burn, 21. For the various Furness ironworks, Marshall, *Furness*, 254–7, 380, 393. Burn's figure of 101 for 1875 is exaggerated, and must include South Lancashire furnaces.

(90) See Wood, 276, for Cumberland figures; also *Mineral Statistics of the United Kingdom* and Lancaster and Wattleworth (for Cumberland), Appendix 5, 163. See the reservation in the foregoing note. Small charcoal iron furnaces like that at Duddon were likely to be counted.

(91) Marshall, *Furness, passim.*

(92) Quoted in Lancaster and Wattleworth, 13. This referred to the year 1885.

(93) Lonsdale Accounts, the Record Office, Carlisle, D/Lons; annual figs. by courtesy of Dr Oliver Wood.

(94) *Ibid.*

(95) *Ibid.*

(96) *Ibid.* for further striking examples; it appears that the Lowthers lost little by ceasing to run their own collieries.

(97) Simmons, *The Maryport and Carlisle Railway* 21; Pollard 'North-west coast railway politics' 176.

(98) Simmons, 21–2.

(99) Gradon, *Furness Railway*, 20.

(100) *Ibid.*, 96–100.

(101) *WN* 22 August 1872. This dividend was soon to crash catastrophically.

(102) Lancaster and Wattleworth, 44; see *WCT* 29 May 1875.

(103) Simmons, 18.

(104) Information by courtesy of Mr David Joy.

(105) Half yearly meeting ref., *WN*, 20 August 1872.

(106) Samuel Griffiths, *Guide to the Iron Trade of Great Britain* (London 1873), 164.

(107) Lancaster and Wattleworth, 44–5, 53–5, 58–9, 62–3, 82; for the non-Scottish firms, 37–8, 47ff, 84, 94.

(108) For capitals and investors in the major Scottish enterprises, see also PRO BT 31, 2152/9971 and 7312/51672 (the Lowther companies); 3194/18567 (The Lonsdale Company); 3190/18539 (the Maryport Haematite Iron Co.). For some early history of Ayrshire ironmaking, thanks are expressed to Prof. R. H. Campbell.

(109) Lancaster and Wattleworth, 66ff.

(110) For the major Cumbrian bankers, see W. F. Crick and J. E. Wadsworth, *A Hundred Years of Joint Stock Banking* (London, 1935), 120–24. On the subject of the banking 'raid', see J.

M. Reid, *The History of the Clydesdale Bank, 1838–1938* (Glasgow 1938), 165–6.

(111) Lancaster and Wattleworth, 54.

(112) Wood, 279.

(113) Lancaster and Wattleworth, 7, giving statistics from Meade, *Coal and Iron Industries of the United Kingdom* (London, 1882).

(114) *Journal of the Iron and Steel Institute, 1874*, 356–7. See also Burn, 48–50. Snelus was also a regional pioneer in the use of ferro-manganese; *Journal of the Iron and Steel Institute*, 1877, 89. In addition, he experimented with the Siemens open-hearth furnace for steelmaking at the West Cumberland steelworks (1880), and even took out a patent (1872) for the 'basic' Bessemer lining before Thomas and Gilchrist; Lancaster and Wattleworth, 50.

(115) *WN*, 8 February 1872.

(116) Table of dividends given by Simmons, *Maryport and Carlisle Railway*, 35, Appx. 1.

(117) *Reports of the Inspectors of Mines and Mineral Statistics of the United Kingdom, 1882–96*, which give tabulations of general price trends (e.g. in the annual vols for the mid-1890s).

(118) *Ibid.*

(119) *Ibid.*

(120) See MSS. of the Greenside Mining Co., at the Record Office, Kendal, and J. Lawson, 'Statistics of mineral production of the Pennines; Part 2, Westmorland and the Lake District', in *Memoirs of the Northern Caves and Mine Research Society*, vol. 2, no. 2, August 1972, 44ff.

(121) *WN*, 31 October 1889.

(122) Lancaster and Wattleworth, 84–5.

(123) Marshall, *Furness*, 336.

(124) Lancaster and Wattleworth, 87.

(125) *Ibid.*, 89.

(126) *Ibid.*, 88.

(127) *WN*, 26 March 1885.

(128) *WN*, 3 September 1885.

(129) Lancaster and Wattleworth, 163, Appendix 5.

(130) Directors Minutes (MS.) of the Furness Railway Co., 20 May 1879.

(131) *WN*, 7 March 1889. In 1878–9 the Gilchrist–Thomas process had been developed in South Wales, by bringing the phosphorus in pig-iron, and originally in many low-grade ores, into contact with a converter lining of limestone, which would absorb the impurity; see Burn, 74–7. The process could be used in the converter and in the open-hearth furnace, and it is worth noticing that G. J. Snelus of Workington had a similar idea, for which see Lancaster and Wattleworth, 3, 50.

(132) Lancaster and Wattleworth and *WN passim*, for the following four months, for the strike.

(133) Harris, *Cumberland Iron*, App., 117.

(134) Pollard, 177, for useful calculations; *WN*, 20 August 1885, 14 February 1889; Gradon, *Furness Railway*, *passim*, for dividends based on half-yearly general meetings.

(135) Half-yearly general meeting in *WN*, 4 September 1879.

(136) Gradon, *History of the Cockermouth, Keswick and Penrith Railway*, 9–11.

(137) Data in meeting report, *WN*, 22 August 1889.

(138) *B. Times*, 31 August 1889 and *passim*.

(139) *WN*, 18 January 1872.

(140) FR report in *WN*, 4 September 1879.

(141) PRO Abstracts of Exports and Imports (MS.), Customs 23, s.v. Barrow.

(142) See Burn, 23, 36–7.

(143) Lancaster and Wattleworth, 122ff.

(144) Harris, *Cumberland Iron*, 107.

(145) *Ibid.*

(146) *Ibid., passim.*

(147) Harris, 93–4.

(148) See Lancaster and Wattleworth, 117; Gradon, *Furness Railway*, 103.

(149) Lancaster and Wattleworth, 58ff.

(150) *Ibid.*, Appendix 5, 163; see also Jewkes and Winterbottom, 82, which shows the Cumberland area producing over 10 per cent of national pig production in 1913.

(151) General trends are indicated in Jewkes and Winterbottom, 97. See, however, the following note.

(152) The figures of output per head in Table 2.3 (*a*) & (*b*) are to be treated with the greatest caution, even though the general output trends for Cumberland and Furness may not in themselves be misleading. The 1870–74 figure for persons employed is from the occupational census of 1871; later figures are from the Inspectors of Mines Reports. As late as 1894, it was possible for C. Le Neve Foster, in his *Annual General Report on the Mineral Industry of the United Kingdom*, 10, to point out that iron ore *mines* were required to supply statistics, but that *quarries* were not. *The Mineral Statistics of the United Kingdom* by Sir Robert Hunt, which are perforce used by researchers for the years before 1882, show aggregate output figures which are corrected in later years, and which do not always literally agree with the aggregate of the outputs of the different ore mining areas of Cumberland. In some instances the small Eskdale mines output is omitted. Dr Oliver Wood's assistance is acknowledged, but he is not in any way responsible for the use of his kindly provided comments and material.

(153) Some fairly typical data are given in *VCH Cumb.*, ii, 384, for the year 1900. But the report for HM Inspector of Mines, J. L. Hedley, for the year 1901, gives a decidedly lower figure for men and lads employed in Cumberland mines, so much so that one is inclined to think that a strike or strikes must have been in progress when the employment figure was compiled; see *WN* 5 June 1901. Here, again, is yet another reason for caution, for discontent was endemic in the industry, and trade unionism grew steadily in West Cumberland coalmining throughout our period.

(154) *Report of Inspectors of Mines and Mineral Statistics of the United Kingdom* (from the series cited), 1885, 205.

(155) The *VCH Cumb.* figure for collieries, and that of the Inspector's report for 1901 (see note 153 above) are here roughly in agreement.

(156) *Report of Inspectors* for year, *loc. cit.*

(157) Jewkes and Winterbottom, 96, Table 1.

(158) Jewkes and Winterbottom, 115, Table 1.

(159) Lancaster and Wattleworth, 8, 60.

(160) *Reports of Inspectors*, price tables, *passim.*

(161) *Reports of Inspectors* (1885), 31 and *passim.*

(162) E.g., Jewkes and Winterbottom, 96.

(163) See pp. 46–7 above.

Chapter three
Cumbrian farming 1851–1914

(1) William Dickinson. 'On the farming of Cumberland', *JRAS*, xiii, 1853, 254, 256.

(2) *Ibid.*, 257.

(3) See E. L. Jones, 'The changing basis of English agricultural prosperity, 1853–73', *Agricultural History Review*, x, 1962, 105 and *passim.*

(4) *Ibid.* and Edith M. Whetham, 'Livestock prices in Britain', *Agricultural History Review*, xi, 1963, esp. 28–31.

(5) *Ibid.*, 29. Calculations of market prices in the text are based on data in the *Ulverston Advertiser* and the *Ulverston Mirror*.

(6) The writer is indebted to Mr David Linsell for these calculations.

(7) F. Garnett, *Westmorland Agriculture, 1800–1900*, (Kendal, 1912), 112–13.

(8) Based on an analysis of the farming accounts for the Holker estate at the Lancashire CRO, DD/Ca, by Mr David Linsell.

(9) *WG*, 13 December 1862.

(10) The lists of owners for Cumberland and Westmorland respectively are in *BPP*, 1874, lxxii, Part I, 193ff, and Part II, 485ff.

(11) Crayston Webster, 'On the farming of Westmorland', *JRAS*, xix, 1868, 11.

(12) *Ibid.*

(13) A Cumberland Landowner, *A Few Hints to Landowners and Cultivators; Horn or Corn, Which Pays Best* (1873) (quoted in E. L. Jones, (note (3) above), 109).

(14) Given in *JRAS*, 2nd series, x, 1874, and reproduced *in extenso* in *WCT*, 12 June 1875.

(15) Dickinson, 218.

(16) *Ibid.*, 219.

(17) *Ibid.*, 221. This was not wholly romanticism; some Lowther tenancies remained in the same families for generations. See *WN*, 30 April 1914.

(18) J. H. Tremenheere's evidence in Report of Women and Children in Agriculture, *BPP*, 1868–9, xiii, 135, para. 11.

(19) Garnett, 249.

(20) *Ibid.*, 251; also Tremenheere (see note (18)), 144, for Netherby.

(21) See *Census of 1851*, Population Tables, Part II, Occns of the People, *BPP*, 1852–3, lxxxviii, 802.

(22) Garnett, 249.

(23) Report of A. Wilson Fox to Royal Commission on Agriculture, *BPP*, 1895, xvii, 10.

(24) *Ibid.*

(25) A. L. Bowley, 'Rural population in England and Wales', *Journal of the Royal Statistical Society*, lxxvii, Part VI (May, 1914) Appx III, 645.

(26) P. J. Perry, *British Farming in the Great Depression, 1870–1914* (Newton Abbot, 1974), esp. Chap. 3 and *passim*.

(27) *Ibid.*, 26–7. By 1891–3, however, there were relatively more bankruptcies in Cumbria.

(28) *N. Lonsdale Express*, 18 September 1886; see also Perry, 30.

(29) See Coleman's report to the Richmond Commission, *BPP*, 1882, v, 42–3 (for N. Lancs. only), and Royal Commission on Agriculture, *BPP*, 1895, xvii, 24–7.

(30) Wilson Fox, 26, which gives the totals of farms on the respective estates (1895).

(31) *Ibid.*, 31.

(32) Perry, 44–5, 113–14.

(33) T. W. Fletcher, 'Lancashire farming in the Great Depression', *Agricultural History Review*, ix, 1961, quoted in Perry, 90.

(34) *Ibid.*

(35) Webster, 16.

(36) *Ibid.*, 13.

(37) Garnett, 138–9.

(38) *WG*, 27 November 1886 and *passim*.

(39) Webster, 27.

(40) Perry, 103.

(41) Wilson Fox, 1895 report, 8. But for the cattle trade, see *WN*, 7 May, 21 May 1914.

(42) See, for example, *WN*, 30 April 1914, and details of show beasts.

(43) Coleman's report, 41–2.

(44) *Ibid.*
(45) Marshall, *Furness and the Industrial Revolution* (Barrow, 1958), 390–91, and *Barrow Herald* and other Furness press items, *passim.*

Chapter four
The search for better things: migration from the Cumbrian countryside, 1841–1914

(1) M. Capstick, *A Study of North Westmorland* (Kendal, 1970), 7–8. It should be borne in mind that in the more 'residential' areas of Westmorland, with their strong element of retired persons, natural increase in the middle of the twentieth century has been very low. See also the epilogue to this volume (chapter 10).
(2) The figures in the table will give some idea of the gaps between birth and death rates in Cumberland and Westmorland in the period under discussion. The Westmorland figures give a useful notion of the rural natural increase rates for the region.

Estimated crude birth and death rates, per 1000 population, in Cumberland and Westmorland

	1856–60	*1861–65*	*1866–70*	*1871–75*	*1876–80*
Birth rates					
Cumberland	32·0	34·8	34·9	35·5	35·1
Westmorland	29·1	30·6	30·2	30·7	30·8
England	34·2	35·3	35·5	35·5	35·4
Death rates					
Cumberland	21·1	23·2	22·1	23·3	20·1
Westmorland	17·9	18·3	17·7	17·6	17·4
England	21·8	22·7	22·4	22·0	20·7

Sources: *18th* to the *35th Reports of the Registrar-General.* See also *45th Report*, 1882, Table 17, xlv, and Table 20, xlvii.

(3) The actual total, calculated from Distribution of the Enumerated Natives of Counties, *Census of 1891*, vol. 3, *BPP*, 1893–4, cvi, Table 9, 482, was 107 368.
(4) *Census of 1881*, vol. 4, General Report, *BPP*, 1883, lxxx, 51.
(5) William Dickinson, 'On the farming of Cumberland', *JRAS*, xiii (1852), 277.
(6) Census enumerator's schedule, 1851, HO 107/2439/573, for Milburn.
(7) Troutbeck schedule, in the same series, Westmorland Library, Kendal.
(8) E.g. for Ravenstonedale (1851, 1861, and 1871) in the same series and location.
(9) Dickinson, 218.
(10) *Ibid.*, 220.
(11) C. J. Hunt, *The Lead Miners of the Northern Pennines*, (Manchester, 1970), 145–51.
(12) Crayston, Webster, 'On the Farming of Westmorland', *JRAS*, xix, 1868, 30.
(13) J. D. Marshall, *Furness and the Industrial Revolution* (Barrow, 1958), 354–5.
(14) Commissioner Mitchell on Weardale miners, in Royal Commission on Child Employment in Mines, *BPP* 1842, xv, 722, quoted by Hunt, 194.
(15) Poor Law Commission, *Reports on the Operation and Administration of the Poor Laws*, Appendix B.1 (1834), 'Answers to rural queries' for Cumberland and Westmorland parishes, Question 38.
(16) Quoted in Hunt, 194.
(17) Diary of Thomas Sopwith, 23 June 1866, quoted in Hunt, 96.
(18) See Chapter 7, esp. pp. 156–7.
(19) M. Anderson, *Family Structure in Nineteenth Century Lancashire* (Cambridge, 1971), esp. Chapter 8, and *passim.*

(20) Hunt, 198–9.
(21) The figures, as given by Bowley, are as follows for Cumberland and Westmorland. Leicestershire figures, given comparatively, serve as an English median farm labourers' wage in the years given:

	1861	1870	1880	1892	1902	1907
Cumberland	13s. 6d.	14s. 9d.	18s. 0d.	18s. 0d.	18s. 4d.	19s. 3d.
Westmorland	15s. 9d.	16s. 1d.	–	–	18s. 4d.	19s. 1d.
Leics.	12s. 0d.	13s. 1d.	13s. 0d.	15s. 0d.	15s. 9d.	16s. 7d.

Source: A. L. Bowley, 'Rural Population in England and Wales', *Journal of the Royal Statistical Society*, lxxvii, May 1914, 645, Appx III. These are, of course, day labour wages, given as weekly totals.
(22) Anderson, 35–6, Maps 1 and 2.
(23) *Census of 1891*, vol. 3, Ages, Marriage, Occupations, Birthplaces etc. BPP, 1893–4, cvi, 385ff, Table 8.
(24) Anderson, Map 1.
(25) *Census of 1891*, vol. 3, 387.
(26) See, in this connection, the advertisement for the Whitehaven steampacket in *PW*, 276ff.
(27) Dickinson, 220.
(28) R. Lawton, 'The population of Liverpool in the mid-nineteenth century', *Transactions of the Historical Society of Lancashire and Cheshire*, vol. 107, 1955, 100ff, Figs. 9a, 9b, and 10.
(29) Lawton, 94–5. Liverpool was a great centre of commercial and service activities in 1851.
(30) *Bulmer Cumb. 1901*, 842.
(31) *Census of 1871*, Accts and Papers, Part II, *BPP*, 1872, lxvi, 504, notes.
(32) *Ibid.*, 505.
(33) Terry Coleman, *The Railway Navvies*. (London, 1965), 24–5.
(34) *Census of 1871*, *BPP*, 1872, lxvi, 503–4.
(35) R. N. Thompson, 'The New Poor Law in Cumberland and Westmorland, 1834–1871.' (Ph.D. thesis, University of Newcastle, 1976).
(36) *Census of 1851*, Population Tables, Part I, Nos. of the Inhabitants, vol. 2, *BPP*, 1852–3, lxxxvi, 43, note (f).
(37) *Ibid.*, 47, note (e).
(38), *Ibid.*, 45, note (a).
(39) *Census of 1871*, *BPP*, 1872, lxvi, 505, note (n).
(40) Tremenheere's evidence to Select Committee on Women and Children in Agriculture, *BPP* 1868–9, xiii, 138.
(41) Royal Commission on Agriculture, *BPP*, 1895, xvii, Report on Cumberland and Westmorland by A. Wilson Fox, 11.
(42) Tremenheere's evidence to S.C., *BPP*, 1868–9, xiii, 138.
(43) *Census of 1871*, *BPP*, 1872, lxvi, 505, note (o).
(44) *Ibid.*, 503, note (a).
(45) *Ibid.*, 505, 506.
(46) J. D. Marshall, *Furness*, 237, for examples from the 1861 Census relative to Furness.
(47) *Ibid.*, 506.
(48) T. H. Bainbridge, 'Cumberland population movements, 1871–81', *Geographical Journal*, 108, 1946, 82–4.
(49) *Ibid.*, 83, and Marshall, 'Cleator and Cleator Moor', *CW2*, lxxvii, 1978, *passim*.
(50) *Census of 1871*, *BPP*, 1872, lxvi, 505–6.
(51) Lancaster and Wattleworth, *The Iron and Steel Industry of West Cumberland: An Historical Survey* (Workington, 1977), 131; Chapter 2 above pp. 46–7.

(52) Quoted by Tremenheere (see note (40)), 139, para. 38.

(53) *WN* 15 February 1872.

(54) Joseph Arch, *The Story of His Life* (London, 1898), 68ff. Arch held his famous Wellesbourne meeting on 7 February 1872.

(55) J. P. D. Dunbabin, *Rural Discontent in Nineteenth Century Britain* (London, 1974), *passim*. This valuable survey covers much of northern England and Scotland, but omits Cumbria from consideration.

(56) *Ibid.*, Chapter VII, and especially 155.

(57) *Ibid.*, 161.

(58) *WN* 29 February 1872.

(59) *WN* 21 March 1872.

(60) *WN* 11 April 1872.

(61) *WN* 29 February 1872.

(62) *WN* 28 March 1872.

(63) *WN* 11 April 1872.

(64) *Ibid.*

(65) *WN* 16 May 1872; this meeting was followed by a public demonstration in Egremont market place, and a body of men who refused the farmers' terms were said to be going off to Cockermouth hiring to seek better arrangements there; see also *WN* 23 May 1872.

(66) *Agricultural Gazette*, 24 November 1879.

(67) Dunbabin, 162–3.

(68) *WN* 16 May 1872.

(69) *Ibid.*

(70) *Agricultural Gazette*, 1 December 1879.

(71) See, for this tradition, A. W. Rumney, *Tom Rumney of Mellfell, 1764–1835* (Kendal, 1936), 29 and *passim*; K. Lovet Watson, *The Hewetsons of Ravenstonedale* (priv. pub., 1965, copy at CRO Kendal), *passim*; 'A Borrowdale Farmer', in *Lancaster Gazette*, 16 February 1822 ('Our sons talk of nothing but Wellington boots, overhauls, dandy waists and neck collar'); microfilm copy of the MS. Diary Volumes of William Fleming of Pennington 1770–1829, at the University of Lancaster, Barrow Library, and CRO Preston, which shows a powerful sense of social aspiration. Each of these references relates to small landowner or yeoman families.

(72) Royal Commission on Agriculture, *BPP* 1895, xvii, I, 33–4.

(73) *Ibid.*, 30.

(74) *Ibid.*, 40.

(75) *Ibid.*

(76) *Lancaster Gazette*, 1 May 1886. I owe this reference to Mrs. J. Chatterley of Warton, Lancs.

(77) See, for general background, W. Ashworth, *An Economic History of England, 1870–1935* (London, 1960) esp. 65.

(78) W. M. Williams, *Gosforth: the Sociology of an English Village* (London, 1956), esp. 45ff.

(79) *Census of 1851*, Population Tables, Part II, vol. 1 Introduction, xlii–iii, *BPP*, 1852–3, lxxxvii.

(80) *Census of 1881*, General Report, *BPP*, 1883, lxxx, 95, Table 25.

(81) The overall proportion of married and widowed persons (added together) for England and Wales was 61·2 per cent for males and 67·8 per cent for females, whereas Cumbrian proportions (all age-groups) were as much as 10 per cent lower; see *Census of 1891*, vol. 3, Summary Tables, v, *BPP*, 1893–4, cvi, Table 2, and Northern Counties, Table 5 (Condition as to Marriage), 463. For a method of obtaining mean marriage ages from distributions of the kind discussed here, see J. Hajnal, 'Age at marriage and proportions marrying', *Population Studies*, 7, 1953, 130.

(82) Registration district totals in the *24th* to the *45th Annual Reports of the Registrar-General*, and Table 15 in the introductions to the later volumes in this series. Tables 4.1 and 4.2, derived from these volumes, point up the comparative data. In 1877, the *40th Report*, xxi, actually argued for a connection (involving, *inter alia*, Cumberland) between high spinsterhood rates and illegitimacy.

(83) For examples of the arguments used in the controversy, *WG* 10 June, 4 November, 21 October, 18 November 1865; and Tremenheere, reported in *WG*, 8 January 1870, and his evidence cited (note (40), 139–40.

(84) This, perhaps for some fairly obvious reasons, is a topic upon which little serious research has been done. However, I am assured by Mr J. F. Cottam, Socio-Economic Adviser, Ministry of Agriculture (ADAS), Carlisle, who commented, in the light of several decades of knowledge of northern hill farming, that such events are 'known' within communities to have taken place, and that the background pressures were certainly felt after very long periods of courtship.

(85) These are acknowledged, for Cumbria, in Dickinson, *Cumbriana* (London, 1876), 90–91. There was a long tradition of late-night visiting by swains. The *Saturday Review*, 28 October 1865, 542, viewed the Scottish problem with that of northern England, and remarked that 'Any restraint upon marriage, whether legal or prudential, will to a certain extent be attended by an apparent increase of vice . . . Their proverbial caution (i.e. of Scots and northerners) makes them sacrifice a certain amount of virtue to gain additional comfort.'

(86) For some illuminating comments bearing on this topic, see T. C. Smout, 'Aspects of sexual behaviour in nineteenth century Scotland', in A. Allen Maclaren (ed), *Social Class in Scotland* (Edinburgh, 1976), 68, where it is noted that the fathers of illegitimate children in Wigtownshire were rarely traced, but that farm servants made up between one-half and three-quarters of known fathers. This suggests that numerous unknown ones were likely to have been such persons also, a point which could well prove to have some significance for Cumbria.

(87) *Ibid.*, 67ff; see also Dr J. M. Strachan's evidence in Report of the Royal Commission on the Laws of Marriage, *BPP*, 1867–8, xxxii, QQ. 1458–1503. For evidence of a certain permissiveness on the part of Poor Law Guardians in Cumbria, see also R. N. Thompson, 220ff.

(88) A tentative case for the linkage of literacy and the desire to migrate is put in J. D. Marshall, 'Some aspects of the social history of 19th-century Cumbria: (I) migration and literacy', *CW2* lxix, 1969, 280ff, which points to the lack of clerical and commercial opportunity in Cumbria itself (302ff). The matter of literacy *per se* is dealt with more thoroughly in Chapter 6 of this volume. Research on a large sample of migrants' careers, having regard to representativeness in origin or *milieu*, might yield interesting results.

(89) The census figures are of course useful, like those in the 1891 Census (cited in note (81)), but the material evidence is in the *35th* to the *38th Annual Reports of the Registrar-General* inclusive, which give marriages and baptisms for the registration districts concerned, and cover the population 'surge' of in-migrants referred to in note (92) above. There is a marked increase of both marriages and baptisms between 1870 and 1873.

(90) Marshall, *Furness*, 353–4.

(91) Even in 1851, the Cumbrian rural districts like Penrith, Brampton and Longtown had remarkably high combined percentages of bachelors and spinsters over 20 years, i.e. of total population in that group, of the order of 37 to 38 per cent. The equivalent figure for Lancashire was just over 30 per cent. Needless to say, these Cumberland districts were also areas of high illegitimacy. Durham's percentage was lower than 27 per cent, and reflected a highly industrialised region. The foregoing calculations are from *Census of 1851*, Population Tables, Part II, vol. 2, *BPP*, 1852–3, lxxxviii, 753. The later reports continue to support the idea of such proportions.

(92) In *38th Report of the Registrar-General* (1875), xxxix.

(93) *Ibid.*

(94) Marshall, *Furness*, 321.

(95) *Ibid.* 335ff.

(96) *Census of 1871*, Occupation Tables, cited.

(97) Anderson, *Family Structure*, *passim* but especially 43ff.

(98) PRO, RG/9/3951, Enumeration District IG, Book I.

(99) *Royal Commission on the State of the Irish Poor in Great Britain*, BPP, xxiv, 1836, Appendices on individual towns, s.v. *Whitehaven*, which gives the then Whitehaven Irish population as *c.*400; see also O. Wood, 'The Development of the Coal, Iron and Shipbuilding Industries of West Cumberland, 1750–1914.' (Ph.D. thesis, London, 1952), 320. Irish were working in Whitehaven in the late eighteenth century; *see* Cumberland and Westmorland Antiquarian and Archaeological Society, Parish Register Series XLI, *The Registers of Whitehaven, St James*, Part I, Baptisms, 1753–1837.

(100) *Census of 1851*, Birthplaces of the People, Northern Counties, 807. There had been 4881 Irish in the whole of Cumberland in 1841; Wood, 320. It is fairly clear that large numbers sought refuge in West Cumberland, as elsewhere, during the period of the potato famine.

(101) Census schedules, PRO HO 107–2437/1A.

(102) *Census of 1851*, Birthplaces of the People, Northern Counties, 807. Gratitude is expressed to Dr Wood for supplying cross-checking information; see also his thesis, 320–23.

(103) Marshall, *Furness*, 239, surveying similar data in, for example, *Census of 1861*, Population Tables, vol. 1, Population, Numbers and Distribution, BPP, 1862, l, 661.

(104) Harris, *Cumberland Iron*, 42, quoting a correspondent in the *Millom Advertiser* (1881).

(105) Wood, thesis, 321.

(106) J. T. Smith's evidence as manager of Barrow Iron and Steelworks, given in *Proceedings of an Enquiry into the Division of Dalton-in-Furness* (1871, pamphlet in Barrow Library, Local History Collection), 73.

(107) *Census of 1871*, Population Tables, vol. 3, Population Abstracts, Birthplaces etc. Data for Barrow are given separately in this Census, Population Tables, vol. 3, Population Abstracts Birthplaces of the People, Division VIII, N. Western Counties, BPP, 1873, lxxii, Table 14, 430ff. It should be stressed that many of these aggregations need rechecking from the original census schedules, and that the printed totals are used here only as general indicators.

(108) St Perran's Chapel, Roose, was named after the patron saint of Cornish tin miners.

(109) Data from successive Censuses, *passim*; for Dronfield, see Lancaster and Wattleworth, 86.

(110) *B.Her.*, 25 January, 1 March, 22 March, 14 June 1873.

(111) See B. Trescatheric, 'The Furness colony', *University of Lancaster Regional Bulletin*, No. 21, vol. 7, Spring 1978, 4–6, for details of the Wadena Colony, set up in Minnesota; the colony organising committee in Barrow consisted 'mainly of temperance men'. The Northern Pacific Railroad colonies did in fact prohibit the sale of alcohol. The writer is grateful to Mr Trescatheric for further information derived from a Nuffield Grant Award project.

(112) For Barrow examples, *B.Her.*, 6 September, 13 September 1873.

(113) See Chief Constable's Reports to Westmorland Quarter Sessions (which included Cumberland data in what was a joint county police force), Kendal CRO, WQF, 15 October 1872 and *passim*.

(114) *WN*, 16 January 1879.

(115) *WN*, 22 May 1879.

(116) *WN*, for 1879, *passim*.

(117) See Jewkes and Winterbottom, *An Industrial Survey of Cumberland and Furness* (Manchester, 1933), 27–8; also *WN*, 3 April 1902.

(118) *WN*, 24 January, 7 March, 25 March, 12 September 1889.

(119) *WN*, 2 January 1879.

(120) *WN*, 29 January, 5 February 1885.

(121) *WG*, 26 December 1885.

(122) R. N. Thompson, thesis, *passim*; the Whitehaven Guardians were in any case known to be very parsimonious, as frequent reports in the *Whitehaven News* show by implication. Their attitude to 'vagrants', widely shared by Cumbrian Guardians, would in itself encourage mobility; in this period and region, Edwin Chadwick's intention of encouraging a fluid labour market may well have borne some rather sour fruit.

(123) *Bulmer Cumb. 1884*, 549ff.

(124) *Ibid.*, 495ff.

(125) *Ibid.*, 303ff.

(126) *Ibid.*, 224ff.

(127) *The Barrow-in-Furness Directory* (published by the *Barrow Times*, 1875), *passim*.

(128 Gradwell's obituary is in *B.News*, 9 September 1882; his forbears appear frequently in the Lowick chapel registers. Many similar cases of yeoman out-migration could no doubt be authenticated in this way.

(129) Although many of these long-established Cumbrian surnames continued to appear in the main West Cumberland towns into the present century, there was a noticeable dilution of them in Barrow by the early 1900s, and a greater variety of surnames is visible in Workington by 1901; *Bulmer Cumb. 1901*, *passim*; Barrow News and Mail, *The Barrow and District Yearbook for 1909*, *passim*.

(130) Chapters 6 and 7, *passim*.

(131) Robert Rawlinson, *Report to the General Board of Health: Whitehaven* (1849), 13.

(132) G. T. Clark, *Report to the General Board of Health: Kendal* (1849), 20.

(133) Rawlinson, *Report . . . Carlisle* (1850); and *Penrith* (1851). For the latter, see also A. Duxbury, 'Formation . . . of the Penrith Board of Health' (M.A. dissertation, University of Lancaster, 1974).

(134) Rawlinson, *Report . . . Carlisle*, 10.

(135) Rawlinson, *Report . . . Keswick* (1852), 35.

(136) Rawlinson, *Report . . . Ulverston* (1855), 16.

(137) A fine account of the work of the General Board of Health is given *in extenso* in R. A. Lewis, *Edwin Chadwick and the Public Health Movement, 1832–1852* (London, 1952), *passim*.

(138) Marshall, *Furness*, 289, citing MS. Minutes of the Ulverston Guardians, 14 July 1864, and *B.Her.*, 16 July 1864.

(139) *Ibid.*

(140) Rawlinson, *Report . . . Keswick*, 38.

(141) *WCT*, 10 April 1875.

(142) *WCT*, 3 April 1875.

(143) The activities of these local boards are reported in detail in *WG*, *passim*, and in the *English Lakes Visitor and Keswick Guardian* (1877–1910), at the British Museum Newspaper Library.

(144) *Supplement to the 55th Report of the Registrar-General* (1895), *passim*. It may be added that even in 1851–60, diarrhoea, cholera and dysentery were far less serious in Cumbria than in other parts of the north, although phthisis was common even in the region's rural districts; see also *25th Report of the Registrar-General* (1864), lxiii, cxi.

(145) John Coleman to the Richmond Commission, (RC, Agric. 1879–82: Report on Lancs., Northumberland and Cheshire, August 1882), 142.

(146) See *55th Report of the Registrar-General*, analytical tables of diseases by districts, 665ff.

(147) *Ibid.*

(148) *Ibid1*, Table 575.

(149) *Supplement to 55th Report*, Part I, occupational survey, para. 84.

(150) *C. Jnl.*, 26 January 1875.

(151) *WN*, 30 July 1885.

(152) *Ibid.*

(153) *WN*, 11 April 1872.

(154) *38th Report of the Registrar-General*, xxxviii. Such a development was of course a result of the 1872 Public Health Act.

(155) *WCT*, 17 July 1875.

(156) *Ibid.*

(157) *WCT*, 24 July 1875; *WN*, 7 August 1879.

(158) *WN*, 5 September 1889.

(159) Marshall, *Furness*, 370, 407–8; *B. News*, 10 January 1885 and *passim*; *B. Her.*, 25 July 1889.

(160) *WN*, 25 April 1889.

(161) A. Harris, 'Millom, a Victorian New Town', *CW2*, lxvi, 1966, 463.

(162) J. D. Marshall, 'Cleator and Cleator Moor', *CW2*, lxxviii, 1978, 170–71.

(163) *C. Pacq.*, 7 March 1889.

(164) *WN*, 10 October 1889.

(165) *WN*, 4 September 1902.

(166) *Census of 1891*, Accts and Papers vol. 2, Northern Counties, *BPP*, 1893–4, cv, Table 6, 1025ff.

(167) *Census of 1891*, vol. 4, General Report, *BPP*, 1893–4, cvi, Table 29, 118.

(168) *Ibid.*

(169) Marshall, 'Cleator and Cleator Moor', 167.

(170) Marshall, *Furness*, 348, 413.

(171) *Report, Cost of Living of the Working Classes; Board of Trade Enquiry into Working Class Rents, Housing and Retail Prices in the Principal Industrial Towns* (Cmd. 3864), 1908, s.v. Barrow-in-Furness, 63.

(172) *WN*, 1 February 1872.

(173) *Census of 1891*, vol. 1, Area, Houses and Population, *BPP*, 1893–4, civ, Table 2, 1008. There was a 71 per cent increase of houses inhabited and uninhabited in Workington between 1881 and 1891.

(174) Harris, *Cumberland Iron*, 44–6, and Appendix, 117.

(175) Concrete Square at Millom was one of the more unprepossessing examples.

(176) See 1891 Census data in overcrowding, as given in note (166). Averages can be misleading; Westmorland, with 5 per cent of two-roomed and 10 per cent of three-roomed dwellings, was worse off than most Midland or West Country agrarian counties or districts.

(177) See Appendix 8. The 'yard' type of town in Cumbria can be examined through ordnance survey and other maps used in conjunction with the census schedules; it is clear that overcrowding could be intense in these places, although this topic, too, would gain from a thorough study.

(178) *WN*, 12 July 1866, gives a few details relevant to the Haverigg incident.

(179) *WN*, 28 February, 7 March 1889 and *passim*; *C. Pacq.*, 28 March, 4 April, 11 April 1889 and *passim*; Harris, *Cumberland Iron*, 86.

(180) Harris, *Cumberland Iron*, 93–4.

(181) G. J. Holyoake, *Fifty Years of an Agitator's Life* (London, 1906), Chapter XLVI, *passim*.

(182) *WN*, 7 March, 14 March, 25 April 1872; Riot Papers, CQ/PW/8, CRO Carlisle.

(183) Riot Papers, CQ/PW/9, CRO Carlisle.

(184) Quarter Sessions report in *WN*, 18 January 1872; Canon Simpson in *WN*, 12 August 1872; see also the 'disappearance of crime' in Cumberland as reported to Q. Session, *WN*, 2

Sports (London, 1911).

(38) Lake District National Park Centre, *Brockhole, Windermere* (Ambleside, 1971), pamphlet, n.p. and album data in the possession of the Centre, by courtesy of Mr J. Nettleton.

(39) E. Hughes, *North Country Life in the Eighteenth Century; Cumberland and Westmorland* (London, 1965), Chapter 2, *passim*.

(40) Walford, *County Families of the United Kingdom, passim*.

(41) The Mannex *Directory of Westmorland* (1849) shows no fewer than 40 large houses within 8 miles of Ambleside, 30 within 4 miles of Kendal, and 16 within 4 miles of Kirkby Lonsdale. The calculations for magistrates are derived form *MW 1847* and *Bulmer Cumb. 1901*; for Westmorland, the 1851 Mannex (*Westmorland with Lonsdale and Amounderness*), and *Bulmer West. 1905*. The ratios are obtained, of course, from Census figures.

(42) The totals for North Lonsdale JPs are derived from list in *Eleventh Annual Furness Year Book* (Ulverston, 1904), 153, and those for Barrow from *The Barrow and District Year Book for 1909* (Barrow), 84.

(43) R. Tufft, 'The Social and Political Composition of the Early Cumberland County Councils, 1889–1914' (M.A. dissertation, University of Lancaster, 1976), 28.

(44) J. D. Marshall and M. E. McClintock (eds), *The History of Lancashire County Council, 1889–1974* (1977), Chapter 1, 10–11.

(45) *WN*, 21 February 1889.

(46) *C. Pacq.*, 24 January 1889.

(47) *WN*, 28 February 1889.

(48) Tufft, 51.

(49) Tufft, Appendix 5, Table 1.

(50) See p.111.

(51) For biographies of a number of these personalities, including McInnes, see E. Gaskell, *Westmorland and Cumberland Leaders* (n.d., but c. 1910), *passim*. For McGowan, cf. *The Whitehaven News Centenary, 1852–1952* (pamph. in Whitehaven P.L.), 17–26.

(52) *WN*, 8 May 1902.

(53) J. Bruce C. Hanson, 'A Charmed Circle of Landlords and Employers; a Study of the Composition of the Westmorland County Council, 1889–1914' (M.A. dissertation, University of Lancaster, 1976), 17.

(54) *Ibid.*, p. 21.

(55) For Cropper and other leading personalities, see *The County Council Yearbook* (1892) 410 etc.; for the connections of the Mounseys, Heyshams and Wakefields with local banking, W. F. Crick and J. E. Wadsworth, *A Hundred Years of Joint Stock Banking* (London, 1935), 120–24.

(56) See Chapter 2 notes (108) and (110).

(57) For Feldtmann (who had at least one relative resident in St Bees, as an 'ore merchant'), *C.Pacq.*, 17 January 1889; there are further details in PRO BT31, 3190/18539, in the lists of shareholders from 1888, Maryport Haematite Iron and Steel Co.

(58) Lancaster and Wattleworth, *The Iron and Steel Industry of West Cumberland: An Historical Survey* (Workington, 1977), 59.

(59) For Stirling (a typical account), *WN*, 8 August 1889; see also R. J. Barber, *Iron Ore and After* (Whitehaven, 1977). Kirkconel appears largely in the MS. Minute Books of Cleator Moor Local Board (1864–), at the CRO, Carlisle, and in local press reports, *WN, passim*.

(60) For Duffield, see A. J. Coles in *Regional Bulletin* (University of Lancaster, No. 13, Summer 1975), 8; Lancaster and Wattleworth, 139.

(61) Gaskell s.v. Randles; Lancaster and Wattleworth, 143.

(62) Marshall, *Furness*, esp. 202 and *passim*.

(63) The most extended account of its history to 1923, drawn mainly from press reports, is W.

McG. Gradon, *The Furness Railway: Its Rise and Development 1846–1923* (Altrincham, 1946).

(64) Pollard, 'North-west coast railway politics in the eighteen-sixties', *CW2*, lii, 1953, 168–9.

(65) *Ibid.*, 176–7.

(66) Lancaster and Wattleworth, 84.

(67) See *Barrow News, passim,* for reports of company dinners.

(68) *WN*, 9 July 1885.

(69) *WN*, 18 April 1889.

(70) Accounts of local board proceedings, in *English Lakes Visitor and Keswick Guardian,* and in *WG, passim*; see also J. K. Walton in O. M. Westall (ed.), *Windermere in the Nineteenth Century* (Centre for North-West Regional Studies, University of Lancaster), 26, 31ff.

(71) D. S. Tate, 'The Kendal Elite – their Cohesiveness and their Challengers.' (M.A. dissertation, Lancaster University, 1976), 5.

(72) *Ibid.*, 33–40; also S. M. Brown 'The Growth of Middle Class Leadership in Kendal Society and its Influence on politics, 1790–1850.' (M.A. dissertation, Lancaster University, 1971), *passim*; J. D. Marshall and C. A. Dyhouse, 'Social transition in Kendal and Westmorland, 1760–1860', *Northern History*, xii, 1976, 127–57.

(73) Data in *Bulmer West. 1905*, 417ff.

(74) Obituary of Peter James Dixon, *C.Jnl.*, 1 February 1895.

(75) *Ibid.*

(76) Frederick Chance, *Some Notable Cumbrians* (Carlisle, 1931), 93ff.

(77) The composition of the Carlisle town council, as set out in 1895, and identified in directory entries, was: minor gentry, 4; minor professions, 4; small businessmen & managers, 15; shopkeepers & publicans, 7; other, 4.

(78) *C.Jnl., passim* for mid-1895.

(79) *C.Jnl.*, 21 June 1895.

(80) *WCT*, 8 May 1875.

(81) *Bulmer Cumb. 1901*, 788.

(82) *WN*, 11 April 1872.

(83) For example, *WN*, 4 April 1889.

(84) *B. News*, 10 January 1885 and *passim*.

(85) F. Barnes, *Barrow and District* (1st edn, Barrow, 1951), 117.

(86) *B. News*, 10 January, 17 January, 1885.

(87) Marshall, *Furness*, Chapter 17 and *passim*.

(88) A. Harris, 'Denton Holme, Carlisle', *CW2*, 1967, lxvii, p. 206ff.

(89) *B.Her.*, 13 October 1866. The nomination was very largely a formality.

(90) Cannadine, 'Landowner as millionaire', 86–7.

(91) *WN*, 3 September 1885.

(92) MS. Diary of the 2nd Earl of Lonsdale, 15 July 1853, at the Record Office, Carlisle, D/Lons.

(93) D. Hay, *Whitehaven, A Short History* (Whitehaven, 1966), 87.

(94) C. O'Neill, 'The progress of paternalism in Whitehaven, 1830–90' (M.A. dissertation, Lancaster University, 1977), 83–98.

(95) Hay, 24.

(96) Douglas Sutherland, *The Yellow Earl* (London, 1965), 108–12, 166.

(97) *Bulmer Cumb. 1901*, 405, 408.

(98) *Barrow and District Yearbook*, 1909, 93.

(99) *Ibid.*, 93–4.

(100) *Ibid.*, 95.

(101) *WN*, 4 July 1872.

(102) *WN*, 31 July 1902.

(103) See pp. 10–11.

(104) *WCT*, 20 March 1875, 1 May, 22 May 1875. This last was inspired by a rather limited Lancashire miners' union movement, for which see R. C. Challinor, *The Lancashire and Cheshire Miners* (London, 1971), esp. Chapter 8.

(105) *WCT*, 1 May 1875, 3 July 1875.

(106) *WN*, 29 January, 16 February, 5 March 1885 and *passim*; Thomas Barlow-Massicks, who is extensively reported on 7 March, was joint manager at both Millom and Askam, and the two firms merged in the following year; Lancaster and Wattleworth, 94.

(107) Information by courtesy of Dr Oliver Wood.

(108) I am especially grateful to Dr Wood for making available the results of his own researches into Cumberland labour history.

(109) Lonsdale MSS. at the CRO Carlisle (quotation by courtesy of Dr Wood).

(110) *WN*, 7 March 1889.

(111) Much of this story is in *WN* from 7 March, *passim* to 1 August. References to Walls and Snow are in, especially, 21 March, 4 and 18 April, 16 May, 13 June and 11 July 1889. Also, full accounts of the proceedings are in *C. Pacq.*, 21 and 28 February, 7 March, 14 March and *passim* to 18 July, when the strike was collapsing.

(112) Lancaster and Wattleworth, 141.

(113) The date of formation of the Dalton and District Working Men's Association is given, almost certainly wrongly, as 1888 in Marshall, *Furness*, 307. But see *B.News*, 31 March 1885.

(114) *Ibid.*

(115) *WN*, 16 May 1889.

(116) *WN*, 19 September 1889.

(117) *Ibid.*

(118) *B.News* 6 August 1890.

(119) *WN*, 2 May, 16 May 1889.

(120) Barber, 42–3.

(121) *WN*, from 1907, *passim*.

(122) *WN*, 31 July 1902.

(123) Tufft, for details of council representation.

(124) *WN*, 31 July 1902.

(125) Barber, 43.

(126) For early co-operative societies, see Cole, *A Century of Co-operation* (1944), 68; the Kendal venture of 1831 is described in the *Lancashire and Yorkshire Co-operator* for 1832, otherwise n.d. (file at the Manchester Central Reference Library).

(127) William Lawson and Charles D. Hunter, *Ten Years of Gentleman Farming* (London, 1875), 16–31.

(128) *Ibid.*, 87.

(129) For early beginnings of these societies, *WN*, 25 July 1889 (Cleator Moor and Millom); for progress at Dalton, *B.Her.*, 26 November 1870, and pamphlet, *Dalton-in-Furness Co-operative Society, 1861–1961*, based on a 50th anniversary statement by James Peters, the first secretary (Dalton, 1961), 3.

(130) *WN*, 9 April 1885.

(131) *WN*, 7 March, 5 September 1885.

(132) *C.Jnl.*, 5 January 1892; see Tufft, Appx 2, also Walls's obituary in *Workington Evening Star*, 28 October 1932.

(133) Tufft, Appx 2.

(134) Walls had a national headquarters in Exchange Building; see F. W. Pethick-Lawrence and

Joseph Edwards (eds), *The Reformer's Yearbook* (1904), 103.

(135) *WN*, 31 July 1902.

(136) *Ibid.*

(137) Hay, *Whitehaven*, 89.

(138) *WN*, 14 May 1914 and *passim*.

(139) J. Mowat and A. Power, *Our Struggle for Socialism in Barrow* (Barrow, 1949), 7.

(140) *B.Her.*, 4 November 1871 and *passim*.

(141) The 1883 total is from a TUC proceedings report in *Nottingham Journal*, 11 September 1883 (the Congress was then held in that town), and the figures may be exaggerated; later figures for the 1890s, are in specimen *Annual Reports of the Barrow Trades Council* at Barrow Public Library.

(142) *C.Jnl.*, 9 July 1895.

(143) Mowat and Power, 11ff.

Chapter six

The training of the human being: formal institutions, 1830–1914

(1) *P & P*, 380–81.

(2) *WN*, 11 July 1872. For relative church attendances, see B. I. Coleman, *The Church of England in the Mid-Nineteenth Century* (Historical Association, London, 1980).

(3) T. Sanderson (ed.), *Poetical Works of Robert Anderson* (Carlisle, 1820), xlv.

(4) Schools Enquiry Commission, 1867, xix, Reports on Northern Division, 159–293, 295–465. *See also P & P*, 344.

(5) Directories for the region provide convincing evidence of the incidence of private academies; their occasional press advertisements give further illumination, if of a fitful kind.

(6) Curwen, *Kirkby Kendal*, 386–7; *BJ*, 203; *PW*, 186, 267.

(7) Royal Commission on Popular Education, *BPP*, 1861, xxi, I, 595, quoted by Pamela Horn, *Education in Rural England, 1800–1914* (New York, 1978), 124.

(8) Tremenheere's evidence to Select Committee on Women and Children in Agriculture, *BPP* 1868–9, xiii, 137, 142–3.

(9) *Census of 1851*, Occupation Tables, Classifications of Schools, Div. X, Northern Counties, 198–200. Otherwise the totals of 'scholars' are as given in the general occupation tables in these volumes, as are those of teachers of both sexes, for 1851 and 1871.

(10) *Ibid.*

(11) Canon J. S. Simpson before Select Committee on Education, *BPP*, 1866, vii, Q. 211.

(12) *See* the Abstracts of Marriages in 18th and 22nd *Reports of the Registrar-General*, and the 35th to the 39th *Reports* inclusive. These give the numbers of persons making marks in the registers, by registration districts as stated, for the years shown in the text. Means are given for these years.

(13) Select Committee on Women and Children in Agriculture, paras 88 and 89, for quotation. The matter of the general development of literacy is raised by E. G. West, 'Literacy and the industrial revolution', *Economic History Review* 2nd Series., xxxi, No. 3, Aug. 1978, esp. 378ff, and by authorities there cited, including Sanderson and Schofield. As the present chapter suggests, 'industrialisation' could have a very adverse effect on literacy indeed.

(14) T. G. Goodwin, 'Provision for Elementary Education and the Growth of Literacy in Lonsdale, 1834–94.' (M.A. dissertation, University of Lancaster, 1970) 99ff.

(15) *Ibid.*, 69.

(16) *Ibid.*, 91.

(17) *Ibid.*, 71.

(18) *Report of the Committee of Council on Education ... 1871–2* (London, 1872), 243–5.

(19) *Ibid.*, 348–9.

(20) See the especially valuable tabular analysis in Gillian Sutherland, *Policy-Making in Elementary Education, 1870–1895* (Oxford, 1973), Table 2, 352–3.

(21) *Ibid.*

(22) See data in *Report of the Committee of Council . . . 1874–5*, xxiiff., xxxv–xxxvi, lii. Cf. also John Burgess, *A History of Cumbrian Methodism* (Kendal, 1980), 111–12. It is worth noticing that Methodist societies in the Eden valley suffered from the results of population loss; *op. cit.*, 116–17.

(23) *Ibid.* and *Report . . . 1871–2*, xxxii–iii.

(24) *Report . . . 1876–7*, 526, for report by a regional HMI, the Rev. C. H. Parez.

(25) *Ibid.*, 526–7.

(26) *Ibid.*

(27) Goodwin, 79.

(28) *Ibid.*, 91–3.

(29) *Ibid.*, 60, 82.

(30) *Ibid.*, 78.

(31) *Report of the Committee of Council on Education*, 1876–7, 527.

(32) *Ibid.*, 528.

(33) *Ibid.*

(34) *C. Pacq.*, 14 March 1889.

(35) *WN*, 12 September 1889.

(36) D. Hay, *Whitehaven, A Short History* (Whitehaven, 1966), 116.

(37) *Report of Committee of Council on Education . . . 1897–8*, 153.

(38) J. F. Chadderton, *Barrow Grammar School for Boys, 1880–1960* (Barrow, 1961), esp. Chapters 1–4.

(39) Some examples of religious conflict are in *C.Jnl.*, 12 January 1875, but see the regional press, *passim*, for this period.

(40) *WN*, 19 January 1889.

(41) *WN*, 29 January 1885; 17 and 24 October 1889.

(42) Described in D. Sutherland, *The Yellow Earl* (London, 1965), 245–57.

(43) Goodwin, 85.

(44) Sutherland, Chapter 5, *passim*.

(45) Regional press, *passim*.

(46) *WG*, 31 January 1885.

(47) Sutherland, 162; *WG*, 31 January 1885.

(48) Published reports, Royal Commission on Secondary Education, 1894, ix, 20–22, 142–8.

(49) L. C. Loveday, *A History of the Nelson Thomlinson School* (Wigton, 1976), 71–5.

(50) MS. Minutes, Secondary Education Sub-Committee of Cumberland Education Committee, 6 April 1903, at CRO Carlisle.

(51) E.g., *WN*, 25 September, 23 October 1902.

(52) *WCT*, 20 December 1902, for census of religious attendance, showing relative distribution of strengths in west Cumberland.

(53) See also printed Minutes of Cumberland Education Committee, from 1903, at CRO Carlisle, *passim*.

(54) *Ibid.*

(55) Report of the Consultative Committee on Devolution in County Education Authorities, *BPP*, 1908, lxxxii, 478–83 (for Westmorland) and 497–8 (Cumberland). For Lancashire, see Marshall and McClintock (eds), *The History of Lancashire County Council* (London, 1977), 80–81.

(56) Minutes of the Cumberland Education Committee, vol. 2, 1904–5, 13–14.

(57) *Ibid., passim*, and 1912–13, 26.

(58) Minutes, vol. 4, 1906–7, Appx. E.

(59) *Ibid.*, xviii–xix.

(60) *Ibid.*, vi.

(61) Minutes, 1912–13 (10th Annual Report of the Cumberland Education Committee), 102.

(62) *Ibid.*, 15–16.

(63) See also Chapter 4, p. 99.

(64) E.g. *WG*, 21 October 1865, 18 November 1865.

(65) *Census of 1851*; Religious Worship, Reports and Tables, *BPP*, 1852–3, lxxxix, pp. ccxxvii and cclxxiv, Table G.

(66) E.g., *Wesleyan Methodist Magazine* (4th Series), vol. iv, 1848, 535–7; *Wesleyan Methodist Association Magazine*, 1848 vol., 375; *ibid.*, 144; 1851 vol., 102–3; 1853 vol., 592–4; Hunt, *Lead Miners of the Northern Pennines*, 220. Cf. also Burgess, *Cumbrian Methodism*, 111.

(67) J. Burgess, 'Wesleyan Methodism in Cumbria' (dissertation, n.d., at CRO Carlisle), 11.

(68) Letter in CRO Kendal, given *in extenso* in *Quarto* (Abbot Hall, Kendal), vol. XIV, No. 2, July 1976, 5.

(69) *WN*, 7 March 1872.

(70) *WN*, 11 July 1872.

(71) *WN*, 8 August 1872.

(72) *WN*, 18 July 1872.

(73) *Ibid.*

(74) See H. J. Hanham, *Elections and Party Management* (London, 1959), 84, 303–7, 396, which stresses Murphy's inflammatory role.

(75) *WN*, 16 April 1885.

(76) *WCT*, 20 December 1902.

(77) Classification of schools in 1851 Census (see note (9) above).

(78) *WN*, 4 July, 5 September 1889.

(79) *WN*, 2 May 1889.

(80) *WCT*, 20 December 1902.

(81) *Ibid.*, and also directories, *passim*.

(82) *WN*, 6 June 1889.

(83) Marshall, 'Kendal in the late seventeenth and eighteenth centuries', *CW2*, lxxv, 1975, esp. 223; see Mannex, *History, Topography and Directory of Westmorland* (1851), 291, with its impressive list of dissenting chapels, and the other directories, given in this work, covering Kendal and Westmorland.

(84) *Bulmer West. 1905*, s.v. the places mentioned.

(85) These Lakeland communities and their institutions are touched upon in, for example, *WG*, 6 December 1862, which describes Milnthorpe's mechanics' institute, and *WN*, 24 January 1889, for Ambleside's numerous activities, and the regional press, *passim*. Places which attracted new settlers usually acquired a variety of institutions fairly quickly.

Chapter seven
The culture of communities

(1) W. R. Mitchell, *The John Peel Story* (Clapham, 1968), 44ff, 52.

(2) J. M. Denwood, *Cumbrian Nights: Red Ike's Poaching Nights* (London, 1932), *passim*; see also E. R. and Marley Denwood, *Oor Mak o' Toak; An Anthology of Lakeland Dialect Poems* (Carlisle, 1946), Introduction.

(3) J. M. Denwood, xv.

(4) F. Barnes and J. L. Hobbs, *Handlist of Newspapers Published in Cumberland, Westmorland and*

North Lancashire (*CW* Tract Series No. XIV, 1951), *passim*.

(5) P. J. Lucas, 'Publicity and power; James Ramsden's experiment with daily journalism', *CW 2* LXXV, 352–75.

(6) *Ibid.*, 369.

(7) *WN*, 14 March 1872.

(8) *WN*, 21 January 1889; *WG* 6 December 1862.

(9) *Census of 1851*, Census of Education, Reports and Tables, *BPP*, 1852–3, xc, 255–6.

(10) C. H. Parez in *Report of Committee of Council on Education . . . 1876–7*, 534.

(11) *Ibid.*, 536.

(12) *WN*, 3 February 1885.

(13) *WN*, 28 May 1885.

(14) *WN*, 3 February 1885.

(15) *Ibid.*

(16) See indicative reports in *WN* 7 March, 11 April, 31 October 1889, which show extension classes also in Carlisle, Cockermouth and Penrith.

(17) *Ibid.*

(18) *B. Times*, 5 March 1881, and *Barrow and District Yearbook, 1909*, 121.

(19) Proceedings of the Association, *passim*.

(20) Published Proceedings of the Cumberland and Westmorland Association, *passim*.

(21) Lists of members in the Old Series, *CW*, *passim*.

(22) T. Sanderson (ed.), *The Poetical Works of Robert Anderson* (vol. 1, Carlisle, 1820), xlv.

(23) Schools Enquiry Commission, *BPP*, xxviii, 1867–8, Pt 16, Reports on Schools in Cumberland and Westmorland, esp. 203–47; the lists of trustees for grammar schools at Drigg, Kirkland, Thursby, Uldale, Wetheral, Aikton, Bowness, Bolton near Morland, Grayrigg, Bootle and other places are of interest.

(24) Sanderson, xlvi.

(25) R. Malcolmson, *Popular Recreations in English Society, 1700–1850* (Cambridge, 1973), *passim*.

(26) Sanderson, xlvi–ii, is clear on this point.

(27) *Ibid.*

(28) *Ibid*, liii.

(29) See pp. 80–82.

(30) *BPP*, 1868–9, xiii, 140 (Tremenheere's evidence).

(31) See E. E. Beattie (ed.) *A Short History of Caldbeck*, n.d., 16.

(32) Sanderson, liv–v.

(33) *WG*, 1 January 1870.

(34) *WG*, 4 March 1848.

(35) Melvyn Bragg, *Speak for England* (London, 1976), 51.

(36) *WN*, 5 March 1914.

(37) *Wesleyan Methodist Magazine*, 4th Series, vol. iv, 1848, 536.

(38) Sanderson, lviii.

(39) See John Phillips, *A Warning to the Wicked, Together with a Dissertation on Drunkenness*, Tract 6.082, Local Collection, Workington Public Library.

(40) *WCT*, 3 April 1875.

(41) W. Whellan, *A History and Topography of Cumberland and Westmorland* (Pontefract, 1860), 479.

(42) Harriet Martineau, *A Complete Guide to the Lakes* (2nd edn, 1855), 142.

(43) J. Sullivan, *Cumberland and Westmorland Ancient and Modern: The People, Dialect, Superstitions and Customs* (London and Kendal, 1857), 164.

(44) For examples of the persistence of this custom, *WN*, 26 March, 9 April 1914.

(45) *WN*, 4 April 1872.

(46) Sanderson, lviii.

(47) *WN*, 10 January 1889.

(48) See Chapter 4, pp. 76, 78–9.

(49) Pamphlets in Barrow-in-Furness Public Library; but for contemporary opinion on Dalton Fair, see also *K. Chron.*, 17 September 1831.

(50) *WN*, 18 January 1872.

(51) See the vivid description in *WN*, 23 May 1872.

(52) Regional press, *passim*, but also F. Garnett, *Westmorland Agriculture, 1800–1900*, (Kendal, 1912), 214ff.

(53) *VCH, Cumb.*, II, 487–8.

(54) *Ibid.*

(55) Although cock-fighting was officially suppressed, it persisted, 'as the police know to their discomfort' (*Agricultural Gazette*, 10 November 1879, 431, with ref. to Furness), and was the subject of large-scale raids in West Cumberland; *WN*, 28 May, 4 June 1885. It may even occur today.

(56) Bragg, 24.

(57) *WN*, 18 July 1872.

(58) *WCT*, 10 April 1875, 3 July 1875.

(59) *B. News*, 6 August 1890.

(60) *Ulverston Advertiser*, 28 November 1850.

(61) *Barrow and District Yearbook*, 1909, 122.

(62) *WN*, 22 August 1889, 8 January 1914.

(63) For the early progress of this festival, *Penrith Observer* 3 February 1891 and *passim*, and for general comment, Millward and Robinson, *The Lake District* (London, 1970), 288.

(64) *C. Jnl.*, 28 January 1910.

(65) James Clark, *History of Cricket in Kendal, 1836–1905* (Kendal, 1909), 7; *C. Jnl.*, *passim.*, K. Smith, *Carlisle* (Clapham, 1970), 54.

(66) James Clark, *History of Football in Kendal, 1871–1908* (Kendal, 1908), 6.

(67) *Ibid.*

(68) *Ibid.*, 52ff.

(69) *C. Jnl.*, 3 May 1850.

(70) *WN*, 8 May 1879.

(71) *WN*, 23 March 1914.

(72) *WN*, 31 July 1879.

(73) *WN*, 15 January 1885.

(74) *Ibid.*

(75) *WN*, 23 May 1889.

(76) O. Wood, 'The Development of the Coal, Iron and Shipbuilding Industries of West Cumberland.' (Ph.D. thesis, University of London, 1952), 321; see *WN*, 17 April 1879.

(77) Clark, *Football*, 8–9.

(78) *Ibid.*, 6. For general background, see J. Walvin, *The People's Game* (London, 1975), 43ff and 66ff.

(79) *Ibid, passim.*

(80) *Ibid.*, 9.

(81) *VCH Cumb.*, ii, 493–4.

(82) Clark, *Football*, 6.

(83) Regional press, *passim*.

(84) *WN*, 4 April 1889.

(85) *VCH Cumb.*, ii, 491.

(86) *WN*, 4 April 1889.

(87) *WN*, 21 March 1889.

(88) *WN*, *passim*.

(89) *WN*, 16 April 1914.

(90) *WN*, 2 April 1914.

(91) *WN*, 23 April 1914.

(92) H. W. Machell, *Some Records of the Annual Grasmere Sports* (Carlisle, 1911), *passim*.

(93) *WN*, 26 March 1914.

(94) *WN*, 19 March 1914.

(95) *WN*, 7 May 1914.

(96) *WN*, 14 May 1914.

(97) *WN*, 2 January 1901.

(98) *A List of the Friendly Societies in the County of Westmorland*, HMSO, 1857, CRO Kendal, WQR/SFB.

(99) See 'F. W. Parrott, a reliable antiquary', *Cumbria*, April 1979, 24.

(100) *Bulmer West. 1905*, 438.

(101) Analysis from *Barrow and District Yearbook, 1909*, 131.

(102) *Ibid, passim*.

(103) See the examples for Gosforth, Silecroft, Bootle, Millom, Corney, Waberthwaite, Kirkby Ireleth, Dearham and Ambleside in *WN*, 13 June 1889.

(104) *WN*, 28 May, 1885.

(105) *Ibid*.

(106) *WN*, 12 March, 4 June 1914.

(107) Royal Commission on Friendly and Benefit Societies: Reports of Assistant Commissioners on Scotland and Northern Counties, *BPP* 1874, xxiii, II, 152.

(108) *WN*, *passim*; pamphlet, *Dalton-in-Furness Co-operative Society 1861–1961* (Dalton, 1961); data on smaller societies in *Co-operative Wholesale Societies Annual for 1888* (Manchester and Glasgow, 1889), 383–5.

(109) *WN*, 31 January 1889.

(110) *Ibid*.

(111) *WN*, 7 February 1889.

(112) *WN*, 2 May 1889; see also article of 5 September 1889, 'Aspatria and its institutions'.

(113) *C.Jnl.*, 24 April 1903.

(114) *C.Jnl.*, 2 January 1903, for example; regional press, *passim*.

(115) *C.Jnl.*, 22 May 1903 for examples, and press, *passim*.

(116) *C.Jnl.*, 2 January, 20 January 1903.

(117) *C.Jnl.*, 2 January, 9 January 1905.

(118) For a most thorough analysis for the two counties see R. N. Thompson, 'The New Poor Law in Cumberland and Westmorland, 1834–1871.' (Ph.D. thesis, University of Newcastle, 1976). Basic indoor and outdoor pauperism in Westmorland in 1885 and 1886 worked out at rather less than 2 per cent of population in those years; for typical figures, *WG*, 11 December 1886.

(119) Information from Mr D. Hay, now in correspondence in Whitehaven Public Library.

(120) See the comments of the late Lawrence Mahon, a specialist in the history of entertainment in the Barrow district, *North-West Evening Mail*, 2 October, 30 October 1970.

(121) *C.Jnl.*, *passim* for this period.

(122) *WN*, 7 February 1889.

(123) *Penrith Observer*, 26 February 1889.

(124) *WN*, 13 March 1879.

(125) *WN*, 31 January 1889.

Chapter eight
The tourist trade and the holiday industry

(1) See J. A. R. Pimlott, *The Englishman's Holiday: a Social History* (1947; reprinted Hassocks, 1976), *passim*.

(2) See especially N. Nicholson, *The Lakers* (1955), and L. A. Williams, *Road Transport in Cumbria in the Nineteenth Century* (1975), 116–28.

(3) *PW*, 309–11; Census enumerators' books, 1841; *C. Jnl.*, 30 July 1836 (we owe this reference to Mrs June Barnes); *C. Jnl.*, 8 July 1859.

(4) *PW*, 439–41; A. B. Granville, *The Spas of England, and Principal Sea-bathing Places* (1841; reprinted Bath, 1971), 1, 314–25; *C. Jnl.*, 27 August 1858, 30 August 1859; *C. Pacq.*, 27 August 1872.

(5) Granville, I, 330–39.

(6) *PW*, 320, 342.

(7) Nicholson, *passim*.

(8) Williams, 116–21.

(9) See Table 2.2, p. 25.

(10) *PW, MW 1847, Mannex 1849, passim*.

(11) *PW, passim*; J. D. Marshall, *Old Lakeland* (Newton Abbot, 1971), Chapter 11; J. K. Walton and P. R. McGloin, 'Holiday resorts and their visitors', *Local Historian*, May 1979; census enumerators' books.

(12) Edward Baines jr., *A Companion to the Lakes* (1834 edition), 93–4, 171–5.

(13) Calculated from the printed Census returns.

(14) We owe this information to Miss Marjorie Shufflebottom.

(15) O. M. Westall, 'The retreat to Arcadia: Windermere as a select residential resort in the late nineteenth century', in Westall (ed.), *Windermere in the Nineteenth Century* (Lancaster, 1976), 43–4 and Appendix; 1871 census enumerators' books.

(16) J. K. Walton, 'The Windermere tourist trade in the age of the railway', in Westall (ed.), 22.

(17) Westall, 40–41, 48–50; *WG*, 10 May 1873, 22 March 1890.

(18) *Lakes Chronicle*, 19 May 1875.

(19) *Ibid.*, 14 August 1885.

(20) Walton, in Westall (ed.), 24–5.

(21) Directories: Mannex 1849, Slater 1869, Bulmer 1885, Kelly 1894.

(22) Walton, in Westall (ed.), 25.

(23) *WG*, 12 May 1883, 30 August 1890.

(24) Walton, in Westall (ed.), 24.

(25) *WG*, 10 May 1890, 6 July 1912, 31 August 1912; Walton, in Westall (ed.), 28–32.

(26) *Lakes Chronicle*, 29 January 1892.

(27) *WG*, 25 August 1883; CRO Carlisle, DSO/24/7/2, F. S. Jackson to Canon Rawnsley, 21 April 1890.

(28) Westall, 46–7.

(29) Walton, in Westall (ed.), 34–5.

(30) CRO Carlisle, minutes of evidence on the Ambleside Railway Bill, 1887, 50.

(31) *WG*, 7 June 1890.

(32) *WG*, 1 September 1883.

(33) Slater's *Directory*, 1869.

(34) *WG*, 21 October 1876.

(35) Marshall, *Old Lakeland*, 181 for Grasmere.

(36) *WG*, 13 July 1912.

(37) *C. Pacq.*, 8 September 1831, 28 September 1847, 30 July 1850.

(38) *C. Pacq.*, 28 June 1836.

(39) *C. Pacq.*, 14 July 1835, 12 July 1836.

(40) *C. Jnl.*, 25 July 1862.

(41) P. R. McGloin, 'The Impact of the Railway on the Development of Keswick as a Tourist Resort,' (M.A. dissertation, University of Lancaster, 1977) 16, 72 and *passim*.

(42) *Ibid.*, 59–60, 76–7.

(43) J. M. B. Baddeley, *The Lake District*, Thorough Guides Series (1902), 125.

(44) McGloin, 10, 56.

(45) *Ibid.*, 74; *Bulmer Cumb. 1901*, 71–2.

(46) Black's *Guide to the Lake District* (1868), 132.

(47) *Ibid.*, 133.

(48) Black's *Guide* (1896), 170.

(49) *Ibid.*, 161, 171.

(50) Black's *Guide* (1868), 207.

(51) *Whitehaven Free Press*, 3 March 1883; cutting in CRO Carlisle, DSO/24/7/1.

(52) Baddeley (1913 edition), xii.

(53) *Bulmer Cumb. 1901*, 361.

(54) Baddeley (1902 edition), 176; T. Bulmer, *Directory of Furness and Cartmel (1909)*, 249.

(55) *C. Jnl.*, 28 July 1899, 11 August 1899.

(56) *WG*, 12 April 1890.

(57) CRO Carlisle, Ambleside Railway Bill minutes, 1887, 49.

(58) *Lakes Chronicle*, 23 June 1875, 4 August 1875, 28 June 1876, 13 September 1899; McGloin, 62.

(59) Walton, in Westall (ed.), 26.

(60) *Ibid.*, 26–7, 31; McGloin, 63–4; *WG*, 10 May 1879, 16 August 1890.

(61) *WG*, 23 August 1873, 19 August 1876, 23 August 1879; Baddeley, (1902 edition), 107.

(62) *WG*, 30 August 1890.

(63) CRO Kendal, WDX/269, S. Read to A. B. Taylor, 5 June 1880.

(64) *WG*, 2 September 1876; CRO Kendal, WDX/269.

(65) CRO Kendal, WDX/269.

(66) CRO Carlisle, D/MG/73/2, J. Holland to Musgrave, 15 October 1896.

(67) See Chapter 9.

(68) CRO Kendal, WDX/269, W. Wilson to English Lake District Association, 11 March 1882.

(69) CRO Kendal, WDX/269, *passim*.

(70) McGloin, 72–3.

(71) CRO Kendal, WDX/269; CRO Carlisle, D/MG/73/2; McGloin, 80.

(72) McGloin, 73–6.

(73) *WN*, 2 July 1833 (we owe this reference to Mr C. O'Neill); *C. Pacq.*, 25 August 1835.

(74) Marshall, *Old Lakeland*, Chapter 12; CRO Carlisle, D/Sen/Rlys/Silloth Bay/8, 1861 minutes of evidence, 13–15, 28–9.

(75) *C. Jnl.*, 4 August 1899.

(76) Visitors' lists, e.g. in *C. Jnl.*, 24 June 1853.

(77) For Silloth, see J. K. Walton, 'Railways and resort development in Victorian England: the case of Silloth', *Northern History*, 1979.

(78) *C. Jnl.*, 24 March 1854, 5 May 1854, 7 September 1855, 6 March 1857.

(79) *C. Jnl.*, 7 September 1855, 4 September 1857.

(80) CRO Carlisle, D/Sen/Rlys/Silloth Bay/8, 13.

(81) *C. Pacq.*, 9 September 1862.

(82) Slater's *Directory* for 1869.

(83) Walton, in *Northern History*.

(84) CRO Carlisle, SRDWB 1/1/1–2, 27 July 1876 to 22 March 1883, especially 3 August 1882.

(85) *C. Jnl.*, 4 July 1899, 1 July 1910.

(86) Carlisle Museum newspaper cuttings file, 'Seaside Resorts', by courtesy of Mr D. Perriam.

(87) See *WN*, 26 April 1880 for a proposed rail link which came to nothing.

(88) This was also true of South Wales and the North-East.

(89) Williams, *Road Transport in Cumbria*, 136–8.

(90) *C. Pacq.*, 22 July 1856.

(91) *C. Pacq.*, 28 September 1847, 3 September 1850.

(92) Black's *Guide*, 1868, 204–210.

(93) See below, note (97).

(94) Marshall, *Old Lakeland*, 186.

(95) *C. Pacq.*, 4 June to 24 September 1891.

(96) *C. Jnl.*, 18 August 1882.

(97) *C. Pacq.*, 3 March 1892 (we owe this reference to Mr C. O'Neill).

(98) *C. Pacq.*, 25 June 1891.

(99) Marshall, *Old Lakeland*, 193 and *passim*.

(100) See also A. Harris, 'The seaside resorts of Westmorland and Lancashire North of the Sands', *Historic Society of Lancashire and Cheshire*, 115 (1963); and J. Gill, 'The Origins and Development of Grange-over-Sands', (M.A. dissertation, University of Lancaster, 1969).

(101) Pimlott, 172–3.

(102) J. K. Walton, 'Residential differentiation and social conflict in three North-Western resorts, 1840–1914', SSRC conference paper, University of Hull, 1976.

(103) H. J. Perkin, 'The "social tone" of Victorian seaside resorts in the North-West', *Northern History*, 12 (1976 for 1975).

Chapter nine
The defence of Lakeland

(1) Ernest de Sélincourt (ed.), Wordsworth's *Guide to the Lakes*, (Oxford, reprint of 1970) 69–92.

(2) *Ibid.*, 151, 162 and *passim*.

(3) Edward Baines jr., *A Companion to the Lakes* (1834 edition), 59–64, 101–2.

(4) L. A. Williams, *Road Transport in Cumbria in the Nineteenth Century* (1975), 161.

(5) J. K. Walton, 'The Windermere tourist trade in the age of the railway', in O. M. Westall (ed.) *Windermere in the Nineteenth Century* (Lancaster, 1976), 20–22.

(6) House of Lords Record Office, Select Committee (Commons) on the Cockermouth, Keswick and Penrith Railway Bill, 1861, 42–3.

(7) Black's *Guide*, 1868, 21.

(8) *Ibid.*, 159–60.

(9) J. M. B. Baddeley, *The Lake District*, Thorough Guides Series (1891), 174.

(10) *WG*, 18 March 1876, 8 April 1876.

(11) A copy of the pamphlet is in CRO Kendal WDX/422.

(12) E. F. Rawnsley, *Canon Rawnsley* (Glasgow, 1923), 36.

(13) *WG*, 5 February 1876.

(14) *WG*, 22 January 1876.

(15) CRO Kendal, WDX/422, Somervell pamphlet, 24.

(16) J. J. Harwood, *History and Description of the Thirlmere Water Scheme* (Manchester, 1895). See also A. Redford, *The History of Local Government in Manchester* (London, 1939), i,

333–52.

(17) Harwood, *passim*; CRO Kendal, WDX/422.

(18) *Ibid.*, Appendix, especially 229–30; *Punch*, 74 (1878), 49.

(19) *Hansard*, (1878), 237, col. 1506.

(20) *Ibid.*, col. 1528.

(21) *Ibid.*, col. 1524–5.

(22) Harwood.

(23) *Ibid.*, and Rawnsley, 81.

(24) Walton, in Westall (ed.), 33–4; CRO Kendal, Rawnsley letters, prospectus of Lake District Defence Society.

(25) CRO Carlisle, DSO/24/6, DSO/24/7/1; *WG* 14 April 1883.

(26) CRO Carlisle. DSO/24/7/1; *WN*, 12 April 1883, 26 April 1883.

(27) *WN*, 12 July 1883, 19 July 1883.

(28) CRO Carlisle DSO/24/7/1.

(29) CRO Kendal, Rawnsley papers.

(30) *WN*, 15 February 1883, 8 March 1883, 31 May 1883.

(31) Calculated from the membership list in CRO Carlisle, DSO/24/9/1.

(32) CRO Carlisle, DSO/24/7/1–2.

(33) CRO Kendal, Rawnsley papers.

(34) CRO Carlisle, Ambleside Railway minutes, *passim*.

(35) See for example CRO Kendal, WDX/422, G. Wordsworth to Hills, 18 November 1885; CRO Carlisle, DSO/24/4, correspondence on White Moss Quarry, 1908.

(36) CRO Carlisle, DSO/24/4.

(37) CRO Carlisle, D/Mg/74/3, Musgrave to Aslett, 25 January 1911.

(38) CRO Carlisle, D/Mg/72, Lamonby to Harker, 11 April 1889.

(39) CRO Carlisle, D/Mg/193/1, Bell's report 13 June 1896, and Memorandum of subscriptions 16 January 1897.

(40) Letter in CRO Carlisle, D/Mg/193/1.

(41) CRO Carlisle, D/Mg, *passim*.

(42) Cutting in CRO Carlisle, D/Mg/193/1.

(43) Walton, in Westall (ed.), 34–5; Rawnsley, 222–3; CRO Carlisle, DSO/24/4.

(44) CRO Carlisle, DSO/24/4.

(45) CRO Kendal, WDX/422, 1895 County Council election papers.

(46) CRO Kendal, WDX/422; CRO Carlisle, DSO/24/7/2.

(47) B. L. Thompson, *The Lake District and the National Trust* (Kendal, 1946), 40–45; Rawnsley, 108–14.

(48) It was being fairly widely used in the 1880s, especially in the opposition to railway schemes.

Epilogue
The twentieth century: variations on a theme

(1) Norman Nicholson, *A Local Habitation* (London, 1972), 31.

(2) References to the eighteenth-century societies are in *Local Chronology* (Kendal 1865), but see also p. 16 (Chapter 1); in *K. Chron.*, 3 August 1813; *WG*, 10 May 1845, 12 January 1856, 7 March and 25 April 1868, and *passim*. That a Westmorland Society existed in London throughout much of the nineteenth century is certain.

(3) *WN*, 12 February, 9 April, 23 April 1914. The report of 9 April is full and helpful.

(4) M. N. Fulcher and J. Taylor, *Cumberland and Westmorland Facts and Figures* (University of Lancaster, Economics Dept Occasional Paper, No. 5, 1965), 27.

(5) *Ibid.*

(6) J. Jewkes and A. Winterbottom, *An Industrial Survey of Cumberland and Furness* (Manchester, 1933), 76.

(7) Fulcher and Taylor, 27–8.

(8) See Saville, *Rural Depopulation* (1957), 49 (Table IV(a)); 55; 56–7 (Table V).

(9) Jewkes and Winterbottom, esp. 8–9.

(10) See *Ministry of Labour Report of Investigation into the Industrial Conditions in Certain Depressed Areas* – I, *West Cumberland and Haltwhistle*, Cmd 4728, 1934, esp. 10–14.

(11) Jewkes and Winterbottom, 78.

(12) *Ibid.*

(13) *Ibid.*, 87–9.

(14) *Ibid.*, 88–9.

(15) *Ibid.*, 86, 89.

(16) *Ibid.*, 109.

(17) *Ministry of Labour Report*, (note (10)), 13–14.

(18) Lancaster and Wattleworth, 74.

(19) Jewkes and Winterbottom, 79–80.

(20) Lancaster and Wattleworth, 114.

(21) Jewkes and Winterbottom, 96.

(22) *Ibid.*, 80. It is a matter of interest that the great Hodbarrow mine remained independent; see A. Harris, *Cumberland Iron* (Truro, 1970), *passim*.

(23) Jewkes and Winterbottom, 107; *Lancashire Industrial Development Association, The Furness Area* (Industrial Report No. 1, 1948), 26–7.

(24) *The Furness Area*, 27.

(25) Jewkes and Winterbottom, 107.

(26) Harris, Appendix, 117.

(27) But see Ross Barber, *Iron Ore and After* (for Cleator Moor 1976); fortunately local history societies keep some reminiscences.

(28) Some moved into public works construction in the 1920s; see Jewkes and Winterbottom, 109.

(29) Lancaster and Wattleworth, Appendix 1, 158.

(30) Jewkes and Winterbottom, 99.

(31) *The Furness Area*, 31.

(32) *Ibid.*, 16–17.

(33) A. J. Coles, 'The moral economy of the crowd; some twentieth century food riots', *Journal of British Studies*, xviii, No. 1, 1978, 157ff. Mr Coles shows the strong element of political militancy that developed in the Cumberland Miners' Association in the early twentieth century (168–71).

(34) J. Mowat and A. Power, *Our Struggle For Socialism in Barrow* (Barrow, 1949), 21, quoting *North-West Daily Mail*, 28 November, 29 December 1922.

(35) *Ibid.*

(36) *The Furness Area*, 12–15.

(37) K. Smith, *Carlisle* (cited), 56.

(38) Jewkes and Winterbottom, 65–6.

(39) Smith, 59.

(40) Jewkes and Winterbottom, 19.

(41) *Morecambe Visitor*, 31 May, 1 June 1904.

(42) See figures given in the parliamentary Returns, *Trade and Navigation of the UK*, which show seriously fluctuating but falling imports to Barrow, as the cattle trade failed, and generally diminishing but substantial exports until 1900. Those figures for the inter-war years are

(112) *Ibid.*, quoting *Cumberland and Westmorland Herald*, during January 1968.

(113) Fulcher and Taylor, 8–10.

(114) See p. 226 above, and Cumberland Development Council Ltd. (publication, *The West Cumberland Industrial Exhibition 1948* (Whitehaven, 1948), 7.

(115) G. V. S. Clague, *Growth in Cumbria: A Study of the Problems and Possibilities of Regional Growth, with Reference to Industry in West Cumberland* (for Cumberland Development Council, 1966; copy in Whitehaven Library, 2/CLA 119733), 7.

(116) *Ibid.*, 10.

(117) *Ibid.*, 12–14. One of the activities of the Development Council was to encourage the survey, G. H. J. Daysh and Evelyn Watson, *Cumberland, with Special Reference to the West Cumberland Development Area: A Survey of Industrial Facilities* (Whitehaven, 1951). For a very succinct brief survey, see also Lancaster and Wattleworth, 152–3.

(118) 'Biographies' of local firms are given in *The West Cumberland Industrial Exhibition*, in this instance, p. 81.

(119) *Ibid.*, 71.

(120) *The Furness Area*, 38.

(121) Clague, 15.

(122) See p. 000 above.

(123) *B. News*, 28 September 1979, Industrial Review, 79, vii.

(124) Clague, 9. 16; Fulcher and Taylor, 1–2.

(125) Industrial Review '79, xiv.

(126) *The West Cumberland Industrial Exhibition*, 41, 71.

(127) *Windscale Inquiry Transcript* (1977) Day 92, 57; Day 94, 7, where the evidence seems hard to refute, and whereby the reprocessing proposals could hardly lead to more than a few hundred extra jobs. The Marchon workforce is well over 2000.

(128) For an example of the oral history that is needed, see Elizabeth A. M. Roberts, *Working Class in Barrow and Lancaster 1890 to 1930* (Lancaster, 1976).